"For many years we have all appreciated Dr. Ma[r]... [contri]butions to the mission of the Church. Now he [gives us a sound] doctrinal foundation for understanding and implementing the 'new evangelization.' This is a shot in the arm for bishops, priests, and laity as we respond to the Holy Father's call to 'cast out into the deep' in proclaiming the person, message, and invitation of Jesus Christ. This book is now on my shelf of trustworthy reference points."

— **Timothy Cardinal Dolan**
Archbishop of New York
President, United States Conference
of Catholic Bishops

"On the fiftieth anniversary of the opening of the Second Vatican Council, *are* the missionary purpose and inspiration of the Council is being revisited. Ralph Martin clarifies a doctrinal point that has been often obscured but must be recovered as a necessary foundation for the new evangelization. This is a uniquely important book."

— **Francis Cardinal George, O.M.I.**
Archbishop of Chicago

"The 'new evangelization' involves a personal deepening and renewal of our faith, a confidence in that belief, and a willingness to share it. Dr. Ralph Martin's book *Will Many Be Saved?* contributes significantly to a richer understanding of our faith, helps restore confidence in the gospel message, and engenders a desire to share the truth of Christ's message. An important contribution to the pastoral strategy of the 'new evangelization.'"

— **Donald Cardinal Wuerl**
Archbishop of Washington, D.C.

"If the pastoral strategy of Vatican II has led to 'practical universalism' in certain quarters, this reading of the Council provides a refreshing reminder of the undiminished urgency and validity of the missionary mandate of Jesus to his followers to evangelize."

— **Peter Cardinal Turkson**
President, Pontifical Council
for Peace and Justice

"The Church's call to a new evangelization could be undermined by doctrinal confusion or uncertainty about whether anything ultimate is really at stake. Ralph Martin's book shows how the teaching of Vatican II — both on the possibility of being saved without hearing the gospel and on the significant limitations regarding that possibility — is firmly in continuity with Scripture and tradition. These penetrating reflections will compel us to reassess our pastoral approach to the preaching of the gospel in our present circumstances and will command the attention of all those who take up the challenge of the new evangelization. An important book."

— **Archbishop J. Augustine Di Noia, O.P.**
Vatican City

"At the heart of the Church's mission is the ongoing need for evangelization. Our response to the 'new evangelization' will lack enthusiasm and conviction if we don't realize what's truly at stake here — our eternal salvation in Christ. Ralph Martin's book provides much-needed clarity on these very important issues."

— **Archbishop Robert Carlson**
Archbishop of St. Louis, Missouri

"With depth and clarity, Ralph Martin shows what the authentic teaching of Vatican II actually is regarding the conditions under which it's possible to be saved and, therefore, the urgency of bringing the confident proclamation of the Good News to all. I highly recommend that all Catholics and other Christians concerned with salvation give this important book the attention it deserves."

— **Bishop David L. Ricken**
Chairman, United States Conference of
Catholic Bishops' Committee on
Evangelization and Catechesis

"Here is a scholarly shout, a bracing splash of cold water. The unique vocation Christ gave to Ralph Martin — evangelist-scholar — explains the wonderful tone of this vital work — evangelical and urgent but sober and disciplined in its argument. Life is not about 'drifting' into salvation; it is about choosing to let Christ heal our affection for sin. In this book the teachings of Vatican II come alive again and we rediscover the authentic doctrine of salvation. What a contribution!"

— **Deacon James Keating**
Director of Theological Formation,
Institute for Priestly Formation,
Creighton University

"Martin has written a thoughtful and thought-provoking book. He convincingly demonstrates, in his careful attention to the relevant texts of Vatican II, that what is at stake for many, in whether they hear the gospel or not, is nothing less than eternal life."

— **Thomas G. Weinandy, O.F.M., Cap.**
Executive Director, Secretariat for
Doctrine, United States Conference
of Catholic Bishops

"A good read, long overdue. Martin's book shakes the foundations of theological optimism about the salvation of nonbelievers. His careful, detailed examination of Scripture, tradition, and Vatican II reveals that Rahner's 'anonymous Christianity' and von Balthasar's 'hope' alike suffer from grave deficiencies. Hence Martin calls for a revival of Christian missionary enthusiasm, which has been flagging due to deficient interpretations of Vatican II and a flaccid humanism. The mandate for mission is essential to the Church since Christ founded her for that purpose."

— **Fr. John Michael McDermott, S.J.**
Sacred Heart Major Seminary
Member of International Theological
Commission of the Congregation for the
Doctrine of the Faith (2004–2009)

"The zeal of Catholics for evangelization has been significantly undermined since Vatican II by false interpretations regarding both the nature and the necessity of the proclamation of Jesus Christ to all peoples. Martin unveils the deepest roots of the deception while presenting a pastoral vision aimed at re-awakening the Church to her central mission. It should give us great hope that Pope Benedict XVI has recognized the importance of Martin's insights on the New Evangelization by appointing him as a Consultor to the Pontifical Council for Promoting the New Evangelization."

— **Deacon Daniel Foley**
Member, US Bishops
National Advisory Council

"Even though I'm a businessman without theological training, I found Ralph Martin's book compelling and had a hard time putting it down. It's fascinating to see how well-known theological theories end up weakening the rationale for evangelization. This book cleared up a lot of confusion for me, and I know many other Catholics like me would benefit from it greatly."

— **Chris M. Hall**
President, Repairclinic.com

"A bold yet careful study that addresses the most difficult and pressing theological issues related to the Church's mission and the new evangelization. Martin's close reading of *Lumen gentium* 16 clarifies the urgency of evangelizing for the salvation of souls. A rich blend of theological insight and prophetic wisdom, this is must reading for academics and pastors alike."

— **Scott Hahn**
Professor of Biblical Theology,
Franciscan University of Steubenville

WILL MANY BE SAVED?

*What Vatican II Actually Teaches
and Its Implications for the
New Evangelization*

Ralph Martin

WILLIAM B. EERDMANS PUBLISHING COMPANY
GRAND RAPIDS, MICHIGAN / CAMBRIDGE, U.K.

Published 2012 by

Wm. B. Eerdmans Publishing Co.

2140 Oak Industrial Drive N.E., Grand Rapids, Michigan 49505 /
P.O. Box 163, Cambridge CB3 9PU U.K.

Printed in the United States of America

17 16 15 14 13 12   7 6 5 4 3 2 1

Library of Congress Cataloging-in-Publication Data

Martin, Ralph, 1942-
Will many be saved? : what Vatican II actually teaches and
its implications for the new evangelization / Ralph Martin.
p.   cm.
Includes bibliographical references and index.
ISBN 978-0-8028-6887-9 (pbk.: alk. paper)
1. Salvation — Catholic Church.
2. Catholic Church — Doctrines.
3. Vatican Council (2nd: 1962-1965)   I. Title.

BT755.M35   2012
234.088'282 — dc23
2012022084

www.eerdmans.com

Contents

Preface

The question of whether and how human beings who have not had the chance to hear the gospel can be saved goes back to the beginnings of Christian reflection. It has also become a much-debated topic in current theology, not only in the Catholic Church, but throughout the Christian world. While this book is focused particularly on the situation of the Catholic Church in facing this question today, there is much in it that is relevant to the wider debate happening in many churches.

There is a long history of debate and development on this question, part of which we will trace in this book. The focus of the book, though, will be a particular text from *Lumen gentium,* the *Dogmatic Constitution on the Church* of the Second Vatican Council *(LG)* 16. Although there are other conciliar texts that touch on the question of the possibility of the salvation of those who have never heard the gospel — and we will consider them as well — the *LG* 16 text, along with its important footnotes, is the most extensive treatment of this question in the conciliar documents, and it is a text that is cited in other conciliar documents that touch on this question. It is also the primary text referred to in subsequent papal documents that touch on this issue and its relationship to evangelization. It is an important text, as it is the most recent and highest-level magisterial teaching pertaining to this issue, and it attempts to sum up a long history of doctrinal reflection and development. It is a text that is well known and often cited in works devoted to this and related questions; but, strangely enough, a few important sentences (the last three sentences) are almost always ignored, or if adverted to at all, very briefly and without significant comment. No sustained attention is paid to these last three sentences, and they are not applied to the contemporary challenges facing the implementation of the new evangelization. It is precisely to these sentences that we will devote our primary attention, as they contain a key to overcoming a doctrinal confusion that is hindering our response, as individuals and as a Church, to the recent popes' persistent calls for a "new evangelization."

Because this is a position that is not often argued — namely, that the conditions under which people can be saved who have never heard the gospel are very often, in fact, not fulfilled — the approach and the methodology must be suited to the task. In order to establish the plausibility of the argument, it is necessary, more than usual, to support the position by citing authorities that demonstrate the soundness of my reading of the relevant texts and their history, the accuracy of my interpretations, and the plausibility of my conclusions. To that end, I will be providing the actual words of the authorities in fuller measure than other books might do in order to establish more firmly my conclusions, which otherwise could be viewed as controversial, and to give readers the chance to judge for themselves. While what I consider the most important citations are included in the body of the book — and the book can be read successfully without consulting the endnotes — there is a lot of very important material in the endnotes, both supporting of points that are being made in the text and providing additional very interesting material. This is especially the case in the chapter on Balthasar.

I am also doing this because the interpretation of *LG* 16 for which I am arguing has obvious implications for the life of the Church today and the success of the "new evangelization." Decisions about pastoral strategy need a solid doctrinal base.

The approach employed will be fourfold. First, *LG* 16 will be situated in the overall context of Vatican II, the *Dogmatic Constitution on the Church,* and the "triptych" of *LG* 14, 15, and 16, with some attention to *LG* 13 and 17 as well. The history of the development of the final conciliar text and the most significant commentaries, early and recent, on *LG* will be consulted with a view to articulating what the consensus of the most important commentators is regarding the text in question.

Second, the doctrinal background needed to understand correctly what the Council is teaching will be examined, particularly that doctrinal development that is referenced in the important footnotes of *LG* 16.

Third, the scriptural foundation claimed for the teaching of *LG* 16 in its explicit citations of Romans 1 and Mark 16, and its implicit citation of

Romans 2, will be examined in the light of contemporary Scripture scholarship. An attempt will be made to ascertain whether there is a consensus
among the most important commentators on the meaning and significance of the Scripture texts cited by *LG* 16, and if so, what that consensus is,
and how it affects our understanding of *LG* 16.

Fourth, the usefulness of *LG* 16 as an interpretive tool in evaluating
theories that affect evangelization will be demonstrated by examining Karl
Rahner's theory of the "anonymous Christian" and Hans Urs von
Balthasar's teaching on the duty to hope that all be saved, assessing their
strengths and weaknesses in light of the teaching of *LG* 16. These two theologians have been selected because of the very significant influence they
continue to have on how Catholics — and many other Christians as well
— think about the urgency of evangelization. Conclusions will then be
drawn on the implications that a more precise understanding of the teaching of *LG* 16 has for the current pastoral strategy of the Church and the
shaping of her message, as she responds to the call to a new evangelization.

Acknowledgments

I would like to thank the many who have helped make this undertaking
possible: First of all, Fr. Robert Christian, O.P., who was willing to take
on the significant responsibility of being the moderator of the disserta-
tion that forms the basis of this book; Msgr. Todd Lajiness of Sacred
Heart Major Seminary in Detroit, and Frs. Steven Boguslawski, O.P., and
Gabriel O'Donnell, O.P., of the Pontifical Faculty of the Immaculate
Conception at the Dominican House of Studies in Washington, D.C.; Fr.
Francis Martin, for his generous service as my S.T.L. thesis director; Fr.
John Michael McDermott, S.J., and Dr. Robert Fastiggi, for reading early
drafts of chapters in their specialties and offering comments; Fr.
Wojciech Giertych, O.P., Bishop Thomas Olmsted, and Archbishop Au-
gustine DiNoia, O.P., for being willing to discuss the issues raised in this
book and offering valuable suggestions; Dr. Mary Healy for helping with
formatting issues; Deacon Daniel Foley and Carolyn Dean for their patient proofreading work and useful suggestions; the librarians at Sacred
Heart Major Seminary, Dominican House of Studies, and the Pontifical
North American College; my colleagues and Board at Renewal Minis-
tries, who freed me for this work; Fr. John Horn, S.J., for his spiritual
guidance and encouragement; Archbishop Allen Vigneron, who first as

Rector asked me to begin teaching at Sacred Heart Major Seminary, and then as Archbishop encouraged me in the journey, first to Washington, D.C., and then to Rome; and especially, my wife Anne, who encouraged me to say "yes" to this invitation in the first place and encouraged me to its conclusion.

RALPH MARTIN

Abbreviations

Documents of Vatican II

AG   *Ad gentes divinitus:* The Decree on the Church's Missionary Activity

DV   *Dei verbum:* The Dogmatic Constitution on Divine Revelation

GS   *Gaudium et spes:* The Pastoral Constitution on the Church in the Modern World

LG   *Lumen gentium:* The Dogmatic Constitution on the Church

NA   *Nostra aetate:* The Declaration on the Church's Relations with Non-Christian Religions

UR   *Unitatis redintegratio:* The Decree on Ecumenism

Papal Encyclicals and Apostolic Exhortations

EN   *Evangelii nuntiandi:* On Evangelization in the Modern World. Pope Paul VI

EV   *Evangelium vitae:* The Gospel of Life. Pope John Paul II

FR   *Fides et ratio:* On the Relationship Between Faith and Reason. Pope John Paul II

NMI   *Novo millennio ineunte:* At the Beginning of a New Millennium. Pope John Paul II

RM   *Redemptoris missio:* Mission of the Redeemer. Pope John Paul II

SV   *Spe salvi:* Saved in Hope. Pope Benedict XVI

VS   *Veritatis splendor:* The Splendor of the Truth. Pope John Paul II

Curial Offices and Documents

CDF   Congregation for the Doctrine of the Faith

DI   *Dominus Iesus:* On the Unicity and Salvific Universality of Jesus Christ and the Church. CDF

ME   *Mysterium ecclesiae:* Declaration in Defense of the Catholic Doctrine on the Church Against Certain Errors of the Present Day. CDF

Source and Reference Documents

AAS   *Acta Apostolicae Sedis*

AS   *Acta Synodalia Concilii Vaticani II*

CCC   *Catechism of the Catholic Church*

CSEL   *Corpus scriptorium ecclesiasticorum latinorum*

DS   H. Denzinger and A Schönmetzer, *Enchiridion symbolorum, definitionum, declarationum,* 34th ed., 1967

PG   *Patrologiae cursus completus, series graeca*

PL   *Patrologiae cursus completus, series latina*

NAB   New American Bible

ND   J. Neuner and J. Dupuis, eds., *The Christian Faith* (Bangalore/ New York: Theological Publications in India/Alba House, 7th ed. 2001)

RSV   Revised Standard Version, Catholic Edition

ST   *Summa Theologiae,* Thomas Aquinas

Sullivan   Francis Sullivan, *Salvation Outside the Church? Tracing the History of the Catholic Response* (Eugene, OR: Wipf & Stock, 2002)

Tanner   Norman P. Tanner, English Editor, *Decrees of the Ecumenical Councils*

TI   *Theological Investigations,* by Karl Rahner, 23 vols., trans. Joseph Doncell (New York: Crossroad, 1991)

CHAPTER I

Vatican II and the Priority of Evangelization

The Purpose of Vatican II

When Pope John XXIII stated the reasons for convoking Vatican II, he made it clear that his hope was that the work of the Council would result in an "aggiornamento" that would enable the Church to communicate the gospel more effectively to the modern world. The post–Vatican II popes have shared this understanding of the desired outcome of the Council.

Pope Paul VI issued his influential Apostolic Exhortation, *Evangelii nuntiandi* (On Evangelization in the Modern World), "on this tenth anniversary of the closing of the Second Vatican Council, the objectives of which are definitely summed up in this single one: to make the Church of the twentieth century ever better fitted for proclaiming the Gospel to the people of the twentieth century."[1]

Paul VI hoped that this document would help provide "a fresh forward impulse, capable of creating within a Church still more firmly rooted in the undying power and strength of Pentecost a new period of evangelization."[2]

Pope John Paul II chose the occasion of the twenty-fifth anniversary of the conclusion of the Second Vatican Council, in 1990, to issue the most important recent magisterial document on evangelization, the encyclical *Redemptoris missio* (Mission of the Redeemer), a document that draws liberally from the insights that Paul VI articulated in *Evangelii nuntiandi*. In this important encyclical the Pope made it clear that this "new evangelization" has its roots in the documents of the Second Vatican Council.

The Second Vatican Council sought to renew the Church's life and activity in the light of the needs of the contemporary world. The Council emphasized the Church's "missionary nature." . . . Twenty-five years after the conclusion of the Council and the publication of the Decree on Missionary Activity *Ad Gentes*, fifteen years after the Apostolic Exhortation *Evangelii Nuntiandi* issued by Pope Paul VI, and in continuity with the magisterial teaching of my predecessors, I wish to invite the Church to renew her missionary commitment.[3]

In the document intended to orient the Church as she entered the third millennium, *Novo millennio ineunte* (At the Beginning of a New Millennium), John Paul II again repeated his understanding of the twofold purpose of the Council:

> From the beginning of my pontificate, my thoughts had been on this Holy Year 2000 as an important appointment. I thought of its celebration as a providential opportunity during which the Church, thirty-five years after the Second Vatican Ecumenical Council, would examine how far she had renewed herself in order to be able to take up her evangelizing mission with fresh enthusiasm.[4]

A Focus on Evangelization

Avery Dulles wrote frequently about the significance of Vatican II's focus on evangelization and its emergence as a major theme of the post–Vatican II pontificates.

> In my judgment the evangelical turn in the ecclesial vision of Popes Paul VI and John Paul II is one of the most surprising and important developments in the Catholic Church since Vatican II. . . . All of this constitutes a remarkable shift in the Catholic tradition . . . today we seem to be witnessing the birth of a new Catholicism that, without loss of its institutional, sacramental, and social dimensions, is authentically evangelical. . . . Catholic spirituality at its best has always promoted a deep personal relationship with Christ. In evangelizing we are required to raise our eyes to him and to transcend all ecclesiocentrism. The Church is of importance but is not self-enclosed. It is a means of drawing the whole world into union with God through Jesus Christ. . . . Too

many Catholics of our day seem never to have encountered Christ. They know a certain amount about him from the teaching of the Church, but they lack direct personal familiarity. . . . The first and highest priority is for the Church to proclaim the good news concerning Jesus Christ as a joyful message to all the world. Only if the Church is faithful to its evangelical mission can it hope to make its distinctive contribution in the social, political, and cultural spheres.[5]

When John Paul II speaks of the "new evangelization," he primarily means the need to re-evangelize those traditionally Christian countries[6] that have been weakened by a process of secularization that is choking off faith.[7] In these countries or regions, there may be many people who bear the name of Catholic but do not follow Jesus as disciples and friends.

During John Paul II's pontificate, Cardinal Joseph Ratzinger described the actual situation in stark terms:

We are witnessing a sort of mass apostasy; the number of baptized persons is decreasing drastically. . . . And an undeniable advance of secularism, as we have already pointed out, is also ascertainable, with different features, in the United States. In short, in the Western world the almost complete identity that once existed between European and American culture and Christian culture is dissolving. All this is true. And the number of people in the West who feel that they are really members of the Church will decline further in the near future. We do not know what might happen in fifty years time — such futurology remains impossible — but for the near future we see the process of secularization continuing; we see the faith diminishing; we see the separation between the commonly accepted culture and Christian faith and culture.[8]

John Paul II saw an urgent need to call to conversion the many millions of nominal Catholics who are in this situation throughout the world. In the document that attempts to sum up "what the Spirit has been saying"[9] since the time of Vatican II until the dawn of the new millennium, *Novo millennio ineunte,* he makes the striking statement:

Even in countries evangelized many centuries ago, the reality of a "Christian society" which, amid all the frailties which have always marked human life, measured itself explicitly on Gospel values, is now gone.[10]

3

The Pope also called for a renewed evangelization — *ad gentes* — to the unevangelized peoples of the world, directed to those who have never had a chance to hear the gospel. He asked the whole Church at every level to review its plans and priorities to make sure that evangelization is at the center.

> I sense that the moment has come to commit all of the Church's energies to a new evangelization and to the mission *ad gentes*. No believer in Christ, no institution of the Church, can avoid this supreme duty: to proclaim Christ to all peoples.[11]

Evangelization in the conciliar documents and the important postconciliar documents of Popes Paul VI and John Paul II has a broad meaning that includes many different activities such as good example in the witness of our life, works of charity and mercy, catechesis, and work for justice and peace. But there is a common theme in all these documents, an insistence that if the central activity of proclaiming Jesus with a view to leading people to conversion is missing, the most important element of evangelization is missing.

> There is no true evangelization if the name, the teaching, the life, the promises, the kingdom and the mystery of Jesus of Nazareth, the Son of God, are not proclaimed.[12]

> Evangelization will also always contain — as the foundation, center, and at the same time, summit of its dynamism — a clear proclamation that, in Jesus Christ, the Son of God made man, who died and rose from the dead, salvation is offered to all men, as a gift of God's grace and mercy.[13]

> Preaching constitutes the Church's first and fundamental way of serving the coming of the kingdom in individuals and in human society.[14]

> The proclamation of the Word of God has *Christian conversion* as its aim: a complete and sincere adherence to Christ and his Gospel through faith. . . . Conversion means accepting, by a personal decision, the saving sovereignty of Christ and becoming his disciple.[15]

Although there has been a major emphasis in the post–Vatican II Church on the essentially missionary nature of the Church and the responsibility of all the baptized to take part in this mission of evangelization, evangelization is still often more a slogan or a "flavor" than a regular part of the baptized Catholic's way of life.[16]

Evangelization: What Is Holding It Back?

One reason why evangelization may be stymied is that there seems to be in the minds of many Catholics, and other Christians as well, a lack of conviction that being a Christian is really necessary in order to be saved. If it is not really necessary to become a Christian in order to be saved, why bother to evangelize? The reasons often given for evangelizing include appeals to a "greater richness" or a "greater fullness," or "making explicit what is already implicitly there." In a culture that is characterized by hostility to claims of absolute truth and unique means to salvation, many Catholics apparently find these reasons to be less than compelling.

But, of course, this lack of conviction finds a certain basis in the Church's own teaching.[17] The Church definitely teaches that it is possible for non-Christians to be saved without hearing the gospel or coming to explicit faith in Christ. There is a certain tension between the call to evangelize and the acknowledgment that conversion to Christ and the Church is not absolutely necessary in order to be saved. John Paul II acknowledges this tension in his encyclical on mission.

He repeats the traditional teaching that Christ and the Church are necessary for salvation and then acknowledges that God has provided ways for people who have not heard the gospel to come into contact with these saving mysteries in a mysterious but potentially effective manner. "It is necessary to keep these two truths together, namely, the real possibility of salvation in Christ for all mankind and the necessity of the Church for salvation."[18]

> The universality of salvation means that it is granted not only to those who explicitly believe in Christ and have entered the Church. Since salvation is offered to all, it must be made concretely available to all. But it is clear that today, as in the past, many people do not have an opportunity to come to know or accept the gospel revelation or to enter the Church. The social and cultural conditions in which they live do not permit this, and frequently they have been brought up in other religious traditions. For such people salvation in Christ is accessible by virtue of a grace which, while having a mysterious relationship to the Church, does not make them formally part of the Church but enlightens them in a

way which is accommodated to their spiritual and material situation. This grace comes from Christ; it is the result of his Sacrifice and is communicated by the Holy Spirit. It enables each person to attain salvation through his or her free cooperation.[19]

In these important texts from sections 9-10 of *Redemptoris missio,* John Paul cites as backing for his teaching texts from *Lumen gentium* 14-17, and a text from *Gaudium et spes* 22. There is a similar text to be found in *Ad gentes* 7.

Charles Morerod interprets this text of John Paul II in terms of explicit and implicit membership in the Church.

> All elements of this passage are important: Non-explicit Christians, who had no real opportunity to meet or understand the Gospel, can be saved, but always under two conditions: (1) salvation occurs through a grace that comes from Christ, is communicated by the Spirit, and is related to the Church, and (2) this process involves some free cooperation on their part.[20]

A careful analysis of these texts is necessary to see if the ambivalence of Catholics towards evangelization could be lessened by a more precise understanding of what exactly the Church is teaching about the possibility of salvation for those who have never heard the gospel. While doctrinal ignorance or confusion is certainly a reason for the lack of response to the urgent conciliar and papal calls to evangelization, it is certainly not the only reason. Other reasons would certainly include the lack of personal encounter with Christ that John Paul cites as a necessary basis for becoming an evangelizer, the lack of contact with the power of the Holy Spirit,[21] and certain pastoral mentalities that keep pastoral workers focused on "maintenance" rather than "mission."[22] In this book, we will only attempt to focus on one obstacle to a response to the call to evangelization, namely, a certain doctrinal ignorance or confusion about what exactly the Church is teaching about the possibility of salvation outside the visible bounds of the Church, or of Christianity. It is because evangelization is so essential to the fundamental identity of the Church, particularly at this moment when the whole Church is being called to a "new evangelization," that establishing doctrinal clarity in this area is of great importance. The fullest treatment of this issue in the Council documents is in *Lumen gentium* 16, and we will devote our attention primarily to this text.

CHAPTER II

Lumen gentium *16: Initial Observations*

The Salvation of Non-Christians: The Council's Teaching

We are trying to determine what precisely the Church is teaching regarding one important question: What are the necessary conditions for and actual limitations on the possibility of non-Christians being saved without coming to explicit faith in Christ and membership in the Catholic Church?

The primary text from Vatican II that most thoroughly and authoritatively deals with this question is *LG* 16.[1] There are two other Vatican II texts that deal with this question that need to be taken into account: *AG* 7 and *GS* 22. Since *LG* as a Constitution is considered the "keystone" of the documents of Vatican II, and other documents often explicitly ground their teaching by referencing it, we will focus primarily on the *LG* 16 text.[2] *AG* explicitly relates its teaching to the theological framework of *LG*. *GS* 22 specifically cites *LG* 16 as a basis for its teaching.

We will consider these texts in an attempt to explicate their meaning in terms of their internal structure and referents, their place in the larger context of *LG* and Vatican II, and in light of the theological and magisterial traditions from which they flow. It is worth noting, as Msgr. Gérard Philips does, that the final vote in favor of *LG* was overwhelmingly in favor, with only five *non placet* votes.[3]

Even though *LG* 16 consists of only ten sentences, it is packed with carefully constructed phrases with significant theological import, and very important footnotes.[4] The text first explains how "those who have not yet received the Gospel are related to the People of God in various ways." A footnote here references a text from St. Thomas, *ST* III, q. 8, a. 3, ad 1: "Those who are unbaptized, though not actually in the Church, are in the Church potentially. And this potentiality is rooted in two things — first and principally, in the power of Christ, which is sufficient for the salvation of the whole human race; secondly, in free-will." It is clear that this "relatedness" is not actually salvific, but potentially salvific.[5] Special mention is made first of the Jews, then of the Muslims, and then of unspecified other religions and peoples, "those who in shadows and images seek the unknown God." Buddhists and Hindus are specifically mentioned in *Nostra aetate*, but the text here does not mention them by name since it is not intending to be exclusive or limit its teaching to just the religions it names. The text then affirms God's universal salvific will, citing 1 Timothy 2:4 as a basis for its exploration of how salvation for those who do not know the gospel might be possible. We will designate this first section of *LG* 16 (the first four sentences) as *LG* 16a, although it will not be the focus of our analysis. Later on in the text, which we will cite below, a fourth group of those who have not heard the gospel is added, those who "have not yet arrived at an explicit knowledge of God." We will include here the three sentences of *LG* 16 that treat of how salvation for all four of these categories of non-Christians might be possible.

> Those who, through no fault of their own, do not know the Gospel of Christ or his Church, but who nevertheless seek God with a sincere heart, and moved by grace, try in their actions to do his will as they know it through the dictates of their conscience — those too may achieve eternal salvation. Nor shall divine providence deny the assistance necessary for salvation to those who, without any fault of theirs, have not yet arrived at an explicit knowledge of God, and who, not without grace, strive to lead a good life. Whatever good or truth is found amongst them is considered by the Church to be a preparation for the Gospel[6] and given by him who enlightens all men that they may at length have life.

We will designate the above three sentences of *LG* 16 as *LG* 16b.

> But very often *(at saepius),*[7] deceived by the Evil One, men have become vain in their reasonings, have exchanged the truth of God for a lie and served the world rather than the Creator (cf. Rom. 1:21, 25). Or else, living and dying in this world without God, they are exposed to ultimate

despair. Hence to procure the glory of God and the salvation of all these, the Church, mindful of the Lord's command, "preach the Gospel to every creature" (Mk. 16:16) takes zealous care to foster the missions.

We will designate these concluding three sentences of *LG* 16 as *LG* 16c.

We have already commented on two of the three footnotes attached to *LG* 16 (all three are reproduced in Appendix I). The third footnote is particularly relevant to our study and we will have occasion to examine it at length in the next chapter.

The Council here is teaching that under certain very specific conditions salvation is possible for non-Christians. What are these conditions?

1. That non-Christians be not culpable for their ignorance of the gospel.
2. That non-Christians seek God with a sincere heart.
3. That non-Christians try to live their life in conformity with what they know of God's will. This is commonly spoken of as following the natural law or the light of conscience. It is important to note, as the Council does, in order to avoid a Pelagian interpretation, that this is possible only because people are "moved by grace."
4. That non-Christians welcome or receive whatever "good or truth" they live amidst — referring possibly to elements of their non-Christian religions or cultures, which may refract to some degree the light that enlightens every man (John 1:9). These positive elements are intended to be "preparation for the Gospel." One could understand this to mean either a preparation for the actual hearing of the gospel or preparation for, perhaps, some communication of God by interior illumination.

The Related Council Texts

The two other Council texts we cited must now be considered.

GS 22, when speaking of our incorporation into the death and resurrection of Christ, which gives us hope for our resurrection, has this to say about non-Christians:

All this holds true not for Christians only but also for all men of good will in whose hearts grace is active invisibly. For since Christ died for all, and since all men are in fact called to one and the same destiny, which is divine, we must hold that the Holy Spirit offers to all the possibility of being made partners, in a way known to God, in the paschal mystery.

LG 16 is cited in a footnote as a foundation for this statement.

Being "men of good will" is another way of stating a condition that is more fully explicated in *LG* 16b. *GS* 22 does not try to explain how this possibility of salvation is offered and what response to it must be made for it to be effective. Joseph Ratzinger, in his commentary on *GS*, thinks that the explicit mention of the Holy Spirit in *GS* 22 as the means by which the paschal mystery is made present adds an important element to *LG* 16, which he thinks could be interpreted in too Pelagian a manner, laying too much stress on what man must do to be saved, even though the role of grace is mentioned.[8] I do not share this concern.

Finally, *AG* 7 must be considered.

> The reason for missionary activity lies in the will of God, "who wishes all men to be saved and to come to the knowledge of the truth. For there is one God and one Mediator between God and men, himself a man, Jesus Christ, who gave himself as a ransom for all" (1 Tim 2:4-5), "neither is there salvation in any other" (Acts 4:12). Everyone, therefore, ought to be converted to Christ, who is known through the preaching of the Church, and they ought, by baptism, to become incorporated into him, and into the Church which is his body. Christ himself explicitly asserted the necessity of faith and baptism (cf. Mk 16:16; Jn 3:5), and thereby affirmed at the same time the necessity of the Church, which men enter through baptism as through a door. Hence those cannot be saved, who, knowing that the Catholic Church was founded through Jesus Christ, by God, as something necessary, still refuse to enter it, or to remain in it [*LG* 14 is referenced here]. So, although in ways known to himself God can lead those who, through no fault of their own, are ignorant of the Gospel to that faith without which it is impossible to please him (Heb 11:6), the Church, nevertheless, still has the obligation and also the sacred right to evangelize. And so, today as always, missionary activity retains its full force and necessity.

The obvious intent of this text is to reaffirm the continuing importance of missionary activity. It would appear, though, that relative to the world's population, the numbers of those who know the Catholic Church is founded by Christ and is necessary for salvation but refuse to enter her are relatively small. Correspondingly, for the vast majority, salvation must then be possible without hearing the gospel. Emphasizing that it is the will of God that missionary activity be carried out is certainly, in itself, a compelling reason; but for many people it fails to explain why missionary activity is still important given that people can be saved without it, and leaves the exhortation weaker than it could be.

The Council Historians: *LG* 16 Was Relatively Noncontroversial

Was there much debate on these texts during the Council? Were they controversial? There was little significant debate on *LG* 16.[9]

In fact the original draft of *De ecclesia* prepared by the Curia contains the substance of the teaching that *LG* 16 presents in the final, approved text. Even though *De ecclesia* went through significant revision and reorganization, on this point there was no substantial change. The curial draft, given to the fathers of the Council at its beginning, expressed what eventually became the teaching of *LG* 16 like this:

> As for those ordered by desire towards the Church, these include not only catechumens, who, moved by the Spirit, consciously and explicitly desire to enter the Church, but also those who, even if not knowing that the Catholic Church is the true and sole Church of Christ, still, by God's grace, implicitly and unknowingly desire the equivalent, either because they sincerely will what Christ himself wills or because, though ignorant of Christ, they sincerely desire to fulfil the will of God their Creator. The gifts of heavenly grace will never be wanting to those who sincerely desire and ask to be renewed by the divine light.[10]

Karl Rahner states that he thinks the issues contained in *LG* 16 were of more long-term importance than the issues concerning collegiality, the "new exegesis," the relationship between Scripture and tradition, and other such issues that dominated the Council's attention. He marvels at how little attention was addressed to *LG* 16 and "how little opposition the conservative wing of the Council brought to bear on this point." He considers what he understands to be "this optimism concerning salvation . . . one of the most noteworthy results of the Second Vatican Council."[11] In a later chapter we will evaluate Rahner's claims concerning the newness of this teaching and its discontinuity with the tradition.

When one examines the *relatio*[12] that introduced the amended texts to be voted on by the Council fathers, one is struck at how little attention was focused on *LG* 16 compared to, for example, *LG* 15, which treats of the relationship of non-Catholic Christians to the Catholic Church. The *relatio* as it presents *LG* 15 states:

> *De indole generali paragraphi* aliqui Patres quondam anxietatem manifestaverunt . . .

The Commission's response was "quod timor praedictus non apparet fundatus."[13]

In contrast, the *relatio* for *LG* 16 was the briefest of the four presentations covering *LG* 13-16.[14]

The bulk of the issues considered in the *relatio* had to do with the structuring of the material or with the supporting footnotes. The *relatio* noted that some Council fathers had made suggestions that some things be made more explicit or said more or less strongly, and the Theological Commission thought that the text it was presenting adequately handled these concerns, but there seemed to be no fundamental disagreement or controversy noted and the text of *LG* 16 was overwhelmingly approved.[15]

In fact, when prominent commentators on the work of the Council listed the main areas of controversy or concern during the course of the Council, the teaching about the possibility of people being saved without hearing the gospel was not listed. Joseph Ratzinger, in his book detailing the theological highlights of Vatican II, devoted only a few pages to this issue, and not in connection with *LG* 16 but in connection with *AG*. When he listed the main areas of concern that most drew the attention of the Council, this issue was not present.[16] Stronger concerns about this issue surfaced when the text *Ad gentes* was debated. There were also some interventions throughout the course of the Council in relation to several of the documents that called for a greater mention of the reality of sin, the work of the devil, and the reality of hell,[17] but the focal point of these concerns, to the extent that they surfaced at all, was the debate on *AG*.[18] Even there the focus of the debate was not on the conditions under which it was possible for people who have never heard the gospel to be saved. Rather it was on the need to give a theologically compelling and inspiring account of the need for mission that would provide encouragement to missionaries. There was also much debate and many interventions having to do with how the mission of the Church should be structured in relationship to current and proposed structures, and issues of central authority versus local freedom to adapt, as well as a strong concern to show that mission was the task of each member of the Church, not just the professional missionaries.

The big issues that dominated the debates on *LG* were those that pertained to balancing collegiality and papal primacy[19] and the issues connected with how to understand and relate to non-Catholic Christians, the focus of *LG* 15, which was developed more fully in the Decree on Ecumenism. Other significant issues that consumed attention during the years of the Council were those connected with the relationship with the Jews, the question of religious liberty, and the huge and complex questions about what attitude to take towards the "modern world" and how to "speak" to it. Concerns on the implications for evangelization of the teaching that it is possible to be saved without hearing the gospel did not surface in a noticeable way until the debate on *AG*. Even then it did not result in a close analysis of the *LG* 16 text,[20] which is the text that contains an important aspect of the Council's answer to why ongoing missionary effort is truly necessary. It simply resulted in a strong reaffirmation of the importance of ongoing missionary work. Omitting a strong explanation of the theological rationale about why missionary activity was still urgent undoubtedly contributed to the rapid collapse of missionary activity in the years after the Council.[21]

Some Early Concerns about Theological Currents

Some of the Council fathers were motivated in their call for a strong affirmation of the need for missionary activity, by their reaction to the disturbing pastoral realities of the lack of a really indigenous Asian Christianity, the influence of the critique of colonialism on the mission enterprise, and recent theological theories that questioned basic missionary assumptions about the need for non-Christians to become Christian. Missionary bishops and others submitted interventions that voiced their concern that the confidence of their missionaries would be undermined if there was not a strong reaffirmation of the need for missions. Ratzinger describes the situation of missions and missionaries, even in the early 1960s, as already being one of "crisis."

> The crucial issue, which gravely affected the whole context of the question, especially for the missionary bishops, was the crisis in which the very idea of missions found itself. The cause of this crisis lay in profound changes in modern thinking about the necessity of missions. The

motive which had driven missionaries in the past to bring other people to Christ had increasingly lost its urgency. What drove the great missionaries at the beginning of the modern era to go out into the world, and what filled them with holy unrest, was the conviction that salvation is in Christ alone. The untold millions of people who suddenly emerged from unknown worlds beyond the horizon would thus be hopelessly doomed to eternal ruin without the message of the Gospel. . . . What was involved was either eternal salvation or eternal damnation.[22]

Ratzinger also notes that the trend in theology was very much in the direction of seeing God's salvific activity outside the bounds of the visible Church, which hitherto had been seen, he states, only by way of concession and exception.

It is important to note here that the overwhelming theological and magisterial interpretation of the texts of Scripture on the issue of salvation up until relatively recently has understood Scripture as saying that it is likely that the majority of the human race will be lost. This is the view of Irenaeus, Basil, Cyril of Jerusalem, John Chrysostom, Augustine, Aquinas, Canisius, and Bellarmine, as well as many others.[23]

Ratzinger also identifies the theological trend, which was even then gathering force, to see the non-Christian world religions more positively. These trends were already percolating throughout the Church, and those directly engaged in the missionary enterprise were particularly sensitive to them and understood them to be a significant challenge to the whole rationale of the missionary enterprise. Ratzinger's comments on this are worth noting:

Here, again, closer reflection will once more demonstrate that not all the ideas characteristic of modern theology are derived from Scripture. This idea is, if anything, alien to the biblical-thought world or even antipathetic to its spirit. The prevailing optimism, which understands the world religions as in some way salvific agencies, is simply irreconcilable with the biblical assessment of these religions. It is remarkable how sharply the Council now reacted to these modern views. During the debate on the parallel passages on the text on the Church, it had seemed more amenable.[24]

There is an obvious concern in this text of *AG* that acknowledging the possibility of people being saved without hearing the gospel could undermine the missionary effort of the Church. *AG* strongly affirms the need to continue preaching the gospel, but the fundamental teaching about why this still makes sense is actually contained in *LG* 16. We must return to *LG* 16c to see why the missionary mandate is not undermined by this possibility. After listing the conditions under which it might be possible for non-Christians to be saved without knowing the gospel, it comments on the unlikelihood in many cases of these conditions being met.

> But very often, deceived by the Evil One, men have become vain in their reasonings, have exchanged the truth of God for a lie and served the world rather than the Creator (cf. Rom. 1:21, 25). Or else, living and dying in this world without God, they are exposed to ultimate despair. Hence to procure the glory of God and the salvation of all these, the Church, mindful of the Lord's command, "preach the Gospel to every creature" (Mk. 16:16) takes zealous care to foster the missions.

The witness of Scripture is that the powerful workings of the world, the flesh, and the devil are operative among non-Christians in a less restrained way than they are among those who live within the protection of the means of grace available in the Church. If Christians sometimes stifle the light of conscience or disobey a direct command of Christ or sometimes prefer the darkness to the light, how much more likely for this to happen in the absence of all the help of explicit revelation and sacramental life in the Church?

The Scripture cited is Romans 1:21-25, which indeed testifies to the awful reality of those to whom God has revealed something of himself rejecting that revelation and, "without excuse," turning to idolatry and immorality and, as a consequence, incurring God's wrath.

As Bishop Bonaventure Kloppenburg stated in his commentary on *LG*, in reference to the texts we have just considered on the possibility of salvation for non-Christians who have never heard the gospel:

> It is clear that, for all the surprising and unusual wealth of texts on this point, Vatican II is not simply guaranteeing the salvation of all men. In the Constitution on the Church which we have several times cited here, the Council notes that "very often men, deceived by the Evil One, have become caught up in a futile reasoning and have exchanged the truth of God for a lie, serving the creature rather than the Creator (cf. Rom. 1:21-25). Or some there are who, living and dying in a world without God,

are subject to utter hopelessness" (*LG* 16). In addition, the texts we have quoted make it clear that the Council always requires loyal cooperation with grace, a sincere search, and good will on man's part.[25]

Bishop Kloppenburg reminds us that the possibility of damnation is not just something that the non-evangelized face, but all of us do.

> In addition to reaffirming the possibility of eternal damnation, the Council says in unqualified terms that "whosoever knowing that the Catholic Church was made necessary by God through Jesus Christ, would refuse to enter her or remain in her could not be saved" (*LG* 14), and that "he is not saved . . . who, though he is part of the body of the Church, does not persevere in charity. He remains indeed in the bosom of the Church, but, as it were only in a 'bodily' manner and not 'in his heart'" (*LG* 14).[26]

Kloppenburg is one of the relatively few commentators who even mention this section of *LG* 16, and when they do, it is often in passing, without analysis or extended commentary.[27]

Another brief, but significant commentary on *LG* 16 that appeared shortly after the conclusion of the Council was that of Christopher O'Donnell. He notes the positive orientation of the Council to the possibility of those who have not heard the gospel being saved, but notes also "the profound theological difficulties involved."

> In the present order man can be saved only by an act of supernatural charity. A love of God not inspired by supernatural faith is not sufficient (*ST,* I-II, q. 62, aa. 1-3). . . . This insistence by the Council on the universally operative will to save in God may seem to lead to a paradox: all men are given the grace to be saved yet the Catholic mind does not consider missionary work to be a matter of making salvation easier for the non-believer. Rather is it the firm conviction throughout the ages, and particularly strong today, that the missioner brings salvation, not an easier way to obtaining it. More than obedience to the command of Christ, the voluntary self-exile of the missioner is seen as an act of the highest charity and efficacy. Hence the relevance of the Council's analysis of the difficulties that lie in the way of the unbeliever, sometimes making it almost impossible for grace to work in the distorted nature of man. The missioner can indeed be truly said to bring salvation.[28]

Cardinal Francis George, in an excellent commentary on *AG*, does identify the text in *LG* 16c as significant but does not comment extensively. He notes that *LG* 16b mentions the possibility of people who have never heard the gospel being saved and then comments:

> The constitution goes on, however, to insist that one cannot simply accept this precarious situation as unchangeable. Lacking "the truth of God," open to human weakness and the wiles of the devil, even despite what is positive in their own religions, "they are exposed to ultimate despair." The Church is obliged in her missions to bring the offer of Christ's salvation.[29]

McNamara in his commentary notes the importance of the concluding section of *LG* 16c:

> The concluding remarks of article 16 serve a twofold purpose: they guard against a facile and unrealistic optimism and prepare the way for the theme of the missions, which is the subject matter of article seventeen. There are very many, we are reminded, who, deceived by Satan, do not find their way to God. They turn aside from the truth and they are guilty of the worship of idols or, living and dying completely without God, are deprived of all hope. This severe judgment on the spiritual situation of a considerable section of mankind leads naturally to mention of the missions.

McNamara, writing in 1968, anticipates the "leap" that many would make from the possibility of some being saved without hearing the gospel to the *probability* or even certainty that all or almost all will be saved without hearing the gospel, and sees this last section of *LG* 16 as being placed there to guard against this unwarranted leap, although he interprets it in a minimalist fashion.[30]

> It guards against the opinion which, on the grounds that non-Christians can be saved even if they never hear the gospel, would deny that the Word of God and the sacraments of the Church, bring them a richer and more assured salvation.[31]

Gustave Thils also provides an interpretation, noting that even though the Old Testament itself and some Church Fathers mention nota-

ble "pagans" who seem to be just men, there are far more unfavorable patristic judgments on the state of pagans, and that *LG* 16 takes all of this
into account.

> Is it necessary to add that these positive evaluations are balanced by the
> negative judgments of a large number of ecclesiastical writers? And in
> the Constitution *Lumen gentium* (II, no. 16), one reads that "too often,
> men deceived by the Evil One, have become vain in their reasonings,
> and have exchanged the truth of God for a lie and have served the crea-
> ture rather than the Creator (cf. Rm. 1:21, 25) . . ." At least there remains
> the conclusion that a certain perfection in paganism seems to be a real-
> izable ideal.[32]

Some commentators mention only the second part of the teaching of
LG 16 that we are considering (*LG* 16b), about the possibility under certain
conditions of people who have never heard the gospel being saved, but
skip over lightly or completely ignore the third part of the teaching (*LG*
16c), which points out that very often these conditions are not met.[33]

It is clear from consulting the Council speeches made in connection
with *AG* that the intent of the Council fathers was very "traditional" in
terms of understanding the mission of the Church to involve at its core
"saving souls." Grillmeier, in his commentary detailing the history of the
development of the text, mentions that from the beginning these sections
of *LG* (13-17) had an overarching missionary context.

> In the original draft of 1963 this section (now *LG* 16) took up the mis-
> sionary task of the Church with regard to all non-Christians, and the
> heading was: "Of non-Christians who are to be led to the Church." But
> now Article 16 is made the continuation of Articles 14 and 15 and its
> theme has become the various ways in which non-Christian groups are
> ordained *(ordinantur)* to the "people of God."[34]

The ending of *LG* 16 now provides a transition to the full missionary call,
which is presented in *LG* 17 quite emphatically.

Cardinal George draws our attention to two speeches, one from Archbishop Cordeiro, and one from Cardinal Suenens to illustrate this point.

Cardinal George notes that Archbishop Cordeiro, from Karachi, Paki-
stan, speaking in the name of fifty bishops, emphasized the importance of
drawing people to faith.

This was indeed the council fathers' vision when they insisted that "God is fully glorified only when all men live consciously in the faith of Christ. This is the goal of all missionary activity."[35]

Cardinal George also quotes and comments on a speech of Cardinal Suenens, who was one of the four moderators of the Council and played a very significant role in the leadership of the entire Council, to support the same point regarding the intentions of the Council fathers in *AG*.

"Our aim is not to confirm each one in his own religion as does Moral Rearmament but to preach the Gospel to every creature." This, of course, was a lifelong concern of Cardinal Suenens.[36]

Philips, who perhaps more than any other single theologian was involved in the crafting of *LG* from its very beginnings to its final form, notes that the sequence of sections from *LG* 13-17 presents a panorama of God's universal salvific will (*LG* 13) through the various categories and their relationship to salvation (*LG* 14-16) that culminates in a stirring call to preach the gospel to all those non-evangelized.

The main task was to show how the affirmation of the universal salvific will of God was related to the necessity of preaching the faith to all men. The result was that the last section took the form of an outline of missiology which dealt with the essentials on a high level of thought.[37]

Philips, in his multivolume commentary on *LG*, comments on the whole text of *LG* 16, including its concluding sentences, in greater detail than any other commentator I have discovered, even though it only encompasses nine pages of commentary overall, and only about two pages of the text is on the "very often" (*LG* 16c) section.

Philips traces the patristic and magisterial development of doctrine that supports the teaching of *LG* 16 on the possibility of those who have never heard the gospel being saved, but calls for a balance, which he finds in the text of *LG* 16. It is a balance that avoids the extremes of presuming everyone who has not heard the gospel is lost, or the other extreme, that of presuming that everyone who has not heard the gospel is saved and therefore there is no need for evangelization. As Philips puts it in commenting on the possibility of those who have never heard the gospel being saved, and the picture that Paul paints in Romans 1:

They know him through the creation, writes St. Paul to the Romans, 1:19-20, and they accomplish that which his law has written in their heart (Rom. 2:14-15). The picture of pagan perversion, so somber as it is portrayed by St. Paul, does not permit us to accuse the author of pessimism. A realistic exegesis requires us to recognize an alternation of light and shadows in the exposition of his doctrine.[38]

He continues:

This so-called broader view, so prized in our days, is a reaction against the former preaching which brandished the firebrands in relationship to the perversion of the world and spoke of the ruin of the universe as if the Savior had not come. From one extreme, some go to the other extreme without being realistic. The opposition of the Evil One against Christ is not a medieval myth, yet it is not necessary to present the demon with horns and cloven hooves. In no way does St. Paul excuse idolaters who in their vain and confused reasoning have exchanged the truth for a lie (Rom. 1:20, 25). They have raised up the creature or themselves to the level of God, where they try to suppress God completely, and there only remains for them ultimate despair. The absurd must give a clue to the real. It is urgent therefore to counter the temptation that emanates from primitive idolatry or from a highly intellectual idolatry.[39]

The magisterium does not resolve the issue as to how saving grace can be applied to individual non-Christians but speaks of God acting "in ways known to himself" (*AG* 7), or "in a way known to God" (*GS* 22). The *relatio* on *LG* 16 notes that the Council fathers wanted the "how" left open to theological reflection.[40]

Aloys Grillmeier, in his commentary on *LG* 16, sums up the state of this question like this:

How actual justification (in faith and love) finally comes about is not said in the Constitution, which is only concerned to show that all relationships to God are at once orientated to the acceptance of the God of salvation, and hence are an ordination towards the people of God. This is what is common to the people of God and to those who seek God. . . . Then the Council seeks a final point of insertion for salvation and ordination towards the people of God in those who have inculpably failed to reach express acknowledgment of God, but try to live well with the help of God's grace. All that is affirmed is that God's salutary grace is not denied them. How does this grace effect salvation? Is salvation possible within the bounds of this inculpable, theoretical atheism, say, by means of a theism implicit in the moral life under the influence of grace, which also implies revelation and faith? Or does grace liberate them from such atheism — and when? The text does not answer these questions. But if salutary grace is possible apart from the explicit preaching of the gospel, the first possibility cannot be excluded. In any case, the moral attitude of such atheists is termed a *praeparatio evangelica.* The precise way in which the grace of God uses these presuppositions to take hold of men is not described. But an inward guidance is supposed, as follows from the words of the text, which speaks of "goodness" and "truth" as the gift of him "who enlightens all men so that they may *finally (tandem)* have life."[41]

Bishop Butler, who was also involved in the drafting of *LG*, refers to the beginning of Chapter II's citation of Acts in this regard. "At all times and in every race, anyone who fears God and does what is right has been acceptable to him (cf. Acts 10:35) (*LG* 9)." This is in reference to the Gentile household of Cornelius being disposed to hear the gospel in the preaching of Peter.

He comments:

> The council does not here explain what is meant by this "fear of God and working of righteousness." Later on, however (n. 16), it remarks that "divine providence does not deny help needful for salvation to those who, without their own fault, have not yet reached an express recognition of God and who strive to attain to a life of rectitude — in which striving they are (in fact) helped by God's grace." We shall hardly be going beyond the intention of the constitution if we identify the fear of God with a genuine docility towards the reality of "ultimate concern," and the working of righteousness with a basic obedience to conscience even though conscience is inculpably misinformed.[42]

Avery Dulles, in reflecting on the question of how God might work to give saving grace to non-Christians apart from the preaching of the gospel, cites the opinion (developed by Maurice Eminyan) that

> By a kind of divine illumination at the moment of death, an explicit decision for Christ and the Church might be made possible, and therefore

also required. . . . This view has the merit of reconciling the modern teaching that God's salvific will extends to every individual with the thesis, supported by Augustine, Aquinas, and most scholastic theologians, that no one can be saved in the Christian era without explicit belief in the Trinity and the Incarnation. Even if (as is rather commonly held today) a more implicit type of faith suffices for the salvation of the unevangelized, still it seems likely that God's grace may give special lights and attractions that favor a salvific option at the moment of death.[43]

On the other hand, James O'Connor gives some good reasons why such a "final option" in many cases does not appear likely.

All in all, the theory of the final option must be judged at least improbable. As far as can be discerned, we do not die, freely disposing of ourselves, or recapitulating a life. It is part of our weakness due to sin, our fallen state, that we generally just fall or drift into death with no ability to do anything for ourselves. For most humans, at least, unconscious or semiconscious, numbed or restless with lack of comfort or with pain, beset by fear of what is ahead or regret for what is behind, death is not a summation. It is a loss, a disintegration. We are not Prometheans, but weak and devastated humans.[44]

Yet, there are some remarkable "revelations" given to Catherine of Siena by the Father as recounted in *The Dialogue,* that pertain to this possibility of a final illumination at the point of death.

At this end point of death, when they see that they cannot escape from my hands, the worm of conscience (which, as I told you, had been blinded by their selfish love of themselves) begins to see again. And in the realization that their own sins have brought them to such an evil end, this worm of conscience gnaws away in self-reproach.

If such souls would have light to acknowledge and be sorry for their sins — and not because of the sufferings of hell that are their consequence, but because they have offended me, the supreme and eternal Good — they would still find mercy.

But if they pass the moment of death without that light, with only the worm of conscience and no hope in the blood, or grieving more for their own plight than for having offended me, then they have come to eternal damnation.[45]

The question of how God might act to save outside the "normal channels" remains open.

It is clear that the teaching of *LG* 16 is dependent on a long development of doctrine concerning the necessity of the Church for salvation and on the authority of Scripture, in its citation of Romans 1:21-25. In the next chapter we will take a closer look at this development of doctrine. In a subsequent chapter we will examine the scriptural underpinnings of the Council's teaching.

CHAPTER III

Lumen gentium *16: The Doctrinal Development*

Sometimes tracing the history of the development of an important doctrine can shed considerable light on what precisely are the theological issues involved and can make possible a more nuanced understanding of the doctrine than its current formulation at first suggests. Such is the case with *Lumen gentium* 16.

Some of this development can best be understood by examining the grouping of texts of which *LG* 16 forms a part. *LG* 13-17 form a unit that addresses the issue of how different communities are related to the Church and the implications for evangelization. *LG* 13 provides the framework and introduction.

> All men are called to this catholic unity which prefigures and promotes universal peace. And in different ways to it belong, or are related: the Catholic faithful, others who believe in Christ, and finally, all mankind, called by God's grace to salvation.

We have already conducted an initial analysis of *LG* 16, which continues to be our main focus, but briefly examining *LG* 14 and 15 will contribute to our understanding. Later on in the book, when we are drawing our conclusions, we will consider *LG* 17.

Lumen gentium 14: Fully Incorporated Members of the Church

This section of *LG* is devoted to a consideration of the Catholic faithful, whom the Council describes as being "fully incorporated into the Church."

Citing Mark 16:16 and John 3:5, the Council teaches that Christ himself established the necessity of the Church by asserting the necessity of faith and baptism. It draws the well-known conclusion:

> Hence they could not be saved who, knowing that the Catholic Church was founded as necessary by God through Christ, would refuse either to enter it, or to remain in it.

Full incorporation into the Church is understood by the Council to involve explicit membership, full communion, and the acceptance of "all the means of salvation" found within her, including the profession of faith, sacraments, and governance.[1]

But mere external membership is not enough to be saved. Perseverance in charity is necessary for a Catholic to be saved.

> Even though incorporated into the Church, one who does not however persevere in charity is not saved. He remains indeed in the bosom of the Church, but "in body" not "in heart."[2]

A number of commentators point out the significance of no longer only defining membership in terms of the external criteria but now also emphasizing the importance of the life of the Spirit and charity, the interior union with the Trinity.[3]

The Council develops its teaching that being a "fully incorporated member" of the Church is not enough to assure salvation.

> All children of the Church should nevertheless remember that their exalted condition results, not from their own merits, but from the grace of Christ. If they fail to respond in thought, word and deed to that grace, not only shall they not be saved, but they shall be the more severely judged.[4]

In 1961, just before the Council began, Yves Congar, the French Dominican theologian who was to have a major influence on the Council documents, published a book that raised an alarm about the presumption characteristic of many Catholics in mid-century France who seemed to live their lives not truly believing that there will be a final judgment. This presumption was to become even more widespread and firmly entrenched throughout the Church in the post-Conciliar years.

All the same, I personally am frightened at the ease with which so many men — and I am thinking only of my own acquaintances and those whom I meet every day — calmly banish from their lives the thought of God and of the covenant he offers us in the Gospel of Jesus Christ, of which the Church of the saints is the sign amongst us. They just go quietly on as if the problem did not exist. The bell rings to call them together for the offering of the Sacrifice of love's covenant; they go on doing odd jobs about the house, or they take a walk, or idle about by sea or river. . . . If they had no means of knowing, they would be like the Chinese or the Tibetan. . . . But these men whom I meet *have* the means of knowing, they *ought* to be uneasy. Or they have even known Jesus Christ, they have had a first approach from him; the covenant has been offered them. If they go on turning a deaf ear, the time during which God's patience keeps the offer open will come to an end. Instead, the day of wrath will come. The last penny will have to be paid: those who through light-mindedness or self-centeredness have ignored God's message of peace, those who, as the gospel puts so forcibly and yet gently, have not recognized the time of Christ's visiting them (Lk 29:44) will see the coming of the moment when, the hour for choice being passed, they will have despairingly to harvest the grapes of wrath.[5]

Catechumens, who have "an explicit intention to be incorporated into the Church, are by that very intention joined to her." This is the only place in the Council documents where the word "votum" (desire/intention) is used, even though it has played a much larger role in the development of doctrine and has been applied more widely in the tradition as we shall soon see.

Vatican II represents a major shift in how the Catholic Church viewed the status of non-Catholic Christians. The Council explicitly recognized that the Spirit has been urging Christians towards repentance for our disunity and a renewed desire for union. It mentioned the impact of the "ecumenical movement," acknowledging it as a grace, and cited it as one of the factors that has contributed to the Church's desire to reformulate her understanding of and relationships with the "separated brethren."[6]

Vatican II's decision in *LG* 8 to replace "est" with "subsistit in" was a big step in opening the way for a more positive assessment of the status of non-Catholic Christians and their churches or ecclesial communities.[7]

The official explanation provided by the Theological Commission said that this change was made "so as to be more consonant with the teaching about ecclesial elements to be found elsewhere than in the Roman Church."[8]

There were several other theological keys to this development. While previously, Orthodox and Protestants tended to be viewed primarily as schismatics and heretics, and the whole theological and magisterial tradition in its harsh judgment on these classes of Christians formed a backdrop for prevailing attitudes (namely, the strong and consistent teaching that schismatics and heretics were guilty of grave sin that placed their salvation in jeopardy), there was now an acknowledgment that those who were "born into" schismatic and heretical traditions ought not to be viewed in the same way as those who generated the schisms and heresies.

At the same time though, *LG* 14 restated the traditional understanding:

> Hence they could not be saved who, knowing that the Catholic Church was founded as necessary by God through Christ, would refuse either to enter it, or to remain in it.

However, it was no longer assumed that Orthodox and Protestants knew it was God's will for them to be Catholics. The *Decree on Ecumenism* expresses this explicitly:

> One cannot charge with the sin of the separation those who at present are born into these communities and in them are brought up in the faith of Christ, and the Catholic Church accepts them with respect and affection as brothers. For men who believe in Christ and have been properly baptized are put in some, though imperfect, communion with the Catholic Church. . . . It remains true that all who have been justified by faith in baptism are incorporated into Christ; they therefore have a right to be called Christians, and with good reason are accepted as brothers by the children of the Catholic Church.[9]

Not only does the Church recognize in these documents that most non-Catholic Christians are not to be charged with sin for remaining outside the visible structures of the Catholic Church, but the Church recognizes also that Catholics bear some responsibility for not living in such a way that "the fullness of truth," which is only to be found in the Catholic Church, shines forth convincingly in their lives. This is an instance of the awareness that began to grow with the discovery of the New World, as we will see later on in this chapter, that not just any preaching of the gospel

27

could be deemed adequate, thereby rendering culpable any who would not embrace that preaching.

> For although the Catholic Church has been endowed with all divinely revealed truth and with all means of grace, yet its members fail to live by them with all the fervor that they should. As a result the radiance of the Church's face shines less brightly in the eyes of our separated brethren and of the world at large, and the growth of God's kingdom is retarded.[10]

Another element leading to a reassessment of Catholic/non-Catholic relations was the recognition that what is held in common is in some ways more significant than what is not. The post-Reformation arguments over divisions have tended to overshadow what was nevertheless believed together. To believe together in the Trinity, the Incarnation, and the Redemption is a huge commonality. This new understanding is expressed clearly in *LG* 15:

> The Church knows that she is joined in many ways to the baptized who are honored by the name of Christian but who do not however profess the Catholic faith in its entirety or have not preserved unity or communion under the successor of Peter.

This text lists many areas of commonality including the sacred Scriptures, faith in the Trinity, a common baptism, and those "who indeed recognize and receive other sacraments in their own Churches or ecclesiastical communities."

Even in the "ecclesial communities" that are not hierarchically ordered and sacramentally focused, "there is . . . a sharing in prayer and spiritual benefits; these Christians are indeed in some real way joined to us in the Holy Spirit for, by his gifts and graces, his sanctifying power is also active in them and he has strengthened some of them even to the shedding of their blood."

The *Decree on Ecumenism* elaborates:

> Moreover, some, even very many, of the most significant elements and endowments which together go to build up and give life to the Church itself, can exist outside the visible boundaries of the Catholic Church: the written Word of God; the life of grace; faith, hope and charity, with

the other interior gifts of the Holy Spirit, as well as visible elements. All of these, which come from Christ and lead back to him, belong by right to the one Church of Christ. . . . It follows that the separated Churches and communities as such, though we believe they suffer from the defects already mentioned, have been by no means deprived of significance and importance in the mystery of salvation. For the Spirit of Christ has not refrained from using them as means of salvation which derive their efficacy from the very fullness of grace and truth entrusted to the Catholic Church.[11]

There is a clear recognition in these texts that the salvation of non-Catholic Christians is indeed quite possible because of all the elements of authentic Christian faith and life that obtain among them.

The recognition that the validity of Orthodox and Protestant baptism was generally not in question made possible a significant "attitudinal shift" that allowed Catholics to see Orthodox and Protestant believers not just as "schismatics" and "heretics" but as true brothers in Christ — "separated brethren," but brethren nonetheless. All of this stands in striking contrast to the Decree on the Jacobites (which explicitly applied to "pagans" the exclusions contained in the theological axiom *Extra ecclesiam nulla salus* [henceforth abbreviated as EENS] that had previously been applied primarily to schismatics and heretics) from the Council of Florence in 1442.[12]

It was a long journey from the necessity of visible union with the Catholic Church as understood by so many generations to "a certain union even by unconscious desire" as Pius XII put it and as the Holy Office reaffirmed in the important *Letter to the Archbishop of Boston*. It is a journey that we must trace in order to provide a proper context for the teaching of *LG* 16.

In contrast to centuries of opprobrium, condemnation, and invective, Vatican II, based on a broader theological understanding, encourages the faithful to admire the holiness and truth that one may find in the separated brethren.

Catholics must gladly acknowledge and esteem the truly Christian endowments for our common heritage which are to be found among our separated brethren. It is right and salutary to recognize the riches of Christ and virtuous works in the lives of others who are bearing witness to Christ, sometimes even to the shedding of their blood. For God is always wonderful in his works and worthy of all praise.

Nor should we forget that anything wrought by the grace of the Holy Spirit in the hearts of our separated brethren can contribute to our own edification.[13]

Despite the careful wording of the Council documents and the explicit desire to teach in harmony with the tradition (although a tradition that is living and evolving, and a doctrine that can legitimately develop),[14] the reformulation of the Catholic attitude towards and relations with the "separated brethren" has caused some controversy. The same is true as regards Vatican II's Declaration on the Relations of the Church to Non-Christian Religions *(Nostra aetate).*

In order to clarify the doctrine of Vatican II and its correct understanding in the light of tradition, the Congregation for the Doctrine of the Faith issued a document in 2000, with the approval of Pope John Paul II, titled "On the Unicity and Salvific Universality of Jesus Christ and the Church" *(Dominus Iesus).* While dealing with false understandings of ecumenism and false theologies of religious pluralism, it in no way undermined or contradicted Vatican II regarding its teaching on the salvation of non-Catholic Christians or the status of their churches and "ecclesial communities," although perhaps things could have been said more sensitively to avoid unnecessary misunderstanding and reaction. It added nothing new, but reaffirmed in strong and clear language the uniqueness and necessity of Christ, and the Church, in the salvific plan of God. In Part VI it adopted the words of Pius XII that followers of other religions are, objectively speaking, in a "gravely deficient" situation. Avery Dulles comments that this statement "is not calculated to please non-Christians, but it in no way contradicts Vatican II. Christian missionaries need to be reassured that they are bearers of a salvific message."[15] There is only one "salvific economy," and whatever salvation is possible to the human race is only possible through Christ and the Church, whatever the diverse ways in which it might come about.

As Cardinal George put it in his commentary on *AG:*

It all seems clear enough. Yet the crisis in mission and in interreligious dialogue occasioned another document, *Dominus Iesus,* which repeats what the council had already said clearly in *Ad gentes,* namely, Christianity's claim to absolute validity.[16]

Extra Ecclesiam Nulla Salus

One way of stating the central issue we are dealing with in our study is whether and under what conditions salvation is possible outside the visible confines of the Catholic Church. There is a long, complex, and interesting development of the Church's understanding of the meaning of this doctrine that is very illuminating for the questions we are dealing with.[17]

In this chapter we will be following the chronology of Fr. Francis Sullivan, who has produced the most recent comprehensive treatment of the issue in English.[18]

The theological axiom *Extra ecclesiam nulla salus* (EENS) has an ancient and venerable history. Its first use, in the Fathers prior to Augustine, was directed to schismatics and heretics. Since baptism joins us to the Church, and the Church is Christ's body, to separate ourselves from the Church through heresy or schism is to separate ourselves from Christ. Heresy and schism are viewed as grave sins against both faith and charity. Ignatius and Irenaeus (second century) warn about the consequences of separating from the Church, but the first formulation that approaches the strong wording of the axiom we are discussing was that of Origen (third century).

> So let no one persuade himself, let no one deceive himself: outside this house, that is, outside the church, no one is saved. For if anyone goes outside, he is responsible for his own death.[19]

Cyprian of Carthage, who died as a martyr in 258, is particularly known for his frequent reference to this dictum and gives it a particularly strong interpretation.[20] In speaking of Christians who were disobedient to their bishop, and therefore in danger of excommunication, he warns:

> For they cannot live outside, since there is only one house of God, and there can be no salvation for anyone except in the church.[21]

Arguing from the text of Paul in 1 Corinthians 13:3, which states that even if we give our body to be burned and do it without love, it gains us nothing, Cyprian makes the strong statement, to be taken up by later theologians and Councils:

> Neither baptism of public confession [of the faith under torture], nor of blood [shed for the faith], can avail the heretic anything toward salvation, because there is no salvation outside the church.[22]

Nay, even though they should suffer death for the confession of the Name, the guilt of such men is not removed even by their blood; the grievous irremissible sin of schism is not purged even by martyrdom.[23]

Fr. Sullivan, in his treatment of the development of this doctrine, tries to determine the historical context, the audience to which the statement is addressed, and the intention of the author, using appropriate hermeneutical principles applicable to nonbiblical texts. He demonstrates how to utilize such analysis in a way that avoids "magisterial fundamentalism" while attempting to determine the true meaning of the statement. While there are those who disagree with the conclusions he arrives at as a result of his studies — as we shall see — his effort to apply sound principles of interpretation is impressive.[24]

Fr. Sullivan claims that the axiom under consideration is at this point exclusively applied to actual or potential heretics or schismatics — not just to the initiators of the heresy or schism, but to later adherents as well. It has not yet been explicitly applied, in his view, to Jews or pagans.

Looking back over the texts that we have cited from Ignatius, Irenaeus, Origen and Cyprian, we see that when these early Christian writers spoke of people being excluded from salvation by reason of their being outside the church, they were consistently directing this as a warning to Christians whom they judged to be guilty of the grave sins of heresy and schism. It is quite possible that, if asked, they would have answered that there was no salvation outside the Church for Jews or pagans either. But it is significant for the history of this axiom that we do not find them applying it to others than Christians at this time when Christians were still a persecuted minority.[25]

The situation changed when Christians eventually became a majority in the Roman Empire after the decisions of a series of fourth-century emperors favored the development and eventual dominance of Christianity.

After Christianity became the dominant religion of the Roman Empire, the axiom was then applied to a broader group than Christian heretics and schismatics; it was applied to Jews and pagans as well, since it was now assumed that everyone had had a chance to hear the gospel and that to refuse to become Christian involved personal culpability.

Fr. Sullivan cites Ambrose, Gregory of Nyssa, and John Chrysostom as all firmly holding that those in the Empire who were still not Christian had certainly had adequate opportunity to hear the message and were culpable now of the grievous sin of unbelief. As Chrysostom puts it:

> One should not think that ignorance excuses the non-believer. . . . When you are ignorant of what can easily be known, you have to suffer the penalty. . . . When we do all that is in our power, in matters where we lack knowledge, God will give us his hand, but if we do not do what we can, we do not enjoy God's help either. . . . So do not say: "How is it that God has neglected that sincere and honest pagan?" You will find that he has not really been diligent in seeking the truth, since what concerns the truth is now clearer than the sun. How shall they obtain pardon who, when they see the doctrine of truth spread before them, make no effort to come to know it? . . . It is impossible that anyone who is vigilant in seeking the truth should be condemned by God . . . "but how is it," you ask, "that they have not believed?" It is because they did not wish to. And yet Christ did his part on their behalf; his passion bears witness to that.[26]

Fr. Sullivan also makes the important point that even though many were thought to be excluded from salvation at this point (fifth century) in the development of this doctrine, it is not because God's universal salvific will is in question; it is because of the lack of response to the grace that God offers.[27]

At this point it would be well to note that the question of the salvation of Jews and pagans who had lived before the coming of Christ was generally handled sympathetically by all the writers under discussion, including Augustine, whom we are about to consider. God's justice was seen as having provided for ways of connecting with Christ and the Church by their following of the natural law, honest seeking of God, and life of virtue, assisted by grace, even before the coming of Christ, in anticipation of the merits won by his coming. But after the coming of Christ this was no longer seen as a generally available option.

Bishop Bonaventure Kloppenburg refers to *LG* 2 (and to a similar text in *DV* 3), which affirms that "helps to salvation" were offered to those alive before the Incarnation of Christ, a teaching that is based on themes found in the Fathers. *LG* 2 cites, among others, Augustine, Gregory the Great, and John Damascene as support for this teaching. Bishop Kloppenburg also cites a sermon of Augustine as support for this teaching.

All of us together are the members and body of Christ: not only we who live here, but all of us throughout the world; not only we who live now, but — how shall I put it? — every just man who journeys through this life, from Abel the just down to the end of time, as long as men beget and are begotten.[28]

Concerning heretics and schismatics, though, Augustine could not have been stronger in his condemnation.

Outside the Church he can have everything except salvation. He can have honor, he can have sacraments, he can sing alleluia, he can respond with Amen, he can have the gospel, he can hold and preach the faith in the name of the Father and the Son and the Holy Spirit: but nowhere else than in the Catholic Church can he find salvation.[29]

Augustine repeats the claim of Cyprian of Carthage that even martyrdom for the faith would not avail for salvation if this were to happen outside the realm of charity, which is preserved by membership in the Church. To break unity with the Church was viewed as a grave sin against charity that separated oneself from Christ and his body.

Regarding Jews and pagans, Augustine strongly held to the view that all still outside the Church after having heard the gospel were destined for eternal punishment unless they repented before they died. As Fr. Sullivan puts it:

While it goes against our ecumenical sensibilities, we have to recognize the fact that St. Augustine held out little hope for the salvation of any Christian who died in a state of separation from the Catholic Church. . . . He held out even less hope for the salvation of those who in his day had still not accepted Christian faith and baptism. . . . Augustine applied with total rigor the text of Mark 16:15-16: "Go into the whole world and proclaim the gospel to every creature. Whoever believes and is baptized will be saved: whoever does not believe will be condemned." Augustine was convinced that those who had heard the message of the gospel and had not become Christians must be guilty of sinful rejection of the faith, and of the Church in which alone salvation could be found. Their damnation would be the result of their misuse of their free will.[30]

At one point Augustine became aware of the existence of many African tribes to the south who had not been evangelized, and surmised that there may indeed be others who had not yet even been discovered, who had not heard the gospel. Augustine held that the guilt of original sin was itself sufficient to condemn human beings and it was only by the mercy of God that anyone was saved. He saw no way for people who had not come to faith or baptism, and therefore membership in the Church, to be saved. The guilt of original sin, often compounded by grievous personal sin, led to damnation. Even "innocent children," because of the guilt of original sin, would be in hell but suffer "the mildest punishment of all."[31] Augustine would not see this as a violation of God's justice since the whole human race deserves damnation (a *massa damnata*) as a result of original sin. As Augustine argues:

> If, as truth itself tells us, no one is delivered from the condemnation that we incurred through Adam except through faith in Jesus Christ, and yet, those people, will not be able to deliver themselves from that condemnation who will be able to say that they have not heard the Gospel of Christ, since faith comes through hearing. . . . Therefore neither those who have never heard the Gospel nor those who by reason of their infancy were unable to believe . . . are separated from that mass which will certainly be damned.[32]

One of Augustine's theological followers, who lived almost a century after Augustine, Bishop Fulgentius of Ruspe (468-533), formulated these ideas in a form that was to find its way into a decree of the Council of Florence in 1442 and become a particularly formidable "monument of tradition."

> Most firmly hold and by no means doubt, that not only all pagans, but also all Jews, and all heretics and schismatics who die outside the Catholic Church, will go to the eternal fire that was prepared for the devil and his angels.[33]

Despite Augustine's influence, Fr. Sullivan notes that three elements of his theology were not to be taken up in the mainstream tradition:

> One was his idea that God would condemn unbaptized infants to hell for the inherited guilt of original sin. Another was that, likewise for the guilt of original sin, God would justly condemn adults who had never had a chance to hear the gospel and thus to make an act of saving faith. And a third was Augustine's conclusion that there were some people

whom God simply did not wish to be saved. . . . The mainstream Christian tradition found a better, if not an ideal, solution to the problem of infants dying without baptism; it insisted that God would come to the aid of a person who was inculpably ignorant of the faith; and it took seriously the biblical assurance that "God desires all to be saved and to come to the knowledge of the truth" (1 Tim 2:4) ruling out "double predestination."[34]

Concerning the fate of unbaptized infants, Pope Innocent III, in his letter to the Archbishop of Arles in 1201, expressed what was to become the mainstream tradition:

> The punishment of original sin is the lack of the vision of God; that of actual sin is the torment of everlasting hell.[35]

These consequences are sometimes spoken of as "the pain of loss" and the "pain of the senses."[36]

This distinction also provided a way of understanding the fate of unbaptized adults that eventually became the medieval consensus, namely, that they would not suffer eternal damnation simply because of the guilt of original sin, but only because of their grave personal sin.

Thomas Aquinas, of course, provided insight into these questions that was to remain a major reference point for all subsequent theological reflection.

By the time Thomas wrote, there had been a high-level papal affirmation of EENS in the decree *Firmiter* of Pope Innocent III at the Fourth Lateran Council in 1215. Thomas, in commenting on this decree, taught that the reason why EENS is true is because the only way people can be saved is through faith and the sacraments, which are to be had in the Church.[37]

When considering the possibility of Gentiles who lived before the coming of Christ being saved, Thomas said that the absolute necessity of faith in Christ could sometimes be implicit and actually be contained implicitly in a more generalized faith in God. The Scripture text that Thomas considered the foundation of his teaching about faith as a *sine qua non* is Hebrews 11:6: "Whoever would draw near to God must believe that he exists and that he is the rewarder of those who seek him."[38]

Several commentators point out that Thomas's teaching about every person being a *potential* member of the Church also laid a foundation for future development that went beyond Thomas's own teaching. As Philips puts it:

> St. Thomas himself teaches with insistence: "Even though unbelievers are not actually in the Church, they are in spite of everything potentially in the Church. This potentiality depends on two elements: first of all and most fundamentally on the power of Christ which suffices alone for the salvation of all humanity; secondly, on the free assent of man."[39]

Fr. Sullivan notes, however, that "While St. Thomas allowed for the sufficiency of implicit faith in Christ before the gospel had been promulgated, he was categorical in asserting the necessity of explicit Christian faith in his own day."[40]

When Thomas was asked about the possibility of even one person being saved who somehow, in medieval Christendom, had never heard the gospel, he replied that God would somehow provide the means by which such a person could arrive at explicit faith in Christ. Fr. Sullivan characterizes Thomas's view that now that Christ had come it was necessary for faith in Christ to be explicit as being "exceptionless."[41]

Thomas acknowledges, based on 1 Timothy 2:4, that God does will the salvation of the whole human race and gives grace to lead people to explicit faith in Christ unless the grace is impeded by the person's own fault, by those who "offer an obstacle within themselves to grace."

> Since the ability to impede or not to impede the reception of divine grace is within the scope of free choice, not undeservedly is responsibility for the fault imputed to him who offers an impediment to the reception of grace. In fact, as far as He is concerned, God is ready to give grace to all, indeed "He wills all men to be saved, and to come to the knowledge of the truth" as is said in 1 Timothy. But those alone are deprived of grace who offer an obstacle within themselves to grace . . .[42]

This belief was expressed in a commonly cited axiom among medieval theologians, including Thomas, to the effect that: *Facienti quod in se est, Deus non denegat gratiam* (To one who does what lies in his power, God does not deny grace).[43]

Given the common medieval understanding that Christianity was so widely known and promulgated that invincible ignorance would be extremely rare, it was assumed that nonbelievers were culpable for their unbelief, including Jews and Muslims. When the hypothetical case of a child raised in the wilderness or by animals, who was invincibly ignorant, was brought up, Thomas gave the following reply in a text that has been frequently cited by commentators on this issue:

> If anyone were brought up in the wilderness or among brute animals, provided that he followed his natural reason in seeking the good and avoiding evil, we must most certainly hold that God would either reveal to him, by an inner inspiration, what must be believed, or would send a preacher to him, as he sent Peter to Cornelius.[44]

This hypothetical case is to figure prominently in Fr. Sullivan's further explorations.

> In the *Summa* Thomas seems to adopt a more Augustinian solution to the problem of "invincible ignorance" of the gospel, perhaps because he has become more aware that there are many more than the "child raised in the wilderness" who have not heard the gospel. That is, he sees original sin as itself a justification for the justice of God not providing special help to bring to faith, with salvation being sheer mercy. There is debate about whether this is his final word on the subject since this is his last work, but others point out that his commentary on Romans, which still holds out the possibility of God giving sufficient grace to the invincibly ignorant under certain conditions to come to an explicit faith in Christ for salvation, was written about the same time.[45]

In any case Thomas clearly teaches that while people who have never heard the gospel and therefore do not come to faith are not damned because of that, they may be damned because of "their other sins, which cannot be taken away without faith."[46] Thomas believed that Jews and Muslims had certainly heard enough about Christ for their unbelief to be culpable, and therefore, unless they repented and believed, they were subject to condemnation. The most culpable and grave sin of unbelief, though, was that of Christian heretics.[47]

Thomas strongly affirms the necessity of baptism because of the command of the Lord, but also because it is, in fact, the means by which the saving actions of Christ are applied to the individual. This is spoken about in the theological tradition as not just a "necessity of precept" but a "necessity of means," although this terminology was not taken over into the

Council texts we are considering. However, Thomas clearly accepts the reality of "baptism of desire" in the case of someone who had the intention of being baptized but died before it was carried out — which would be explicit desire.

> Such a person can obtain salvation without being actually baptized, on account of the person's desire for baptism which desire is the outcome of faith that works through charity, whereby God, whose power is not tied to visible sacraments, sanctifies a person inwardly.[48]

Thomas also acknowledges the efficacy of an implicit desire for baptism. Such would be the case of someone who perhaps had just come to faith and the forgiveness of sins and did not yet know about the necessity of the sacrament of baptism, but who nevertheless desired God's will — and thereby, had an implicit desire for baptism.

> A person receives the forgiveness of sins before baptism in so far as he has baptism of desire, explicitly or implicitly, and yet when he actually receives baptism, he receives a fuller remission, for the remission of the entire punishment. So also Cornelius and others like him receive grace and virtues through their faith in Christ and their desire for baptism, implicit or explicit; but afterwards when baptized, they receive a yet greater fullness of grace and virtues.[49]

This is a very important teaching of Thomas. It forms the basis for much of the future development of the doctrine. Thomas himself applied his theology of "desire" to the question of the necessity of the Eucharist, in a way similar to his treatment of the question of the necessity of baptism.

The discovery of America and the subsequent realization that whole continents of undiscovered peoples existed challenged the traditional theological understanding. Most historians of the development of this doctrine would agree that this discovery impinged on the theological conscience of the Church in a very significant way and was a true turning point. Although there is pretty clear evidence that both Augustine and Aquinas knew that there were possibly sizable numbers of people who had not heard the gospel, nevertheless the experience of "Christendom" still shaped their thinking, which is not to say, of course, that their theology on this point is not still extremely relevant even after the "age of discovery."[50] The traditional understanding that was challenged is perhaps most boldly stated in the Bull *Unum sanctam* of Boniface VIII issued in 1302, the last sentence of which is generally understood to intend to define: "Moreover, we declare, state and define that for every human creature it is a matter of necessity for salvation to be subject to the Roman Pontiff."[51]

The mention of the Roman Pontiff is seen by many scholars as simply another way of speaking of the necessity of communion with the Catholic Church.

Another strong, authoritative statement of the theological axiom we are discussing is contained in the Decree for the Jacobites of the Council of Florence (1431-1445). We will see the words of Bishop Fulgentius of Ruspe, Augustine's theological disciple, incorporated here:

> [The Holy Roman Church] firmly believes, professes and preaches that "no one remaining outside the Catholic Church, not only pagans,"* but also Jews, heretics or schismatics, can become partakers of eternal life; but they will go to the "eternal fire prepared for the devil and his angels" (Mt 25:41), unless before the end of their life they are received into it. For union with the body of the Church is of so great importance that the sacraments of the Church are helpful to salvation only for those remaining in it; and fasts, almsgiving, other works of piety, and the exercises of a militant Christian life bear eternal rewards for them alone. "And no one can be saved, no matter how much alms he has given, even if he sheds his blood for the name of Christ, unless he remains in the bosom and unity of the Catholic Church."[52]

The Age of Discovery and Theological Ferment

The experience of the discovery of the "new world" and its multitude of peoples stimulated theological reflection on the fate of the unbaptized who, even though they lived in the "time of Christ," had never heard the gospel. Were there new ways of understanding such "invincible ignorance"?

Dominican theologians took the lead in exploring these questions. Fr. Francisco de Vitoria at first reaffirmed the traditional teaching:

> When we postulate invincible ignorance on the subject of baptism or of the Christian faith, it does not follow that a person can be saved without baptism or the Christian faith. For the aborigines to whom no preaching of the faith or Christian religion has come will be damned for mor-

40

tal sins or for idolatry, but not for the sin of unbelief. As St. Thomas
says, however, if they do what in them lies, accompanied by a good life
according to the law of nature, it is consistent with God's providence
that he will illuminate them regarding the name of Christ.[53]

But then he introduced a new and important consideration about what
would constitute an adequate preaching of the gospel that would oblige
the hearers to accept it.[54]

He challenged the common belief that the gospel was being adequately preached to the indigenous peoples of the new world and that their
rejection of it was fully culpable.[55] He pointed out the reality of colonial
brutality and questioned whether the gospel preached in an environment
of conquest could really be said to be an adequate proclamation. In such
circumstances perhaps its rejection was not blameworthy.

> The Indians in question are not bound, directly the Christian faith is an-
> nounced to them, to believe it, in such a way that they commit mortal
> sin by not believing it, merely because it has been declared and an-
> nounced to them that Christianity is the true religion and the Christ is
> the Savior and Redeemer of the world, without miracle or any other
> proof or persuasion . . . or if before hearing anything of the Christian re-
> ligion they were excused, they are put under no fresh obligation by a
> simple declaration and announcement of this kind, for such an an-
> nouncement is no proof or incentive to belief. Now, I hear of no mira-
> cles or signs or religious patterns of life; nay, on the contrary, I hear of
> many scandals and cruel crimes and acts of impiety. Hence, it does not
> appear that the Christian religion has been preached to them with such
> sufficient propriety and piety that they are bound to acquiesce in it even
> though many religious and other ecclesiastics seem both by their lives
> and example and their diligent preaching to have bestowed sufficient
> pains and industry in this business, had they not been hindered therein
> by men who were intent on other things.[56]

As Fr. Sullivan puts it:

> This is an important advance over the medieval way of thinking about
> non-believers. During the middle ages, it does not seem to have oc-
> curred to Christians to ask whether the Christian message had been
> proclaimed to the Jews in a convincing way, or whether the evil actions

of Christians might have proved an obstacle to their being persuaded of the truth of Christianity.[57]

Another Dominican, Fr. Domingo Soto, in attempting to understand how the peoples of the New World could have been offered salvation before the arrival of the missionaries, postulated that the same implicit faith that was sufficient for those who were born before Christ's coming would also have been sufficient for the people in the new world.[58] This, of course, is a very important "theological move."

A Flemish theologian, Albert Pigge (1490-1542), extended this line of thought even further and surmised that perhaps Muslims' faith in God could be understood in certain cases to contain an implicit faith in Christ, when they were inculpably ignorant of the gospel.

Fr. Sullivan thinks Pigge may have been the first theologian "to suggest that a Muslim's lack of Christian faith might actually be inculpable, and that he could be saved by his faith in God."[59]

As Pigge put it:

> If you say that by now the Gospel of Christ has been sufficiently promulgated in the whole world, so that ignorance can no longer excuse anyone — reality itself refutes you, because every day now numberless nations are being discovered among whom, or among their forefathers, no trace is found of the Gospel ever having been preached, so that to all those people up to our time Christ was simply unheard of. . . . Now if the ignorance of the Christian faith did not prevent Cornelius, even without baptism, from being pleasing to God in Christ, how much less will the much more invincible ignorance of these people prevent them from being able to please God in Christ?[60]

Pigge explicitly applies this to Muslims who were raised in good faith to believe certain things and think they are pleasing God by doing so, being substantially ignorant of Christian revelation and not having seen miracles or heard credible explanations of the Christian faith.

The next development that Fr. Sullivan treats comes during the Reformation and Counter-Reformation. He notes, though, that the Council of Trent does not use the expression EENS or treat of this issue, since it was not an issue that Rome and the Reformers differed on, despite all their other substantial differences, and the theological speculation that had been triggered by the discovery of the new world was not sufficiently mature for a Council to consider. The Council did reaffirm, though, the traditional teaching about the necessity of faith (it cited Heb. 11:6) and the necessity of baptism, although it did recognize "baptism of desire" as a legitimate possibility.[61]

St. Robert Bellarmine (1542-1621) in his work on ecclesiology applied the baptism by desire model to membership in the Church in two cases, that of catechumens and that of an excommunicated person who had nevertheless regained the state of grace through perfect contrition but before being officially reconciled.

> I reply that the saying: "Outside the Church no one is saved," should be understood of those who belong to the Church neither in reality nor in desire, just as theologians commonly speak about baptism. Because catechumens, even though not in the church in reality *(re)* are in the church by desire *(voto)*, and in that way they can be saved.[62]

And concerning the excommunicate who had repented but hadn't been officially reconciled:

> Such a one is in the church with his mind or by desire *(animo sive desiderio)*, which is sufficient for his salvation; however, he is not in the church bodily, that is, by external communion, and it is the latter which makes one in the strict sense a member of the church on earth.[63]

Sullivan comments: "In these passages of Bellarmine's treatise *On the Church Militant*, we have, for the first time, an interpretation of the axiom . . . which explicitly recognizes that a person who is not actually a member of the Church can be saved by the desire of belonging to it."[64] How exactly this happens and under what conditions is not spelled out in detail in Bellarmine.[65]

Francisco Suarez (1548-1619) suggested how this might happen. He reaffirms that since God wills that all men be saved he will therefore provide some means of this happening. Suarez develops the notion that everything in some sense is implicitly contained in faith in God. Therefore he supposes that faith in God can contain in it an implicit desire for baptism and membership in the Church. Suarez explains how God may provide the sufficient help for this to happen in the following terms:

> Another way of explaining this sufficiency is indicated in these words of the first chapter of John: "He was the true light that enlightens every

man who comes into this world" (Jn 1:9). The Fathers understand these words to refer to an internal and supernatural illumination, which they held is communicated to all adult persons, universally, as far as it depends on God. According to this interpretation, even to those unbelievers to whom the gospel or Christian faith has never been preached by men, God provides a way by which they are enlightened and moved sufficiently for an act of faith, provided they put no obstacle in the way. And God does this either by arranging in an extraordinary way that a preacher be sent to them, or by teaching them by the ministry of angels, or by God himself interiorly enlightening and calling them, with the result that this saying will be true for all: "Behold, I stand at the door and knock" (Rev 3:20).[66]

So, in addition to the possible means of sending an angel or a preacher of the gospel, which Aquinas had postulated and which Suarez also affirmed, he adds a universal, supernatural, interior illumination that has the possibility of eliciting saving faith. Since Pope Innocent XI in 1679 had condemned the opinion that people could be saved by a faith in God that they obtained through reason, the supernatural nature of the illumination was necessary.[67]

Fr. Juan de Lugo (1583-1660), a Jesuit, pushed these insights even farther and suggested, as Fr. Sullivan summarizes it, that "heretics, Jews and Muslims might not be damned, as the Council of Florence had said they would, but, on the contrary, might be saved through their sincere faith in God."[68]

This, of course, was a significant departure from the position of Thomas and the medieval theologians, which assumed that the unbelief of the above categories of "unbelievers" was culpable. De Lugo justified his position by pointing out that not every presentation of the gospel was necessarily credible, mirroring Vitoria's challenge to the credibility of the presentation of the gospel to the new world in the context of brutal conquest.

These theologians believed that "in some sense" it must be true that there is no salvation outside the Church, and were trying to determine what that sense might be.

Another Jesuit, Juan Martinez de Ripalda (1594-1648), postulated that every moral act is subject to supernatural elevation even if it is performed by non-Christians. Karl Rahner explicitly cites de Ripalda as a forerunner of his own theories, articulated 400 years later, pointing out that de Ripalda's views have never been condemned.[69]

The suppression of the Jesuits in 1773 by Pope Clement XIV fueled a backlash against their more "liberal" theories concerning salvation. The theological "trend" moved back to the older understanding that unless people came to explicit faith in Christ before they died they were damned.[70]

It is worth noting the response of the nineteenth-century Jesuit theologian, Giovanni Perrone (1794-1876), to the objection that it was charity, and not faith, that determined salvation, based on the judgment scene in Matthew.

> Failure to do the works of charity is not the only reason why some are damned, nor will all who have done such works be saved. Otherwise, one could conclude that, provided that they had done some works of charity, adulterers, drunkards and thieves, and even Jews and Muslims and idolaters, would be saved. But that is absurd![71]

Nevertheless Perrone, by his time the most influential Roman theologian, taught that "only those guilty of culpable heresy, schism or unbelief were excluded from salvation by being 'outside the Church.'"[72] Fr. Sullivan suggests that by the middle of the nineteenth century this "had become the common opinion among Catholic theologians," which was confirmed by Pope Pius IX in 1854 and then most authoritatively, in his encyclical *Quanto conficiamur moerore,* published in 1863.[73] This position essentially prepared the way for *LG* 16.

> It is known to Us and to you that those who labor in invincible ignorance concerning our most holy religion and who, assiduously observing the natural law and its precepts which God has inscribed in the hearts of all, and being ready to obey God, live an honest and upright life can, through the working of the divine light and grace, attain eternal life, since God, who clearly sees, inspects and knows the mind, the intentions, the thoughts and habits of all, will, by reason of his supreme goodness and kindness, never allow anyone who has not the guilt of willful sin to be punished by eternal sufferings.[74]

In the same encyclical, Pius IX also reaffirmed the necessity of the Church for salvation and noted that those who are "contumacious against the authority and the definitions" of the Church or "who are pertinaciously divided" from her "cannot obtain eternal salvation."[75]

It is also worth noting the draft document on the Church that Pius IX had drawn up in preparation for Vatican I. Because it was interrupted by the Franco-Prussian war, only those parts of the document pertaining to the role of the Pope actually made their way into a final Council document, but it is worth noting that the teaching of Pius IX on the issue of the possibility of salvation outside of the visible Church was established enough to be contained in a potential Council document. This, of course, did not happen until Vatican II, where strong resonances of this document can be found in *LG* 16. It is interesting to note that the purpose of the proposed document was explicitly to foster evangelization. Excerpts of the relevant parts are as follows:

> The apostolic charge of Supreme Pastor with which the ineffable Providence of Divine Mercy has invested Us, continually urges Us to neglect nothing that may open wide to all men the way that leads to life and to eternal salvation, so that all may come to the light and knowledge of truth, even those who are still sitting in darkness and in the shadow of death.
>
> Since God Our Savior has confided to his Church as to a rich storehouse the ensemble of doctrinal truths and the treasury of the means of salvation so that she may be for all men a fountain of life, it is important before all else to show those who are in error what the true Church is and to inspire in the faithful a greater esteem for her. By this means the latter will be strengthened to make progress in the way of salvation; the former will be brought to that way. . . . Let all men understand from this that the Church of Christ is a society necessary for salvation. . . . We affirm that she is absolutely necessary, not merely with a necessity of precept, in virtue of the order to enter the Church given by the Savior to all men, but also with a necessity of means, because in the order established by Providence for men's salvation, communication of the Holy Spirit, participation in the truth and in life, can be obtained only in the Church and through the Church of which Christ is the Head.
>
> Moreover, it is a dogma of the faith that no man can be saved outside the Church. At the same time, those who are in invincible ignorance on the subject of Christ and his Church will not be condemned to eternal suffering because of this ignorance. In fact, they are not culpable of any sin in the eyes of the Lord who wills that all men be saved and come to the knowledge of the truth, and who does not refuse, to him who does what he can, the grace which will permit him to reach justifi-

cation and everlasting life. On the contrary, no man will obtain this eternal life if he does not abandon the state of life which is separated by his fault from the unity of faith and communion with the Church. He who is not to be found in the ark will perish in the time of the deluge.[76]

Nevertheless, an important distinction must be kept in mind. Just because people are not culpably ignorant does not mean that thereby they are saved. Their personal response to the illumination that God gives is required. As Fr. Sullivan puts it:

> For the first time in the history of the Catholic Church, we have papal authority for explaining that this axiom means: "No salvation for those who are *culpably* outside the Church." . . . It is important to note *how* Pope Pius said they can be saved, because he has sometimes been taken to mean that people can be saved by ignorance, or merely by keeping the natural law. If one reads his statement carefully, one sees that being "invincibly ignorant of our most holy religion" is a *condition* that must be fulfilled to avoid culpability, but is in no sense a *cause* of salvation. Neither is it correct to say that people are saved merely by keeping the natural law; this would be to fall into Pelagianism, of which Pius IX is surely not guilty. The operative words in his statement are: "through the working of the divine light and grace." It is this that effects salvation, provided, of course, that people freely cooperate with divine grace.[77]

The next major document that affected the discussion was the encyclical of Pope Pius XII, *Mystici Corporis Christi*, published in 1943, which stated that the Roman Catholic Church and it alone is the mystical body of Christ. While non-Catholic Christians were not considered to be "members" of the Church, they could be related to it in various ways, by desire *(votum)*, or even an "unconscious desire." This provoked a storm of theological activity that culminated in the distinctions made about the various degrees of relationships with the Church articulated at Vatican II, most particularly in the *Decree on Ecumenism* and the *Constitution on the Church.*

A significant document, that in some ways is the culmination of this long development, and is cited in *LG* 16 as support for its teaching, is the *Letter of the Holy Office to the Archbishop of Boston*[78] issued in 1949, which reaffirmed the "broader" understanding of EENS that did not require explicit membership in the Church for salvation, but allowed for relatedness by implicit, even unconscious, desire. As late as *Mystici Corporis Christi* in 1943, the "Mystical body of Christ" was simply identified with the Roman Catholic Church (to be repeated by Pius XII in the encyclical *Humani generis* in 1950). And yet it was the Fr. Leonard Feeney case, which was doctrinally resolved by the *Letter of the Holy Office to the Archbishop of Boston* on August 8, 1949, that helped pave the way for a more nuanced interpretation of the teaching of Pius XII. He explicitly approved the *Letter* and accepted its interpretation of his ecclesiological teaching. Pagé considers this the most important document of the pontificate of Pius XII regarding this issue.[79]

This was one of the doctrinal clarifications that helped pave the way for Vatican II's articulation of the possibility of salvation outside of the visible Church, and the *Letter* is indeed cited in a footnote as support for the teaching of *LG* 16. Congar also sees it as background for *AG* 7.[80] Because of its importance for the developments that took place at Vatican II and the way it sums up previous theological development, we should identify the major doctrinal clarifications the *Letter* makes.

What were the issues in the "Fr. Feeney case" and how were they resolved by the Holy Office?

Fr. Feeney, the Catholic chaplain at Harvard, taught a very strict interpretation of the theological axiom *Extra ecclesiam nulla salus*. He believed that only those visibly joined to the Catholic Church could be saved. This excluded not only non-Catholic Christians but everyone else as well. The *Letter* of the Holy Office is important as it gives an authoritative interpretation to the meaning of the theological axiom, which at first sight seems to lend itself to a literal interpretation, especially in light of the magisterial documents Fr. Feeney cited in defense of his interpretation.[81] The *Letter* is also important as it gave an authoritative interpretation of Pius XII's teaching on the identification of the Catholic Church with the mystical body that opened the way for Vatican II's teaching on the Church.

The response of the Holy Office made these important points that are relevant to our current considerations:

1. Fr. Feeney does not correctly understand or interpret the theological axiom.

2. Private interpretation of magisterial teaching cannot take precedence over the teaching authority of the Church as it interprets its own tradition.

3. Regarding the sacraments of baptism and of penance, as the Council of Trent taught (DS 1524, 1543), the graces they confer can also be obtained in certain circumstances when they are able to be accessed "only in desire

and longing." This can also be applied to a certain union with the Church. (The phrase "a certain union" is used here rather than "member," which is reserved for what Vatican II calls "fully incorporated" Catholics.)

> In His infinite mercy God has willed that the effects, necessary for one to be saved, of those helps to salvation which are directed toward man's final end, not by intrinsic necessity, but only by divine institution, can also be obtained in certain circumstances when those helps are used only in desire and longing. This we see clearly stated in the Sacred Council of Trent both in reference to the sacrament of regeneration and in reference to the sacrament of penance (DS 1524, 1543). The same in its own degree must be asserted of the Church, in as far as she is the general help to salvation. Therefore, that one may obtain eternal salvation, it is not always required that he be incorporated into the Church actually as a member, but it is necessary that at least he be united to her by desire and longing.[82]

4. This desire for union with the Church need not always be explicit.

However, this desire need not always be explicit, as it is in catechumens; but when a person is involved in invincible ignorance God accepts also an implicit desire, so called because it is included in that good disposition of soul whereby a person wishes his will to be conformed to the will of God.[83]

5. An authoritative interpretation of *Mystici corporis christi* is given.

For in this letter the Sovereign Pontiff clearly distinguishes between those who are actually incorporated into the Church as members, and those who are united to the Church only by desire. . . . Toward the end of this same encyclical letter . . . he mentions those who "are related to the Mystical Body of the Redeemer by a certain unconscious yearning and desire," and these he by no means excludes from eternal salvation, but on the other hand states that they are in a condition "in which they cannot be sure of their salvation" since "they still remain deprived of those many heavenly gifts and helps which can only be enjoyed in the Catholic Church" (DS 3821). With these wise words he reproves both those who exclude from eternal salvation all united to the Church only by implicit desire, and those who falsely assert that men can be saved equally well in every religion (DS 2865, DS 1641, DS 1677).[84]

6. A rather "high level" of implicit desire is required for the possibility of salvation.[85]

> But it must not be thought that any kind of desire of entering the Church suffices that one may be saved. It is necessary that the desire by which one is related to the Church be animated by perfect charity. Nor can an implicit desire produce its effect unless a person has supernatural faith: "For he who comes to God must believe that God exists and is a rewarder of those who seek Him" (Heb. 11:6). The Council of Trent declares (Session VI, chapter 8): "Faith is the beginning of man's salvation, the foundation and root of all justification, without which it is impossible to please God and attain to the fellowship of His children" (DS 1532).[86]

Many of the commentators who treat of the history of the development of this doctrine cite the importance of the *Letter* in response to the Fr. Feeney case as summing up and advancing this development.[87]

Sullivan assesses the significance of this *Letter:*

> It is not difficult to see that in this explanation of the necessity of belonging to the Catholic Church for salvation, the holy office has given authoritative approval to an interpretation of *Extra ecclesiam nulla salus* which began with Bellarmine and Suarez in the sixteenth century and in modern times was most fully developed by Franzelin. The holy office has given official sanction to the *in re-in voto* solution.[88]

In certain parts of the text of *LG* 16 that pertain to the matter we have been discussing, the salvation of non-Christians, one can see the importance of the clarity that has been achieved over the centuries of theological and magisterial reflection, and the continued importance of the distinctions between culpable and inculpable ignorance, explicit and implicit faith, the universal salvific will of God, the absolute necessity of grace for supernatural faith, etc. As one rereads the relevant sections of *LG* 16, it is apparent how much of the long history of doctrinal development is embedded in its succinct formulations.

> Those who, through no fault of their own, do not know the Gospel of Christ or his Church, but who nevertheless seek God with a sincere heart, and moved by grace, try in their actions to do his will as they know it through the dictates of their conscience — those too may

achieve eternal salvation. Nor shall divine providence deny the assistance necessary for salvation to those who, without any fault of theirs, have not yet arrived at an explicit knowledge of God, and who, not without grace, strive to lead a good life. Whatever good or truth is found amongst them is considered by the Church to be a preparation for the Gospel and given by him who enlightens all men that they may at length have life. But very often, deceived by the Evil One, men have become vain in their reasonings, have exchanged the truth of God for a lie and served the world rather than the Creator (cf. Rom 1:21, 25). Or else, living and dying in this world without God, they are exposed to ultimate despair. Hence to procure the glory of God and the salvation of all these, the Church, mindful of the Lord's command, "preach the Gospel to every creature" (Mk 16:16) takes zealous care to foster the missions.

There continues to be significant theological reflection on how exactly it might be possible for someone who is inculpably ignorant[89] of the gospel to actually come to supernatural faith and charity without the "propositional clarity" of positive revelation. Rahner points to the probability of there being more dimensions to human consciousness than we have traditionally understood.

> There must be more dimensions to human consciousness in its knowing and free decision making, more foreground and background, more data, verbalized or not, accepted or repressed, than traditional theology has explicitly recognized.[90]

Both Pagé[91] and Journet cite Maritain as one who has made a significant contribution in understanding how this might be possible. Journet posits two kinds of "lights" that come to human beings from God. One is "prophetic light," which illumines things that we must perceive for our salvation. The other is "sanctifying light," which calls us to assent to what is illumined in the prophetic light.[92] Journet extensively quotes Maritain[93] on how this process may possibly take place in a "pre-conceptual" manner among those who do not know the gospel. Maritain himself bases his reflections on the teaching of St. Thomas (*ST* Ia-IIae, q. 89, a. 6) concerning the theological significance of the first human act of an unbaptized child.[94] Maritain's point, following Thomas, is that contained in that first moral act — if it is an act that chooses the good — there may be an embryonic or rudimentary response to a prophetic and sanctifying light given by God that may actually involve a supernatural faith that is salvific, although quite vulnerable and perhaps unstable if it does not come to consciousness.

> With this pre-conceptual, pre-notional knowledge, through the will, of the "good which brings salvation," of the "good by which I shall be saved," we receive the least degree of prophetic light necessary in order that theological faith should be able to come into action and make the understanding, really, actually, supernaturally, assent to the mystery of the God who "exists," and who "rewards those who try to find him." [Based on Hebrews 11:6, the two foundational beliefs — credibilia — that must be present for salvation.]
>
> But this is a provisional, unstable, dangerous state of faith, a state of childhood; and knowledge of the mysteries of salvation will require that it should leave the shadows, be perfected, reach an adult state, and find its first conceptual expression in the two basic "credibilia."[95]

Étienne Hugueny makes an even stronger point about the instability and fragility of such a first moral choice.

> The good influences of the environment are unfortunately insufficient to prevent the falls and often the corruption of the will in formation; indeed, few there are who are able to resist the evil influences of the environment in which they are developing. It's therefore common that the young unbeliever, in a pagan environment, will follow the inclination of his corrupt nature and the evil example of the environment where he lives, when the hour arrives for him to choose his primary orientation to his moral life. Avoiding therefore the call of God, the number of negative infidels [this refers to unbelievers who have not yet made a positive choice against God but are unbelievers because of the environment of unbelief in which they grow up] will grow, who by a first sin against God who presented himself to their reason, have placed an obstacle to interior illumination or to exterior revelation, through which God would have given them the gift of faith, bringing to perfection their first religious idea.[96]

Conclusion

It is important to see that the development of doctrine that formed the basis for *LG* 16 was a painstaking process. Some points that we must particularly keep in mind as we proceed are as follows:

1. Christ's coming has radically changed the situation of the human race by offering it salvation. But with this gratuitous gift comes the urgency of proclaiming to the whole world the treasure that is being offered and the need to accept it.

2. To hear the gospel and understand it, and not accept it is to jeopardize one's salvation. To depart from it after having accepted it is also to jeopardize one's salvation. To depart from the Catholic Church or not to enter it, knowing it to be the Church of Christ, is to jeopardize one's salvation.

3. Not every proclamation of the gospel can be deemed "adequate," either because of deficiency of content, manner, or witness of life, and therefore not everyone who apparently rejects such an "inadequate" preaching of the gospel can be judged culpable of unbelief.

4. Just as those who lived before the coming of Christ could be saved if they responded with saving faith to the light they were given and acted in accordance with conscience, under the influence of grace, likewise those who are inculpably ignorant of the gospel today also have the possibility of salvation under similar conditions, even though Christ has come.

5. There is some precision as to what must be involved in this saving assent to God where the gospel has not adequately been presented. It must involve supernatural faith and supernatural charity.[97] It must involve a dedication to do the will of God as he makes it known.

6. Just because salvation is possible for people who are inculpably ignorant of the gospel or have not heard a presentation that is adequate, does not mean they are thereby saved.[98] It is essential that the initial, mysterious "yes" that is said to God be followed by perseverance in that "yes" to the end. Inculpable ignorance of the gospel is a condition of, not a cause of, salvation.

Not knowing this painstaking process of development can easily lead one to take a superficial and cavalier attitude towards the possibility of being saved without explicit faith in Christ and membership in the Church. Such an attitude has, in my opinion, become prevalent in the contemporary Catholic Church. Some theologians have claimed that this "salvation optimism" is indeed one of the intended and significant fruits of the Second Vatican Council. Distinctions are necessary.

Salvation Optimism?

Karl Rahner has declared "this theological optimism of the Council regarding salvation"[99] one of the most significant (and unnoticed) accomplishments of Vatican II. In an upcoming chapter we will examine whether his claims and interpretations of this "theological optimism" are in harmony with the actual teaching of the Council or not.

Fr. Richard McBrien, in his commentary on *LG*, also identifies this "salvation optimism."

> This principle [the Church as a sacrament] must be seen in the context of one of the most important developments in contemporary Catholic theology, linked especially with the work of the late Karl Rahner; namely, the shift away from an Augustinian pessimism about salvation to a more hopeful, universalistic outlook, as reflected in this and other documents of the Council. The human race is no longer seen as a *massa damnata* from whom a few are saved to manifest the glory and mercy of God, but as an essentially saved community from whom a few may, by the exercise of their own free will, be lost.[100]

We have already seen how unwarranted such a statement is by our examination of the actual text of *LG* 16 and its supporting footnotes, the doctrinal development that provides a context for its proper interpretation. We are also about to examine, in the next chapter, the scriptural foundation that undergirds *LG* 16c.

Even Francis Sullivan, who provides such a valuable history of the development of the doctrine EENS, seems to have strong views about how the doctrine should keep developing in a certain direction, and he invokes the "optimism" of Vatican II as support.

He speaks sometimes as if a total reversal has been made from "pessimism" to "optimism" even though he himself has traced out the painstaking and precise development of the doctrine, which as we see is rather nuanced. He approvingly cites Rahner's judgment of Vatican II's salvation optimism.[101]

In his treatment of *LG* 16, he simply does not comment[102] on the significant qualification that *LG* 16 puts on its "salvation optimism," namely *LG* 16c. In addition, he seems in his overall treatment of Vatican II to conflate the rather significant changes contained in *LG* 14 and 15 regarding the status of non-Catholic Christians (with which I agree) with, as this book is arguing, the much more modest development in the teaching about the status of non-Christians.[103] If one ignores, or glosses over, *LG* 16c, one cannot possibly give a balanced judgment about the teaching of the Council on the status of non-Christians.

In his defense of Jacques Dupuis and his book, *Toward a Christian Theology of Religious Pluralism*, Fr. Sullivan notes that the CDF published a "Notification"[104] about this work, asking that certain ambiguities be clarified, and stating that certain points in the book have "no foundation in Catholic theology."

Fr. Sullivan's response to the CDF's objection was that there was indeed a foundation in Catholic theology for Fr. Dupuis's views in the theology of Karl Rahner, which Fr. Sullivan claimed that Vatican Council II supported.

> He found support in the optimism that council expressed about the salvation of people of other religions, an optimism he described as one of the most noteworthy results of the council.[105]

Fr. Sullivan does not cite the basis for this statement in the article, but goes on to the question in which he is most interested, namely, whether the non-Christian religions, as religions, can be viewed with the same optimism. He points out that Rahner gives an affirmative answer to this question.

An important distinction must be made, it seems to me, about an "optimism" that sees the possibility of people who have never heard the gospel, or who have never heard it "adequately," having a possibility of being saved under certain very specific conditions (spelled out in *LG* 16 but also in previous theological and magisterial documents), and an "optimism" that presumes that "possibility" means in fact "probability." It is a short step from an assumed "probability" concerning salvation to the widespread assumption now common in the culture of the Church as well as in the culture at large, that virtually everyone will be saved. Fr. Sullivan even claims that the Council's optimism implies a "general presumption of innocence" among those who have not heard the gospel, without citing any texts to that effect.

> It would take several centuries more for the limits of the psychological horizon to expand sufficiently so that the presumption of guilt, which was characteristic of the medieval judgment concerning all those outside the Church, would gradually change, first into a recognition that

some of them might be in good faith, and then into the general presumption of innocence which is now the official attitude of the Catholic Church.[106]

Unfortunately, no sources are indicated for the alleged "presumption of innocence" that is supposedly the "official attitude" of the Church. Huge leaps in logic are being made here.

All of this seems to neglect the pervasive scriptural testimony — scarcely a "medieval judgment" — to the deeply ingrained tendency of a fallen race to resist interior illumination and/or the explicit preaching of the gospel, because they prefer, as Scripture says, the darkness to the light. We must now turn towards the fundamental scriptural underpinning on which *LG* 16 relies as authority for the next important element of its teaching.

CHAPTER IV

The Scriptural Foundations of Lumen gentium 16

We are focusing our attention on *LG* 16c, which states that even though it is possible for people who have not heard the gospel under certain conditions (the conditions we have already considered) to be saved, "very often" this is not the case. This is an absolutely essential part of the teaching of *LG* 16, but it is very rarely cited. Most commonly, *LG* 16b is cited to support the view (rightly) that it is possible to be saved without coming to explicit faith in Christ and membership in the Church, but it is, unfortunately, rarely mentioned that this possibility may often not be realized in the actual lives and choices of non-Christians. The basis for this claim of *LG* 16c is the teaching of Romans 1, which is explicitly cited, and Romans 2, which is implicitly alluded to. Msgr. Philips, who made a major contribution to the drafting of *LG* — Cardinal Ratzinger calls him the "principal author"[1] — explicitly states in his commentary that the basis for the teaching of *LG* 16 on conscience is indeed Romans 2:14-15.[2] We will review the text in question with particular attention to the oft-neglected *LG* 16c.

> Those who, through no fault of their own, do not know the Gospel of Christ or his Church, but who nevertheless seek God with a sincere heart, and moved by grace, try in their actions to do his will as they know it through the dictates of their conscience — those too may achieve eternal salvation. Nor shall divine providence deny the assistance necessary for salvation to those who, without any fault of theirs, have not yet arrived at an explicit knowledge of God, and who, not without grace, strive to lead a good life. Whatever good or truth is found amongst them is considered by the Church to be a preparation for the Gospel and given by him who

enlightens all men that they may at length have life. But very often, deceived by the Evil One, men have become vain in their reasonings, have exchanged the truth of God for a lie and served the world rather than the Creator (cf. Rom 1:21, 25). Or else, living and dying in this world without God, they are exposed to ultimate despair. Hence to procure the glory of God and the salvation of all these, the Church, mindful of the Lord's command, "preach the Gospel to every creature" (Mk 16:16) takes zealous care to foster the missions. (*LG* 16)

The Council clearly acknowledges the possibility that those who have never heard the gospel may, under certain conditions, be saved. But it immediately goes on to state that "very often" (*at saepius*) these conditions are not met and that the salvation of non-Christians who do not meet these conditions is significantly tied to the gospel being effectively preached to them.

In postconciliar theological and pastoral commentary, the possibility of being saved without hearing the gospel has often been commented on, so much so, that many have made the leap from "possibility" to "probability" to "presumed universal salvation." Whether it be Rahner's citation of *LG* 16b to claim magisterial backing for his theory of the "anonymous Christian," or the "grass roots" preaching of parish clergy and religious education personnel, this commentary on the possibility of everyone or almost everyone being saved almost always ignores the Council's statement that "very often" the conditions under which such salvation may be obtained are not fulfilled. This is a very serious omission.

Since the "hinge" on which *LG* 16's argument for the continued urgency of evangelization turns is its citation of Romans 1:21, 25, my task in this chapter will be to examine exactly what is being claimed in these texts. To do so, I will consult a range of well-respected commentators. Because of the importance of establishing the meaning of these texts clearly, I will cite more amply than might be usual the actual words of many of the contemporary commentators, which, surprisingly, are in remarkable agreement about the basic meaning and significance of the texts, providing very strong backing, indeed, for *LG* 16c.

Romans: The Overall Context

This is the epistle that contains at its core the longest sustained theological exposition of Paul's understanding of the gospel and, in particular, the status of both Jews and Gentiles as regards salvation. It is, perhaps, the Pauline epistle that has been commented on most frequently and continues to play a major role in theological reflection on justification, faith and works, and now on the relationship between Christianity and Judaism. C. E. B. Cranfield calls it "the most systematic and complete exposition of the Gospel that the NT contains."[3]

The main theological point that Paul is attempting to make in the epistle is that everyone is in need of the salvation won by Christ — Jew and Gentile — and that justification is impossible apart from faith in Christ. This, of course, raises some complex theological questions, not all of which Paul explicitly addresses, and many of which are being energetically discussed even today.

The texts that *LG* 16c cites are part of a section of the theological argument that is generally understood to include Romans 1:18-32,[4] although we will also need to comment briefly on texts in chapters 2 and 3. We will also draw on the broader argument of Romans as it is useful.[5]

Joseph Fitzmyer sums up the overall argument of these first chapters like this:

> The topic in vv. 18-32 is God's wrath as a reaction to human wickedness and unrighteousness, and in 2:1–3:9 it will be God's wrath manifested against the unrighteousness of those who try to achieve it by observance of the law. The status of humanity without the gospel is thus characterized as one under the wrath of God; in contrast the new status will be one under the uprightness of God (3:21-31).[6]

Brendan Byrne characterizes this whole section from 1:18 to 3:20 as "a prophetic declamation within the framework of Jewish apocalypticism."[7] He identifies the "eschatological perspective" as being key to an understanding of Romans where the issue of salvation in the light of the final judgment is overarching.

> The key hope was to be "saved" from the "wrath" (and consequent eternal separation from God) through being found "righteous" (= "being justified") at the final judgment (2:3-16; 5:9-10; 8:2, 31-39). Those "found righteous" would enter into the blessings of salvation promised to Abraham "and to his seed" (4:13) — that is, to the Israel of the end-time, the eschatological People of God.[8]

We will begin our consideration, however, with the four verses that immediately precede this section in which Paul states his overall purpose.

Romans 1:14-17

> I am under obligation both to Greeks and to barbarians, both to the wise and to the foolish: so I am eager to preach the gospel to you also who are in Rome. For I am not ashamed of the gospel: it is the power of God for salvation to everyone who has faith, to the Jew first and also to the Greek. For in it the righteousness of God is revealed through faith for faith; as it is written, "He who through faith is righteous shall live."

Paul states his purpose in writing: to preach the gospel. A large part of Romans is an exposition of the gospel with the focus on why we need to be saved and how we can be saved. He is very aware of his special mission to the Gentiles — not only the Greek speakers but the "barbarians" (non-Greek speakers). At the same time, as a Jew himself, who often preached in synagogues and met with house churches that contained both Gentile and Jewish Christians, he is concerned to make clear that the gospel, and the faith that it proclaims and engenders, is essential for both Gentile and Jew alike. His statement that the gospel "is the power of God for salvation to everyone who has faith, to the Jew first and also to the Greek," announces the universal scope of the gospel. While in different parts of the epistle he may be speaking specifically at different times of non-Christian Gentiles, Jews, Christian Gentiles, and Jewish Christians, an overarching concern is the universal scope of the need for salvation and the universal solution that the gospel announces.

The message of the gospel is very radical, and Paul is aware that both Gentiles and Jews will find the claims he is about to make astounding. He is not ashamed to be the bearer of the shocking message he is about to proclaim because he knows that the message is true and that the power of God is contained in it and released by its proclamation. When the hearer of the gospel responds positively to the truth that is heard — believes in it, has faith — the faith that is engendered by the work of the Spirit (the power of the gospel) brings the hearer into a relationship with the righteousness of God which saves one from God's "wrath." Paul, having seen this happen innumerable times, knows that the gospel is not just a "religious theory" or Gnostic "myth" but that it releases spiritual power when responded to in faith, changing lives in significant ways. It is significant that Paul particularly stresses that the "righteousness" or holiness of God is revealed by the gospel. We will see how this occurs in a twofold manner: (1) the revelation of the unrighteousness of sinful man, and (2) the revelation of the holiness of God in the preaching of the gospel, and revealed most starkly in the events of the paschal mystery, which the gospel proclaims.

Byrne emphasizes that this twofold revelation — of God's wrath and his righteousness — are both important.

> The two "revelations" are related, even causally . . . in the sense that the revelation of God's wrath means that the final reckoning is under way and human beings are being found wanting in God's sight. The "thesis" to be developed here is that there is "no righteousness" on the human side (3:20). If there is to be any rescue whatsoever, it can only come about through a righteousness stemming totally from God and appropriated by human beings as pure gift through faith. The revelation of God's wrath, then, indicates the circumstances which require that the way of *God's* righteousness, appropriated through faith (1:17), be the sole, necessary and sufficient path for human beings to arrive at salvation (1:16).[9]

Jewett brings out how deeply this revelation cuts through the defenses, illusions, and rationalizations of the proud human heart.

> Paul is operating on the assumption that the gospel of Christ (1:17) reveals the shameful "secrets of the heart" (2:16; 1 Cor 14:25) that humans attempt to suppress. The cross of Christ reveals the unacknowledged tendency to stamp out the truth and to wage war against God so that humans and institutions can maintain their guise of superior virtue and honor. The resurrection of Christ exposed this vicious secret at the heart of the human endeavor, and reveals the shocking truth about the nature of the attempted reversal in the roles of humans and God. In their competition for honor, they claim a status due only to God and end up in shameful distortion. The present preaching of the gospel "reveals" this hidden reality.[10]

The citation at the end of verse 17 is from Habakkuk. It is significant that Paul quotes it here at the beginning of his exposition since one of the main points he will make in dealing with the significance of the "privilege" of the Jews is that, properly understood, the Covenant, the Law, circumcision, and the Prophets, and in particular Abraham, the founding father of the Jews, were all pointing to faith as the essential core of salvation, and were "approved" by God for their faith-filled obedience, which now needs to be directed to Jesus.[11]

Romans 1:18

> For the wrath of God is revealed from heaven against all ungodliness and wickedness of men who by their wickedness suppress the truth.

There is an immense amount of truth communicated in this single verse. God's wrath is frequently mentioned in both Testaments. The truth that is being conveyed is not of an emotionally unstable God who is given to bursts of anger. It is not talking about the "emotional state" of God or the emotion of "anger." The truth that is being conveyed is of the utter incongruity between the depth of God's holiness and the sin of men. There can be no "integration" or "synthesis" of the two. There can be no "tolerance" or "coexistence" of the two. Ultimately only one who is willing to become holy will be able to dwell with God. One who is unwilling to become holy will be "lost," "destroyed," consigned to the "outer darkness," to the "second death," to the everlastingness of "hell." Becoming holy is to be saved. Refusing to be transformed by the grace of God, through faith, is to remain lost. To die refusing the grace of repentance and faith is to be lost forever. God's wrath can only be understood when one grasps in some dim way the utter horror and evil of sin, the blasphemous idolatry of sin. It is not a matter of the emotion of "hatred"; it is about the eternally holy Being of God and the impossibility of dwelling in the presence of such holiness without oneself becoming holy.

Lyonnet, drawing on Thomas Aquinas, points out that one way of understanding God's wrath *(la colère de Dieu)* is not a change in God but what human beings experience subjectively when they are not in right relationship with God.

> It is evidently a metaphor, as is jealousy, hatred, etc. and it is not a changeable emotion in God himself, as St. Thomas often comments, as if God first of all is irritated and then appeased; the change, says St. Thomas, is only in the effect, that is to say, in man himself.

In fact, this metaphor aims to illustrate the effect produced in the sinner, first of all of *the absolute incompatibility which exists between God and sin,* and similarly, between God and the sinner, in so far as he is separated from God by his sin.[12]

Cranfield points out that, as we reflect on human life, not to be angry at evil being done to people or injustice being done is a grave character flaw, indicating lack of love and wisdom. And yet human "anger" or "wrath" is always imperfect and shadowed with sin. God's anger is perfectly righteous and totally one with his love. Cranfield wonders, if God "did not react to our evil with wrath," could he really be good and loving?[13]

God's wrath will be fully manifest on the "day of Yahweh," on the "last day" at the "final judgment" at the "parousia" when the definitive and final judgments of God will be made manifest on all of human history and on each person's life, and the human race will be finally and definitively separated into the eternally saved and the eternally lost. This apocalyptic and eschatological framework is deeply embedded in both the OT and NT and is firmly held to and taught by Paul.[14]

Cardinal Ratzinger points out the need to restore the truth about God's "wrath" in the contemporary pastoral situation of the Church.

From this one can understand what the "wrath of God" and the anger of the Lord are all about: necessary expressions of his love that is always identical with the truth. A Jesus who is in agreement with everybody and anybody, a Jesus without his holy wrath, without the toughness of the truth and of true love, is not the true Jesus as Scripture shows him but a miserable caricature. A presentation of the "gospel" in which the seriousness of God's wrath no longer exists has nothing to do with the biblical gospel. True forgiveness is something quite other than weakly letting things be. Forgiveness is exacting and makes demands on both the person who forgives and the person who receives forgiveness in that person's whole being. A Jesus who approves of everything is a Jesus without the cross, because the tribulation of the cross would not then be needed to bring men and women salvation. In fact to a noticeable extent the cross is being interpreted out of theology and its meaning changed so as to become merely an unpleasant accident or a purely political affair. The cross as atonement, the cross as a way of forgiving and redeeming, does not fit into a certain modern pattern of thought. . . . Forgiveness has to do with truth, and for that reason it requires the cross of the

Son and it requires our conversion. . . . A pastoral practice of appease-
ment, of "understanding everything and forgiving everything" (in the
superficial sense of this phrase) stands in glaring contrast to the biblical
evidence. The correct pastoral practice leads to the truth, arouses love
for the truth, and helps people to accept the pain of the truth. It must itself be a form of accompanying people on the difficult but beautiful way
into new life that is also the way to true and lasting joy.[15]

While God's wrath will be fully and finally manifest at the final judgment, it is also partially manifest in discernible ways throughout history.[16]
The examples of judgments in history are multiple: the judgment of Adam
and Eve (Gen. 3:14-24), the judgment of Cain (Gen. 4:8-16), the judgment
of the Flood (Gen. 6:5-8), the judgment at the Tower of Babel (Gen. 12:5-9),
the judgment of Sodom and Gomorrah (Gen. 19:12-14), and the innumerable prophetic warnings about judgments and subsequent judgments of the
Exile, the judgment of the destruction of the temple, the judgment of de-
feats in battle, the judgment of idolatry, the judgment of mocking God's
anointed, the judgment of infidelity and immorality, of relying on human
means rather than God, etc. The NT tells us that these judgments in history have been recorded "for us, as a warning" (1 Cor. 10:11-12).

Jesus himself spoke of the impending judgment of the Jewish people
in history as a consequence of their rejection of him, in the destruction of
their temple and their existence as a people with a land and a form of national governance, in their dispersal among the nations (Luke 20:41-44).

Jesus himself spoke frequently of the consequences of rejecting the
mercy that was present in him and the deadly consequences of such rejection that will become apparent on the Day of Judgment when he warns it
will go worse for many than it went for Sodom (Matt. 11:20-24). It is not
just Paul who speaks of God's wrath and the various equivalent concepts
connected with judgment. It is the teaching of Jesus that is carried forward
in the apostolic preaching. In order to appreciate what it is to be saved, we
need to know what we are saved from and that we are indeed in need of
such saving (1 Thess. 1:9-10; 5:9; Rom. 5:9).

It is also significant that Paul speaks of God's wrath being "revealed
from heaven." He is making clear that what he is about to describe as wrath
in history is not just the "natural" consequences of sin but something that
ultimately is founded in the Being of God.

It is important also to note that the "ungodliness and wickedness" that
Paul refers to is particularly rooted in the specific activity of "suppressing

the truth." What we are seeing in these verses is not only a revelation of the righteousness of God but a revelation also of the truly wicked and ungodly condition of the human heart, most particularly, in its perverse "suppressing" of the truth.[17]

Fr. Francis Martin speaks of the often subtle individual responsibility in this suppression, but he also recognizes the creation of a *culture* that is constructed on a suppression of the truth. In commenting on the Greek word for "suppression," Martin says:

> The verb used here designates the source of all that follows, pointing as it does to the way of a culture that has designed itself to be impervious to the evidence of God. However, the expression speaks most of all of a subtle interior movement by which what is dimly grasped is prevented from growing into full knowledge.[18]

Most commentators focus on the individual's responsibility, but Martin broadens the discussion, which is important for the situation we are facing today, to include the reality of a culture of suppression and the particular responsibility of the leaders in constructing such a culture.

> It is important to realize that this suppression is initially personal, on the part of some leaders who shape the culture, and then also communal or cultural in . . . the resulting lack of the knowledge of God and the consequences of this becoming embodied in the institutions and thought world of the society. Paul is condemning a *culture* and is uncovering . . . the root cause of an aberration that is so mysteriously easy to generate and perpetuate and finally results in a culture that becomes a bondage.[19]

The actual condition of the culture in which theology happens can very much influence its preoccupations and even its conclusions. The theology done in a Christendom situation was different than theology done when the Church was illegal and persecuted. As we transition into a post-Christendom situation in the West and deal increasingly with cultures that are hostile to Christianity, our theology and our pastoral strategies will be impacted. Parts of Scripture that did not "resonate" or "make sense" will again make sense. The analysis of personal and social decay found in Romans 1, which wasn't applicable in the same way at other times in the Church's historical embodiments, is becoming increasingly applicable and relevant to our own contemporary situation.[20]

Lyonnet believes that the Greek word translated in English here as "suppression" can also be translated as *"refuser accueil"* (to refuse welcome), which has significant resonances with John 1:11-13.

> He came to his own home, and his own people received him not. But to all who received him, who believed in his name, he gave power to become children of God; who were born, not of blood or of the will of man, but of God.

Lyonnet cites a number of exegetes who describe this "refusal to welcome" as the fundamental sin of injustice towards God.[21]

Cardinal Ratzinger comments on Romans in several of his writings, emphasizing both the culpable suppression of the truth and the remarkable applicability of these verses to our current situation.

> The apostle offers a surprising response to this metaphysical and moral cynicism of a decadent society dominated only by the law of the jungle. He declares that, in reality, this society knows God very well. . . . According to the apostle, the truth is accessible to them, but they do not want it, because they refuse the demands that the truth would make on them. . . . For Paul, the moral decadence of society is nothing more than the logical consequence and the faithful reflection of this radical perversion. When man prefers his own egoism, his pride, and his convenience to the demands made on him by the truth, the only possible outcome is an upside-down existence. Adoration is due to God alone, but what is adored is no longer God; images, outward appearances, and current opinion have dominion over man. This general alteration extends to every sphere of life. That which is against nature becomes the norm; the man who lives against the truth also lives against nature. His creativity is no longer at the service of the good: he devotes his genius to ever more refined forms of evil. The bonds between man and woman, and between parents and children, are dissolved, so that the very sources from which life springs are blocked up. It is no longer life that reigns, but death. A civilization of death is formed (Rom 1:21-32). The description of decadence that Paul sketches here astonishes us modern readers by its contemporary relevance.[22]

The objection can rightfully be raised that not all Gentiles participate in all or even most of the behavior that Paul describes here and in the following verses. Cranfield makes the point that, even though the particular behavior described is widespread, "every" Gentile does not participate in it. Nevertheless, he points out, all Gentiles and Jews try to justify themselves in some other way than the way given by God: the gracious gift of Christ, illumined by the preaching of the gospel, responded to in faith and loving obedience. The passion to "suppress the truth" and engage in "futile reasoning" leads to the idolatrous efforts to devise our own religion to accommodate our deeply rooted rebellion and disordered passions, both intellectual and bodily. As Cranfield puts it:

> It is not Paul's judgment of his contemporaries that we have here, but the gospel's judgment of men, that is, of all men, the judgment the gospel itself pronounces, which Paul has heard and to which he has himself submitted. The section depicts man as he appears in the light of the cross of Christ. It is not a description of especially bad men only, but the innermost truth of all of us, as we are in ourselves.[23]

Fitzmyer puts it this way:

> Nevertheless, he [Paul] is not saying that every individual pagan before Christ's coming was a moral failure. He speaks collectively and describes a de facto situation. Moreover, he does not limit his discussion merely to contemporary Greco-Roman society . . . for he has already made mention of "barbarians" along with "Greeks" (1:14). He has in mind the totality of pagan society.[24]

Another way of talking about this, of course, is as "original sin," that primordial rebellion against God that has left its profound wound on every person. Lyonnet describes the truth about this universal, original sin as the very foundation of Christianity without which the redemption of Christ makes no sense.[25]

Käsemann is in accord:

> For the apostle, history is governed by the primal sin of rebellion against the Creator, which finds repeated and universal expression. It is thus governed by the wrath of God, which throws the creature back on itself, corresponding to its own will, and abandons it to the world.[26]

Cranfield goes on to point out that before the wrath of God is revealed in the proclamation of the gospel it is revealed in the events that the gospel proclaims, namely the crucifixion of the Holy One of God, Christ. He believes on the basis of his exegesis that the most important thing about the wrath of God "is that we do not see the full meaning of the wrath of God in the disasters befalling sinful men in the course of history: the reality of the wrath of God is only truly known when it is seen in its revelation in Gethsemane and on Golgotha." The horror of sin is seen as its full fury falls on the innocent one, the holy one, Jesus himself. The torture and humiliation of the Lamb of God reveals what is in the human heart, and the death that sin causes and deserves. Cranfield's contention is that Paul is indicating that "the wrath, as well as the righteousness is being revealed in the Gospel, and that the righteousness no less than the wrath is being revealed from heaven."[27]

Jewett makes the point that clearly all humanity is being addressed here in verse 18, from the very beginning:

> The target of divine wrath is against "all impiety and wrongdoing of humans," an encompassing description of what is wrong with the human race as a whole. Despite a later reference to characteristically pagan failures (1:23), the formulation with "all" indicates that Paul wishes to insinuate that Jews as well as Romans, Greeks, and barbarians are being held responsible.[28]

Jewett points out that what is "wrong" with humanity is revealed most starkly in "the cross of Christ that revealed the complicity of all parties in the attempt to suppress the truth he represented. The cross reveals a fundamental distortion of honor-shame systems in which a universal desire for superior status ends up in a hostile assault on God."[29] He also adds the useful comment: "For Greeks and Romans *impietas* is the most heinous crime — the failure to respect deity, especially in the civic cult."[30]

Romans 1:19-20

> For what can be known about God is plain to them, because God has shown it to them. Ever since the creation of the world his invisible nature, namely, his eternal power and deity, has been clearly perceived in the things that have been made. So they are without excuse.

These are very important verses. Some things about God can be known by human beings apart from "positive revelation." God reveals himself as Creator as human beings ponder the reality of the creation. The creation implies a Creator. This is not just "unaided human reason" fortu-itously figuring things out but an intentional communication from God to the creature by means of the creation.[31] There is a vast literature on whether Paul is enunciating the basis for a "natural theology" in these verses.[32] It is not necessary for our purposes to address this issue. What we need to note is that it is possible to "clearly perceive" certain truths about God that imply a certain response in return. Not to perceive these truths, not to perceive the Creator through the creation, is a result of a truly wicked suppression of the truth, not because God is not revealing himself. Paul's conclusion is that human beings who fail to perceive the Creator and the implications of such are truly "without excuse."

Romans 1:21-23

> For although they knew God they did not honor him as God or give thanks to him, but they became futile in their thinking and their sense-less minds were darkened. Claiming to be wise, they became fools, and exchanged the glory of the immortal God for images resembling mortal man or birds or animals or reptiles.

A communication is made by God. Knowledge is given. There is an ex-tensive literature that discusses what type of knowledge this could be. Lyonnet expresses what seems to be the prevailing opinion on this. It is not a "positive revelation" such as has been made to Jews and Christians. Nor is it, as some have speculated, a revelation given to Adam and transmitted to his posterity. It is, as Lyonnet puts it, a revelation *"through the created world and an interior light."* In any case, ignorance cannot be claimed.[33]

Francis Martin ties together, more closely than Latourelle does, the "natural" revelation of creation and the call to personal relationship:

> He is not saying that God's self-manifestation in and through creation presents itself as "compelling evidence." It is rather an invitation to yield to the evidence and follow its lead. Refusal to do this is a form of human action, a praxis that can create an anti-culture. . . . Created realities bear witness to their Source, but the person must be willing to follow their beckoning, and yield as well to the light given by God to grasp the true meaning of this witness which, in the present order of things, leads to love and praise of God. I say "in the present order of things" to indicate

that there is not any purely "natural order" in which the witness of creation can end with a knowledge of God divorced from his call to a personal relationship of obedience and trust.[34]

Byrne points out that a space for a "sincere atheism" cannot be found in Paul and acknowledges how challenging this is for the modern mind to accept.[35] It is also a challenge to some of the texts of Vatican II, which appear to hold the opposite.[36]

Fitzmyer understands the knowledge to be "vague, unformulated knowledge or experience of God" but not the "real, affective knowledge of God that includes love, praise, reverence, and thanksgiving."[37] With this understanding of the different types of "knowing" of God, it is possible to understand 1 Corinthians 1:21 ("For since in the wisdom of God the world did not come to know God through wisdom, it was the will of God through the foolishness of the proclamation to save those who have faith") in a sense, then, that does not contradict Romans 1:21.[38]

Käsemann describes how fundamental this knowledge is, however one wants to define it, and how unavoidably every human encounters it:

> Knowledge of God does not relate speculatively to his nature but to his claim to lordship and the creatureliness that we experience therewith. . . . With his existence in the world a person stands before God even before religion discloses that to him and before he reflects on it in his attempts at theology. Already required of him is reverence, thankfulness, and a humanity which is not arrogant and does not flee responsibility.[39]

They[40] actually had knowledge of God but suppressed it, and the act of suppressing the truth initiated a chain of false and foolish reasoning ("vain" or "futile" reasoning is an important concept in the Bible;[41] likewise, the contrast between the foolish and the wise) that led them farther and farther away from life-giving truth into death-dealing lies. They thought they were "smart" in turning away from God and to their own desires, but, blinded by their self-delusion, they actually were turning into "fools." Rather than worshiping, as is fitting, the Truth, they turned to the utter folly of idolatry, worshiping "nothings."

Jewett points out how truly outrageous this "exchange" is:

> The "wise" who claim superiority in this world are actually morons in the light of the gospel and the prospect of wrath. They need the gospel

as much as the "uneducated" if they are to recognize the truth about themselves.

The height of folly is idolatry, which Paul depicts not as a silly mistake but as the ultimate expression of the human campaign to suppress the truth.[42]

Jewett sees a clear reference to the golden calf episode as recounted in Psalm 106:20 and Jeremiah 2:11, but thinks that "the aggressive intentionality that this wording would have conveyed to his audience has not been clearly perceived."

> There was no question of "exchanging" the glory for a preexisting "facsimile" in this psalm; the statue of the calf was fashioned by Aaron and his colleagues, making it the archetypal episode of idolatry in biblical literature . . . [suggesting] the "glory of God" as the target to be displaced by the idol . . . a preposterous level of delusion. . . . The usual translation "exchange" likewise tends to reduce the matter to a trade of one option for another. But the associations with the Eden and golden calf stories demand the recognition that the option of the false image was actively created by humans rather than merely being selected from preexisting alternatives.[43]

G. K. Beale has published a major study on the theme of idolatry in both Testaments and concurs with the view that there are numerous allusions to Old Testament depictions of idolatry and its consequences woven into Paul's words in Romans 1. He too understands Paul to be teaching that idolatry is the root sin of all other sins, and that it extends not just to actual "wooden idols" but to any trust in the world, self, or things of the world that is not trust in the Lord, and that the consequence of idolatry is becoming like what we worship — empty, lifeless, deformed.[44]

The New Testament itself, of course, extends the concept of idolatry to cover such things as the "belly" (Phil. 3:19), covetousness (Col. 3:5), and what is immoral, impure, or covetous (Eph. 5:3-6).

> For many, of whom I have often told you and now tell you even with tears, live as enemies of the cross of Christ. Their end is destruction, their god is the belly, and they glory in their shame, with minds set on earthly things. (Phil. 3:18-19)

Put to death therefore what is earthly in you: immorality, impurity, passion, evil desire, and covetousness, which is idolatry. On account of these the wrath of God is coming. (Col. 3:5-6)

But immorality and all impurity or covetousness must not even be named among you, as is fitting among saints. . . . Be sure of this, that no immoral or impure man, or one who is covetous (that is, an idolater), has any inheritance in the kingdom of Christ and of God. Let no one deceive you with empty words, for it is because of these things that the wrath of God comes upon the sons of disobedience. (Eph. 5:3-6)

Byrne points out that our creation "in the image of the eternal God is the basis for human destiny to eternal life; the 'exchange' also involves losing the destiny to eternal life."[45] The great sin here is turning away from the knowledge of God that is given, and refusing to acknowledge God as God.

As Käsemann puts it: "The reality of the world and the basic sin of mankind consist in not recognizing God in his reality that opens itself to us."[46]

Jewett, citing Plato among others, points out how even the pagan philosophers knew that man had a duty to thank and praise God. Particularly striking is his citation of the words of Epictetus to the effect that "to be consistent with the nature of humankind, one must praise God: 'If, indeed, I were a nightingale I should be singing as a nightingale; if a swan, as a swan. But as it is, I am a rational being, therefore I must be singing hymns of praise to God.'"[47]

The human intellect is profoundly affected by the Fall and tends on its own towards "vain" or "futile" reasoning. Refusing to honor God in his "invisible nature, eternal power and deity" is "without excuse." The primary sin of the creature is not acknowledging our contingent being, by honoring and thanking the one to whom we owe our existence.[48]

Jewett holds that "Leading the human race to this recognition in restoring the proper stance of humans in glorifying God is the goal of Paul's missionary project that the entire letter seeks to advance, as 15:6 and 9 make plain." Jewett further points out that this was widely experienced and understood in the early Church as the Jewish tradition of giving thanks at mealtimes was adopted and the central sacrament named the "Eucharist."[49]

Byrne, as we have seen, describes Paul's understanding of the Christian mission as bringing "an overflow of thanksgiving to God on the part of human beings."[50]

Fitzmyer comments: "Paul regards this futility of thinking and misguided conduct as manifestations of the wrath of God, not provocations of it. He realizes that *only the apocalyptic light of the gospel can penetrate such darkness.*"[51]

Käsemann points out the irony that, though thinking they are guided by "reason," they are, in effect, in bondage to the disordered, blind desires of the fallen "will."[52]

Jewett comments: "Life that does not take account of the reality of God is doomed to the unreal world of self-deception."[53] He goes on to state that "foolish persons and nations" that fail to recognize the ultimate power of God are "doomed to frustration and defeat" and that the human ability to perceive correctly "is disabled when God is unacknowledged."[54]

There is a great debate in the commentaries about whether allusions to the Fall (Gen. 3:1-7)[55] and to the worship of the golden calf (Exod. 32:1-34),[56] and, later on, to Sodom (Gen. 19:1-28),[57] are intended here by Paul.

It seems reasonable to conclude after surveying the range of opinion that there almost certainly are allusions here to the golden calf and Sodom stories, whether they are explicit textual allusions or allusions from the oral tradition.[58] In any case, Paul understands the historical examples of idolatry and immorality in the history of Israel that are alluded to in the text as applicable to the Gentiles as well, and illustrative of the universality of the wound of sin. Cranfield puts it this way:

> The implication would seem to be that Paul himself reckoned that, by describing — as he certainly was doing in 1:18-32 — the obvious sinfulness of the heathen, he was, as a matter of fact, describing the basic sinfulness of fallen man as such, the inner reality of the life of Israel no less than of that of the Gentiles. . . . We understand these verses as the revelation of the gospel's judgment of all men, which lays bare not only the idolatry of ancient and modern paganism but also the idolatry ensconced in Israel, in the Church, and in the life of each believer.[59]

Or, as Käsemann puts it, the historical events pertinent to Israel, including the worship of the golden calf, now illumine the experience of all humanity, as they reveal the perverse rebellion against God, suppression of the truth, and turn to idolatry and immorality. He sees the historical events such as the golden calf and the Fall itself as prototypes illumining the experience of all humanity.[60]

Romans 1:24-25

> Therefore God gave them up in the lusts of their hearts to impurity, to
> the dishonoring of their bodies among themselves, because they ex-
> changed the truth about God for a lie and worshiped and served the
> creature rather than the Creator, who is blessed forever! Amen.

The reason why "God gave them up in the lusts of their hearts" is that
they suppressed the truth of God's revelation and rather than give him the
honor and thanks that is fitting, worshiped creatures, constructed idols,
and in their vain reasonings, made a god in their own image, creating a "religion" to accommodate their lusts. Exchanging the truth for a lie is a tragic
and unspeakably foolish exchange. Jesus identified Satan as the "father of
lies and a murderer." The atmosphere of the demonic is present here.[61]

Jewett comments that the "lie" is not just any lie, but "*the* lie" (Fitzmyer calls it the "big lie"), the lie that led to the Fall that he sees at work
throughout the history of God's people, culminating in the crucifixion of
Christ.

> The singular use of "the lie" in Romans implies an antecedent act from
> which all later lies about God derive, namely the primordial desire of
> humans to "be like God" and to define evil and good for themselves
> (Gen 3:5). In the light of the gospel, Paul has radicalized the story of the
> fall by emphasizing the elements of willful distortion.[62]

Paul sums up the "bottom line" a little later on in the epistle (6:23)
when he declares that "the wages of sin is death." It is important to be clear
about the sequence of events:

1. God reveals himself to his creatures in the creation.
2. Human beings suppress the truth of God as he reveals it to them in the
   creation.
3. They refuse to honor him or give him thanks.
4. They construct "gods" in the image of creatures, choosing the evil of
   idolatry.
5. The rejection of the truth and embrace of a lie leads them to create an
   idolatrous religion that accommodates their unchained lusts.
6. They now are servants of "creatures" rather than the Creator, slaves of
   sin, blinded by delusions.

The horror of what has transpired is such that Paul feels the need to react to it with an exclamation of honor and praise of God.

Romans 1:26-27

> For this reason God gave them up to dishonorable passions. Their women exchanged natural relations for unnatural, and the men likewise gave up natural relations with women and were consumed with passion for one another, men committing shameless acts with men and receiving in their own persons the due penalty for their error.

Paul is underlining again the root cause of the immorality — the suppression of the truth and the refusal to honor and thank God. Now, for the second time, he also indicates that it is God who has given them up. On one level we are dealing here with the "natural consequences" of sin. On another level we are encountering again the wrath of God as human rebellion shatters against the Being of God. Käsemann acknowledges that the creation and human reality are abandoned to "chaos," but this is a decision of what he calls the "hidden judge," who will become unmistakably manifest at the final judgment.[63] It is God who decides to "hand them over" to the consequences of their rebellion.

Cranfield notes that some modern commentators shy away from attributing divine intentionality to the "wrath" and unfolding consequences of sin. Cranfield believes this is not warranted by the text, and the thrice-repeated declaration of Paul to the effect that God handed them over "is surely so emphatic as to suggest that a deliberate, positive act of God is meant."[64] Käsemann agrees with this position, as does Jewett.[65] This, of course, does not exclude aspects of the judgment that can partially be described as including the natural consequences of rebelling against the order of reality, the withdrawal of divine protection, the "inevitable results," etc.[66]

The perversity of suppressing the truth and refusing due honor and thanks to God leads to the human construction of a false religion, a religion that is idolatrous. The turn from God to "self" ironically brings with it a distortion of the "self," which expresses itself in the twisting of our basic sexual identities as male and female in the perverse use of the sexual faculty. The perverse exchange of the truth of God for a lie leads to the perversion of the procreative capacity of men and women.

Fitzmyer describes it like this:

Paul sees homosexual conduct as a symbol of the perversion stemming from idolatry. For him it is a way in which human beings refuse to acknowledge the manifestation of God's activity in creation. The human being who fails to acknowledge God and turns from him who is the source of life and immortality, seeks rather a vicarious expression of it through the misuse of the natural procreative faculty. . . . Homosexual behavior is the sign of human rebellion against God, an outward manifestation of the inward and spiritual rebellion. It illustrates human degradation and provides a vivid image of humanity's rejection of the sovereignty of God the creator.[67]

The darkening of the human understanding that was a consequence of the rebellion, and the perverse exchanges rooted in the refusal to honor God, lead to the base dishonoring of the human person in perverse sexual immorality.[68] The penalty for their own error that they receive in their own person is variously interpreted.

1. The bondage to sin, which is a consequence of their actions, is itself a punishment.
2. The distortion of the human personality, of the male/female identities, that occurs in homosexual behavior is a punishment.[69]
3. Bodily damage and sexually transmitted diseases are a penalty.

It seems as if the first possibility is most widely accepted as the probable meaning of Paul, although the other possibilities also illumine *de facto* consequences of homosexual behavior. As Cranfield puts it: "It has been recognized from early times that the reference is more probably to their sexual perversion itself as the punishment for their abandonment of the true God than to a necessary or appropriate but unspecified punishment for their sexual perversion."[70]

There is, of course, an extensive literature and vigorous debate concerning how Paul's teaching on homosexuality does or does not apply to contemporary understandings of homosexuality. For the purposes of this book this is not a debate we need to consider.

Romans 1:28-31

And since they did not see fit to acknowledge God, God gave them up to a base mind and to improper conduct. They were filled with all manner of wickedness, evil, covetousness, malice. Full of envy, murder, strife, deceit, malignity, they are gossips, slanderers, haters of God, and insolent, haughty, boastful, inventors of evil, disobedient to parents, foolish, faithless, heartless, ruthless.

Jewett and others see a threefold progression in the "giving over": first on the level of false worship, second on the level of sexual perversion, and third on the public level of social disintegration or, as Jewett puts it, "criminal and sociopathic behavior."[71] Jewett also thinks that "base mind" would be better translated as "'reprobate instinct,' a mindset that is perversely unfit for humane purposes."[72]

For the third time, Paul repeats the primary reason why this descent into bondage to immorality is happening and underlines the fact that this is not just "natural consequences" but a divine intentionality at work. Because "they did not see fit to acknowledge God, God gave them up to a base mind and to improper conduct." The disordered conduct flows from the rejection of the light, the suppression of the truth. Now, not only is there grave sexual perversion and disorder, but also "all manner of wickedness, evil, covetousness, malice."

Byrne points out that the "acknowledging of God" spoken of here "means more than mere awareness of God's existence and chief attributes. It implies the deep personal knowledge (cf. 3:20; 10:2; Phil. 1:9; also Col. 1:9-10; 3:10) that goes along with due creaturely response to God (cf. v. 21a)."[73] Jewett shares this view.[74]

Jewett also points out that "in contrast to the Greek outlook, the flaw in the human race does not lie in ignorance that can be excused or modulated through education but rather in a direct and multifaceted campaign to disparage God and replace him/her with a human face or institution."[75]

Commentators debate whether in the listing of the disorders one can see a somewhat orderly description of the violation of the two tablets of the Decalogue; violation of the first tablet in lack of proper reverence to God, and violation of the second tablet in destructive social relationships. There is sharp disagreement on this point, but it is not central to our concern.

There is further debate about whether there is a particular order to the listing of the types of wickedness. Various kinds of groupings can be discerned by different commentators and the many similar listings of vices found in other books of the NT pointed out.[76] Again, this is not a concern that is immediately germane to our analysis.

Käsemann's description of the listing of vices as something like the opening of "Pandora's box" seems to characterize well the effect that Paul's listing has on the reader.

> He who leaves his Lord loses control over himself together with his sense of the order of being, and can no longer be summoned to responsibility. His conduct demonstrates that he is no longer restrained by the conventional limit of what is "seemly," and even the humanity that Gentiles honor means nothing for him. . . . The meaning here is unmistakable: Idolatry opens the floodgates for vices which destroy society and turn creation back into terrible chaos. In this way the curse of God's wrath accomplishes its purpose. . . . There is no longer any protective dike in this cosmos. . . . The vices just spring out in rapid succession as from Pandora's box.[77]

Jewett sheds additional light:

> The source of all these evils is the human race as a whole, dominated by the "unfitting mind." Here we have a social pathology that is oriented not to the character flaws of individuals or groups but to the collective experience of the human race since the corruption of creation, viewed in the radical new light shed by the gospel. This catalogue undercuts in the most sweeping manner any potential claims of individual, group, or national exceptionalism. Pursuant to this aim, the 21 evils are drawn from Greek, Latin, and Jewish catalogues, no one of which tallies completely with Paul's scheme.[78]

Romans 1:32

> Though they know God's decree that those who do such things deserve to die, they not only do them but approve those who practice them.

A number of commentators point out that only some of the many vices/crimes listed bear with them the death penalty in either Gentile or Jewish law or, for that matter, any known law code.[79] There is a general consensus that Paul probably does not have in mind a specific "decree" where God declares that these vices deserve death, although the general decree following the Fall where death is decreed as the consequence of disobedience may have formed the backdrop for this statement. In what way the Gentiles could know of this decree is left unspoken, and many commentators think that probably Paul assumes that the light of conscience he speaks of in Romans 2, as well as the revelation given in creation, gives pagan Gentiles enough of a sense of the existence of God and right and wrong to know that the wickedness Paul describes is, in some way, deserving of death. Byrne sums it up well:

> The presumption appears to be that, along with the original knowledge of the existence of God (vv. 19-20), went a sense also of the divine will for human behavior, the "unwritten law" inscribed in conscience (2:14-15). This sense of moral responsibility before God included an awareness of the sanction (life or death) hanging over human behavior. The divine enactment *(dikaioma)* to this effect, which the Jews found in their law (cf. esp. Deut 30:15-20), was available through conscience to the rest of humankind. Hence the continuance in wrongdoing on the part of some and the approval given by others shows the foolishness and delusion holding the world in its grip. Humans *know* such behavior leads to death, yet they persist in it and even persuade themselves that it is laudable. . . . Ultimately it is the underlying alienation from God, rather than the individual vices, that leads to the penalty of death and the death that is envisaged is not so much physical death (though Paul does see that connected with sin: Rom 5:12-14; 8:10) but death in the eschatological sense of permanent separation from God.[80]

Käsemann speaks of almost a despairing, desperate knowledge on a deep level that knows a sentence of death has been passed that will be executed at the final judgment but that "we suffer already in the perversion of creation. It does not keep us either from doing wrong or from the applause that enjoyably accompanies all vice."[81]

Fitzmyer also is in agreement that it is the final death or "second death" of definitive exclusion from the kingdom of God that Paul is thinking of here.

> It might seem at first to refer to physical death as a punishment for the vices listed, but it is difficult to establish that pagan consciences would recognize death as such a penalty for all these vices. Rather, Paul is probably thinking of "total death" (5:12, 19), the lot of all sinners; it amounts

to exclusion from the kingdom of God (I Cor 6:10; Gal 5:21). This clause, then, expresses Paul's verdict about the lot of pagan idolaters: "They deserve to die." This is but another way of saying what Paul says in 6:23, "the wages of sin are death."[82]

There is a further wickedness that Paul points out: not only doing wickedness oneself, but also approving others who do it. Some commentators find this additional statement of Paul harsh, but there is a clear echo of this teaching throughout the Scripture that condemns those who encourage others in their wickedness. Cranfield points out that in the history of the interpretation of Romans there is strong agreement with Paul's teaching about the evil of encouraging others in wickedness, and he offers some reasons why this is well founded:

> The man who applauds and encourages others in doing what is wicked is, even if he never actually commits the same wicked deed himself, not only as guilty as those who do commit it, but very often more guilty than they. . . . Those who condone and applaud the vicious actions of others are actually making a deliberate contribution to the setting up of a public opinion favorable to vice, and so to the corruption of an indefinite number of other people. So, for example, to excuse or gloss over the use of torture by security forces or the cruel injustices of racial discrimination and oppression, while not being involved in them directly, is to help to cloak monstrous evil with an appearance of respectability and so to contribute most effectively to its firmer entrenchment.[83]

Jewett provides an interesting comment on the mode of communication of Paul in this chapter as he attempts to "make a case more radical than had ever been made before, namely that the human race was involved in a consciously vicious campaign to suppress the truth."

> The case is overwhelmingly strong on rhetorical grounds and can be understood as an outgrowth of Paul's reflection on the implications of the cross event. Yet neither here nor elsewhere in the early chapters of Romans is the argument watertight in a strictly logical sense. It is a matter of rhetoric driven by faith that was designed to be effective for the audience of Roman house and tenement Churches in 57 C.E. Its persuasive power, measured against the social standards prevailing in that cultural setting, must be acknowledged as formidable.[84]

While this section of text is the immediate context in which the two verses (1:21, 25) are cited in the *LG* 16 text, we also must briefly review Romans 2 and 3 in order to grasp the overall teaching. The teaching of *LG* 16 on the possibility of salvation for those who try to guide their actions by the "dictates of conscience" is scripturally grounded in Romans 2 and specifically in verses 11-16.

Romans 2: The Rhetorical Trap

Paul springs his "rhetorical trap"[85] in chapter 2. In chapter 1 he has primarily described an idolatry and vicious lifestyle that the Jew would be accustomed to attributing to the Gentile pagans,[86] but now Paul attempts to show that the Jew too will be subject to God's wrath because he does some of the same things that the Gentiles do but more universally. In addition he relies on his "privileged position" and presumes on God's favor rather than understanding the true meaning of the Covenant, the Law, and the Patriarchs, which were intended by God as signposts towards justification by grace through faith expressed in loving obedience. Even though the hypothetical person whom Paul is addressing in the second person is not immediately identified, the explicit identification of the Jews is made in verse 17. While there is a great deal of debate about whom exactly Paul is talking to prior to verse 17, it is clear in verse 17 that he applies what he has said to the Jews. Cranfield claims that it is strongly probable that Paul has the Jews in mind from the beginning of chapter 2.[87]

Commentators struggle with the incongruity of charging the Jews (vv. 1-5, 21-24) with the same crimes as the Gentiles.[88] As a matter of fact, at this time in Israel, idolatry in the usual forms was not prevalent, nor was the practice of homosexuality. On the other hand, Jesus has established that righteousness with God must involve not only refraining from certain external wickedness but also from the rejection of the internal nurturance of evil thoughts and desires, that the righteousness required to enter the Kingdom must be greater than that of the scribes and the Pharisees, and must involve an interior transformation (Matt. 5:21-48).[89]

Not only must there be an interior righteousness that Paul emphatically teaches is generally impossible, for both Jew and Gentile, apart from incorporation into Christ and life in the Spirit, but there must also be a humility that characterizes the grateful recipient of salvation. Fleshly pride in being "chosen," "having the law," "being circumcised," "having Abraham as our Father" (Matt. 3:9) without the humility of faith and the obedience of love will avail nothing.

As Byrne puts it:

> Paul does not contest that God is kind and patient. He challenges, however, the attitude that falsely takes these attributes to mean that God's judgment of sin will not be severe. Such an attitude, in effect, "despises" them. Whereas the truth of the matter is that God's kindness, forbearance and patience are there to provide a space for repentance before the inevitable judgment falls (cf. Wis. 11:23). What distinguishes Israel from the rest is not the prospect of milder judgment, but the staying of God's hand to provide opportunity for conversion *(metanoia)*. Jews may not be now in the same situation as the Gentiles, in whose pattern of life the wrath is already revealed (1:18). But this does not mean that the wrath will not apply in their case. . . . The wrath already fallen upon the Gentiles in the shape of the vices to which they are "given up" (1:24, 26, 28) will fall no less severely upon the chosen people unless they repent.[90]

Käsemann brilliantly describes the complacency and presumption that can easily predominate when one has been blessed with many gifts, as the Jews were. When God's forbearance is taken for weakness, his kindness despised, "judgment is not escaped, but confirmed."

> The danger of the pious person is that of isolating God's gifts from the claim which is given with them and of forgetting to relate forbearance and patience to the Judge of the last day. Humans always crave security. They seek to obtain it through moralism, worshipping the gods, or trusting the divine goodness. The Lord who is known as Judge, however, does not ensure security; he destroys it.[91]

Various commentators cite rather startling extrabiblical Jewish writings of the time to the effect that physical circumcision guaranteed entrance to the Kingdom, or that Abraham would check everybody at the gate and, if they were circumcised, they went in. The Jewish prophets, and Jesus himself, directly confronted this misplaced presumption in the strongest of terms.

Käsemann continues:

> The gifts given us are then regarded as our booty with which we may protect ourselves against the Giver himself, as though he were our en-

emy. When this happens we have the same paradoxical process as that depicted in 1:22ff. God actually becomes what we see in him and make of him, namely, the wrathful adversary.[92]

This is remarkably similar to what Catherine of Siena reports receiving from God the Father in prayer:

These souls [those who die in friendship with the Lord] wait for divine judgment with gladness, not fear. And the face of my Son will appear to them neither terrifying nor hateful, because they have finished their lives in charity, delighting in me and filled with good will toward their neighbors. The different appearances of his face when he comes in majesty for judgment will not be in him but in those who are to be judged by him. To the damned he will appear with just hatred, but to the saved, with mercy and love.[93]

Bernard of Clairvaux makes a similar observation:

You see, the gaze of the Lord, though ever in itself unchanged, does not always produce the same effect. It conforms to each person's deserts, inspiring some with fear but bringing solace and security to others.[94]

Besides making the point that relying on externals without interior transformation falls short, Paul introduces the startling possibility (vv. 25-29) that a Gentile, without being circumcised, can be a "real Jew," while physically circumcised Jews who are not interiorly transformed are not real Jews.[95] Again, there is a vigorous debate among the commentators about whether Paul is talking about Gentile Christians here or whether he is opening the possibility of Gentile pagans keeping in some measure aspects of the law of God (they obviously would not be keeping the ceremonial and other particularly Jewish aspects of the law).

When he writes here (vv. 14-21) about keeping the law which is written on their hearts, and their consciences accusing or excusing them, who is Paul talking about? Some major theological voices, such as Augustine and Aquinas, argue strongly that in the overall context of Paul's teaching on justification he must certainly be talking here and in verses 7 and 10 and verses 25-29 about Gentile Christians, who now have the law written on their heart through the work of the Holy Spirit, seeing here an explicit reference to Jeremiah 31:33, which strengthens the argument that Paul is referring to Gentile Christians. Augustine took this interpretation in order to avoid a Pelagian understanding of these texts, namely, that pagans could keep the law without the grace of Christ. Augustine did acknowledge the possibility of some pagans keeping the law in some fashion; but this would not justify them, although it would lessen their punishment.[96] Aquinas also takes this interpretation for the same reason as Augustine, to avoid a Pelagian interpretation.[97] Cranfield favors this interpretation also, although with an opening to a theological development that is broader than Paul ever explicitly states.

> On the whole . . . Paul was probably actually thinking only of Christians [in vv. 7 and 10, and then later in vv. 12-16, and vv. 25-29]; but there is little doubt that, had he been asked whether what he was saying also applied to OT believers, his answer would have been affirmative, and it may well be that he did also recognize the possibility that among the heathen there were those in whose deeds God would see evidence of a secret faith unknown except to Himself.[98]

Other commentators suppose that those who are keeping the law written on their hearts are not Gentile Christians but rather pagans, but that this keeping of the law, such as it is, disposes them to justification, but does not in itself justify them, since there is no doubt that Paul clearly teaches that the keeping of the law can justify no one, but only faith in Christ.[99] Whatever keeping of the law is possible for pagans orders them towards justification, but is not in itself justifying. For that, a response to an interior grace that leads to supernatural faith and charity is necessary.

This would seem to be that "sincere seeking of God and attempting to do his will as they know it through conscience" that *LG* 16 is speaking about, which makes salvation possible, but does not automatically achieve it. When *LG* 16 speaks about conscience, it does not explicitly cite Romans 2:14-16 but it seems obviously to be basing its teaching on these texts, and as we have seen, Msgr. Philips, who was deeply engaged in the revisions of this text, affirms this to be certainly the case.

Byrne comments on verses 14-15:

> Paul need not have more than a few outstanding individuals in mind (so that what is stated here does not really counter the pessimistic judgment on the Gentile world as a whole formulated earlier on [1:19-32; cf. 3:9, 23]). Nor does he mean that these few "righteous Gentiles" carry out the

law in its entirety. The point is that their exceptional pattern of life over-throws any exaggerated claims made for the law as sole moral guide and criterion of judgment.... In the end, of course, on Paul's fuller explana-tion of the gospel (cf. 3:20-30), the eschatological justification can only rest on a "performance" that is entirely the achievement of God's grace (5:17-19; cf. 8:4). In that light, any justification envisaged could apply solely in the case of believers.[100]

Byrne goes on then to make the connection to the subsequent theo-logical discussion and doctrinal development that raises the possibility of implicit faith.

Paul's acknowledgement in this passage of at least the possibility that those beyond the law (the Gentiles) could live righteously and attain justification invites a reflection upon the contemporary situation where Christian believers constitute only a small proportion of the total popu-lation of the world. The sense of God's judgment in Christ reaching be-yond externals to grasp the moral capacity hidden in the depths of hu-man beings promotes a view of divine grace as something ranging well beyond the bounds of explicit Christian faith. However distant Paul's argument may seem from contemporary concerns, it at least gives a hint that God's work in Christ, as well as initiating a process and a movement of explicit belief, also offers a paradigm of salvation for those who do not explicitly believe.[101]

For our purposes, it is not necessary or possible to get into a discus-sion of the "apparent" faith/works tension in Paul's teaching in Romans (vv. 6-13) other than to say that many convincing attempts to harmonize these emphases exist that respect the clarity of the teaching of justification by faith and judgment by deeds.[102]

What is important to note clearly is that the eternal destiny of each and every human being is at stake in his or her response to the revelation that God makes of himself. The destinies of the human race diverge in two irreconcilable paths: one to eternal life,[103] and the other to "wrath and fury."

Käsemann describes this contrast strikingly:

Blessing and curse are prophetically proclaimed here on those who con-form or rebel in face of the law of the last day (v. 6).... In face of this criterion there is an eschatological division of mankind which relativizes the distinctions between Jew and Gentile in the same way that this happens in the proclamation of justification. This is a fresh indication that the message of judgment in Paul must be understood in the light of his doctrine of justification and is posited along with it. Where the gospel is preached there is spread abroad (2 Cor 2:16) both the fragrance of life to life and also that of death to death, and those who are called to salvation are separated from those who go to perdition (1 Cor 1:18; 2 Cor 2:15). . . . We have here a strict parallel to the transition from 1:16f. to 1:18. When salvation is revealed, perdition is also disclosed, and the uniqueness of our passage lies not in the thought of judgment as such but in the apocalyptic, universal dimension of its proclamation.[104]

Romans 3: All Have Sinned

Every verse, indeed almost every word of Romans, has been subject to close analysis and vigorous scholarly debate, and the limits of this chapter do not allow the exploration or even the acknowledgment of many of the issues raised by chapter 3. However, we do need to take note of the conclusion to the argument that Paul has been moving towards beginning with the Romans 1:18-32 segment to which we have paid most attention in order to have in mind the "big picture," at least in this part of the epistle.

In chapter 3 Paul strongly states his conclusions that flow from his analysis and argumentation in chapters 1 and 2. We will only consider here verse 9 to the end of the chapter.

At this point we simply want to note Paul's conclusion without exploring the numerous issues that are also raised in this chapter: Everyone falls short of the glory of God. Everyone is under the power of sin. No one can justify himself by his works or by keeping the law by his own efforts. If he attempts to do so, he will soon discover the depth of his sin and incapacity. Salvation from the "wrath to come" or the "present wrath" is possible only through the gift of God's grace and mercy, given in Jesus, and accessible to all through faith.

The issue is sometimes raised that perhaps what Paul is saying is not universally applicable to the whole human race, but perhaps just to the cultural situation of his own time. Of course there is no indication in the text that Paul is limiting his statements in their applicability, but rather, just the opposite. In addition, can anyone deny that the cultural situation

Paul is describing is increasingly identical with many of the post-Christian Western cultures? As Cardinal Ratzinger put it, shortly before he was elected Pope:

> Can we really say that his affirmations possess a value that goes beyond this specific historical constellation? Certainly we would need to modify the details. Nevertheless, Paul's words are essentially painting the picture, not of some particular historical situation, but of the permanent situation of humanity, of man, vis-à-vis God.[105]

And again, speaking of the applicability of Paul's analysis in Romans 1 of the pervasive suppression of the truth and rejection of God, to our current situation, Ratzinger concludes:

> Does this apply today in a completely nonreligious culture, in the culture of rationality and its technological application? I think it does.[106]

Most commentators would understand that when Paul claims that "everyone" falls short, he is speaking generally. While he does not really tackle this question in a specific enough manner to settle the question, most commentators believe Paul would not find it unthinkable that the sincere Gentile, through some response in faith to the revelation of God in creation or in conscience, or in the case of the Jew, to the positive revelation to which he is heir, under the influence of grace, could be justified. But if someone wishes to argue this (as *LG* 16 does), they would also have to admit that Paul clearly believes that this is not often the case. *LG* 16c explicitly acknowledges this to some degree.

Cranfield identifies verses 21-26 of this chapter as the center and heart of the entire epistle and has this to say about its meaning:

> It proclaims the fact that the one decisive, once for all, redemptive act of God, the revelation both of the righteousness which is from God and also of the wrath of God against human sin, the once for all revelation which is the basis of the continuing revelation of the righteousness (1:17) and of the wrath (1:18) in the preaching of the gospel, has now taken place. It shows that the heart of the gospel preached by Paul is a series of events in the past (not just the crucifixion of Christ — for the Cross by itself would have been no saving act of God — but the crucifixion together with the resurrection and exaltation of the Cru-

cified) a series of events which is *the* Event of history, an act which as the decisive act of God is altogether effective and irreversible. It attests to the fact that what we have to do with in the gift of righteousness, with which Romans is concerned, is nothing less than God's costly forgiveness, which, whereas forgiveness on cheaper terms would have meant God's abandonment of His faithful love for man and the annihilation of man's real dignity as His morally accountable creature, is altogether worthy of the righteous, loving, faithful God, who does not insult or mock His creature man by pretending that his sin does not matter, but rather Himself bears the full cost of forgiving it righteously — lovingly.[107]

Mark 16:14-16

After *LG* 16 cites the verses from Romans 1 that we have most closely examined, as well as its implicit citation of Romans 2, it then quotes Mark 16:15 and cites Mark 16:16 as the texts that embody the right response to what Paul states in Romans 1 and 2. As we have done with the verses cited from Romans, we will take a look at the immediate context of the citation from Mark. We will not at this time comment at length or give an account of the major commentaries[108] but simply conclude our considerations with the conclusion at which *LG* 16 arrives, an affirmation of the need to preach the gospel.

> Afterward he appeared to the eleven themselves as they sat at table; and he upbraided them for their unbelief and hardness of heart, because they had not believed those who saw him after he had risen. And he said to them, "Go into all the world and preach the gospel to the whole creation. He who believes and is baptized will be saved; but he who does not believe will be condemned. And these signs will accompany those who believe: in my name they will cast out demons; they will speak in new tongues; they will pick up serpents, and if they drink any deadly thing, it will not hurt them; they will lay their hands on the sick, and they will recover." So then the Lord Jesus, after he had spoken to them, was taken up into heaven, and sat down at the right hand of God. And they went forth and preached everywhere, while the Lord worked with them and confirmed the message by the signs that attended it. Amen. (Mark 16:14-20)

Jesus has to call his disciples out of their "unbelief and hardness of heart" since "they had not believed those who saw him after he had risen" (v. 14). Once awakened by the voice of the Lord and called to belief, the disciples are then given their mission — to become witnesses themselves and extend the message of the risen Christ to the whole world (v. 15).

We have seen from our study of Romans that the natural condition of the human heart after the Fall is self-seeking, rebellious, and prone to deception, idolatry, and immorality. For the vast number of people who are in this situation, it is sobering to realize, as Fitzmyer puts it, that only the "apocalyptic light of the gospel can penetrate such darkness."[109]

This is precisely what *LG* 16 proposes. Since "very often" human beings do not respond to the communication that God gives through creation and conscience, it is imperative that "all these" (those who reject the light of creation and conscience) be given a chance to hear the gospel, preached with the assistance of the Lord (vv. 17-20) in power. "He who believes and is baptized will be saved; but he who does not believe will be condemned" (v. 16).

There are many issues raised by these verses that cannot be dealt with in a chapter of this length. What constitutes an "adequate" preaching of the gospel, such that those who reject it are truly rejecting God?

Again, it is sobering to reflect that the greatest preaching of the gospel that ever took place, that of Jesus, was widely rejected. The Gospel of John tells us why.

> For God so loved the world that he gave his only Son, that whoever believes in him should not perish but have eternal life. For God sent the Son into the world, not to condemn the world, but that the world might be saved through him. He who believes in him is not condemned; he who does not believe is condemned already, because he has not believed in the name of the only Son of God. And this is the judgment, that the light has come into the world, and men loved darkness rather than light, because their deeds were evil. For every one who does evil hates the light, and does not come to the light, lest his deeds should be exposed. But he who does what is true comes to the light, that it may be clearly seen that his deeds have been wrought in God. (John 3:16-21)

The Scriptures indicate that it is tragically possible to love the darkness rather than the light and to prefer deeds of darkness and worlds of illusion to the momentary pain of conversion — reality therapy — and the long-term "glorious freedom" of the children of God.

Preliminary Conclusions and Some Additional Questions: Implications for the New Evangelization

1. Paul and the commentators on Paul that we have consulted strongly suggest that before we can appreciate the gift of salvation, we need to be aware of our condition apart from Christ. As Lyonnet describes it, this is the "methodology" of Paul, and we must consider what part this should play in our announcing of the gospel.

> It is not therefore surprising that before describing the revelation of the saving justice of God (Rom. 2:21ff.), Paul makes us aware of another revelation, that of the wrath or anger of God.
>
> It is necessary to add that in the dialectical methodology of the apostle the revelation of the wrath of God plays an essential role: in order to be able to receive justification as a *purely gratuitous gift of God,* it is necessary that a man be deeply aware of his sin (Rom. 3:19-21).[110]

2. *LG* 16 states that "very often" people who are not Christian (and the same can be applied to many who are Catholic in name only) are not sincerely seeking God and living according to the light of their consciences. The Council, citing Romans 1:21, 25, declares that many have been deceived by the evil one and rejected the truth for a lie and are in effect idolaters. This statement of the Council and the underlying texts from Romans that support it fly in the face of a mentality that presumes that almost everybody is a "good person" and of course will go to heaven, and that God could not really be a good God and let people go to hell. This naïvely optimistic position unfortunately is evidence of the "futile thinking" that is a result of the darkened mind that comes from rejecting the light of God.

The "very often" statement of the Council is extremely well supported by the texts of Romans that it cites, and these are not isolated texts. The whole message of the NT is that one does not enter the Kingdom by drifting along with the prevailing culture, the "broad way" of Matthew 7:13-14.[111]

> Enter by the narrow gate; for the gate is wide and the way is easy, that leads to destruction, and those who enter by it are many. For the gate is narrow and the way is hard, that leads to life, and those who find it are few. (Matt. 7:13-14)

These verses aptly describe the picture one gets from pondering Paul's powerful assertions concerning the situation of the human race apart from Christ that we have just examined.

One of the biggest obstacles to evangelization is the belief that all will be saved in their own way. The truth is, of course, that God has appointed one way to be saved: faith in the gratuitous gift of salvation offered to us in the person of his Son. And indeed, this one way to salvation, under certain conditions, can be found, even apart from explicit faith in Jesus. The clarity that Romans gives us, not only about the reality of sin and the wrath of God and the darkness and rebelliousness of the human heart, but also about the pervasiveness of this participation in darkness, is essential knowledge in the shaping of our message and is an important motivation for the urgency of the mission.

3. Romans shows us that something is really at stake: eternal salvation or damnation. The gospel is a chance to "escape the wrath to come." Judgment continually happens in history, but the "day of wrath," the "day of the Lord," will definitively pass sentence on the entire human race, and there will be a permanent separation between those who believed and obeyed and those who did not. Indeed, one of the most insistent messages of both Testaments is that there are two ways set before the human race: one way leads to life, the other way leads to death. This is not just a theoretical possibility or an empty warning. The witness of the entire Bible — and indeed of all of human history — is to the actual historical realization of choice for and against God.

4. There are those who choose the way that leads to life and others who choose the way that leads to death, those who choose the blessing and those who choose the curse (Deut. 30:15-20). We see the difference between the wise and the foolish (Sir. 21:11-28), between those who serve God and those who refuse to serve him, between those who fear the Lord and trust in him and those who wickedly defy him and trust in themselves (Mal. 3:16-21), between those who believe and those who refuse to believe, between those who truly know the Father and those who do not, between those who grieve and quench the Spirit and those who do not, between those who worship the one God in Spirit and truth and those who have exchanged the truth of God for a lie and worship the creature, between the city of God and the city of man, between those who love the brethren and those who do not, between the good and the wicked. There are those who are "vessels of mercy" and those who are "vessels of wrath" (Rom. 9:22-23), those for whom Christ is the "cornerstone chosen and precious" and those

for whom he is a stumbling stone and scandal (1 Pet. 2:6-8). There are those who eagerly await the return of the Lord and cry out "Come Lord Jesus!" (Rev. 22:20) and there are those who cry out to the mountains "Fall on us and hide us from the face of him who is seated on the throne, and from the wrath of the lamb, for the great day of their wrath has come, and who can stand before it?" (Rev. 6:16-17). This separation was signaled on the hill of Calvary when one thief humbly turned to Christ with faith, hope, and love, and the other thief bitterly mocked and blasphemed him (Luke 23:32-43).[112] This separation, which exists even now, is finalized and the eternal reward and punishment appropriate to each individual is carried out definitively on the great Day of Judgment.

Jesus reveals many things but occasionally he emphasizes, with solemnity, that what he is about to say is of special importance:

> Truly, truly, I say to you, the hour is coming, and now is, when the dead will hear the voice of the Son of God, and those who hear will live. For as the Father has life in himself, so he has granted the Son also to have life in himself, and has given him authority to execute judgment, because he is the Son of man. Do not marvel at this; for the hour is coming when all who are in the tombs will hear his voice and come forth, those who have done good, to the resurrection of life, and those who have done evil, to the resurrection of judgment. (John 5:25-29)

As we have seen so far in our study of *LG* 16, we know it is possible that those who have never heard of him can be saved. We have also seen, though, that this is a possibility fraught with danger and uncertainty and that "very often" those for whom salvation is possible do not avail themselves of the possibility. What we know for certain, on the authority of Christ and his Spirit, is that "everyone who calls upon the name of the Lord will be saved" (Rom. 10:13), and for those who are in Christ Jesus "there is no condemnation" (Rom. 8:1). It matters whether the gospel is preached or not. It matters if people believe and are baptized or not.

CHAPTER V

Rahner and "Anonymous Christians"

The balanced interpretation of Scripture and incorporation of the history of the development of doctrine which is represented in *LG* 16, as well as its status as the most recent authoritative magisterial pronouncement on the subject, makes it an invaluable tool in assessing the strengths and weaknesses of contemporary theories concerning salvation, in particular as they pertain to evangelization.

There are two contemporary theories that have been very influential in shaping the thinking of many Catholics, both on a popular and an academic level, on the question of salvation apart from explicit faith in Christ and membership in the Church. One is Karl Rahner's elaboration of a theory concerning "anonymous Christians." The other is Hans Urs von Balthasar's speculation concerning the possibility that everyone might be saved and our duty to hope for such. In order to demonstrate the usefulness of a proper understanding of *LG* 16 and the Scripture and doctrine that undergird it, the next two chapters will be devoted to an explication and evaluation of these theories, in the light of *LG* 16.

We will begin with Rahner, as his name has come up a number of times already in this book. His interpretation of the theological "optimism" of Vatican II has been widely influential, both in the academy and among educated Catholics in general. Even if they have never read a word of his theology, it is a rare person who has not at least heard of the "anonymous Christian" with some general idea of what it means.

In addition, Rahner continues to be a major referent point for contemporary theology as it confronts the question of the salvific import of the world religions.[1]

The Supernatural Existential

Within Rahner's theological system, his theory of "anonymous Christianity" is based on his theological anthropology. In reflecting on "nature and grace," Rahner posits a "supernatural existential" by which he means to suggest that the supernatural is present and active in "nature" and most especially human nature, apart from explicit faith or incorporation into Christ.[2] Rahner defines it as such:

> This self-communication by God offered to all and fulfilled in the highest way in Christ rather constitutes the goal of all creation and — since God's word and will *effect* what they say — even before he freely takes up an attitude to it, it stamps and determines man's nature and lends it a character which we may call a "supernatural existential."[3]

Or, as one of his commentators put it:

> Using his idea of a non-objectified, pre-categorical revelation freely offered by God to the subjectivity of all human persons as an a priori horizon of their knowing and loving, Rahner developed the supernatural existential.[4]

Rahner claims that human nature never exists without this "supernatural existential." From the moment of conception it is always present. Rahner acknowledges that in the abstract there is a distinct human nature, apart from the supernatural existential — what he calls a "remainder concept" — but in fact, it never actually exists without the supernatural existential. He wants to safeguard Catholic doctrine which, based on Scripture, teaches that salvation and ultimately, the beatific vision, is not owed to human nature but is a pure gift of grace.[5]

Rahner posits that human nature in the abstract contains within itself a natural spiritual openness, a natural, transcendent dynamic ordered to the horizon or ground of all being. But, from the moment of conception God calls this being to a higher destiny, to a supernaturally elevated participation in the being of God. Because of this call of God, a new orientation is immediately part of the human person, a "supernatural existential" which is now transcendently ordered to eternal life with the Trinity.[6]

As Patrick Burke expresses it:

Because in the concrete order all men in fact have been called by God to a supernatural destiny (and man in "pure nature" does not exist, nor ever has existed), they always and originally exist under the influence of this supernatural elevation. This is precisely what Rahner means by human nature's "supernatural existential." It orients man to the reception of "strictly supernatural grace," so man experiences it not as a datum of knowledge or as an abstract and merely consequent summing up of what is common to many individual objects, but as the a priori horizon, given in consciousness, under which everything is grasped as an object.[7]

Rahner is clear that this "supernatural existential," while a form of grace — perhaps best called prevenient grace — does not in itself bring about justification.[8] The individual's response to this supernatural existential is critical.

Burke detects three levels of "grace" in Rahner's thought.

First, man is created as a dynamic natural openness to all being. As such, he is dynamically open to the supernatural and finds in God, and ultimately in Christ, his absolute fulfillment. However, this fulfillment is not owed to him, and he apparently can find fulfillment in a lesser natural good. This is the "grace of creation." Second, man is endowed originally and always with a "supernatural existential" that elevates his natural dynamic transcendence, unconditionally orienting him toward God. This is not a "grace of creation," but neither is it apparently "strictly supernatural grace." Finally, man is offered "strictly supernatural grace," traditionally called "uncreated grace," which is the indwelling of the Holy Spirit, the self-communication of God himself.[9]

This obviously has implications for the development of Rahner's theory of the anonymous Christian.[10] As Burke puts it:

It follows then, that even outside the process of official revelation, the history of human religion is a product not merely of natural reason and sin, but also and more profoundly of the natural spirit and grace. Thus, when an individual is summoned by the message of faith from the visible Church, it is not the first time that he comes into spiritual contact with the reality preached by the church: such conceptual knowledge is not primary.[11]

The Conditions under Which the
Salvation of Non-Christians May Be Possible

Rahner makes explicit in a number of different essays written over a period of years the implications of this "supernatural existential" for the question of the salvation of those who have never effectively heard the gospel, namely, his theory of the "anonymous Christian."[12]

> The supernatural grace of faith and justification offered by God to men does not need to be conceived of as an isolated intervention on God's part at a particular point in a world which is itself profane. On the contrary, it can perfectly well be interpreted on the basis of God's universal will to save as a grace which, as offered, is a constantly present existential of the creature endowed with spiritual faculties and of the world in general, which orientates these to the immediacy of God as their final end, though of course in saying this the question still remains wholly open of whether an individual freely gives himself to, or alternately rejects, this existential which constitutes the innermost dynamism of his being and its history, an existential which is and remains continually present. . . . It does this effectively at all times and in all places in the form of the offering and the enabling power of acting in a way that leads to salvation. And even though it is unmerited and "supernatural" in character, it constitutes the innermost *entelecheia* and dynamism of the world considered as the historical dimension of the creature endowed with spiritual faculties.[13]

Even though this "supernatural existential" is embedded in human nature *qua* human nature, apart from any explicit knowledge of or response to God, Rahner does elaborate in several places what kind of response to the "innermost dynamism" is needed for salvation to be effected.

> The man of today is first and foremost a man who feels himself at one (at that point at which he truly achieves the fulness of self-realization) with mankind as a whole . . . if he wills to recognize and as a Christian must recognize a *single* meaning and a *single* dynamism running through the whole history of mankind, then he must simply have a single answer as to how and in what way he can recognize in every one of his fellows a brother in the sense in which Christianity recognizes every individual as a brother, a sense, that is, which is not merely humanist

but truly Christian. There must be a Christian theory to account for the fact that every individual who does not in any absolute or ultimate sense act against his own conscience can say and does say in faith, hope, and love, Abba within his own spirit, and is on these grounds in all truth a brother to Christians in God's sight. This is what the theory of the anonymous Christian seeks to say, and, in so far as it is valid, what it implies.[14]

The first condition, therefore, that Rahner stipulates for someone being an "anonymous Christian"[15] is first of all that he does not act against his conscience in "any absolute or ultimate sense."

He then postulates that whenever someone makes a moral decision in his life it can be an act that actually contains within it supernatural faith, and thus, salvation. Rahner states that this can be the case even when, to all appearances, there is actual estrangement from God.

We can say quite simply that wherever, and in so far as, the individual makes a moral decision in his life . . . this moral decision can also be thought to measure up to the character of a supernaturally elevated, believing and thus saving act, and hence to be more in actual fact than merely "natural morality." Hence, if one believes seriously in the universal salvific purpose of God towards all men in Christ, it need not and cannot really be doubted that gratuitous influences of properly Christian supernatural grace are conceivable in the life of all men . . . and that these influences can be presumed to be accepted in spite of the sinful state of men and in spite of their apparent estrangement from God.[16]

This position, of course, has some resonance with the teaching of St. Thomas on the "first moral act" of the individual,[17] which we have considered in an earlier chapter.

This raises some important questions that Rahner does not address here. We know that there can be a merely "metaphysical" belief in God that is neither supernatural nor salvific. Can there be a merely "natural" moral decision that is not a "supernaturally elevated, believing, and thus saving act"? Most important, what is the basis for presuming that grace offered is therefore accepted?

Another way in which Rahner expresses what is required for this response to the "supernatural existential" to be salvific is for someone to "accept himself completely."

But he also already accepts this revelation whenever he really accepts *himself completely,* for it already speaks *in* him. Prior to the explicitness of official ecclesiastical faith this acceptance can be present in an implicit form whereby a person undertakes and lives the duty of each day in the quiet sincerity of patience, in devotion to his material duties and the demands made upon him by the persons under his care. . . . In the acceptance of himself man is accepting Christ.[18]

This acceptance of oneself seems to involve a life of daily fidelity, responsibility, virtue, and loving service. Because of the "supernatural existential," to accept oneself is also to accept one's orientation to saving union with God. Conversely, a decision not to accept this orientation to the supernatural is to deny one's own self. As Conway puts it:

A decision against God's self-communication involves the human being not only in a contradiction with God but also with his deepest self, for once the supernatural existential is present, the human being is no longer in a state of "pure unimpaired nature." Therefore those who decide against God's self-communication find themselves in contradiction not only with God but also with themselves.[19]

Rahner also postulates that even though someone may be an avowed atheist — perhaps because of misconceptions about Christianity — as long as he does not deny God "in his heart" he may be an anonymous Christian.

It is true that it would be wrong to go so far as to declare every man, whether he accepts the grace or not, an "anonymous Christian." Anyone who in his basic decision were really to deny and to reject his being ordered to God, who were to place himself decisively in opposition to his own concrete being, should not be designated a "theist," even an anonymous "theist"; only someone who gives — even if it be ever so confusedly — the glory to *God* should be thus designated. Therefore no matter what a man states in his conceptual, theoretical and religious reflection, anyone who does not say in his *heart,* "there is no God" (like the "fool" in the psalm) but testifies to him by the radical acceptance of his being, is a believer . . . (and) can be called with every right an "anonymous Christian."[20]

One of Rahner's main concerns in developing his theory of the "anonymous Christian" was to find a way to think about the growing atheism in the Christian heartland of Europe that did not lead to despair. In his theory he is seeking to make a distinction between someone who claims to be an atheist but "in his heart" has not rejected his fundamental orientation to God, and the notional or "categorical" believer — one who says he is a Christian — but has turned away from his fundamental orientation to God "in his heart" — and is in fact, an atheist. The traditional view of atheism in Catholic theology was that a persistently, long-held explicit atheism must be culpable. Rahner points to the various texts in the documents of Vatican II on atheism and claims that this is, in fact, an open question.[21]

> Fifty years ago when I was studying theology, we young theologians were taught as certain doctrine that in the long run positive atheism could not exist in a person without grave personal guilt . . . for this doctrine, the existence of God was so clear and so easy to demonstrate from reason, and the concept *God* in the statement "God exists" so obvious that, given normal intelligence and sufficient length of time, only a scoundrel could fail to be convinced of the existence of God. . . . During the Council nobody ever mentioned this traditional doctrine, not even the most conservative bishops and theologians; nor was it mentioned in the context of the conciliar debates and deliberations, where one would have expected it to come up. No serious discussions arose when the Council [considered *LG* 16 and *GS* 22]. . . . For a Church that is resolved at all costs to be faithful to both divine revelation and tradition, such statements in the history of her awareness of the faith are milestones to which she will not return.[22]

He correctly points out that the texts of Vatican II do not repeat the long-held theological opinion that persistently held atheism must eventually become culpable. To the objection, by some of his critics, that the teaching of *LG* 16 should be understood only in the sense that atheists can possibly be saved only by coming to explicit faith, Rahner replies, correctly I believe, that the statement of *LG* 16 would not make sense if all it meant is that the atheist can be saved if he comes to faith, namely, when "he ceases to be one."[23] On the other hand it must be noted that *LG* 16 does not explicitly mention atheists, although the inclusion of certain "atheists of good will" can be supported by the teaching of *GS* on the various types of atheisms (*GS* 19-23).

Rahner's Assessment of the Probability
of the Salvation of Non-Christians

Rahner not only establishes the possibility of non-Christians being saved apart from explicit faith in Christ and membership in the Church, and outlines the conditions that must obtain for this to happen, he also assesses the probability of this happening.

Since he wishes to posit not only the possibility but, as we shall see, the probability of most non-Christians being saved apart from explicit knowledge of Christ, even those living in the state of objective mortal sin, he makes much of the distinction between objectively grave sin and subjective guilt.[24]

> We must consider the immeasurable difference — which it seems right to suppose to exist even in the Christian sphere — between what is objectively wrong in moral life and the extent to which this is really realized with subjectively grave guilt. Once we take all this into consideration, we will not hold it to be impossible that grace is at work, and is even being accepted, in the spiritual, personal life of the individual, no matter how primitive, unenlightened, apathetic and earth-bound such a life may at first sight appear to be.[25]

Rahner goes considerably beyond Vatican II in postulating that not only individuals within the non-Christian religions, but the religions *qua* religions, mediate salvific grace. Even when all appearances are to the contrary, Rahner postulates they nevertheless may be mediating saving grace.

> Catholic moral theology, however, admits that an objectivity objectively [sic] and as such opposed to God's will can nevertheless mediate a positive moral act; it must consequently be recognized that such objectivities may in principle be ways of mediating positive religious acts, even though objectively and implicitly they are in a certain sense opposed to God. It is, for example, quite possible for a polytheist to act positively in regard to the true, absolute God, for whom in his objective, verbalized consciousness he finds a name from his polytheistic pantheon. In their institutions and theoretical objectifications non-Christian religions can be categorical mediations of genuine salvific acts, both because they always retain some truth (at least the postulate of a transcendentality of man beyond the field of his immediate experience) and also because

even false and debased religious objectivity can be a way of mediating a genuine and grace-given transcendentality of man.[26]

But despite what Rahner posits being a theoretical possibility it is also necessary to add, as Cardinal Ratzinger did in his book, a "no."

The theology of our own day, as we said, has particularly brought to light the positive aspect [of non-Christian world religions] . . . but it is equally aware of a decided No to other religions and sees in them a means by which man seeks to shield himself from God instead of leaving himself open to his demands. . . . The man of today will for the most part scarcely respond with an abrupt No to a particular religion's claim to be true; he will simply relativize that claim by saying "There are many religions." And behind his response will probably be the opinion, in some form or other, that beneath varying forms they are in essence all the same; each person has his own way.[27]

Rahner rejects, without detailed argumentation, a position held by some in the Catholic tradition, that, because of original sin, or because of "subjectively grave offenses against the natural law," God might withhold the possibility of salvation from some of those who have not heard the gospel.

It is senseless to suppose cruelly — and without any hope of acceptance by the man of today, in view of the enormous extent of the extra-Christian history of salvation and damnation — that nearly all men living outside the official and public Christianity are so evil and stubborn that the offer of supernatural grace ought not even to be made in fact in most cases, since these individuals have already rendered themselves unworthy of such an offer by previous, subjectively grave offences against the natural moral law.[28]

Rahner starts from the widely taught and well-founded view that salvation is offered to everyone, and goes on to presume, problematically, almost universal acceptance. This is a very important text, and we need to look at it closely.

If one gives more exact theological thought to this matter, then one cannot regard nature and grace as two phases in the life of the individual that follow each other in time. It is furthermore impossible to think that this offer of supernatural, divinizing grace made to all men on account of the universal salvific purpose of God, should in general (prescinding from the relatively few exceptions) remain ineffective in most cases on account of the personal guilt of the individual. For, as far as the gospel is concerned, we have no really conclusive reason for thinking so pessimistically of men. On the other hand, and contrary to every merely human experience, we do have every reason for thinking optimistically of God and his salvific will which is more powerful than the extremely limited stupidity and evil-mindedness of men. . . . Christ and his salvation are not simply one of two possibilities offering themselves to man's free choice; they are the deed of God that bursts open and redeems the false choice of man by overtaking it. In Christ God not only gives the *possibility* of salvation, which in that case would still have to be effected by man himself, but the actual salvation itself, however much this includes also the right decision of human freedom which is itself a gift from God. Where sin already existed, grace came in superabundance. And hence we have every right to suppose that grace has not only been offered even outside the Christian Church (to deny this would be the error of Jansenism) but also that, in a great many cases at least, grace gains the victory in man's free acceptance of it, this being again the result of grace. Of course, we would have to show more explicitly than the shortness of time permits that the empirical picture of human beings, their life, their religion and their individual and universal history does not disprove this optimism of a faith which knows the whole world to be subjected to the salvation won by Christ.[29]

While it is certainly true that God offers sufficient grace for salvation to every human being, and that where sin abounds, grace abounds even more, it is not "impossible to think" some of the things that Rahner claims to be unthinkable. The whole testimony of Scripture and the theological tradition of the Church do not make it impossible to think that only "in a relatively few exceptions" will the offer of salvation be rejected. On the contrary the scriptural witness to the "many and the few," to the "called and the chosen," indicates something quite different. Nor is it impossible to think that the unrepented, personal guilt of an individual could be an obstacle to salvation. As we have shown, Scripture and the Church teach just the opposite. The lists of personal sins that will definitely exclude people from the Kingdom are rather clearly stated. Contrary to Rahner, the "extremely limited stupidity and evil-mindedness of men" seem quite sufficient to refuse definitively the offer of salvation. Apart from the scriptural and magisterial witness to the contrary, even from an empirical point of view it is difficult to understand Rahner's optimistic view of human beings' response to what he postulates as the supernatural existential. He acknowledges that his optimistic theory of the "positive response rate" of human beings needs to be tested against empirical observation of actual human beings and what we can observe of their response. The puzzling empirical fact is that he spent virtually his whole priesthood (1932-1984) first under Nazi rule and then, after World War II, with half of Germany under Soviet communism. He published his first major works in 1939 and 1941. He spent the whole of World War II in Nazi Germany and Nazi-occupied Austria, free to lecture although not at a university. From 1939 to 1944 he lectured in Leipzig, Dresden, Strasbourg, and Cologne, laying the theological groundwork for his theories.[30] Consider the slaughter of so many tens of millions — including the firebombing of Dresden; the horrifying reality of the campaign to exterminate the Jews and the millions of concentration camp deaths — including those of many Polish Catholics; the fiendish medical experimentation. Did this not give pause to his theory that almost everybody says "yes" to the offer of salvation contained in the "supernatural existential" apart from any hearing of the gospel? Is it at all credible to posit that the grace of God has "overtaken" the "false choices" of men in these and many other empirically observable situations?

Even when Rahner admits that perhaps the empirical situation of the human race does not appear to verify his theory, he nevertheless clings to it, with something very much like a Balthasarian "hope."[31]

> We do not know, but today we are permitted to hope that, in spite of all ideological differences and in spite of so much horror in the profane history of the world, many, perhaps even all human beings, belong to those in whom the free, gratuitous and overflowing grace of God is victorious. This is a conviction that one can and, indeed, must have. . . . I fear eternal damnation in particular cases and yet I hope for the possibility of a final apokatastasis panton (salvation of all), in spite of the fact that this hope is constantly being undermined by our empirical experience.[32]

Again, in a manner similar to that of Balthasar, he dismisses those who hold a different evaluation of the biblical and empirical evidence, in a startling *ad hominem* insult:

With all respect to Saint Augustine, he must be asked: "How can you believe in the victory of the cross of the eternal Son of God and at the same time see no problem in the fact that apparently enormous numbers of people are damned? Does this not testify to an indescribable coldness in your heart?"[33]

What would one then have to say about Jesus' heart, whose teachings on the "many" and the "few" are a basis for Augustine's thought?

Even those very sympathetic to Rahner's speculative theology note that the condition of the human race is not as rosy as speculative theology sometimes asserts. Robert Sears, in a sympathetic account of Rahner's theories, notes that even secular scholarship has lifted the curtain on the fallen condition of humanity, and makes the likelihood of "self-transcending love" being the default position of the human race extremely unlikely.[34] He points out the need to verify "optimistic" evaluations of what is happening in the hearts of human beings and brings forward some evidence that gives pause to such optimism.

> Experience shows that the initial experience of love is no firm criterion; for the dark side very soon appears with its jealousies, angers, and destructive drives. . . . In the deeper regions of the human person, even our most "altruistic" intentions often prove to be efforts to see ourselves as valuable, and the fidelity of our commitment is shaken by lack of response in the other. A depth analyst such as Freud concluded toward the end of his life that some blocks to that freedom which is the basis of any true love are all but insurmountable, and that the drive to self-destruction is all but irresistible.[35]

Sears also provides testimony that not only is individual "self-transcending love" uncommon, but the effort to embody it in social, political, and economic structures is even more challenging. He cites John Bennett in this regard.

> Enthusiasm for a cause is not enough. There is a phase in a particular struggle when the cause may simplify one's life, make decisions clear, enable one to know with whom to stand. But complexities finally overtake such simplifications. One discovers there are no total solutions, that even successes create new and unanticipated problems, which actual alternatives call for new and troublesome decisions. Those who

have been most political and activistic often find the people with whom they have worked split away over strategies and develop a shocking hostility towards one another.[36]

Sears also notes that Reinhold Niebuhr came to a similar conclusion.

> He concludes that the moral obtuseness and self-interest of human collectives make a morality of pure disinterestedness impossible, so that any overly optimistic expectation of it must come to terms with a history that evidences the contrary.[37]

Sears refers us to the experience of Fr. Leo Mahon in Panama as an illustration of his point.

> When he went there in 1963, he organized a group of 500 men, using methods learned under Saul Alinsky in Chicago. This group disintegrated almost immediately. He realized that what was needed was a "new man" and began to evangelize the people and to seek conversion of life.[38]

Richard Schenk comments that Rahner's fascination with his speculative theories led him to lose touch with the common experience that, ironically, he claims to be theorizing about.

> The price of favoring the dynamic towards perfection so absolutely over its counter-dynamic is shown not only in the new implausibility of reprobation, but in the loss of touch with common experience, one of the central bases claimed by Rahner's theology. Understandably, optimism is not the dominant experience of our times.[39]

Rahner acknowledged that his theory must be tested against considerable scriptural testimony to the contrary, and the actual empirical situation of human beings — severe tests indeed. His ultimate appeal, though, as backing for his theory, is the teaching of Vatican II.

Assessing the Basis of Rahner's Theory

Rahner is clearly aware of the tradition of the development of doctrine concerning the possibility of salvation for those who do not hear the gospel or come to explicit faith in Christ and membership in the Church. In the essays, where he expounds his theory of the "anonymous Christian," he does not spend a lot of time recapitulating the tradition. He gives short summaries in several of the essays that seem to trace accurately enough the history of the development of doctrine on this issue, but does not claim to find the theory of the "anonymous Christian" as he presents it, in the tradition before Vatican II.[40]

After tracing the history of the development, he declares that the "final stage is the teaching of the Second Vatican Council."[41] He singles out the text of *LG* 16 as of special importance and claims it as validation for his theory of the "anonymous Christian": "What is meant by this thesis of the anonymous Christian is actually also taught materially in the Constitution on the Church of Vatican II (no. 16)."[42] Since this is his most extended treatment of *LG* 16, we shall quote his comments at length.

> According to this document those who have not yet received the gospel and this *without any fault* of their own (and this possibility is clearly presupposed as a real one) are given the possibility of eternal salvation (*"aeterna salus,"* which can only be understood of supernatural salvation). The only condition is, from the point of view of *God,* *"gratiae influxus"* (or *"divina gratia"* as it is also called), and from the point of view of *man,* *"Deum sincero corde quaerere eiusque voluntatem per conscientiae dictamen agnitam operibus adimplere."* This fulfillment of the duty of conscience is explicitly supposed as possible also in the case of those *"qui sine culpa ad expressam agnitionem Dei nondum pervenerunt."* That an inculpable atheism of this kind can last a long time whether individually or collectively is not stated, but not excluded either. Since this atheism is seen only in opposition to *"expressa agnitio Dei,"* there is a clear indication that beneath such an atheism there may very well lie an unreflected, merely existentially actualized theism (precisely by a radical obedience to the dictates of conscience). . . . In its statements the Constitution on the Church is in no way implying, that here in these cases salvation is achieved as it were in a substitute fashion by means of a purely natural morality. This would indeed contradict Scripture and the magisterium (DS 3867 sqq.) . . . although in the face of this theological optimism of the Council regarding salvation it remains the task of theology to show why the necessity of the gospel, of the Church and the sacraments are not thereby devalued, it is quite impossible to doubt that what is *meant* by the "anonymous Christian" (the

name itself is unimportant) is compatible with the Council's teaching, indeed is explicitly stated by it.[43]

I think it is clear that part of *LG* 16's teaching is compatible with Rahner's speculation about how such salvation might be possible, although not everyone would agree with his interpretation that the text in question is referring to atheists. The difficulty is that neither here nor anywhere else in his writings does he advert to the entire teaching of the Council on this point as contained in *LG* 16. Surprisingly, he cites in various essays only the first, *LG* 16a, or, more frequently, the middle part of the text, *LG* 16b, and omits the crucial third part, *LG* 16c, which, citing Romans 1:21, 25, declares that the conditions under which it is possible for non-Christians who have never heard the gospel to be saved are "very often" *(at saepius)* not met, and therefore it is important for the Church to carry out her mission of preaching the gospel to "all these," that is, those who are not meeting the conditions for salvation enunciated in *LG* 16b.

Rahner's completely optimistic description of the conciliar teaching on the salvation of non-Christians is only possible when the complete text is ignored (along with the New Testament texts and empirical evidence that he admits are relevant but doesn't himself confront), and yet he persists in claiming a one-sided optimism as the teaching of the Council. Ratzinger calls it an "astonishing optimism."[44]

Rahner speaks of "this theological optimism of the Council regarding salvation,"[45] and declares that "this optimism concerning salvation appears to me one of the most noteworthy results of the Second Vatican Council."[46] And, in speaking of *LG* 16, *AG* 7, and *GS* 22, he notes that "the authentic content of salvation, acknowledged in a spirit of vast optimism must be found in the [non-Christian] religions themselves."[47] He also comments that "this optimism with regard to salvation remains one of the most astonishing phenomena in the development of the Church's conscious awareness of her faith in this development as it applies to the secular and non-Christian world, the awareness of the difference between saving history as a whole and the history of explicit Christianity and of the Church."[48] He again rejects Augustine's teaching, assuming "what may be called this radically optimistic view (contrary to an Augustinian conception of history)."[49]

Eamonn Conway, one of Rahner's most careful interpreters, sums up Rahner's teaching on this issue. "Though the Christian must refrain from judging others, he nonetheless must also have unlimited optimism for the salvation of all. Not to profess such optimism is to doubt the success of the Christ-event."[50]

In a fine doctoral dissertation that astutely evaluates Balthasar's severe criticism of Rahner's theory of the "anonymous Christian," Eamonn Conway assumes as a "given" the "optimistic" views of Vatican II on salvation.[51] Conway, despite several references to *LG* 16 as a foundation for Rahner's theory, never comments on or even alludes to the concluding three sentences of *LG* 16, the sentences that significantly qualify the "optimism" of the preceding sentences. In his much later essay, he again omits any reference to the limiting sentences of *LG* 16c when speaking of the optimism of Vatican II, and defending Rahner from the charge that his theories undermine the missionary work of the Church.

> It is not Rahner's idea in itself, but the way in which it was misinterpreted and misused that seemed to undermine mission. More fundamentally, however, it will be suggested that it was the re-discovery of the Church's own authentic teaching on salvation outside the Church that undermined a certain kind of missionary activity, activity which with hindsight we recognize as having been founded upon an unwarranted and theologically misguided pessimism regarding the possibility of salvation of non-Christians. Rahner's theology merely contributed, along with the work of others, to the re-emergence of the Church's hope regarding the salvation of all, as we find articulated in the documents of the Second Vatican Council. . . . The reality is that the theology of the Second Vatican Council demanded a whole re-think with regard to the basis for the Church's missionary activity. For fallen human nature, fear is often a more powerful motivation than love. By emphasizing the sincerity and efficacy of God's salvific will, Rahner helped to replace fear not with certainty, but with genuine Christian hope, hope that God's salvific will would not be eternally frustrated. At the same time Rahner, more than Balthasar, took care to avoid postulating a general *apocatastasis*.[52]

I believe that this "optimistic" interpretation is possible only when *LG* 16c — and its foundational references to the scriptural and doctrinal foundations of its teaching — is excluded from consideration. It is remarkable that many of the finest commentators on Rahner's theory, and on related issues, also completely ignore the final section of *LG* 16 and seem to assume almost as a "given," without critical examination, the alleged "optimistic teaching" of Vatican II.[53]

Those who read the text of *LG* 16 more closely, including *LG* 16c, must certainly qualify any use of the word *optimistic*.

In commenting on the possibility of there being "just" men and women before Christ, even among the pagans (men like Socrates, for example), Gustave Thils and others also remind us that not everyone was a Socrates or an Aristotle.[54]

Concerning the scriptural foundations of his theory, Rahner does not really establish in these essays what these foundations are but makes rather sweeping statements about what the "gospel" warrants us to assume, believe, etc. He acknowledges that his interpretation of this "salvation optimism" has to overcome "very great obstacles which are inherent in the New Testament statements concerning the necessity of salvation coming through the Gospel which is preached in its power."[55]

He does not address these New Testament statements.[56] Schenk points out that Rahner's theological anthropology, influenced by German idealism, led Rahner not to feel compelled to examine Scripture and tradition thoroughly.

> This system freed Rahner, in the issue under discussion here, from the need to examine individually the texts of Scripture and tradition which seemed to point towards final loss, of which he apodictically declares that they are all meant as mere threats, with an uncertainty not characteristic of their parallel promises.[57]

Pagé points out that it is a "ridiculous optimism" that ignores the vast scriptural testimony to the pervasive and deep reality of the profound resistance to God and hatred for him that is found in the work of the evil one and in the human heart given to sin.

> However, the Constitution does not veer towards a ridiculous optimism which would not be able to see the errors threatening those who do not enjoy the benefits of the full gospel revelation.[58]

Pagé goes on to list two pages of scriptural references that witness to the profound resistance to God's will found in the world, the hearts of men and the devil, and the overwhelming scriptural evidence that God's light and love are often rejected.[59] Such biblical themes undergird the "very often" *(at saepius)* phrase of *LG* 16c.

Philips acknowledges that we cannot write off the "tableau of pagan perversion" depicted by Paul in Romans 1 if we are engaging in realistic exegesis.

> The picture of pagan perversion, so somber as it is depicted by St. Paul, does not permit us to accuse the author of pessimism. A realistic exegesis requires us to take into account the alternation of light and darkness in the exposition of his doctrine.

Philips recognizes that in the most extreme case envisioned by *LG* 16 — the case of self-professed atheists — while God's grace is being offered even there and it is possible that some people in this situation are responding to it by their commitment to justice or solidarity or some other concept, it is unlikely that such a commitment can be sustained in an ongoing way without it being founded on the divine.

> It is possible, for men of integrity, that God remains hidden under the form of an absolute value or imperative, under the concept of Justice, of Solidarity, or under some other concept. One must not draw the wrong conclusions however. An unconditional human solidarity which does not recognize a divine foundation will not last a long time. To be fully a human being with our fellow human beings, means that a human being must go beyond himself.[60]

Assessing Pastoral Implications for Evangelization

It is clear that Rahner is actually motivated by pastoral concerns and is trying to preserve "hope" in those who are discouraged by the prospect of evangelizing in the cultural context Rahner was most sensitive to — the post-Christian European intellectual culture of his time. In a way not unlike that of the sixteenth-century Dominican and Jesuit theologians, who attempted to come to grips theologically with the shock of the discovery of vast peoples in the "new world" who had never heard the gospel, Rahner is attempting to come to grips theologically with the shock of the collapse of Christendom and the ascendency of an aggressive anti-Christian international secular culture in the Christian heartland, as well as the continued existence of vast numbers of people of "other religions" who show no signs of conversion to Christianity in significant numbers. He is explicit in stating this as a motivation for his work. Rahner writes movingly in one of his most personally empathetic essays about the suffering of Catholic family members who are seeing their relatives abandon the Church.

> The Christian of today lives in a Diaspora which penetrates deep into the circle of his relatives. . . . He lives in a family circle whose members although originally Catholic, not only are not zealously "practicing," but if the truth is to be told have become completely without faith, sometimes to the point of being actively hostile, of officially leaving the Church. . . . These are persons who are "related" to us, whom we love, to whom we are bound with a thousand ties of blood, of shared feelings, of life and destiny, of love. . . . How many questions are involved in this situation, how much anxiety and pain! Are there tears more bitter than those shed by a Christian mother, when her son renounces the faith of his fathers which is also hers? How does the heart of a mother not tremble when she asks herself whether it will be her belief or the unbelief of her surroundings which will triumph in the hearts of her children? How wounding can ridicule and mocking rejection be, when it comes from those whom we love.[61]

Yet he knows that this is not just a deeply personal issue for many but is really indicative of a major transition point in Church and world history.

> The West is no longer shut up in itself; it can no longer regard itself simply as the centre of the history of this world and as the centre of culture, with a religion which . . . could appear as the obvious and indeed sole way of honoring God to be thought of for a European.[62]

> Prior to the modern age European theology had no true idea of the enormous numbers of individuals outside Christianity or of the immense length of non-Christian history.[63]

> In the ancient cultures of Asia it has never been able to gain a foothold, and in the West where it became one of the historical roots it is still steadily losing in importance and influence . . . the saying about the little flock will become still more true in spite of all the Church's pastoral and missionary efforts.[64]

> In a world in the process of evolution, offering less and less ground out of which a genuine Christianity could grow, things go more and more

downhill, and we can neither understand why God should permit times so unfruitful for Christianity nor foresee any end to them. We can therefore only go on being depressed (this too is concealed and unadmitted), because we cannot "get out" and yet — fortunately — don't have to expect the end in our own lifetime.[65]

But the Christian who finds himself in a diaspora situation which is becoming increasingly acute, the believer who finds his faith and his hope sorely tried at the sight of his unbelieving brothers, can derive from it (the theory of the anonymous Christian) comfort and the strength of objectivity . . . this knowledge will keep him from panic.[66]

Others writing at the same time offered observations about the psychological and theological impact that the growing numbers of non-Christians were having on the Church. Joseph Ratzinger comments:

As far as the future is concerned, it seems likely that, in the view of the proportion between the growth of the Church and the growth of the world's population, the Church's influence in the world will constantly decrease. The numerical triumph of Catholicism over other religions, which today may still be granted, will in all probability not continue much longer.[67]

After briefly reviewing the development of the doctrine of the necessity of the Church for salvation, he notes the possibility of those who have never heard the gospel being saved. Ratzinger then indicates that the issue now, given that people can be saved without hearing the gospel or without explicit faith in Christ or membership in the Church, is why someone would still want to be a Christian or belong to the Church. As he puts it:

In a certain sense we may say that for the men of today, the problem has shifted. The question that worries us is no longer primarily whether and how "the others" are saved. We know for certain, through our faith in God's mercy, that they can be saved: how this is done we may safely leave to God. The question which preoccupies us is, rather, this: Why — despite the wider possibility of salvation — is the service of the Church and the full service of faith and life through and in the Church still necessary? In other words, Christians today are no longer really troubled by the question whether their unbelieving brethren can attain salvation. Rather, they want to know what is the meaning of their clinging to Christ's all-embracing demand and to the Church.[68]

Rahner is also writing to give hope to those who are deeply distressed by how far the concrete Church of "today" is from being an appealing witness to the treasure it contains. He knows how embarrassing it is for Catholics hoping for friends and relatives to be attracted to Christ and the Church to encounter "clerical primitiveness and doubtful political opinions." He bemoans the prevalence of sermons of unpredictable quality. He is painfully aware that sometimes "good secularists" exhibit more of "Christian virtue" than those who bear the name of Christ do. Sometimes, as Rahner puts it, "One feels glad when an ecclesiastic appears slim and has clean finger-nails."[69]

Nevertheless, Rahner is very aware that his theory of the "anonymous Christian," besides on the face of it not being in harmony with the Scripture, seems to have serious negative consequences for evangelization.[70] He directly addresses these concerns in some of his essays. He realizes that after reading his work the question spontaneously arises: Why bother to evangelize if almost everybody is an "anonymous Christian"? Virtually every commentator — defender and critic — of Rahner's theory recognizes that this is a question that immediately springs to mind. If people can be saved without hearing the gospel, and if except for a few, rare exceptions we can presume that almost everybody is saved, why bother to preach it? As one commentator poses and answers the question:

> Here we need to front up to an objection that has been alluded to more than once. There is a fresh awareness today that (I) salvation is offered to all men, (II) that Christianity cannot boast of any monopoly of the Spirit, (III) that Christ is hiddenly at work beyond the confines of Christianity, (IV) that, therefore, salvation does not depend unconditionally on the preaching of the gospel. Why, then, bother about the foreign missions? Does not the doctrine of the anonymous Christian effectively dig the grave of missionary endeavor?[71]

And then his answer:

> The Theology of anonymous Christianity, properly understood, far from paralyzing the missionary thrust, will simply make it more precise

and sophisticated.... They [missionaries] will seek to render objective, conceptualized and explicit a faith in Christ already held in an implicit, unthematic and existential form.[72]

Another missionary/theologian raises the issue in a similar manner. In speaking of the theory of the anonymous Christian he comments:

The implications of this notion have contributed notably to the so-called "crisis in the missions." The missionary in the field tends to state the question something like this: "If men can be saved without visibly belonging to the Church, then where is the urgency of missionary work?" ... It is not enough simply to repeat over and over again that missionary activity is necessary, and that it involves the salvation of the whole world somehow, because the Church is essentially missionary. This is profoundly true, but why?[73]

Conway acknowledges that Rahner's theory of the anonymous Christian "demolishes the assumption which was central to the traditional theology of mission" and that "the missionary who previously believed that his work was necessary if souls were not to be lost, might now feel that his or her task had been robbed of much of its urgency and importance."[74]

Rahner himself attempts to respond to the obvious concern about what sense it still makes to preach the gospel by making a number of points concerning the link between "anonymous Christianity" and "explicit Christianity."[75]

1. The inner dynamic of anonymous Christianity tends towards explicit, conscious Christianity.

[Anonymous Christianity] strives towards an explicit expression, towards its full name. An unfavorable historical environment may impose limitations on the explicitness of this expression so that this actuation may not exceed the explicit appearance of a loving humaneness, but it will not act against this tendency whenever a new and higher stage of explicitness is presented to it right up to the ultimate perfection of a consciously accepted profession of Church membership.[76]

There seems to be some oscillation in Rahner's comments on this issue, as is to be expected in a career that spanned many decades. In a somewhat earlier essay he seemed to indicate that even when confronted with "explicit" Christianity the "anonymous Christian" may not respond positively, and yet still be an "anonymous Christian."

> It may therefore very well be the case that someone has bowed before God in faith in some remote level of his conscience which is only with difficulty or not at all accessible to us and that the process of the unfolding of this saving event to full ecclesiastical Catholic Christianity has at some point, perhaps very early, come up against some insurmountable obstacle (in forms of thought, reactions of sensibility, habits, prejudices on both sides, etc.) so that in point of fact the person who in the core of his being is in a state of grace finds it impossible to realize that what he is meeting in such Christianity is only the embodiment in a more articulated and further specified form of what he already is in the depths of his being.[77]

2. While not essential for salvation, explicit Christianity makes salvation more assured.

> The proclamation of the gospel does not simply turn someone absolutely abandoned by God and Christ into a Christian, but turns an anonymous Christian into someone who now also knows about his Christian belief in the depths of his grace-endowed being by objective reflection and in the profession of faith which is given a social form in the Church. . . . The reflex self-realization of a previously anonymous Christianity is demanded (1) by the incarnational and social structure of grace and of Christianity, and (2) because the individual who grasps Christianity in a clearer, purer and more reflective way has, other things being equal, a still greater chance of salvation than someone who is merely an anonymous Christian.[78]

3. The "anonymous Christian" is the only possible hearer of the gospel.

> The missionary task, therefore must be one that can exist together with anonymous Christianity because on theological grounds we must hold that this missionary task presupposes the existence of the anonymous Christian as the only possible hearer of the gospel message. . . . Even though anonymous Christianity is prior to explicit Christianity it does not render it superfluous. On the contrary, it itself demands this explicit Christianity in virtue of its own nature and its own intrinsic dynamism.[79]

Rahner cites approvingly the statement of a Japanese student chaplain who mentioned to Rahner that "the theory put forward here constitutes the indispensable condition for him such that it is only on this condition that he can perform his missionary work, precisely because he can then appeal to the anonymous Christian in the pagan and not simply seek to indoctrinate him with a teaching *ab externo*."[80]

Rahner is convinced that, even though it appears that his theory will undermine missionary efforts, the opposite will be the case. After painstakingly attempting to help family members of unbelievers, persons who have even explicitly repudiated their faith and the Church, understand that, buried under the apparent rejection, there may actually be an affirmation of faith, he affirms his belief in the efficacy of his theory of the "anonymous Christian" in stimulating missionary efforts.

> No matter how much the contrary may appear to be the case at first sight, in the *long* run a more courageous and more intense apostolate will develop where one is convinced that ultimately every apostolate is an uncovering of that Christianity which God in his grace has already hidden in the hearts of those who think that they are not Christians.[81]

It is difficult to read these texts and not understand Rahner to be claiming that almost everyone is already an "anonymous Christian" because "Christianity" is "already hidden in their hearts," and, therefore, evangelization is simply bringing to explicitness an assent to God that has already been made. But as we have seen in our study of *LG* 16c, Scripture and tradition indicate otherwise. Rahner seems to ignore the strong testimony of Scripture and the weight of empirical experience that indicate that a strong resistance, even rejection, of God can be hidden in the hearts of people.

Rahner invites us to test this theory by an evaluation of the empirical situation. He himself does not do this. It seems apparent from the testimony of the Scriptures and the entire missionary history of the Church that there are many who reject the gospel when they hear it, as well as many who accept. And this certainly cannot always be attributed to an inadequate proclamation of the saving message. Paul testifies that "in their wickedness, they suppressed the truth, and so are without excuse" (Rom. 1:18-20). The Scripture testifies that those who refused to come to Jesus were choosing to remain in the darkness and to keep doing their deeds of darkness rather than undergoing the pain of conversion (John 3:19-21).

The "loving humaneness" that seems to be what Rahner proposes at some points as the minimal, empirical evidence of an anonymous Christian, seems oftentimes to be in short supply.

4. Even if salvation is no longer at stake, duty will be a sufficient motivator for evangelization to go forward.

> If man is consciously aware of whom [sic] he is and what he is making of himself of his own freedom, the chance that he will succeed in this self-achievement of his and arrive at a radical self-fulfillment is greater than if he merely possesses and fulfils his own humanity at a merely inert and unconscious level. Hence the conscious self-realization of a hitherto anonymous Christianity brought about through missionary preaching implies on the one hand the achievement of a more radical dimension of responsibility and on the other a greater chance of this Christianity interiorly bestowed by grace being brought to its fulness in all dimensions precisely as an explicit Christianity and in a state of radical freedom. Nor let it be said that if the only difference between explicit Christianity and anonymous Christianity is that the opportunity of achieving salvation afforded by the former is greater (instead of saying that salvation is initially bestowed by that explicit Christianity), this must after all have the effect of weakening missionary zeal. It is perfectly possible for there to be an absolute duty in human life to offer one's neighbour a greater chance of freely achieving the fulness of himself even when in principle the chance of such full self-realization was present all along even without offering him this further opportunity.[82]

Rahner believes Christians will see that, even if people can be saved without ever coming to explicit faith or Church membership, Christians have a responsibility to bring the fullness of the grace of salvation to people.

> And even if we knew with absolute certainty that in their case as it is their ultimate salvation was already secure, this would not relieve apostolic zeal from all meaning and obligation in their regard. The Church and we in her do not have an apostolic mission towards others merely (and perhaps not even primarily) because these others might otherwise be lost, but because (even prescinding from this) God wills his Christ and his grace and truth and salvation to acquire visible and palpable form and presence in the history of mankind even here below.[83]

It would seem that it would be the rare person indeed who would see it as an "absolute duty" to help his neighbor achieve more of the "fulness of himself" or to acquire "visibility." The evidence of motivation for missionary endeavors in the Church's tradition is rooted in the foundational belief that the salvation of unbelievers is in jeopardy.

5. Mission should now focus not on the salvation of the individual but on the evangelization of cultures.

> Making Christ, his gospel and his grace present among all peoples as such in their own specific histories and cultures. . . . Once and for all Christianity is not intended merely to assure a salvation . . . for the individual in the other-worldly dimension, but is rather intended to make God's grace manifest here below in all its possible forms and in all historical spheres and contexts. . . . It is precisely not merely the other world that belongs to God and his Christ, as though he secretly rescued a few isolated individuals out of a merely secular world. On the contrary this world too belongs to him, the earthly dimension, history, the peoples, and also the history which present day humanity itself sets itself actively to shape, instead of merely passively enduring it. . . . This new interpretation of the theology of mission in no sense involves any assertion that mission has no connection whatever with the personal salvation of the individual. . . . It is obvious that mission improves the situation in which salvation can be achieved and the opportunity of salvation for the individual.[84]

6. The mission of the Church is to be a sacrament of salvation.

Rahner frequently speaks of the primary mission of the Church in terms of its being a sacrament, manifesting among a relative few what God is doing among the many in an anonymous way.[85] He thinks it important, then, that this sacrament of the Church be present in every geographical location and every culture so that the world might see what it is called to and what it to a great extent is already participating in, in an anonymous way. Certainly the image of the Church as sacrament received prominence in the documents of Vatican II and is a rich and valid image.[86] On the other hand, when coupled with the "salvation optimism" of Rahner, it seems to take on a reductionist cast that dulls the missionary urgency. One of the most important "church as sacrament" biblical texts is worth paying attention to.

I gave them your word, and the world hated them, because they do not belong to the world any more than I belong to the world. I do not ask that you take them out of the world but that you keep them from the evil one. They do not belong to the world any more than I belong to the world. Consecrate them in the truth. Your word is truth. As you sent me into the world, so I sent them into the world. And I consecrate myself for them, so that they also may be consecrated in truth. I pray not only for them, but also for those who will believe in me through their word, so that they may all be one, as you, Father, are in me and I in you, that they also may be in us, that the world may believe that you sent me. And I have given them the glory you gave me, so that they may be one, as we are one, I in them and you in me, that they may be brought to perfection as one, that the world may know that you sent me, and that you loved them even as you loved me. (John 17:14-24 NAB)

First of all, we see very clearly the contrast between the "world" and the church. The world is under the control of the evil one and the disciples no longer belong to the world (1 John 5:19). Jesus prays for his disciples to be protected from the evil one, to be consecrated in truth, and he sends them into the world on the mission of proclaiming the truth and drawing others to faith in Jesus. The sacramental life of the Church, and the quality of the disciples' relationship with each other and the Lord, are intended to draw others to explicit faith, true hope, knowledge of the Father's love, and participation in the communion of the Church. This active missionary dimension with the specific goal of preaching for conversion is considerably muted when "church as sacrament" is interpreted in tandem with "salvation optimism." It tends to present a passive picture of the Church as seemingly saying, "Look at us; we are a sign of what you may already be; would you be interested in joining us?" The picture we get from the New Testament, both in the type of training that Jesus gave to his disciples in teaching, preaching, healing, casting out devils, and his explicit commands to "go" to the entire world, as well as the picture we get of the active evangelization carried out by the Apostles and the early Christians, shows the active missionary life that accompanied the community life. Of course, both dimensions are necessary, the witness of the life and the going out to proclaim. As Rahner puts it, responding to concerns about the numerical diminishment of the Church:

If we clearly realize the essentially theological nature of the Church as the basic sacrament of salvation, promising salvation to the world and not merely to itself, if in our modern ecclesiology we prefer the metaphor of the basic sacrament to the older metaphor of the Church as the sole ark of salvation on the sea of a perishing world, then we can look more impartially to the future. The Church is everywhere: in the last resort its nature and its function remain independent of the question of its numerical relationship to the total world-population.[87]

The center of gravity, in Rahner's interpretation of Church as sacrament, definitely shifts from drawing people to become members of the Church to being a sign of God's anonymous work of salvation outside the visible boundaries of the Church.

> The Church is the sacrament of universal salvation. What does this mean? She is a historically tangible sign, willed by God, a sign that God loves the world as a whole, that he does not release it from the grip of his powerful love, and that he intends to lead it to its blessed consummation in ways that are not known to us. The Church is the great sacramental sign of all these things. But a sign is never simply identical with what it signifies. Therefore, while the Church is the sacramental sign of the world's salvation, we know that salvation extends far beyond it.[88]

In speaking of local parishes/communities he further elaborates:

> Such a community is an oasis in a world that is secretly always filled with God's grace but that, seen from without, socially, looks very unholy, very pagan. The community is the visible sign of salvation that God has established in this seemingly godless world. Through this community God says: I am here in this world and I remain with my grace; secretly I fill the deepest depths of humanity, keeping people in the love that I, the eternal God, have for my only-begotten Son, the Incarnate Word.[89]

Rahner then anticipates the logical question: Why is it important to be part of the "sign" when the whole world is being saved anonymously? Why undertake the additional responsibility of being part of explicit Christianity when being saved by "following your conscience" and "loving your neighbor" works just as well?[90]

> At this point a Christian might say: If that is true, I myself might make my life easier. I am going over to the world, which, according to what we have

just said, is not living outside of God's salvific will, which can attain its salvation even outside the visible Church. I will therefore forgo explicit Christianity with all the obligations that go with it: Sunday Mass, receiving the sacraments, being controlled by church authorities, and so on.[91]

Rahner's reply is that once you know explicitly that Jesus and the Church are willed by God it is impermissible to go back to an anonymous Christianity and to do so would endanger one's salvation, since one has been chosen by God to express one's salvation explicitly.[92] Somehow, though, the compelling arguments that salvation is widely available, and received, outside of the visible Church seem to have more influence than Rahner's caveat that the sacramental view of the Church, as sign of a wide salvation, "by no means implies that Christians would be allowed to break away, as it were, from this sign to which they belong in order to join anonymous Christianity, for which God's salvific will is at work mysteriously — albeit always on account of Christ."[93] Rahner also argues that those who have been called to explicit membership in the Church have an obligation to see that "the sign does not perish" and that others also come to an "awareness of this innermost blessing of grace."[94] While few seem to reject Christ and the Church explicitly and "go over to the world," many seem to feel quite comfortable in not accepting the doctrine, morality, and missionary responsibility of the Church and still consider themselves Christians whose salvation is not in jeopardy. And even that minority who do explicitly reject Christ and the Church and declare themselves atheists, Rahner tells us, may be only "categorical atheists" and not "transcendental atheists."

Preliminary Conclusions

Before we formally draw our conclusions, it would be useful to consider why, despite Rahner's many distinctions, so many who read him or hear a reasonably accurate account of what it means to be an anonymous Christian lose missionary conviction. As Avery Dulles put it:

Although Rahner denied that his theory undermined the importance of missionary activity, it was widely understood as depriving missions of their salvific importance. Some readers of his works understood him as teaching that the unevangelized could possess the whole of Christianity except the name. Saving faith, thus understood, would be a subjective attitude without any specifiable content. In that case, the message of the gospel would have little to do with salvation.[95]

Peter Phan, in an overall sympathetic treatment of Rahner's eschatology, identifies why this loss of missionary conviction occurs despite Rahner's caveats to the contrary.

> One may wonder whether the scarce attention and space Rahner has dedicated to sin and hell, on the one hand, and on the other, the strong emphasis he placed on the certainty of the salvation of the world as a whole as well as his speculation on apocatastasis (even only as an object of hope) do not lead one to make light of the threat of eternal self-loss. His repeated protests against the calculation of the number of the damned and his insistence on our ignorance of whether anyone will actually be lost at all may ironically produce another surreptitious calculation that affirms that there is and there will be no one in hell.[96]

1. Rahner himself makes statements that seem to overshadow his distinctions. Let us look again at a text that we have already considered in another context.

> If one gives more exact theological thought to this matter, then one cannot regard nature and grace as two phases in the life of the individual which follow each other in time. It is furthermore impossible to think that this offer of supernatural, divinizing grace made to all men on account of the universal salvific purpose of God, should in general (prescinding from the relatively few exceptions) remain ineffective in most cases on account of the personal guilt of the individual. For, as far as the gospel is concerned, we have no really conclusive reason for thinking so pessimistically of men. On the other hand, and contrary to every merely human experience, we do have every reason for thinking optimistically of God and his salvific will which is more powerful than the extremely limited stupidity and evil-mindedness of men. . . . Christ and his salvation are not simply one of two possibilities offering themselves to man's free choice; they are the deed of God which bursts open and redeems the false choice of man by overtaking it.[97]

He seems to be clearly saying that it is the exceptional few who are not already anonymous Christians, because the grace of God "overtakes" the "extremely limited" sinfulness of human beings. And:

It is only the history of salvation and revelation in and after Jesus Christ as the eschatological and unsurpassable Word of God, by which God has irreversibly promised himself to the world in *historical* tangibility, that excludes and renders obsolete an ultimate denial by human freedom of the grace-given existentiality of history.[98]

Although rejecting a theoretical doctrine of universal reconciliation, the Church in the Council and in its practical conduct starts out from the assumption that God's grace is not only offered to man's free decision, but also that it largely prevails universally in this freedom.[99]

Texts like these seem to say that the ultimate "no" to God is now virtually obsolete. We know from other texts that he holds that an ultimate "no" is theoretically possible, but texts like those above tend to overshadow the others.

2. Rahner presents the teaching of Vatican II regarding salvation outside of the visible Church as a very significant change and characterizes it as a change from pessimism to optimism, as a veritable *caesura*, "which can be compared perhaps only with the transition from Judaeo-Christianity to Gentile Christianity."[100] He acknowledges at one point that there is really nothing new about the doctrinal teaching about the possibility of salvation outside of the visible Church.

The theological reasons for the caesura were indeed present at an earlier stage: the assumption of God's universal salvific will in Christ, the doctrine of the opportunity of salvation without sacraments, of the implicit desire of membership of the Church, of the validity of baptism even outside the Catholic Church, and so on. These ever-present theological truisms might give the impression that nothing has really changed in the relationship between the Church and the rest of mankind.[101]

He acknowledges that there has been a long development from what he characterizes as Augustinian pessimism to Vatican II optimism. Nevertheless, he insists on characterizing Vatican II's acknowledgment of the universal will of God for the salvation of the human race and its acknowledgment of the opportunity that God gives to every person to be saved, even if they have not heard the gospel, as a major turning point. He rightly identifies some major attitudinal, perspective, and policy changes in pastoral strategy — especially in the embrace of the ecumenical movement and

the official recognition of positive elements in non-Christian religions —
but gives the impression that they are indicative of doctrinal change.

> Of course it could be said that this optimism of the Council in regard to
> universal salvation also remains hypothetical, that it could break down
> as a result of an individual's final culpability, that in this hypothetical
> way it was the normal teaching of the Church even before the Council.
> It is indeed true that even after the Council the Church has not pro-
> claimed any doctrine of universal reconciliation (apokatastasis) and be-
> fore it had also taught God's universal salvific will. But this preconciliar
> teaching was understood in a very abstract way and qualified with not a
> few ifs and buts, which cannot be maintained after the Council. The
> Council tacitly buried the doctrine of "limbo" for children dying before
> baptism.[102]

3. Rahner presents Vatican II as being primarily a pastoral council that
offered only a "start" on further dogmatic development.

> That means that the Council did not clearly and explicitly teach and in-
> terpret doctrines of a dogmatic sort; rather, it said things that are a start,
> a suggestion, an invitation to further dogmatic reflection and elabora-
> tion. Therefore I cannot quote any clear and unquestionable doctrines
> of the Council for my purpose. I can only point to conciliar statements
> that lead theologians to new questions requiring further reflection.[103]

In commenting on the limited usefulness of Vatican II for the German
Synod of 1971:

> This council has certainly a lasting importance for the Church as a
> whole and so too for the German Church. . . . But in the positive deci-
> sions of the council, if we look at them quite coolly, there is much that is
> already obsolete — in the decree on the liturgy, for example. Many of
> the council's statements simply express the Christian faith and that, of-
> ten enough, in the light of presuppositions and horizons of understand-
> ing which cannot simply be regarded as those of today or tomorrow.[104]

Ratzinger identifies this interpretation of Vatican II as a "jumping off
point" for further development as a significant factor in the post–Vatican II
confusion.

An interpretation of the Council that understands its dogmatic texts as mere preludes to a still unattained conciliar spirit, that regards the whole as just a preparation for *Gaudium et spes* and that looks upon the latter text as just the beginning of an unswerving course towards an ever greater union with what is called progress — such an interpretation is not only contrary to what the Council Fathers intended and meant, it has been reduced *ad absurdum* by the course of events. . . . The real reception of the Council has not yet even begun. What devastated the Church in the decade after the Council was not the Council but the refusal to accept it.[105]

He specifically applies this open-ended development to the question of universal salvation.

Although rejecting a theoretical doctrine of universal reconciliation, the Church in the Council and in its practical conduct starts out from the assumption that God's grace is not only offered to man's free decision, but also that it largely prevails universally in this freedom. This attitude of the Church came into existence of course only after a very long period of development. But it became clear and irreversible in the Second Vatican Council; for such a hope can certainly grow, while it can no longer really decline.

Formerly theology asked apprehensively, how many are saved from the *massa damnata* of world-history. Today we ask whether we may hope that all are saved. This question, this attitude, is more Christian than the former and is the fruit of a more mature Christian awareness that has grown over a long period and is slowly coming to terms more closely with the ultimate basic message of Jesus on the victory of God's Kingdom.[106]

It is unsettling that Rahner would call his understanding of universal salvation more Christian than a central element of Jesus' own teaching:[107]

Enter through the narrow gate; for the gate is wide and the road broad that leads to destruction, and those who enter through it are many. How narrow the gate and constricted the road that leads to life. And those who find it are few. (Matt. 7:13-14 NAB)

Someone asked him, "Lord, will only a few people be saved?" He answered them, "Strive to enter through the narrow gate, for many, I tell you, will attempt to enter but will not be strong enough. After the master of the house has arisen and locked the door, then will you stand outside knocking and saying, 'Lord, open the door for us.' He will say to you in reply, 'I do not know where you are from.' And you will say, 'We ate and drank in your company and you taught in our streets.' Then he will say to you, 'I do not know where (you) are from. Depart from me, all you evildoers!' And there will be wailing and grinding of teeth when you see Abraham, Isaac, and Jacob and all the prophets in the kingdom of God and you yourselves cast out. And people will come from the east and the west and from the north and the south and will recline at table in the kingdom of God. For behold, some are last who will be first, and some are first who will be last." (Luke 13:23-30 NAB)

It seems that Rahner in his overall theological work on this topic has reached the point that Newman says we can never legitimately reach — where the words of the gospel have become reversed — and the many headed towards destruction have now become the few, and the few headed to salvation have now become the many;[108] where the "strive (agonize) to enter" of Jesus' urgent exhortation has now become the "accept yourself, follow your conscience" of Rahner. It does not seem that this is a place that we can afford to stay as a Church; out of loyalty to the inspired Word of God, and out of concern for the salvation of the "many."

Summary Conclusions

1. Rahner's theory of the "anonymous Christian," despite its good pastoral intentions and theological seriousness, has, in my opinion, greatly weakened the impetus to evangelization. It is very easy to get the impression from Rahner's essays on the topic that almost everyone, if not everyone, is already in a saving relationship with Christ, and what remains is to "enrich" or "improve" such a person's life.[109] This, in my opinion, is not sufficient motivation to undertake the effort to evangelize. Along with this "salvation optimism" is a strange "existential pessimism" that definitely is relevant to the direction in which he takes his theology. He sometimes speaks as though we are facing the radical de-Christianization of Western culture rather helplessly, puzzled about our own doctrine and moral teaching, still rather foolishly clinging to the belief that if the world accepted Christ and the Church it would be better off.

The Council wishes to get rid of triumphalism, but some of it has lingered on. The idea that, if only the unbelieving world were to accept the living Church and her message, it would find salvation and happiness, is subconsciously present and continues to be voiced frequently in declarations of the magisterium. That the Church herself is a Church of sinners, that even her true and salutary doctrines lead to riddles, that the Church too, in the final analysis, does not know exactly, clearly, and convincingly how we should go about it, is not the most clearly voiced conviction of the living Church. . . . Do Christians simply capitulate before the insuperable darkness of existence and honestly admit that they are capitulating? Or do they simply ignore their perplexity and become right away persons who have victoriously overcome the hopelessness of life? Is it possible for Christians neither simply to despair nor overlook in a false optimism the bitter hopelessness of their existence? It seems to me that it is not easy to answer these questions theoretically. Yet the questions and their answers are of the greatest importance for Christian life, even if they occur only in the more or less unconscious praxis of life, even if the very question about this Christian perplexity falls under the law of this same perplexity. This situation makes it impossible to give clear answers to the questions.[110]

2. Apart from motivation, it seems to me that Rahner has an overly optimistic view of the "response rate" of the human heart to the grace of God. There is a significant scriptural testimony regarding the capacity of the human heart to reject truth, light, grace, and Christ himself. Rahner himself, late in life, acknowledged that perhaps he did not sufficiently take into account the reality of sin.

Let it be admitted here, even if with some anxiety, that in my theology the topic of sin and the forgiveness of sins, stands, in what is certainly a problematic way, somewhat in the background in comparison with the topic of the self-communication of God.[111]

3. Rahner distorts the teaching of Vatican II by neglecting important texts of *LG* 16 that speak of the real possibility of people who do not know the gospel being saved, under certain conditions, "very often" not being fulfilled.

Ultimately, despite the good motivation and many valid points in his theology of the "anonymous Christian," there are serious defects in how he takes into account the whole testimony of Scripture, tradition, and the teachings of Vatican II on this point — serious issues of truth, the neglect of which, unfortunately, can put in serious jeopardy the salvation of souls.

We now need to consider the teaching of Hans Urs von Balthasar, who along with Rahner has been a major influence on the "culture of universalism" that pervades the climate of the Church today.[112]

CHAPTER VI

Balthasar: Dare We Hope That All Be Saved?

Along with Karl Rahner, whose theory of the "anonymous Christian" we have considered in the previous chapter, Hans Urs von Balthasar is one of the most influential theologians in the past century. Both of them are particularly relevant to our exploration of what constitute the limits on the conditions of salvation for those who do not hear the gospel, limits that are stated in *LG* 16c. Both theologians' theories have had a wide acceptance not only in theological circles but in the Church at large and have significantly contributed to overshadowing the teaching of *LG* 16c.[1]

In Catholic theological circles, as we will see, their views on the possibilities of universal salvation are cited as the basis of a prevailing consensus among Catholic theologians in favor of a strong hope that everyone may be saved and a rather skeptical attitude toward the possibility of human beings ultimately being capable of definitively saying no to the saving love of God. This theological view, in its extreme form, is often referred to as "universalism" or as "apokatastasis."[2] John Sachs, a Jesuit theologian, in a lengthy article on universal salvation that appeared in *Theological Studies,* expresses what he claims is the current Catholic theological consensus.

> We have seen that there is a clear consensus among Catholic theologians today in their treatment of the notion of apocatastasis and the problem of hell. . . . It may not be said that even one person is already or will in fact be damned. All that may and must be believed is that the salvation of the world is a reality already begun and established in Christ. Such a faith expresses itself most consistently in the hope that because of the gracious love of God whose power far surpasses human sin, all men and

women will in fact freely and finally surrender to God in love and be saved.

When Balthasar speaks of the duty to hope for the salvation of all, he is articulating the broad consensus of current theologians and the best of the Catholic tradition. Like other theologians, notably Rahner, he intentionally pushes his position to the limit, insisting that such a hope is not merely possible but well founded. . . . I have tried to show that the presumption that human freedom entails a capacity to reject God definitively and eternally seems questionable. And, although this presumption enjoys the weight of the authority of Scripture and tradition, it would seem incorrect to consider this possibility as an object of faith in the same sense that the ability of human freedom in grace to choose God is an object of faith.[3]

Richard Bauckham comments:

The history of the doctrine of universal salvation (or *apokatastasis*) is a remarkable one. Until the nineteenth century almost all Christian theologians taught the reality of eternal torment in hell. . . . Eternal punishment was firmly asserted in official creeds and confessions of the churches. It must have seemed as indispensable a part of universal Christian belief as the doctrines of the Trinity and the Incarnation. Since 1800 this situation has entirely changed and no traditional Christian doctrine has been so widely abandoned as that of eternal punishment. . . . Universal salvation, either as hope or as dogma, is now so widely accepted that many theologians assume it virtually without argument.[4]

Bauckham traces the history of universalism's attempts to come to grips with the Scriptures in three stages: first, universalists tried, through word study, to claim that the "eternity" of hell was really not eternal. Bauckham notes that twentieth-century exegesis has ruled out this approach.

Few would now doubt that many NT texts clearly teach a *final* division of mankind into saved and lost, and the most that universalists now commonly claim is that alongside these texts, there are others which hold out a universal hope (e.g. Eph 1:10; Col 1:20).[5]

In the second and third stages, he notes that universalists have attempted to deal with the situation either by claiming that the texts that appear to

teach definitively a final separation of the human race are really only warnings that will not be carried out, or by admitting that the Scriptures do not
actually support the universalist position but that the "spirit" of the New
Testament allows us to go beyond the texts, allegedly led by the Spirit, into
a deeper understanding of the final victory of God's love.[6]

Richard Schenk, in a very important article, acknowledges the influence that Balthasar has had in this remarkable shift among Catholics.

> Whatever the final theological judgment on Balthasar's calling into
> question the facticity of ultimate loss may turn out to be, there can be
> no doubt that his proposals that we bracket out (set in *epoché*) the as-
> sumption that the possibility of any final loss will ever be realized have
> added their own considerable weight to a far more widely motivated
> shift in the way the burden of proof at these proceedings is allocated. . . .
> Today, due in no small part to Balthasar's works themselves the burden
> of proof has shifted to those who consider this newly prescribed hope
> dubious. . . . The hermeneutical situation of any possible discussion,
> then, is marked today by an already completed, widespread shift in
> mainstream Catholic attitudes, prior to any conceivable efforts in sys-
> tematic or biblical theology, a shift away from the existential conviction
> that there really will be any kind of final loss.[7]

These comments of Schenk express accurately the remarkable shift in
both theological and popular sentiment regarding the possibility of eternal
loss. In my contacts it seems that many even of the most orthodox and spiritual people seem to have almost imperceptibly drifted into a position very
close to universalism. When *Dominus Iesus* and the subsequent *Doctrinal
Note on Evangelization* were issued, many thought that the most serious
doctrinal confusions affecting evangelization were definitively refuted. But
these documents only addressed one part of the problem. These documents
firmly restate the absolute uniqueness and necessity of Christ and the
Church for salvation. There is only one savior for the whole world, and no
one is saved except through Jesus Christ and some manner of link with the
Church, however implicit it may be. Both Rahner, and, as we shall see,
Balthasar, agree with this central truth: no one is saved apart from Christ.
The problem is that they do not acknowledge unambiguously the authoritative teaching of Christ, as carried forward in the tradition and rearticulat-
ed in *LG* 16, that "very often" human beings are not living their lives in a way
that will lead them to salvation, and there is a real probability of many being

lost unless they are addressed with a call to repentance, faith, and baptism, and positively respond to such a call, an effective renewed evangelization. These documents deal with the issues raised by a theology of religious pluralism and a certain relativism, but they do not deal with the problem of a *de facto* or even theoretical universalism, which agrees with everything these documents assert but still assumes that virtually no one will be lost.

In his encyclical *Mission of the Redeemer,* John Paul II expresses his concern about how various theological confusions have resulted in a widespread undermining of the missionary work of the Church.

> Nowadays the call to conversion which missionaries address to non-Christians is put into question or passed over in silence. It is seen as an act of "proselytizing"; it is claimed that it is enough to help people to become more human or more faithful to their own religion, that it is enough to build communities capable of working for justice, freedom, peace and solidarity.[8]

Catholics who have not read a single theological essay have heard the substance of this "consensus" and experienced the pervasiveness of this "shift." This has contributed to the general atmosphere of universalism that pervades the mindset of many Catholics today.[9]

Avery Dulles identifies what he calls a prevalent "thoughtless optimism" regarding salvation:

> Quite apart from what theologians teach, popular piety has become saccharine. Unable to grasp the rationale for eternal punishment, many Christians take it almost for granted that everyone, or practically everyone, must be saved. The Mass for the Dead has turned into a Mass of the Resurrection, which sometimes seems to celebrate not so much the resurrection of the Lord as the salvation of the deceased, without any reference to sin and punishment. More education is needed to convince people that they ought to fear God who, as Jesus taught, can punish soul and body together in hell (cf. Mt 10:28).[10]

Cardinal Ratzinger also identified fear of the Lord, which includes fear of losing our salvation, as important for the life of the Church today.

> "The fear of the Lord is the beginning of wisdom," says Scripture (Ps. 111:10), and this saying remains true even today. Being able to sin be-

longs to our fundamental situation as creatures ever since the Fall, and this danger we are in is as it were the ontological ground of proper and properly ordered fear. A Christian upbringing cannot aim at ridding man of every kind of fear: it would then be in contradiction to what we are. Its task must be to purify fear, to put it in its proper place, and to integrate it with hope and love so that it can watch over and aid these. Thus it is possible for the right kind of courage to grow, courage that man would not need if there were not reason to fear. . . . Anyone who loves God knows that there is only *one* real threat for man, the danger of losing God. For that reason we pray: "Lead us not into temptation, but deliver us from evil" — that is, from the loss of faith, from sin in general. . . . The lack of the fear of God is the beginning of all folly. When the fear of God that has its proper place at the heart of the love of God no longer holds sway, people lose their standard, their criterion: fear of man exerts its domination over them, there emerges an idolatry of what appears, and thus the door is wide open for every kind of folly.[11]

A quite interesting contemporary witness has emerged as to the salutary effect the fear of damnation can have on the conversion of someone far from the Church. Peter Hitchens, whose brother Christopher was the aggressive atheist, writes of his experience while contemplating Rogier van der Wyden's "The Last Judgment."

No doubt I should be ashamed to confess that fear played a part in my return to religion, specifically a painting: Rogier van der Weyden's 15th Century Last Judgment, which I saw in Burgundy while on holiday. I had scoffed at its mention in the guidebook, but now I gaped, my mouth actually hanging open, at the naked figures fleeing towards the pit of Hell. These people did not appear remote or from the ancient past: they were my own generation. Because they were naked, they were not imprisoned in their own age by time-bound fashions. On the contrary, their hair and the set of their faces were entirely in the style of my own time. They were me and people I knew. I had a sudden strong sense of religion being a thing of the present day, not imprisoned under thick layers of time. My large catalogue of misdeeds replayed themselves rapidly in my head. I had absolutely no doubt that I was among the damned, if there were any damned. Van der Wyden was still earning his fee, nearly 500 years after his death. At about the same time I rediscovered Christmas. . . .[12]

Already, in 1972, Dulles had written an article describing how new theological, cultural, and political trends were affecting mission work. He noted that only seven years after the Second Vatican Council there were "many complaints that the missions are dying."[13]

As we have seen in the preceding chapter, Rahner attempts to "dive under" the words of Scripture as they have been traditionally understood, and finds in his anthropology of the human being a transcendental subjectivity that is already addressed by God and is most likely positively responsive to the "supernatural existential," and therefore justified. In doing so he claims magisterial backing for his theory but simply ignores the text from *LG* 16c that we have been considering. Balthasar, on the other hand, attempts to "jump over" the words of Scripture as they have been traditionally understood and posit extrabiblical possibilities, which overshadow the biblical teaching and therefore the teaching of *LG* 16c as well. This chapter will devote proportionately more space to a consideration of Balthasar's theory than we have to other chapter topics, both because of its complexity and also because of Balthasar's very high standing and influence among current Church leadership. In this regard it is important to note that the overall theological work of Balthasar has been highly praised by leading theologians and Church leadership, including John Paul II and Cardinal Ratzinger.[14] The approach this chapter will take is to focus on the particular work in which Balthasar most fully explains and defends his theory, which also happens to be among the last works he wrote before he died in 1988. The chapter will also reference other parts of his writings, which, though written earlier, provide important insights into his theory and show its continuity. We will proceed first of all by briefly summarizing Balthasar's arguments and final conclusions. We will then consider in some detail the main arguments he makes for his positions and the methodology he employs; we will then offer our evaluations, drawing on some of the most important secondary literature from both his defenders and critics. We will then offer our own conclusions. It is important to be clear that we will not be considering Balthasar's impressive and massive work as a whole, except as it relates to the particular theme that we are examining. It is also important to be clear that while our evaluation will, indeed, be critical of his work on this theme, this is not to be taken as an estimation of his work as a whole.

An Overview of Balthasar's Argument

Although Balthasar had elaborated many of his thoughts on the possibility of universal salvation in earlier works,[15] it was not until a press conference he had given, and an article he had written in response to the questions raised at the press conference was reprinted in *L'Osservatore Romano,* that an intense debate broke out that resulted in his book-length defense of his theory which was published in German in 1986. The English translation that appeared shortly afterwards also includes the original article, "A Short Discourse on Hell," with some revisions, and a third work, published as an epilogue, which is the text of a lecture he gave shortly before he died: "Apokatastasis: Universal Reconciliation." All three works were published in English translation in one volume, under the title *Dare We Hope "That All Men Be Saved"? With a Short Discourse on Hell.*[16]

Balthasar had a career-long interest in the minority theological stream among some of the Fathers that openly advocated (Gregory of Nyssa) or sympathetically speculated (Origen) on *apokatastasis* — the theory that holds that in the end, all mankind will be saved.[17] Some variations also include speculation that this might ultimately include even the demons. Early in his career he had written book-length treatments devoted to an exposition of the thought of some of these authors. He also had a strong interest in the modern Protestant theologian Karl Barth, who advocated a position close to universalism, the exact nature of which is still being debated in scholarly articles.[18]

Since the theory of *apokatastasis* was condemned as heretical by the Emperor Justinian and then by the Councils of Constantinople (543, 553),[19] and since Balthasar frequently declared his intention to write and live as an orthodox Catholic theologian, he was always clear that he was not intending to teach universalism as a doctrine, but simply arguing for it as a hope, as a possibility. As this chapter proceeds, though, we will see, despite his protestations, that a strong case can be made that it is indeed what he believes, and he is, in fact, teaching it, while stopping short of holding it "formally."

Balthasar's Pastoral Concern

Balthasar, despite his elaborate theological speculation, professes to be writing on this topic out of a pastoral concern. He is concerned that if we are sure that there is even one person in hell we cannot any longer hope for the salvation of all and cannot take seriously the universal salvific will of God. He believes this will result in a diminishment of Christian charity in our prayer for the salvation of all.[20] He is also concerned that it will foster the development of Pharisaical attitudes that see the "other" as on the way to hell but oneself as on the path of salvation. An even deeper concern for Balthasar is his belief that for contemporary man belief in a God who sends people to hell is incompatible with an image of that God as Love, and therefore contributes to widespread unbelief. He speaks of attitudes that find expression such as this: "Many are enraged by the idea of eternal punishment and do not want to serve so hard a Judge."[21] He states that it is necessary to look at the texts that speak of the possibility of hell, "our feelings of revulsion, notwithstanding."[22] He is also concerned, although this is more on a theological level, that if there is anyone in hell, Christ's sacrifice will have been without its proper fruit, and "in fact, would frustrate God's universal plan of salvation."[23]

In his interpretation of Scripture and theological reasoning he is attempting to show that while we cannot deny that hell may be a *possibility*, there may indeed be no one there, so great is the power of God's love and the power of Christ's redemptive acts to overwhelm or even "outwit" human freedom.[24]

The Challenge of Scripture and Tradition

Balthasar realizes that his argument faces formidable challenges in interpreting the many Scripture passages that seem to indicate clearly that hell is populated. He also is aware that the mainstream of Catholic tradition has considered this a settled question, and the greatest theologians, including Augustine and Aquinas, consider it apparent that Scripture indicates that there are "many" in hell and that there will certainly be a twofold division of the human race made manifest on the solemn Day of Judgment.[25]

Balthasar is clear that the doctrine of "universalism" was a minority position that did not arise until the third century, and that disappeared soon after its condemnation by the Councils of Constantinople and Augustine's powerful refutation of it in his work.[26] Dulles says that Balthasar's position

> seems to me to be orthodox. It does not contradict any ecumenical councils or definitions of the faith. It can be reconciled with everything in Scripture, at least if the statements of Jesus on hell are taken as minatory rather than predictive. Balthasar's position, moreover, does not under-

mine a healthy fear of being lost. But the position is at least adventurous. It runs against the obvious interpretation of the words of Jesus in the New Testament and against the dominant theological opinion down through the centuries, which maintains that some, and in fact very many, are lost.[27]

Dulles points out how clear and constant the tradition has been on the two destinies of the human race, quite clearly understanding that many, even most, might be lost. He acknowledges that "the relative number of the elect and the damned are not treated in any Church documents, but have been a subject of discussion among theologians."[28] He notes that the Greek Fathers — Irenaeus, Basil, Cyril of Jerusalem, and John Chrysostom — all interpret passages such as Matthew 22:14 ("For many are invited, but few are chosen") as meaning that the majority will refuse to avail themselves of the gift of salvation and be lost. Augustine, basing himself on the texts in the Book of Revelation speaking of the "multitudes" before the throne of God, states that many will be saved, but even more will be lost. Thomas Aquinas wrote that the number of the elect is only known to God but that it is likely that most will be lost.[29]

After Thomas, Francisco Suarez, writing in the late sixteenth and early seventeenth centuries, in his treatise on predestination, specifically asked the question: How many will be saved? Dulles summarizes Suarez's conclusions by saying that outside of the Catholic Church most will be lost, but within the Church most will be saved, "since many die before they can sin mortally, and many others are fortified by the sacraments. Suarez is relatively optimistic in comparison with other Catholic theologians of his day. Peter Canisius and Robert Bellarmine, both Doctors of the Church, for example, were convinced that most of the human race is lost."[30] By the early twentieth century, Dulles notes, theological studies indicated "there was a virtual consensus among the Fathers of the Church and the Catholic theologians of later ages to the effect that the majority of humankind go to eternal punishment in hell."[31] Dulles notes that even though there was a strong consensus to this effect, he believes it is not against official Church teaching to entertain the possibility that the majority are saved. Dulles indicates that "about the middle of the twentieth century, there seems to be a break in the tradition. Since then a number of influential theologians have favored the view that all human beings may or do eventually attain salvation."[32] We have seen earlier in this chapter that Sachs claims there is now a consensus among theologians, which is the direct opposite of the earlier consensus. Dulles mentions a posthumous "reverie" by Maritain where he speculates that even the "damned" may eventually end up in a limbo-like state, as well as the writings of Rahner and Balthasar, as examples of this break with the tradition.[33]

Dulles summarizes the clear consensus of the tradition:

> The constant teaching of the Catholic Church supports the idea that there are two classes: the saved and the damned. Three General councils of the Church (Lyons I, 1245; Lyons II, 1274; and Florence, 1439) and Pope Benedict XII's bull *Benedictus Deus* (1336) have taught that everyone who dies in a state of mortal sin goes immediately to suffer the eternal punishments of hell. This belief has perdured without question in the Catholic Church to this day, and is repeated almost verbatim in the *Catechism of the Catholic Church* (CCC #1022, 1035).[34]

Balthasar knows the relevant Scripture and tradition well. He probably would not disagree with Dulles's account of the weight of Scripture and tradition.

Balthasar acknowledges that there is a constant stream of clear teaching on the reality of hell. "Following Matthew 25, which remains the leading text, the reality of hell is adhered to without exception: beginning with the martyrdom of Polycarp (in 156) through Justin and Tertullian . . . all the way down to Augustine and his descendants."[35] He cites Basil's and Chrysostom's sermons as evidence of how deeply and widely the "two-fold judgment" message of Scripture was literally understood. "[They] popularized a doctrine that was understood since the beginning of Church history, both by simple believers and — as we have seen — by many theologians, as the straightforwardly literal interpretation of the 'two-fold judgment' in Matthew 25 and other New Testament statements."[36]

As Edward Oakes summarizes it: "Ever since the condemnation of Origenism in the fifth century, the Christian Church has pretty much taken it for granted, at least in the West (which has lived so much under the shadow cast by that giant of the spirit, St. Augustine), that hell is rather more populated than heaven."[37]

Despite the weight of Scripture and the authoritative interpretation of the magisterial and theological tradition, Balthasar claims that we should not try to harmonize the two streams of Scripture, one of which speaks clearly of the twofold judgment, and the other of which seems to speak of universal salvation. "We shall not try here to press these biblically irreconcilable statements into a speculative system."[38] He counsels the abandonment of such efforts in favor of an "agnosticism" about the results of judgment.

"Let us cast aside what leads to such dead-ends and limit ourselves to the truth that we all stand under God's absolute judgment."[39] Casting aside two thousand years of profound theological reflection on the unity and harmony of these "conflicting" streams of Scripture seems a bit radical.

Grisez claims that, despite his admonition, in fact Balthasar does try to reconcile these two streams of passages but precisely in a universalist direction.[40]

Part of Balthasar's methodology is to acknowledge the thrust of the combined witness of Scripture and tradition in various places in his work, and then boldly seek to counter it. He does this first of all, as we have noted, by asserting that the various streams of Scripture on this topic cannot be reconciled, effectively neutralizing Scripture. He then attempts to show that there is wider support in the tradition for the "minority" position than commonly understood. He then rejects the traditional theological synthesis which attempts to reconcile the universal will of God to save all with the reality of human freedom which manifestly is capable of rejecting grace. He insists that the "saints" should have the "last word," and claims them as support for his position. Having done this, he summarizes his conclusion by utilizing a text of Edith Stein which, he affirms, "expresses most exactly the position that I have tried to develop."[41] She speculates on how grace can secretly work in the souls of apparent unbelievers as "all-merciful love" descends to everyone.

> And now, can we assume that there are souls that remain perpetually closed to such love? As a possibility in principle, this cannot be rejected. *In reality,* it can become infinitely improbable — precisely through what preparatory grace is capable of effecting in the soul. . . . Human freedom can be neither broken nor neutralized by divine freedom, but it may well be, so to speak, outwitted.[42]

Balthasar often "stands behind" theologians that he favorably quotes, but seldom is he as direct in his endorsement of their views as he is here in his claim that Stein's views most exactly represent his position. In the end, then, Balthasar is teaching that even though it is theoretically possible for someone to be damned it is "infinitely improbable." We will now examine in some detail Balthasar's main arguments and some of the most important commentary on them.

Balthasar's Approach to Scripture

One of Balthasar's most active expositors and defenders, Edward Oakes, frankly states that "the whole value and validity of Balthasar's theology for the Church in the coming millennium will hinge on the validity of his approach to the Scriptures."[43] This would be true really of any theologian, since Scripture is the soul of theology. Because of the importance of assessing Balthasar's use of Scripture in order to arrive at a proper evaluation of his speculative theology, we need to devote adequate space to it in this chapter. First we need to look at what Balthasar specifically says about some of the main hermeneutical principles he is utilizing in his approach to Scripture.

Despite his severe criticism of Rahner's theories on the anonymous Christian, and his critique of the subordinate role that Rahner gives to Scripture,[44] Balthasar appeals to Rahner's approach to eschatological texts as support for his understanding of them as simply warnings and not predictions about actual future events. What then is the Rahnerian approach that Balthasar adopts?

In his significant essay on hermeneutics Rahner makes some rather sweeping assertions.[45] He claims that any eschatological assertion that cannot be reduced to Christology and anthropology should be viewed, dismissively, as "apocalyptic."

> It can therefore also be said that Christ himself is the hermeneutic principle of all eschatological assertions. Anything that cannot be read and understood as a Christological assertion is not a genuine eschatological assertion. It is soothsaying and apocalyptic, or a form of speech which misunderstands the Christological element, because couched in a style and an imagery borrowed from other sources.[46]

He claims that any challenge to his approach can only be accepted if it shows that an interpretation is restricting an assertion about Christology or dogmatic anthropology.

> Where the line cannot be clearly drawn between content and mode of assertion in an eschatological assertion of Scripture or tradition, a minimizing interpretation can only be contested when it can be proved that such a restriction also meant in fact a restriction applied to the assertions which are at the base of eschatology, the assertions of Christology and dogmatic anthropology.[47]

Rahner claims that the "two ways" theme of the Bible is really an Old Testament theme and does not carry over into the New Testament. One of the "ways" (the way of blessing and salvation) is an established fact and should be focused on; the other "way" (the way of curse and condemnation) is only an existential possibility for the individual to reflect on for himself and should only be mentioned as a theoretical possibility.[48] As in other theses that he puts forward, he admits that there could be some challenges to his approach to eschatological hermeneutics, and he mentions one such possibility. He notes that Jesus might actually know about and be speaking about actual future events and not just be making existential appeals to present decisions.[49] Of course, if Jesus did actually know and teach about future outcomes, this would completely undermine Rahner's and Balthasar's approach to Scripture. Rahner also once again casually mentions that his theory of how to interpret apparent statements about the future as present existential appeals would have to be tested against a detailed exegesis of "the various texts of the magisterium and of Scripture," but claims that "it is evidently impossible to do these studies here."[50] A cursory glance at the eschatological statements of Scripture and their traditional interpretation, as represented in the Catechism of the Catholic Church, shows that many of the eschatological assertions of Scripture are indeed understood by the Church as statements about future events (CCC 992-1060). Peter Phan gives a sympathetic account of Rahner's hermeneutical approach to eschatological statements but also acknowledges some significant weaknesses.

> With regard to hell, Rahner reiterates that eschatological assertions are not "advance coverage" of the beyond or of what is going to happen at the end of time. The biblical statements about eternal punishment and the various images used to describe it do not offer a preview of future punishment but should be interpreted in keeping with their literary genre of "threat discourse." . . . Because biblical statements on hell are not factual descriptions but a summons to personal decision for God, it is not possible to know from them whether there are people in hell or how many. . . . For Rahner, then, the doctrine of *apocatastasis* is justified by the virtue of hope, not as a statement of fact or an apodictic prediction, but as an object of hope and prayer. . . . What is Rahner's strength may arguably be his limitation. Since his anthropology is basically transcendental Thomism, his eschatology, which is based upon it, is liable to the weaknesses this anthropology entails. For example, it has been

pointed out that Rahner's brand of Thomism is too indebted to Hegelian and Kantian legacies to be able to incorporate fully biblical data on various eschatological themes. For instance, his notion of freedom as the capacity for definitive and final self-determination has been criticized for not giving full scope to the biblical understanding of sin. . . . This notion has also led to Rahner's endorsement of Gisbert Greshake's controversial theory of immediate resurrection in death and to the eclipse of the biblical teaching on the resurrection as an event at the end of time. . . . Another objection to Rahner's *anthropologische Wende* is that his concept of eschatology as an "extrapolation" into the future of what has already happened in human history does not leave much room for the *novum* of the still-to-be-realized kingdom of God.[51]

It is clear that Rahner's hermeneutics of eschatological statements is radically reductionist, but Balthasar nevertheless adopts it as his own.

Balthasar's approach is to acknowledge the many passages that speak of a division of the human race between those who say "yes" to the grace of God and live in accordance with the light they receive, and those who apparently say "no" to the grace of God and live in a way that Scripture indicates will lead to exclusion from the Kingdom. He then points out that there are a number of Scripture passages that seem to point in the direction of the possibility of all being saved. He acknowledges that theology and the teaching Church over the centuries have seen their role as synthesizing these passages into an intelligible whole — an effort he argues should not be attempted — which has resulted in a widely accepted interpretation that can be summarized like this:

While God wills that the whole human race be saved, and the offer of salvation be extended to every human being, even to those who never have had the chance to hear the gospel, and while where sin abounds grace abounds even more, and while the redemption of Christ is more powerful than the sin of Adam, and while the atonement of Christ is more than sufficient to save the entire human race, God wills that there has to be a freely given "yes" on the part of each human being to accept the grace of redemption and live in accordance with it, in order for an individual to be saved. The testimony of Scripture gives the impression that while many say "yes," many more say "no."

Balthasar claims that even though a theological synthesis like the above paragraph has been accepted by the Church throughout her history as a reasonable harmony of the various Scriptures on the subject, such a synthesis of these Scriptures should not be accepted and should no longer be attempted.[52] He claims that these texts should simply be left to stand side by side in their contrasting emphasis, with no conclusions drawn, no syntheses attempted. Kevin Flannery points out that he offers no argument to support this unusual position.[53] Into this stalemate, then, theological speculation can tread. However, as Wainwright puts it, Balthasar has difficulty preserving the stalemate, and clearly tilts towards a universalist "synthesis."

> He will offer an account that handles "universalist" interpretations of the complex data *gently* while drawing the *sting* out from the "double outcome" verses, so that he at least risks what in principle he denies as legitimate, namely, the "possibility of subordinating one [series of scriptural texts] to the other" (ET 1, 267). . . . There is no mistaking where Balthasar's sympathies lie. In one heavily sarcastic passage in particular, he castigates the "infernalists" for making distinctions that, while retaining the notion of God's benevolent will, nevertheless allow it to be frustrated by man's wickedness (DWH, 183-186). For his part, Balthasar admits that the "double outcome" passages "weaken the force" of the "universal" ones, but he denies that they invalidate them (DWH, 186-187). He consistently questions taking the New Testament's "extreme warnings as implying the factual existence of a populated hell" (DWH, 179).[54]

Flannery makes a similar point.

> It is apparent that Balthasar does not really believe that the two types of passage should be left with a "cleft" between them (*Dare We Hope*, 23), since he attempts to resolve the tension between them himself. . . . Balthasar closes the gap by giving more weight to the second type of passage (interpreted in a particular way), thereby "conditionalising" the first type.[55]

Schenk comes to a similar conclusion:

> However, despite these reflections and the frequently repeated rhetoric of treating the "real possibility" of final loss with an "uncompromising seriousness," . . . it becomes clear with time that Balthasar sees this only as an "infinitely improbable possibility," no more likely than the possi-

bility that God would have to view creation as an ultimate failure. . . . The one side of the apparent option is treated with scorn: "I do not wish to contradict anyone who, as a Christian, cannot be happy without denying the universality of hope to us so that he can be certain of his full hell" (*Dare We Hope*, 187). With that, the appearance of any antinomy is dissolved, and the second alternative becomes the only one with any semblance of plausibility or decency.[56]

Balthasar also explores an approach which would attempt to divide the NT canon between what he first describes as the pre-Easter gospel accounts of Jesus' own teaching, and the "more enlightened" post-resurrection accounts of the Epistles.[57] In *Theo-drama* IV, he bluntly says: "It must be said at the outset that all the words of the Lord that point to the possibility of eternal perdition take place before Easter."[58] This, of course, is to ignore the harmony between the words of Jesus in the Gospels on the final judgment with the same post Resurrection two-outcome result carried forward in the apostolic teaching and preaching. It is also to ignore, as Oakes points out, that these very words of Jesus on judgment, including all the judgment parables, were treasured by the early Church, after they had experienced the immense enlightenment of the Easter and Pentecost experiences, and incorporated into catechetical teaching and preaching.[59] When Balthasar comments on the words of Jesus in John's Gospel (John 9:30 "For judgment have I come into the world") he invokes the commentary of Adrienne von Speyr, which he quotes: "It is one of those words of the Lord that are still spoken before the actual redemption on the Cross, at a time when the light had not yet fully penetrated the darkness."[60] Eventually, as Balthasar thinks through this thesis, he is forced to admit that the Gospel accounts themselves were post-resurrection texts, and the Epistles themselves contain strong affirmation of the two destinations of the human race at the final judgment (e.g., Rom. 1:17–2:11; 1 Cor. 3:11-15; 2 Cor. 5:10; 1 Thess. 1:10; 2 Thess. 1:5-10; Heb. 6:4-8; 10:26-31; John 3:18-21, 36; 5:29; 12:48; 1 John 2:18-25). In a footnote concerning Balthasar's insistence that the parables of judgment are warnings, not declarations of what will happen, Oakes acknowledges that to interpret certain parables in this manner — and he especially mentions the Parable of the Sheep and the Goats — seems to be a stretch, "and if Balthasar's exegetical ground is shaky there, it will prove unstable everywhere else as well."[61] Germain Grisez states his comments on Balthasar's "everything is only a warning" approach more bluntly.

The claim that the Scripture passages which speak of the future damnation of unrepentant sinners are threats that may not be actually realized in the way stated implies that those making the threats — and, therefore, the Holy Spirit, who asserts whatever the human authors of Scripture assert (see DV 11) — may have been bluffing, that is, may have lied.

Indeed, in suggesting that Jesus' warnings — for example, those quoted by Vatican II — may have been empty threats, von Balthasar implies that Jesus himself may have misrepresented the Father, making him seem other than Jesus knew him to be. But the Holy Spirit cannot have lied, and Jesus cannot have misrepresented the Father. So, von Balthasar's attempt to deal with those Scripture passages is unacceptable. Nor does he help matters by suggesting, as he sometimes does, that such Scripture passages can be understood as warnings that tell us nothing about what will actually happen in the future but are meant only to motivate present repentance and fidelity. For the very notions of threat and warning imply a reference — truthful or not, accurate or not — to what *will* happen if a certain condition is fulfilled, in this case if one dies in unrepented mortal sin.[62]

At one point Oakes comments on Balthasar's endorsement of Speyr's interpretation of the above-mentioned judgment text in John's Gospel: "It seems odd to call the discourses of Jesus in John unaffected by the resurrection."[63] Wainwright, in his essay on Balthasar's eschatology, points out the same puzzling approach to Scripture.[64] If Balthasar's approach to the interpretation of the judgment teaching of the Scriptures misses the mark, so will his theological speculations. Alyssa Pitstick provides an important analysis of his faulty approach to Scripture in his inconsistent evaluation of "culturally conditioned" aspects of Scripture, especially in his pivotal interpretations of "Sheol." "In order to found his theology of Sheol, Balthasar explicitly excludes certain books of Scripture."[65] Also, "Despite his own explicit acknowledgments of the divine inspiration of Scripture, Scripture passages that would conflict with his position are either glossed into compatibility, dismissed as interpretations of the human author or well-meant additions to what really happened, or simply omitted."[66] Whether it be Balthasar's lifelong attraction to theories of universalism or Speyr's alleged revelations, something other than an objective interpretation of Scripture is at work here.

W. T. Dickens has written a sympathetic account of Balthasar's writings on biblical hermeneutics, pointing out Balthasar's many affirmations of the need to treat the Bible as a harmonious whole, and interpret one part of Scripture in the light of the rest of Scripture, what is today called "intratextuality." Yet regretfully, Dickens concludes: "Notwithstanding the clarity of his pronouncements in this regard, Balthasar frequently failed to follow his own counsel. There are numerous examples in the volume on the Old Covenant in *The Glory of the Lord* in which he based his exegesis on a reconstructed *Urtext*."[67] O'Connor also comments on some of the problems connected with Balthasar's treatment of Scripture.[68]

Schenk insightfully identifies Balthasar's strained approach to both Scripture and tradition.

> To reach the position that the one line of statements in Scripture and tradition suggesting the facticity of some final loss meant to affirm nothing more than an infinitely implausible possibility, Balthasar, as he himself admits, adopts what must appear to be a highly selective approach for his scriptural interpretations, reminiscent of the dualistic division between letter and Spirit common in Reformed hermeneutics from their beginning. . . . A similar approach must be taken with regard to the theological tradition as well, although here Balthasar seems more willing to dismiss openly one side of the tradition reaching back beyond Jesus of Nazareth. Given the greater reliance of Balthasar's method on scriptural and traditional texts, given the less general or merely fundamentally theological aim of his theology, the predominance given here to a "hermeneutics of suspicion" represents more of an internal methodological crisis than similar statements in Rahner's work.[69]

This same criticism, as we will soon see, is also applicable to his interpretation of the mystics. He sometimes argues a point, attempting to gain some traction with it in support of his thesis, but later has to acknowledge that it is not a strong point, perhaps thinking that a weak point is better than no point.[70] Balthasar's approach to Scripture is not only in tension with the historical-critical method but in tension with the whole tradition of interpretation, both theological and magisterial, on the texts that he considers. The impression one gets as Balthasar wrestles with the texts of the twofold judgment is that he is doing everything but taking the claim on its own terms. Oakes claims that "The defense of the faith of the 'simple' . . . is an important theme in Balthasar's writings, especially in his shorter works."[71] It is ironic then that the approach to Scripture on the twofold judgment that Balthasar takes would be shocking to the "simple" as they read these texts themselves and interpret them as the tradition has always interpreted them. His interpretations would be shocking also to the cloud of witnesses among the saints that he so frequently invokes as a *locus theologicus,* as well as the whole theological and magisterial tradition.

O'Connor points out reasons why many contemporary approaches to eschatological assertions contained in the Scripture trail off into vagueness, especially mentioning the hermeneutical approaches of both Rahner and Balthasar. The philosophical pressure of Heidegger and the exegetical pressure of Bultmann loomed large over Catholic theology in Germany. Ratzinger points out that Bultmann's rejection of the Ascension and second coming of Christ as "mythological" put great pressure on eschatological reflection among Catholics.[72]

O'Connor expands this insight:

> The lack of concreteness in many theological treatises on the life to come occurs, I believe, because, not infrequently, theologians have accepted as axiomatic the theorem that Biblical language about the future is *merely* symbolic, figurative, or metaphorical. This inadequate perception is found in too much of the writing about the *hermeneutics* or meaning of eschatological statements.[73]

Because Balthasar was against some post–Vatican II trends, including liberation theology and the ordination of women, and because he defended the Pope and favored obligatory celibacy for the clergy, he has been viewed as a conservative by many.[74] Oakes calls Balthasar's eschatology, which he developed as a result of his approach to Scripture and tradition, his "single greatest innovation in theology" and acknowledges his departure from the consensus of Scripture and tradition in a theory "teeming with optimism and hope" as a reason for not pigeonholing Balthasar under a "conservative" label.[75]

Specific Texts: The Judgment Texts

We will now take a look at some of the texts[76] that Balthasar thinks are most challenging to his thesis that damnation is only a highly unlikely theoretical possibility.[77]

The principles of interpretation that we will employ will be those contained in *Dei verbum* (Dogmatic Constitution on Divine Revelation). The important teaching of *DV* 11 will form the backdrop for our consideration of the following texts, most particularly the inspired authorship and the unity of Scripture.

> Since, therefore, all that the inspired authors, or sacred writers, affirm should be regarded as affirmed by the Holy Spirit, we must acknowledge that the books of Scripture firmly, faithfully and without error, teach that truth which God, for the sake of our salvation, wished to see confided to the Sacred Scriptures. (*DV* 11)

As Cardinal Ratzinger put it: "The Catholic tradition . . . trusts the evangelists; it believes what they say."[78] And he continues:

> But since sacred Scripture must be read and interpreted with its divine authorship in mind, no less attention must be devoted to the content and unity of the whole of Scripture, taking into account the Tradition of the entire Church and the analogy of faith, if we are to derive their true meaning from the sacred texts. (*DV* 12)[79]

Perhaps the text to which Balthasar refers most often is the well-known judgment scene in Matthew's Gospel, where judgment is based on how the least of the brethren have been treated.

> When the Son of Man comes in his glory, and all the angels with him, he will sit upon his glorious throne, and all the nations will be assembled before him. And he will separate them one from another, as a shepherd separates the sheep from the goats. He will place the sheep on his right and the goats on his left. Then the king will say to those on his right, "Come, you who are blessed by my Father. Inherit the kingdom prepared for you from the foundation of the world. . . ." Then he will say to those on his left, "Depart from me, you accursed, into the eternal fire prepared for the devil and his angels. . . ." And these will go off to eternal punishment, but the righteous to eternal life. (Matt. 25:31-46)

Another text that Balthasar frequently notes as a challenge to his theory is the text that transmits the solemn words of Jesus to the effect that everyone will be raised from the dead, some to glory and some to damnation.

> Amen, amen, I say to you, whoever hears my word and believes in the one who sent me has eternal life and will not come to condemnation,

but has passed from death to life. . . . Do not be amazed at this, because the hour is coming in which all who are in the tombs will hear his voice and will come out, those who have done good deeds to the resurrection of life, but those who have done wicked deeds to the resurrection of condemnation. (John 5:24, 28-29)

As to the text of the missionary sending as reported in the Gospel of Mark, Balthasar claims it should be interpreted not as a report of actually different outcomes but as a current challenge to decide.[80]

He said to them, "Go into the whole world and proclaim the gospel to every creature. Whoever believes and is baptized will be saved; whoever does not believe will be condemned." (Mark 16:15-17)

The text that he says he finds most challenging is the somber warning of Hebrews that speaks of the impossibility of being saved if the salvation given and once accepted is spurned.[81]

For it is impossible in the case of those who have once been enlightened and tasted the heavenly gift and shared in the Holy Spirit and tasted the good word of God and the powers of the age to come, and then have fallen away, to bring them to repentance again, since they are recrucifying the Son of God for themselves and holding him up to contempt. Ground that has absorbed the rain falling upon it repeatedly and brings forth crops useful to those for whom it is cultivated receives a blessing from God. But if it produces thorns and thistles, it is rejected; it will soon be cursed and finally burned. (Heb. 6:4-8)

And also:

If we sin deliberately after receiving knowledge of the truth, there no longer remains sacrifice for sins but a fearful prospect of judgment and a flaming fire that is going to consume the adversaries. Anyone who rejects the law of Moses is put to death without pity on the testimony of two or three witnesses. Do you not think that a much worse punishment is due the one who has contempt for the Son of God, considers unclean the covenant-blood by which he was consecrated, and insults the spirit of grace? We know the one who said: "Vengeance is mine; I will repay," and again: "The Lord will judge his people." It is a fearful thing to fall into the hands of the living God. (Heb. 10:26-31 NAB)

He claims that even though these texts, and many others,[82] appear to be definitively declaring that there will be a final separation of the human race and that some will be saved and some will be lost, and even though the overwhelming theological tradition of the Church has read these passages in such a way, on the contrary, they should really only be read as "warnings" that will not necessarily actually happen.

Another text that he finds challenging is the judgment scene found in the Book of Revelation.

> The one who sat on the throne said, "Behold, I make all things new." Then he said, "Write these words down, for they are trustworthy and true." He said to me, "They are accomplished. I (am) the Alpha and the Omega, the beginning and the end. To the thirsty I will give a gift from the spring of life-giving water. The victor will inherit these gifts, and I shall be his God, and he will be my son. But as for cowards, the unfaithful, the depraved, murderers, the unchaste, sorcerers, idol-worshipers, and deceivers of every sort, their lot is in the burning pool of fire and sulfur, which is the second death." (Rev. 21:5-8)

He acknowledges that these words of John are very similar to the warning of Paul:

> Do you not know that the unjust will not inherit the kingdom of God? Do not be deceived; neither fornicators nor idolaters nor adulterers nor boy prostitutes nor sodomites nor thieves nor the greedy nor drunkards nor slanderers nor robbers will inherit the kingdom of God.[83] (1 Cor. 6:9-11)

For an interpretation of the text from Revelation, Balthasar suggests we turn to Adrienne von Speyr, which shows how closely their positions coincide.

> It seems now as if there are also blank pages in the book of life. And it is not known now whether that which seems blank to man is also blank for God. . . . John sees the condemned in the position of being cast down, because he must bear witness to this *possibility;* this witness is part of his mission; he must be able to report that he has seen it, since it belongs, as a possibility, to the essence of judgment, and in order to be able to report it, he must have seen it.[84]

In light of the fancifulness of this interpretation, Balthasar's criticism of Barth would seem to apply in his own case in this respect as well.

> It is not so much a matter of Barth omitting some crucial doctrine as it is a distortion of nuance, an inappropriate coloration to the whole. In Catholic terms, we may call it an exaggeration, an overstatement, a failure of balance.[85]

Or, as Ratzinger put it in connection with some issues concerned with *GS*, the position is "alien to the biblical-thought world or even antipathetic to its spirit."[86]

Both the texts, that of John from Revelation and Paul's text from 1 Corinthians, definitively teach that there are those who will be excluded from the Kingdom, condemned to the second death, if they persist in unrepented serious sin, examples of which are listed. There is the further admonition that this teaching is "trustworthy and true," and there are warnings against being deceived concerning the behavior that will exclude one from the Kingdom.

The ITC in its document on eschatology, in the context of addressing the weakening of many Catholics' grasp on foundational truths of the gospel, puts it like this:

> Death in the Lord implies the possibility of another way of dying, namely death outside the Lord, which leads to a second death (cf. Rev 20:14). For in this death, the power of sin through which death entered (cf. Rom 5:12) manifests to the fullest extent its capacity to separate us from God. . . . The Church believes that the definitive state of damnation awaits those who die burdened with grave sin.[87]

Balthasar provides his own minimizing commentary on the passage from Paul: "In Paul's case, we have a warning and admonition to historically living men that they should mend their ways and not believe that they will automatically enter heaven."[88]

However, Paul's words are both more specific and more strongly put than Balthasar's paraphrase. Paul is saying that we must be on guard against the specific deception that would water down the behavior that will exclude one from the Kingdom, the deception of explaining away the clear message of revelation. From other contexts we know that Paul teaches that the human heart is inclined to seek out teachers who will tell them what they want to hear, that false teachers and prophets are active in the community, and that his readers need to be clear that persisting in certain very specific immoral behaviors will definitely exclude them from the Kingdom.[89]

There are obvious problems with proposing that all these texts be interpreted as simply "existential" warnings for the "now," and that nothing can be claimed on their basis about the future. In fact, it is virtually impossible, just on the basis of a grammatical/literary analysis, to interpret these passages as anything other than declarative statements about what in fact will happen in the future and what will be the outcome of the choices that people make.

The key texts are not presented as warnings of "possible" outcomes but as declarative statements of what will indeed happen if one dies in unrepented, serious sin. Certainly Scripture makes statements about the future that are either explicitly or implicitly conditional. When a question arises about how to interpret Scripture, how that Scripture has been received, understood, and interpreted in the tradition of the Church is critical. The theological and magisterial traditions that relate to this issue have always understood these statements — taking full account of the second series of statements that we will examine shortly that speak of God's universal will for salvation — as declaring certainly that there will be a twofold division of the human race, and that those who die in unrepented, serious sin will be excluded from the Kingdom. When the Scripture uses the future, indicative tense to communicate a meaning, it is specifically not making a conditional statement, and this is how the tradition has understood the statements in question. O'Connor in some detail shows the continuity of this tradition of interpretation from the *Quicumque* (Athanasian Creed, date uncertain, perhaps the fifth century) to the *Firmiter* (Creed of the Fourth Lateran Council of 1215) to the *Benedictus Deus* of Benedict XII of 1336, up until Vatican II and beyond. His comments on *LG* 48, which speaks of the twofold outcome of judgment, are of interest. First, the relevant text of *LG* 48:

> Indeed since we know neither the day nor the hour it is necessary to keep vigil constantly, as the Lord warned us, so that, having completed the one course of our earthly life we may merit to enter the marriage banquet with Him and be numbered among the blessed (cf. Matt. 25:31-46) and so that we not be commanded, like evil and lazy servants, to descend to eternal fire (cf. Matt. 25:41) in the exterior darkness where there

will be "weeping and the gnashing of teeth" (Matt. 22:13 and 25:30). For, before we reign gloriously with Christ, all of us will stand before the "tribunal of Christ, so that each may give an account of what he has done in the body, whether good or bad" (2 Cor. 5:10) and at the end of the world "those who have done good will go to the resurrection of life, those indeed who have done evil will go to the resurrection of judgment." (John 5:29; cf. Matt. 25:46)

O'Connor points out, as have other commentators, that one bishop at the council requested that an explicit text be inserted in *LG* 48 to make clear that there are indeed damned souls so as to rule out damnation as a merely hypothetical outcome. The Theological Commission replied that no additional text was needed, since "In no. 48 there are cited the words of the Gospel in which the Lord Himself speaks about the damned in a form which is grammatically future."[90]

The significance of that remark is that when the Church speaks of damnation of humans she speaks, as Christ himself did, not in a form of grammar which is *conditional* (i.e., speaking about something which *might* happen) but in the *grammatical future* (i.e., about something which *will* happen). And it was with this understanding that the bishops of Vatican II voted upon and accepted *Lumen Gentium*.[91]

O'Connor considers the further objection that these passages are not intended to give us a description of the future and cannot be considered as absolute proof, but only information about the future that clarifies our present choices. He replies:

It is true indeed that the future has not been described for us. Only enough has been revealed to stimulate our hope and desire, and to warn us that not all will share what is to be hoped for and desired. But the indications of what is to be hoped for, and the indications that not all will share those wonderful realities must be taken with equal seriousness.[92]

O'Connor makes the further point that the postconciliar documents adopt the same interpretation and use the same future indicative grammar as the Scripture and the entire tradition.[93]

When the International Theological Commission took up the issue of eschatological statements, it noted that the powerful influence of secularism on contemporary culture exerted great pressure on Christians to be silent about eschatological assertions and reduce them to pious exhortations to live well now, removing from them any real future time referent. In addressing theories of resurrection that make resurrection simultaneous with death, the ITC makes the case that Scripture clearly teaches the existence of the soul apart from the body, and clearly teaches a consummation, including resurrection, that will not happen until Jesus' actual Second Coming, which will be a real event that concludes human history as we know it.

> The New Testament's way of speaking about the souls of the martyrs does not seem to remove them either from all reality of succession or from all perception of succession (cf. Rev 6:9-11). Similarly, if time should have no meaning after death, not even in some way merely analogous with its terrestrial meaning, it would be difficult to understand why Paul used formulas referring to the future *(anastesontai)* in speaking about their resurrection, when speaking to the Thessalonians who were asking about the fate of the dead (cf. 1 Thes 4:13-18).[94]

In citing the Church's liturgical prayers for the dead and affirming that "the law of prayer is the law of belief," the ITC document declares: "It is clear from this text that the resurrection not only belongs to the future — that is, it is not yet in effect — but will take place at the end of the world."[95]

Jesus, John, Matthew, Luke, Mark, James, Peter, and Paul in the multiple texts that talk of the final judgment of the human race are unmistakably declaring that if people persist in unbelief and immorality to the end, they will be eternally lost. There is nothing in Scripture to indicate that there are second chances after death, but rather, just the opposite.[96] Life is emptied of its meaning if our choices do not end up really mattering for our eternal destinies.

As the ITC document puts it:

> In revealing the Father's secrets to us, Jesus wants to make us his friends (cf. Jn 15:15). But friendship cannot be forced on us. Friendship with God, like adoption, is an offer, to be freely accepted or rejected. . . . This consummated and freely accepted friendship implies a concrete possibility of rejection. What is freely accepted can be freely rejected. [No one who] thus chooses rejection "has any inheritance in the kingdom of Christ and of God" (Eph 5:5). Eternal damnation has its origin in the

free rejection to the very end of God's Love and Mercy. The Church believes that this state consists of deprivation of the sight of God and that the whole "being" of the sinner suffers the repercussion of this loss eternally. . . . This doctrine of faith shows equally the importance of the human capacity of freely rejecting God, and the gravity of such a freely willed rejection.[97]

While we cannot judge the state of anyone's soul and what transpires at the moment of death, it certainly appears — from the view of human resistance to grace, and subsequent judgment, contained in the Scriptures and from empirical observation — that many people persevere to the end in their rejection of God and/or in a life of immorality. Balthasar acknowledges as much, but then posits the possible chance(s) after death, for which there is no basis in Scripture or the magisterium. He claims that those who take the traditional interpretation of these texts on judgment, following Augustine (but also Aquinas and the entire theological/magisterial mainstream) — that there will be a definitive separation of the human race based on how people have responded to the grace of God — have "transformed" and indeed, "vitiated" the Scriptures which, he claims, only warn of a possibility and do not teach that there will indeed be a division of the human race into the saved and damned. Such an interpretation seems strained.

Dulles summarizes the meaning of the "two destination" NT passages like this:

As we know from the Gospels, Jesus spoke many times about hell. Throughout his teaching, he holds forth two and only two final possibilities for human existence: the one being everlasting happiness in the presence of God, the other everlasting torment in the absence of God. He describes the fate of the damned under a great variety of metaphors: everlasting fire, outer darkness, tormenting thirst, a gnawing worm, and weeping and gnashing of teeth. . . . Taken in their obvious meaning, passages such as these give the impression that there is a hell, and that many go there; more in fact, than are saved.[98]

Even if one does not want to claim that these passages indisputably reveal that there are people in hell, despite the tradition's understanding, one would at least have to say that from the weight of these Scriptures and the historical testimony of final rejection of God or embrace of immorality, both in Scripture and contemporary history and experience, it is not just a theoretical possibility but probable, that many end up in hell.[99] Flannery acknowledges that a case can be made that Scripture does not imply with the force of logical necessity that there are people in hell. He argues though that the overwhelming weight of Scripture and tradition "approach logical necessity."[100] As O'Connor puts it, these passages and how they have been interpreted by the theological tradition and the magisterium lead us to *presume* that there will be many in hell, a presumption that the Holy Spirit who inspired the Scriptures intends us to have, a presumption imparted to us by a God who is utterly truthful and cannot deceive.

> In the light of what it has been given us to know, we must *presume* that (in numbers completely unknown to us) humans will be included in "the eternal fire prepared for the devil and his angels" (Matt. 25:41), and that we ourselves could be among that number. It is such a presumption that the words of Jesus and the teaching of the Church would appear to have as their own, and better guides in this matter we cannot have. Against such a presumption one cannot have what is properly defined as *theological* hope, but we can and must have a human hope, a wish which expresses itself in prayer and zealous efforts, for the salvation of all.[101]

This "presumption" which is given to us in Scripture and tradition is different from the prevailing "presumption" that everybody or almost everybody will be saved, and that finite human freedom is unable to finally resist the grace of God. The current "theological consensus" as Sachs has stated it is precisely the reverse of what has been revealed to us as it has been understood by the Church throughout the ages.

Specific Texts: The Universal Salvation Texts

The second part of Balthasar's argument is that as definitive as the texts of twofold judgment appear to be, they are actually "contradicted" by other texts that may indicate that everyone will be saved. Some of the main texts he cites in this regard are from Paul.[102]

> First of all, then, I ask that supplications, prayers, petitions, and thanksgivings be offered for everyone, for kings and for all in authority,

that we may lead a quiet and tranquil life in all devotion and dignity. This is good and pleasing to God our savior, who wills everyone to be saved and to come to knowledge of the truth. For there is one God. There is also one mediator between God and the human race, Christ Jesus, himself human, who gave himself as ransom for all. (1 Tim. 2:1-6)

Another text that Balthasar thinks is particularly relevant to his argument is this:

For this we toil and struggle, because we have set our hope on the living God, who is the savior of all, especially of those who believe. (1 Tim. 4:10)

Since his argument is that it is not only possible but that we have a duty to hope that everyone will be saved, he notes the reference to hope in relationship to the salvation of all. However, even within the same chapter it is clear that Paul does not expect everyone to be saved.

Now the Spirit explicitly says that in the last times some will turn away from the faith by paying attention to deceitful spirits and demonic instructions through the hypocrisy of liars with branded consciences. (1 Tim. 4:1-2)

And it is clear that the need to "toil and struggle" is due to the opposition and deception that must be overcome in order for people to come to "knowledge of the truth" and be saved. The "demonic" instructions and the "fables" that people are giving heed to — as the Spirit expressly says — are intended to lead to destruction in this life, and to eternal destruction, for those who give themselves to such teaching.

Attend to yourself and to your teaching; persevere in both tasks, for by doing so you will save both yourself and those who listen to you. (1 Tim. 4:16)

Another text that Balthasar considers significant is 2 Peter 3:9.

The Lord does not delay his promise, as some regard "delay," but he is patient with you, not wishing that any should perish but that all should come to repentance. (2 Pet. 3:9)

But again, the context is ignored. These words are addressed to Christians who are puzzled by the "delay" of the Lord in returning in glory to judge the living and the dead. Paul points out that the delay is in order to give maximal opportunity for repentance. In the very next verse, which Balthasar ignores, Paul points out that there will be a final judgment and because of this it is crucial that Christians redouble their devotion, their lives of holiness, and not be misled. He urges them to be ready so that they will be able to "escape the wrath to come" on the Day of Judgment.

> But the day of the Lord will come like a thief, and then the heavens will pass away with a mighty roar and the elements will be dissolved by fire, and the earth and everything done on it will be found out. Since everything is to be dissolved in this way, what sort of persons ought (you) to be, conducting yourselves in holiness and devotion, waiting for and hastening the coming of the day of God, because of which the heavens will be dissolved in flames and the elements melted by fire. But according to his promise we await new heavens and a new earth in which righteousness dwells. Therefore, beloved, since you await these things, be eager to be found without spot or blemish before him, at peace. . . . Therefore, beloved, since you are forewarned, be on your guard not to be led into the error of the unprincipled and to fall from your own stability. (2 Pet. 3:10-14, 17)

Balthasar, of course, is familiar with the traditional distinction between the "objective" redemption which is available to everyone and the need to appropriate "subjectively" this redemption through repentance and faith. He thinks, though, that there are two texts that cannot be explained this way. The first text is that of Romans 5:12-21. The second text is that of John 12:32. We will consider the Romans text first.

> For if by that one person's transgression the many died, how much more did the grace of God and the gracious gift of the one person Jesus Christ overflow for the many? And the gift is not like the result of the one person's sinning. For after one sin there was the judgment that brought condemnation; but the gift, after many transgressions, brought acquittal. For if, by the transgression of one person, death came to reign through that one, how much more will those who receive the abundance of grace and of the gift of justification come to reign in life through the one person Jesus Christ? In conclusion, just as through one transgression condemna-

tion came upon all, so through one righteous act acquittal and life came to all. For just as through the disobedience of one person the many were made sinners, so through the obedience of one the many will be made righteous. The law entered in so that transgression might increase but, where sin increased, grace overflowed all the more, so that, as sin reigned in death, grace also might reign through justification for eternal life through Jesus Christ our Lord. (Rom. 5:17-21)

It is unclear to me why Balthasar thinks this text should not be interpreted in the traditional way, namely that redemption is available to everyone and is far greater than the sin of Adam, but needs to be received subjectively in order to be personally effective. Since one of the basic principles of Scripture interpretation is that Scripture has to be interpreted in light of Scripture it does not seem credible that this text should be understood as canceling out all the other texts of Paul and the rest of the New Testament that clearly talk about a final judgment which will result in condemnation for whole classes of human beings: unbelievers, the immoral, false teachers, those who deny particular truths, those who lead others astray, etc. As Dulles says: "Some passages in the letters of Paul lend themselves to a more optimistic interpretation, but they can hardly be used to prove that salvation is universal."[103]

The other text to which Balthasar gives great weight is found in John's Gospel: "And when I am lifted up from the earth, I will draw everyone to myself" (John 12:32). Neither when taken in isolation nor, still more, in context is it apparent why this text is supportive of the likelihood of there being an "empty hell." It is clear from the context that Jesus does not anticipate universal assent to his offer of salvation.

"Now is the time of judgment on this world; now the ruler of this world will be driven out. And when I am lifted up from the earth, I will draw everyone to myself." He said this indicating the kind of death he would die. So the crowd answered him, "We have heard from the law that the Messiah remains forever. Then how can you say that the Son of Man must be lifted up? Who is this Son of Man?" Jesus said to them, "The light will be among you only a little while. Walk while you have the light, so that darkness may not overcome you. Whoever walks in the dark does not know where he is going. While you have the light, believe in the light, so that you may become children of the light." . . . Jesus cried out and said, "Whoever believes in me believes not only in me but also in the one who sent me, and whoever sees me sees the one who sent me. I came into the world as light, so that everyone who believes in me might not remain in darkness. And if anyone hears my words and does not observe them, I do not condemn him, for I did not come to condemn the world but to save the world. Whoever rejects me and does not accept my words has something to judge him: the word that I spoke, it will condemn him on the last day, because I did not speak on my own, but the Father who sent me commanded me what to say and speak. And I know that his commandment is eternal life. So what I say, I say as the Father told me." (John 12:31-50)

This is an extremely rich passage about which we can only make a few brief comments. It is obvious from the context that Jesus does not expect his "drawing" of all men to result necessarily in all men allowing themselves to be drawn.[104] In fact, the context of this statement is one of conflict, judgment, rejection, a battle between light and darkness. Those who respond to the light of Jesus and his Word will become children of God; those who do not will be condemned on the last day by the very Word they did not believe, or did not take seriously. The recurring quotation of Isaiah, throughout the New Testament, about the blinding of eyes and hardening of hearts, is revelatory about how the prophecy of Simeon (Luke 2:25-35) will be fulfilled. The encounter with Jesus will reveal what is in people's hearts and will result in the rise of some and the fall of others depending on their response, formed in the deepest recesses of their hearts.[105]

Just as in his earthly ministry Jesus offered salvation to all, seeking to gather all to himself as a mother hen her chicks, but many refused, so too today, as he continues his ministry through the Church and offers salvation to all, there are many who refuse to be gathered.

The Council of Trent gives a definitive interpretation of these texts that seems to rule out Balthasar's interpretations. The Council of Trent is quite clear about the validity of the objective/subjective distinction. Quoting the passage in 1 John 2:2, which states that Jesus is "expiation for our sins, and not for our sins only but for those of the whole world,"[106] the Council goes on to state:

But though *he died for all* (2 Cor 5:15), yet not all receive the benefit of his death, but only those to whom the merit of his passion is imparted. For just as men and women would not actually be born unjust if they were not bred and born from the seed of Adam, since by that descent they incur through him their own state of injustice while they are being conceived; so, if not reborn in Christ, they would never be justified, because by that rebirth there is granted to them, through the merit of his passion, his grace by which they become just.[107]

It is also clear, based on the biblical revelation that the Council so frequently cites, that the transition from the state of injustice, which is the default state of the human race, to the "state of grace and of adoption as children of God (Rom 8:23) . . . once the gospel has been promulgated, cannot take place without the waters of rebirth or the desire for them, as it is written: *Unless a person is born again of water and the holy Spirit, he cannot enter the kingdom of God* (Jn 3:5)."[108]

The Council applies this teaching to every human being, Jew or Gentile.

For a true and genuine understanding of the doctrine of justification, the holy council declares that everyone must acknowledge and confess that since all lost their innocence in the sin of Adam, became unclean (Is. 64:6) and (in the words of the Apostle) *by nature children of wrath* (Eph. 2:3), as is set out in the decree on original sin, they were so far slaves of sin (Rm. 6:20) and under the power of the devil and death, that not only could the gentiles not be freed from or rise above it by the force of nature, but neither could the Jews even by the letter of the law of Moses, though their free will, for all that it had been weakened and sapped in strength, was in no way extinct.[109]

Balthasar's Rejection of the Traditional Theological Synthesis

In order to make room for his theory, Balthasar also needs to dismiss the classic theological attempts to explain how God could will that all men be saved, yet nevertheless not all men actually will be saved. The classic distinction of God's antecedent or conditional will (that all men be saved) and his consequent or absolute will (that all men who accept the offer of salvation be saved) developed by Maximus the Confessor in response to Origenism, carried forward in the tradition by John Damascene and enunciated by Thomas Aquinas and others, and defended ably today by a number of contemporary theologians is dismissed by Balthasar without extensive argumentation.[110]

Balthasar then proposes that even though, based on Scripture, one cannot deny the *possibility* of someone ending up in hell, it is extremely unlikely, given the specific nature of the Redemption that Christ has won for us. Balthasar is well known for his special emphasis on the Holy Saturday "descent into hell" — an article of the Creed that has traditionally been interpreted as the triumphant descent of Christ into the "limbo of the Fathers" where the just awaited their release at the news of Christ's atoning death on their behalf. In this descent, the hell of the damned also is made aware of their eternal destiny because of their rejection of the Redemption that had been offered them in anticipation of the sacrifice of Christ.

Balthasar, though, claims that Christ's descent into hell[111] was actually so that he could experience total rejection by God and experience damnation/hell on behalf of the whole human race, so that no human being would have to suffer this fate. There are serious questions of not only scriptural hermeneutics but also Christological and Trinitarian issues raised by this theory that have been actively challenged by numerous scholars.[112] These issues do not directly concern us here and are obviously beyond the scope of this chapter. Balthasar explains that the entire debt owed to God by the human race has been paid by Christ who literally "became sin" and suffered damnation in such an extreme form that no man now owes anything to God. Everyone, without a violation of justice, can be admitted to heaven. Balthasar further explains that now judgment is totally in Christ's hands since he underwent the "descent" and he can freely choose to pardon or condemn the individuals that appear before him, and without injustice, pardon even those who died unrepentant — or perhaps, he sometimes seems to speculate, there may be another chance for repentance after death.[113]

Pitstick summarizes his position like this:

> Sinful creatures incurred a debt to the Creator Father through their abuse of His loving paternal gift of finite freedom. Having exercised judgment against sin in the Person of Christ, the Father has nothing more to say on the subject, but the Son who suffered that judgment might. Sinners, who were debtors to the Father, have become debtors to the Son, while judgment is the Son's because He has undergone all judgment. By suffering the punishment mankind deserved, He purchased, so to speak, mankind's debt. As a result, He is free to collect it or not.[114]

Oakes regards "the last three volumes of the Theodramatics as the culmination and capstone of [Balthasar's] work, where all the themes of his theology converge and are fused into a synthesis of remarkable creativity and originality, an achievement that makes him one of the great theological mind[s] of the twentieth century." Oakes continues:

> Here, more than anywhere, is where his work should be judged. . . . Describing so densely packed a drama — and one that moreover is shrouded over in darkness by revelation and whose presentation is thus necessarily based on extrapolation and mystical insights — is, it goes without saying, extremely difficult.

Oakes notes that "as the volumes of the Theodramatics progress, the citations from the writings of Adrienne von Speyr grow more frequent (in the last volume she is cited, it seems, on almost every page)."[115]

The same is true of Balthasar's treatment of hell and the Trinity in volume II of *Theo-Logic.* Here Balthasar states that his earlier work, *Mysterium Paschale,* "is an attempt to pave the way for Adrienne von Speyr's bold teaching."[116] His teaching in this section heavily quotes Speyr and puts forth her unusual theory that condemned persons are not in hell but rather their "effigies."[117] Balthasar even suggests that Christ may meet the condemned sinner in hell itself and give him or her a last chance to repent,[118] rather than lose the "gamble" in giving the creature freedom.

Oakes acknowledges that Balthasar is taking "astonishing leaps" that may not be easy to follow or accept.

> We have now come to the point where Balthasar's thought is at its most daring and speculative, where perhaps indeed many will feel left behind, where they feel his thought borders on the very speculative reverie he accuses the nominalists of indulging. How true these reservations are can perhaps emerge only from one's own encounter with his thought. . . .[119]

Oakes thinks Balthasar's effort is fundamentally sound, although he readily admits that these speculations are just that, speculations.

> But he has dared to leap into previously uncharted territory, and we wish both to grant him this speculative freedom and also the right of the Church to assimilate these speculations in her own good time. Private reflections and personal opinions of a theologian, especially one who bases his works so heavily on the graces of a mystic, take time.[120]

Oakes calls Balthasar's teaching — about there perhaps being some mysterious "moment of death" or "after death" last act of God to save everyone so he does not lose his "gamble — after his other arguments have been challenged or rejected," Balthasar's "last trump."

> To which Balthasar has only one response left — his own trump, so to speak, but one that is quite arresting: *if even a single human being is eternally lost by rejecting God and his holy grace, then God has lost the gamble he made with himself when he first created a universe of free beings who were made to receive that love freely.*[121]

When all is said and done, Oakes states, it may all come down to one question: "Perhaps, then, the issue boils down to whether there is a possibility of conversion after death, that is, in hell. Can the Church pronounce on that possibility if revelation has not?"[122]

A strong case can be made, implied in various sections of this chapter, that revelation and the subsequent magisterium as a matter of fact have ruled out the possibility of conversion after death or "conversion in hell."[123]

The Case of the Angels

Balthasar's concern that God will have lost his "gamble" if anyone is lost is considerably weakened and, indeed, runs into the impasse of the fact that the same "gamble" was already and definitively "lost" with the fall of a portion of the angels, also created free. As O'Connor puts it:

> Admitting our very limited knowledge about the history of the angelic order, we know, nevertheless, that some of them rejected God in such a form as to incur eternal damnation. Von Balthasar himself . . . admits this. Yet those spiritual beings were, like us, the work of his [God's] creative love. Creatures of an intelligence and will greater than our own, they too were beings of beauty and, what is more, recipients of divine grace, subjects of his love. Yet, because of their sin, their loving Creator left them to eternal damnation, loving them still — at least to the extent of preserving them in being. Is our love and compassion not to be extended to all those intelligent beings who inhabit this universe with us? Is our love not unreserved because we know that some of them are eter-

nally lost to God and to us? And is it not presumptuous to imagine that we are more worthy of his compassion than they? For one who takes the existence of angels and their history seriously (as von Balthasar does), the damnation of some of them must be a sobering reminder that the all-merciful and just God remains for us beyond our understanding.[124]

Flannery notes, "If God can, without contradicting his own merciful nature, consign an angel to hell, there would seem to be no logical reason why he could not do the same to a human soul."[125]

The solution that the theological tradition has taken in its meditation on the magnitude of the gift of eternal life is that a freely chosen relationship of love with God, necessarily "running the risk" of human freedom, is somehow necessary for the greater good of the human race and the glory of God.

Balthasar claims that because we do not know for sure that there is anyone in hell, not even Judas, and because the will of God is to save all men, and because of the nature of Christ's redemptive sacrifice, we not only can, but have the duty, out of Christian charity, to hope that every human being is saved.

Balthasar acknowledges that he is deeply indebted to Adrienne von Speyr, whose theological reflections on her mystical revelations concerning the descent are, as we have noted, quoted copiously at key points throughout his theological corpus. He insists that her theological reflections based on her mystical experiences not be separated from his theological positions.[126]

While Balthasar knows he is treading a fine line in his argumentation, he nevertheless seems to end up, despite protestations to the contrary, making his theological position very clear, namely, that it is extremely unlikely that there is anyone in hell.

Balthasar, the Fathers, and the Saints

Balthasar devotes considerable attention in *Dare We Hope* to what he claims is a much more widespread support of universalist positions in the Fathers than is commonly recognized. He often speaks of how the early Church writers who either openly or tentatively taught universalism had to be "careful" in their writing. He speaks about how some of them "hinted" in the universalist direction so as to avoid condemnation, and how some intimated at times that only an enlightened elite, who were mature and could handle the knowledge, should be taught this.[127]

> After Emperor Justinian had condemned Origen's teaching, Maximus had to formulate his position on *apokatastasis* very carefully. . . . Maximus himself, like Origen, reserved the teaching about the *apokatastasis panton* for those perfected in love. The doctrine of hell, by then commonly held, he proclaimed in the form of an ascetic admonition. Frequently he uses universalistic formulations like those in Romans 5.[128]

There is some indication, as one might expect would be the case, of Balthasar himself being more open about what he privately held with those he supposed would be sympathetic to his views, and more guarded in his published writings. Barth's biographer, Eberhard Busch, relates several such conversations between Barth and Balthasar, who lived in proximity to each other in Basel. In a conversation with Barth, Balthasar is reported as saying: "That's all right, at last we're quite alone and one can say what one thinks." Busch further reports on the basis of Barth's recollections: "Balthasar first remarked: 'The dogma is that hell exists, not that people are in it.' At any rate, on these evenings Barth discovered to his amazement a Catholic theologian who, he said, 'envisioned a kind of reformation of the Catholic Church and of Catholic theology from within. And now I was to be introduced like a new Trojan horse to bring it about (against Thomas and also against Augustine!).'"[129]

Balthasar's quite conscious effort to affirm orthodoxy while proposing theories that are not consonant with it may account for his puzzling methodology. He frequently affirms sound principles and then proposes positions that *prima facie* do not seem to be in accord with the sound principles, usually making no attempt to explain the inconsistency. Pitstick puts it like this:

> What are intended for such qualifications generally take the form of simple denials of what is implied in his language or simple reaffirmations of traditional doctrines, without explanation of the sense in which the affirmation (or the denial) and the rest of his texts can both stand.[130]

At this point we can no more than mention that patristic scholars have raised serious questions about the accuracy of Balthasar's interpretation of these Fathers, particularly his attempts to enlist them as sympathizers or teachers of universalism. Brian Daley, for example, challenges Balthasar's assertion that Methodius was a universalist. He traces both Origen's thought and its influence on Methodius and Gregory of Nyssa and he concludes that, not only does Methodius not teach this openly, but he does not even hold it secretly: "There seems to be no evidence that Maximus sympathized with the Origenist theory of *apokatastasis* in its classical form."[131]

In his more extensive work on patristic eschatology, he concludes:

> Yet Maximus is not, as has sometimes been argued, a proponent of the theory of universal salvation or apokatastasis in the unqualified form espoused by Origen and Gregory of Nyssa. . . . Maximus makes it clear in a number of passages that the final divinization of rational creatures will only be realized in those who have shown themselves worthy of God's gift. . . . Each person remains free to frustrate the achievement of God's saving purpose in himself by refusing to follow the way of Christ.[132]

Balthasar minimally responds in *Dare We Hope*[133] and in *Theo-Drama*.[134] Thomas Joseph White thinks Balthasar's response is inadequate to the texts that Daley has brought forth from Maximus.[135] Daley's general assessment of Balthasar's portrayal of the Fathers, while respectful and appreciative, is nevertheless strongly critical in a crucial respect:

> Often brilliant commentaries on these authors within the specialized context of Balthasar's theological project, they are usually less than successful in allowing ancient authors to speak clearly to us in their own voices. . . . Like a collector of paintings from every period he has assembled an extraordinary gallery of theological positions, arguments, influences and connections; but because the collection is such an eclectic one, and the arrangement is so carefully controlled by a larger intellectual programme, it tells us, in the end, more about the taste and understanding of the collector than it does about the artists and their work.[136]

O'Connor identifies instances where Balthasar clearly misrepresents the teachings of the Fathers in order to claim precedents for his own theory. For example, Balthasar claims: "Let us return to the Church Fathers. At first, the view still existed among them that no Christians, even if they had sinned grievously, end up in hell. Cyprian already seems to suggest this; Hilary as well; Ambrose remains formal on the matter, and Jerome no less so."[137]

O'Connor comments: "This statement is disappointingly inaccurate. . . . There is no Father of the Church, up to the time of Origen, who teaches that all Christians, even those who sinned grievously, are saved." He finds Balthasar's citation of Cyprian particularly egregious, for the actual text of Cyprian teaches the very opposite; the Christian sinner who sins grievously and then *repents* can be saved.[138] He also points out that, contrary to Balthasar, the earliest Christian writing outside of the NT that attests to the reality of hell was not the *Martyrdom of Polycarp* (c. 156) but the even earlier *Second Epistle of Clement,* which teaches:

> For in reference to those who have not guarded the seal [i.e., the seal of Baptism], it says "Their worm shall not die and their fire shall not be quenched, and they shall be a spectacle to all flesh." So while we are on earth, let us repent. . . . For once we have departed this world we can no longer confess there or repent anymore.[139]

Manfred Hauke also raises questions about Balthasar's invocation of various Fathers in support of his theory, noting that it is precisely those ambiguous teachings of various Fathers that were never accepted by the Church that Balthasar cites for support.[140]

O'Connor describes the situation like this:

> Although he rejects the theory of apokatastasis, von Balthasar is so categorical in denying that we *know* that there are or will be humans who are to be eternally damned, and so forceful in defense of a hope for the salvation of all that *he appears to be saying* that, in fact, no one will be eternally lost.[141]

Roch Kereszty makes a similar observation:

> Does his understanding allow for a definitive free refusal of God's love on the part of any human being? He repeatedly insists on this possibility, but the inner consistency of his thought does not seem to admit it. . . . My reservation regarding his position comes from the suspicion that the logic of his thought leads not just to hope, but to a (consciously denied but logically inescapable) certainty for the salvation of all.[142]

Flannery puts it like this:

> Balthasar reconciles the two strands of scriptural tradition by an argument for the fact of universal salvation and not by an argument for the possibility of hoping and praying for universal salvation. If Balthasar is right, we need not *hope* for universal salvation: it could not *not* be. God could not condemn any men to eternal damnation since this would be to "blunt God's triune will for salvation."
>
> Beginning with the idea that God's "triune will for salvation" may not be "blunted" or "thwarted" by men, Balthasar can only proceed to the conclusion that God cannot condemn anyone to hell lest he violate his own nature (or the nature of his will), but this is to go too far. . . . He quotes with evident approval the remark of Hans Jürgen Verweyen: "Whoever reckons with the possibility of even only *one* person's being eternally lost *besides himself* is unable to love unreservedly." In the light of *Matthew 25* it would seem that Christ's moral character is seriously flawed.[143]

He notes that "only a few marginal figures . . . dared to speak another kind of language . . . but these voices do not suffice," seemingly indicating that the voices of himself and Speyr need to be heard. He then approvingly quotes Adrienne von Speyr: "The truth is not simply an either-or; either somebody is in hell or nobody is. Both are partial expressions of the whole. Thus, too, Ignatius has a right to make his meditations on hell . . . The truth consists in a sum total of partial truths."[144] With comments like these we are departing from the ordinary realm of rational discourse where the laws of noncontradiction apply.

The Mystics

Balthasar cites certain mystics as seemingly implying that all might be saved, but when he gives texts he does so in a way that tries to interpret them as in support of his theory rather than give a careful account of what they actually are saying. He seems to admit as much when after quoting Catherine of Siena in a way favorable to his theory he acknowledges:

> But precisely at this point, someone will come up with the numerous texts providing evidence that Catherine herself and many other mystics

. . . were all convinced, despite everything, that the damnation of many was a fact.[145]

Balthasar makes another sweeping generalization in this regard:

An eschatology that leaves open the outcome of the judgment . . . and renounces any final systemization . . . has always been characteristic of the eschatology of the mystics, for whom the experiences of the "dark night" and of "hell" always had a soteriological meaning. . . .[146]

He acknowledges that he has been criticized for interpreting texts of other mystics (Mechtild of Hackeborn, Angela of Foligno, and Julian of Norwich) in support of his position in a way that does not do justice to their actual teaching. He then changes tack and argues that while the saints do not necessarily hold his view on the possibility of hell being empty they were zealous to save souls from hell, which, of course, is not in dispute, and is not relevant to his theory.[147] Balthasar also claims, without evidence or argumentation, that he is in very good company with his theory and cites the "best of company," which he implies shares his views, as: Przywara, Cardinal de Lubac, "the great Blondel," Claudel, Marcel, "the tempestuous Léon Bloy," Cardinal Ratzinger, Walter Kasper, Romano Guardini, and "last but not least, Karl Rahner."[148] He quotes Bloy approvingly: "The exclusion of a single soul from the wondrous concert of the world is inconceivable and would pose a threat to the universal harmony."[149] He then dismisses scornfully, without argument, a distinguished French theologian who does not agree with him. "I might also note here that Fr. B. de Margerie — in France a traditionalist, scarcely recognized outsider, but in Germany discovered by right-wingers as a theological luminary and often cited in polemic — does not represent an authority for me."[150] Balthasar then makes the sweeping statement: "The last word, here as well, will go to the saints. Regardless of whether they think that there are or are not men in hell, the thought of that possibility remains unbearable to them."[151] Of course, this has no bearing on his theory, is not in dispute, and is virtually impossible to verify. He quotes a text from Teresa of Avila's *Autobiography* that speaks of her anguish at seeing a soul condemned for all eternity to hell. A fair treatment of Teresa would show that she very much held to the traditional interpretation of the biblical passages on judgment and was very much concerned for the evangelization of the "new world" with which she had contact through letters, precisely because she was concerned for the inhabitants' eternal salvation if they didn't have a chance to hear the gospel. One of the most common characteristics of "the saints" is their vivid understanding of and belief in the reality of judgment and the actual, not just possible, eternal consequences.[152] Larry Chapp, in a study of Balthasar's views on revelation, describes why Balthasar values the saints so highly:

> The saints, for Balthasar, are more than mere models of holiness meant to motivate us to imitation. They are the irruption of the persono-logical/eschatological core of Scripture and Church into full historical view and are, therefore, part of the revelatory address from God calling us to decision. Were it not for the visible holiness of the saints, it would be all too easy to dismiss Scripture and Church as ideological deforma-tions of an originating historical event. The holiness of the saints dis-plays something of the compelling beauty of the form of God's revela-tion in Christ, drawing us closer and provoking from us a dramatic decision. The "beauty" of the saints is the evident sanity and reasonable-ness of their trust in God's revelation.[153]

David Moss, writing on how significant the saints were to Balthasar's theology, states: "It is in this way, then, that, through the mediation of the saints, Balthasar claims that the dogmatic tradition becomes available to us as renewed and refreshed in every generation."[154] It is puzzling that the saints are honored for their trust in revelation when what they understood as revealed is the traditional picture of the twofold judgment that includes the certainty that many choose to refuse the offer of salvation "to the end" and are therefore in hell.

Manfred Hauke, in his detailed survey of the scholarship that has at-tempted to assess the accuracy of Balthasar's claims of support for his the-ory from "the saints," comes to this stark conclusion.

> The testimony of the saints is decisively unfavorable to the opinion that hell would be empty. Anyway, with his "slightly risky thesis," he proves the contrary, putting into relief the importance of holiness as a witness for theology. The Balthasarian proposal, to put in first place the saints and mystics, in its actual results, witnesses to the falsifica-tion of the hope in apokatastasis and confirms the existence of a two-fold justice.[155]

The Theological Solution of the Tradition

What Balthasar claims cannot and should not be done — namely, to attempt to find an intelligible theological interpretation for the range of Scriptures relevant to this question — has in fact been done by the greatest theologians of the Church throughout the centuries. It is the task of theology to do so. Aquinas's basic solution, ably defended today by young theologians like Thomas Joseph White, is regarded by many today as providing a permanently valid basis for the harmonization of the Scriptures on this point. It is the interpretation that is implied in the text of *LG* 16 that we are examining.

The basic solution that the theological tradition provides to the "dilemma" that Balthasar sees in the two contrasting sets of Scripture is that of understanding God's will as regards salvation under the aspect of its antecedent and consequent aspects. The Catholic tradition has come to affirm that God indeed wills the salvation of all men and gives grace to every single person sufficient for salvation. (This position is in contrast to an extreme Augustinianism that posits a double predestination, which, prior to foreseen merits or demerits, holds that God creates some for glory and some for damnation; a position that has been rejected by the Church.) At the same time, because of God's profound gift of human freedom, God respects the decisions of his creatures in their acceptance or rejection of saving grace. Thus, his antecedent will is that all men be saved; his consequent will is that creatures be allowed their choice to accept or reject saving grace.[156] Creatures are only saved because of the grace of God; creatures are only damned by their persistent and final refusal of grace. God is responsible for the salvation of all that are saved. He destines no one to end up in hell. Only the creature is responsible for his own damnation. Hell is a place that has come into being through the choice of persistently and finally choosing to reject God, on the part of the fallen angels and men. God never wills moral evil, never entices anyone to moral evil, and always provides sufficient grace for the salvation of each of his creatures. God is truly good. A text from Sirach expresses well this truth of God's mercy and human freedom:

> When God, in the beginning, created man, he made him subject to his own free choice. If you choose you can keep the commandments; it is loyalty to do his will. There are set before you fire and water; to whichever you choose, stretch forth your hand. Before man are life and death, whichever he chooses shall be given him. (Sirach 15:14-17)

Just as Balthasar rather peremptorily declares an "impasse" in reconciling what he sees as competing Scriptures, so also does he sarcastically dismiss, as we have previously noted, the traditional theological understanding.

> Permit us, Lord, to make a small distinction in our will: "God wills in
> advance [*voluntate antecedente*] that all men achieve salvation, but subsequently [*consequenter*] he wills that certain men be damned in accordance with the requirements of his justice" (S. *Th.*, 19:6 ad 1; De Ver.
> 23:2). . . . But what about Jesus' triumphant words when he looks forward to the effect of his Passion? . . . Oh, he will perhaps attempt to draw
> them all but will not succeed in holding them all. "Be of good cheer, I
> have overcome *the world*" (Jn 16:33). Unfortunately, only half of it, despite your efforts, Lord. "The grace of God has appeared for the salvation of *all* men" (Titus 2:11) — let us say, more precisely, to offer salvation, since how many will accept it is questionable. God does not wish
> "that any should perish, but that *all* should reach repentance" (2 Pet
> 3:9). He may well wish it, but unfortunately he will not achieve it.
> "Christ" was "offered once to take away the sins of *all*" (Heb 9:28). That
> might be true, but the real question is whether all will allow their sins to
> be taken away.[157]

With the Scriptures apparently "neutralized," the traditional theological synthesis dismissed, and the support of the Fathers, saints, and mystics claimed, Balthasar strongly argues that we have a duty to hope for the salvation of all. Surely we "hope and pray" for the salvation of all the living, but is this the hope of intercessory prayer, as Balthasar sometimes claims, nothing more than hoping that a sick friend will get well, but uncertain of the outcome? Or is it something more, a supernatural hope based on the sure promise of Christ to save everyone no matter what their response to grace is during their lifetime? The use of the concept of "hope" in Balthasar — a concept so central to his argument — needs to be evaluated before we draw our conclusions.

An Analysis of "Hope" in Balthasar's Argument

Since his argument is that we have a duty to "hope" that all be saved, we need to pay attention to what meaning he is attributing to the word "hope." There is an equivocation in his use of the word. In some places he seems to claim only a very weak meaning for the word, such as when we "hope" that someone overcomes an illness.[158] There can be no objection to "hoping" that all who have not already been condemned to hell, be saved, in this sense of the word "hope." Indeed, we all should have this hope. In other places he seems to claim a stronger meaning for "hope," something more than "mere desire," approaching theological hope that is virtually certain since it is based on the promise of God and his efficacious grace.[159]

> Jesus comes as the light of absolute love . . . in order to save all men. But how will this be, if there are some who consciously draw back from this love and refuse it (Jn. 3:19; 9:40-41; 12:48)? The question, to which no final answer is given or can be given, is this: Will he who refuses it now refuse it to the last?
>
> To this there are two possible answers: the first says simply "Yes." It is the answer of the infernalists. The second says: I do not know, but I think it permissible to hope (on the basis of the first series of statements from Scripture) that the light of divine love will ultimately be able to penetrate every human darkness and refusal.[160]

O'Connor thinks that Balthasar is definitely advocating a *theological hope* that is ill founded, given the weight of Scripture and tradition and the probability if not certainty that hell is actually a realized state for some rather than a hypothetical possibility.[161]

Thomas Joseph White analyzes Balthasar's use of "hope" in the stronger of these two senses.

> [For Balthasar] the possibility of a hell stemming from human sin alone (which Balthasar quite rightly insists upon) is a possibility that is excluded by the presence of effective grace. Therefore, the hope for universal salvation is not a hope that all men may receive the grace of God by which they will be saved if they consent, but that God will choose (in the end: whether in this world or the next) to overcome all human resistances effectively. It is therefore more than a hope that God's grace be offered to all, and that each one have the possibility of salvation. . . . It is in fact also a hope that even if human beings initially refuse grace, God will eventually convert by his effective will the hearts and minds of each person in a way that leaves no ultimate space for damnation, no place for an enduring refusal. This is a *hope,* then for *apokatastasis*

panton in the "last act" of the drama of redemption, in spite of the (temporary) permissions of creaturely evil. . . . True, he does maintain the carefully qualified hope (rather than categorical affirmation) that the will of God will triumph over sin. . . . Yet the gravitational tendency of this thought is toward a conclusion that Christian hope, if it is to be adequate to the mystery of God's infinite freedom in love, should and must aspire to the belief that all will be saved.[162]

Flannery draws on distinctions in Suarez that he thinks are important to keep in mind when praying for the salvation of all, distinctions that parallel the weaker and stronger senses of the meanings of hope.

He says that it is one thing to pray for the salvation of all out of the "simple desire" which would include the condition, expressed or not, that that which is prayed for be subordinate to the will of God. It is another thing to pray out of "absolute and efficacious desire," as Christ did when, according to Suarez, he prayed for those predestined to Glory: "I do not pray for the world but for those whom you have given me." . . . It is permissible, says Suarez, to pray for the salvation of all in the former mode, for the condition attached to it ensures that such prayers do not come into conflict with the revealed will of God. But if we pray in the latter mode for the salvation of all, we must come into conflict with Church teaching, for in this mode we pray with respect to those supposed to be condemned that they not be condemned. As Suarez explains, it is possible to pray for the salvation of all with simple desire, even if we know by revelation that some are damned. . . . To pray, in this fashion is simply to conform our wills to God's, who might will the salvation of all, even knowing that some will refuse it.[163]

Balthasar's defenders also sometimes use the word "hope" in an equivocal way. Margaret Turek, for example, acknowledges that there is an important distinction to be made between supernatural hope based on the certain promises of Christ and a human hope that is contingent upon creaturely response. She claims, though, that the Catechism of the Catholic Church supports Balthasar in permitting supernatural hope even in the case of a hope that goes beyond what is promised in Scripture. She cites a text of the Catechism (# 1821) as evidence, claiming that the last sentence justifies Balthasar's hope as properly supernatural.[164]

We can therefore hope in the glory of heaven promised by God to those who love him and do his will. In every circumstance each one of us should hope, with the grace of God, to persevere "to the end" and to obtain the joy of heaven, as God's eternal reward for the good works accomplished with the grace of Christ. In hope, the Church prays for "all men to be saved" (1 Tim. 2:4).

It is clear that the hope being spoken of in the first two sentences is a conditional supernatural hope based on the promise of God that "those who love him and do his will" and "persevere 'to the end'" in "good works" will come to the glory of heaven. The "hope" spoken of in the last sentence for "all men to be saved" with its citation of 1 Timothy 2:4 is of the same kind, a conditional supernatural hope, and not an absolute supernatural hope. From the context of the immediately preceding texts which speak of a salvation conditioned on human response and on the next verse of 1 Timothy 2, it is clear that the realization of this hope in the glory of heaven is dependent on "coming to the truth" and responding to the proclamation of the gospel.[165]

> For there is one God, and there is one mediator between God and men, the man Christ Jesus, who gave himself as a ransom for all, the testimony to which was given at the proper time. For this I was appointed a preacher and apostle. (1 Tim. 2:5-7)

Turek wants to claim for Balthasar the right to have supernatural hope, as opposed to merely human desire, for the salvation of all, but there remains an ambiguity both in Turek and in Balthasar. Balthasar heaps scorn on the traditional understanding of the antecedent and consequent dimensions of God's will for the salvation of all, and in the last analysis appears to be championing a supernatural hope that is not conditional on human response and cannot be resisted without God having failed. In an interview with Angelo Scola, Balthasar claims:

> Hope must be seen as a theological virtue (*espérance* is more than *espoir*) which is an expectation oriented toward God. There is no such thing as an earthly *espérance*, at best an *espoir*, an expectation that "hopefully" things will turn out well, that the world as a whole will perhaps become better. . . . Saint Bonaventure calls theological hope, by which we desire the divine good, infallible; according to him one may

say that I can always hope for the best from God, which I shall receive, if I persevere in hope. If I lose hope, I lose at the same time its infallibility. If I retain it, I will infallibly receive what I had hoped for.[166]

Do We Know That Anyone Is in Hell?

Balthasar acknowledges that in order to hope for something it has to be viewed as possible. Because of this he expends considerable effort trying to establish that we have no *certain* knowledge that anyone is in hell. He points out, as we have already noted, that the Church has not formally declared that any individual is in hell, not even Judas.[167]

Pitstick makes the penetrating remark that if Judas is indeed enjoying the glory of heaven, or will enjoy such glory, it is hard to make any sense out of Jesus' words about him: "It would be better for that man if he had been never born" (Matt. 26:24). Dulles makes a similar observation:

> The New Testament does not tell us in so many words that any particular person is in hell. But several statements about Judas can hardly be interpreted otherwise. Jesus says that he has kept all those whom the Father has given him except the son of perdition (John 17:12). At another point Jesus calls Judas a devil (John 6:70), and yet again says of him: "It would be better for that man if he had never been born" (Matthew 26:24; Mark 14:21). If Judas were among the saved, these statements could hardly be true. Many saints and doctors of the Church, including St. Augustine and St. Thomas Aquinas, have taken it as a revealed truth that Judas was reprobated.[168]

Roch Kereszty argues that "there can hardly be any question that in the view of the evangelists, Judas is definitely lost."[169] Flannery makes the point that in Revelation 20:10, "apparently, a human soul — i.e., the false prophet — is spoken of as suffering in hell forever."[170]

As the Church has "received" the Word of God in Scripture and as it has subsequently theologically reflected on it, its teaching has come to assume that the "plain sense" of Scripture clearly indicates that there are people in hell. The Church has never felt that she should engage in "negative canonizations" (solemnly defining that a particular soul is in hell), although its solemn anathemas directed to individual heretics and to those who follow their teaching in the canons of the ecumenical Councils, are indeed, quite sobering to read.[171]

Even if one wanted to take a more cautious approach to interpretation than the tradition has, one would at least have to say that it is plausible that there are people in hell. Therefore, hope for the salvation of all would have to be restricted to those presently alive,[172] and, of course, for the faithful departed and those "whose faith is known to you alone." We cannot properly have hope for those who departed this life persisting in their refusal of saving grace and faith, although only God knows who these are. And while we hope and work for the salvation of all those still alive, we do so knowing, based on the words of Jesus and the understanding of the tradition, that it is quite possible that many will refuse the offer of salvation and die unreconciled to God.

Some Evaluations

The foundation of Balthasar's hope is not really the Scripture passages that he cites that are more "universal" in their content, but in his own understanding of the precise nature of the redemption, seeing in it, along with Speyr, an extreme manifestation of Godforsakenness. In brief, as we have mentioned, Balthasar holds that since Christ has accepted experiencing damnation on behalf of the human race, including separation from the Father, and from his own divinity, in his descent into hell, there is now no need for any human being to experience damnation. Despite the controversial Christological and Trinitarian issues raised by this theory, we can, I believe, on the basis of more traditional Christology and Trinitarian theology grant that in principle there is no need for any human being to experience damnation if they avail themselves of the salvation won for them through the paschal mystery, even if through no fault of their own they are ignorant of the message of salvation, and their response contains only an implicit faith and repentance, and they persevere to the end in their response to the grace they are given.

When Balthasar either directly argues for universalism or simply asks questions challenging the traditional understanding but nevertheless making his sympathies clear and his own answer implicit, he, in my judgment, departs from the content of revelation and the mainstream theological tradition of the Church in a way that undermines the call to holiness and evangelization and is pastorally damaging. In the case of Balthasar's interpretation of the "two destinies" texts, his interpretation of them all as mere warnings rather than as statements of real outcomes undermines the traditional motivation for preaching the gospel to all creatures, namely that their salvation is in real jeopardy. Balthasar keeps recommending hell as a subject for personal meditation to keep us humble and nonpresumptuous, but ignores a primary context for many of the words of Jesus and the Apostles, namely, as motivation for preaching the gospel to those who are in danger of perishing.[173] He refers often to Ignatius's meditation on hell in the Spiritual Exercises as a model for how it should function in our own lives,[174] but ignores its function as a vital underpinning to the missionary outcomes of the Exercises as Jesuit missionaries went to the far reaches of the world in order to preach the gospel and rescue — not themselves — but those to whom they preached, from the real danger of hell. The role of hell in Ignatius' meditations is grounded in the traditional belief that hell is real and many are heading there. Reducing hell to a subject for pious meditation, or a rather unlikely possibility, removes it from its structural role in the gospel as an important revelation of truth, out of God's mercy, that must be believed and acted on, not only for one's own salvation, but for the salvation of others. Balthasar seems so concerned about the danger of "consigning the other to hell" that he ignores that fact that the "other" may very well be in danger of hell and true charity means speaking the truth in love to the "other" to give him a chance to repent, believe, and be saved. Or, as *LG* 16c puts it when speaking of those who had a chance to find salvation but who rather exchanged the truth of God for a lie, and worshiped the creature rather than the creator, or have given themselves over to the despair of nihilism:

> To procure the glory of God and the salvation of all these, the Church, mindful of the Lord's command, "preach the Gospel to every creature" (Mk. 16:16) takes zealous care to foster the missions. (*LG* 16c)

In Scripture we not only have a revelation of the saving plan of God and the greatness of the salvation offered to the human race, but we also have a sobering revelation of the depth of sin in the human heart that leads time and time again, historically, actually, to the rejection of that offer of salvation.[175]

The frequent rejection of the Word of God and the person of Christ are clearly testified to in the Scriptures. The rejection of God and his Word is not only a theoretical possibility but a historical actuality. Under the inspiration of the Holy Spirit, Scripture records numerous instances of rejection, as a warning to us, to avoid the same fate by sinning.

I do not want you to be unaware, brothers, that our ancestors were all under the cloud and all passed through the sea, and all of them were baptized into Moses in the cloud and in the sea. All ate the same spiritual food, and all drank the same spiritual drink, for they drank from a spiritual rock that followed them, and the rock was the Christ. Yet God was not pleased with most of them, for they were struck down in the desert. These things happened as examples for us, so that we might not desire evil things, as they did. And do not become idolaters, as some of them did, as it is written, "The people sat down to eat and drink, and rose up to revel." Let us not indulge in immorality as some of them did, and twenty-three thousand fell within a single day. Let us not test Christ as some of them did, and suffered death by serpents. Do not grumble as some of them did, and suffered death by the destroyer. These things happened to them as an example, and they have been written down as a warning to us, upon whom the end of the ages has come. (1 Cor. 10:1-12)

This is a remarkable passage that not only shows the Word's anticipatory presence in the Old Testament, already giving people a chance to accept or reject his salvation, but also shows the sinful depths of the human heart that in the very face of God's mercy can and does choose to reject it, as Jesus would explain later, loving the darkness more than the light, bringing condemnation on themselves, dying in their sins. The relevance to us is that if we, too, indulge in immorality or idolatry or disdain the Word of God and the grace of God, we will experience the judgment of God.

Balthasar speculates that perhaps everyone will be pardoned anyway, even if they die unrepentant, or perhaps another chance will be given after death for repentance to happen, and that we should certainly hope this. Speyr in her mystical visions speaks of people's effigies being in hell but not them. Oakes acknowledges the difficulty in determining exactly what Balthasar is saying about how this universal pardon could happen when it appears that people are dying in mortal sin. Ambiguity surrounds Balthasar's speculations about the encounter of damned souls with Christ in hell. Oakes concludes, as we have previously noted: "Perhaps, then, the issue boils down to whether there is a possibility of conversion after death, that is, in hell."[176] Of course, as we have noted, the view that conversion is possible after death is not in harmony with Scripture or the magisterium of the Church.

Just as it is appointed that human beings die once, and after this the judgment, so also Christ, offered once to take away the sins of many, will appear a second time, not to take away sin but to bring salvation to those who eagerly await him. (Heb. 9:27-28)

By this Constitution which is to remain in force for ever, we, with apostolic authority, define the following. . . . Immediately after death the souls of those who die in a state of mortal sin descend into hell, where they suffer the punishments of hell, "eternal fire." (Benedict XII, DS 1000-1002)[177]

The Council of Florence, in 1439, took up the teaching of Benedict XII from 1336 and reaffirmed it solemnly in its doctrinal decrees. In Session VI, which was devoted to formally defining what must be believed, it stated:

Also, the souls of those who have incurred no stain of sin whatsoever after baptism, as well as souls who after incurring the stain of sin have been cleansed whether in their bodies or outside of their bodies, as was stated above, are straightaway received into heaven and clearly behold the triune God as he is, yet one person more perfectly than another according to the difference of their merits. But the souls of those who depart this life in actual mortal sin, or in original sin alone, go down straightaway to hell to be punished, but with unequal pains. We also define. . . .[178]

Concerned by the confusion surrounding what the Church teaches about death, resurrection, heaven, and hell, in the light of "the unintentional effect on people's minds of theological controversies given wide publicity today, the precise subject and the significance of which is beyond the discernment of the majority of the faithful," the Sacred Congregation for the Doctrine of the Faith issued the "Letter on Certain Questions concerning Eschatology" in 1979.

The element in question is the article of the Creed concerning life everlasting and so everything in general after death. When setting forth this teaching, it is not permissible to remove any point, nor can a defective or uncertain outlook be adopted without endangering the faith and salvation of Christians. . . . In fidelity to the New Testament and Tradition, the Church believes in the happiness of the just who will one day be with Christ. She believes that there will be eternal punishment for the sinner, who will be deprived of the sight of God, and that this punishment will have a repercussion on the whole being of the sinner. She believes in the possibility of a purification for the elect before they see God, a purification altogether different from the punishment of the damned. This is what the Church means when speaking of Hell and Purgatory.[179]

This teaching is confirmed in the *Catechism of the Catholic Church.*

The teaching of the Church affirms the existence of hell and its eternity. Immediately after death the souls of those who die in a state of mortal sin descend into hell, where they suffer the punishments of hell, "eternal fire." The chief punishment of hell is eternal separation from God, in whom alone man can possess the life and happiness for which he was created and for which he longs. (CCC 1035)

Balthasar comes to the point as he ends the defense of his position in the *Short Discourse on Hell* by quoting Edith Stein, from a text that she never published, "which expresses most exactly the position that I have tried to develop."[180] We have briefly looked at a part of this text when we presented an overall preliminary view of Balthasar's argument, but now we need to look at it more thoroughly.

Stein acknowledges that it appears that

Temporal death comes for countless men without their ever having looked eternity in the eye and without salvation's ever having become a problem for them: that, furthermore, many men occupy themselves with salvation for a lifetime without responding to grace — we still do not know whether the decisive hour might not come for all of these somewhere in the next world, and faith can tell us that this is the case.[181]

She speculates on how grace can secretly work in the souls of apparent unbelievers, as "all-merciful love" descends to everyone.

And now, can we assume that there are souls that remain perpetually closed to such love? As a possibility in principle, this cannot be rejected. *In reality,* it can become infinitely improbable — precisely through what preparatory grace is capable of effecting in the soul.

Stein then describes how grace can "steal its way into souls" and gain more ground "in an illegitimate way."

> The more improbable it becomes that the soul will remain closed to it. . . . If all the impulses opposed to the spirit of light have been expelled from the soul, then any free decision against this has become infinitely improbable. Then faith in the unboundedness of divine love and grace also justifies *hope for the universality of redemption,* although through the possibility of resistance to grace that remains open in principle, the *possibility* of eternal damnation also persists. Seen in this way, what were described earlier as limits to divine omnipotence are also canceled out again. Human freedom can be neither broken nor neutralized by divine freedom, but it may well be, so to speak, outwitted.

Balthasar often "stands behind" theologians that he favorably quotes, but seldom is he as direct in his endorsement of their views as he is here in his claim that Stein's views most exactly represent his position. In the end, then, Balthasar is unmistakably teaching that even though it is theoretically possible for someone to be damned it is "infinitely improbable," even if it involves mysterious transactions in the next world. In the end his declaration of a "stalemate" between the contrasting sets of Scripture passages no longer holds, as he makes clear his belief in an all-but-certain universal salvation.

As Pitstick puts it:

> For the reasons discussed above, as well as the fact that Balthasar's primary argument in support of hope for the salvation of all is that the eternal loss of some implies a defect in God's omnipotence, it would appear Balthasar's denials of *apokatastasis* are just as "rhetorical" as those for which he criticizes Karl Barth.[182]

In his own early work on Karl Barth, Balthasar criticizes Barth in a way that could also be applied to his own thought, as it developed.

> In his book on the Creed, Barth warns us of eschatological arrogance. He avers that the "positive doctrine of the *apocatastasis* does not belong to the Creed because it would simply eviscerate it." Internal to history, God's Word will always be a two-edged sword. . . . Nonetheless, despite these demurrals, Barth's doctrine of election does not leave much room open for possibility. There is something inevitable and necessary in his

views. What is definitive in Barth's thought is grace and blessing, and all reprobation and judgment is merely provisional.[183]

Towards the end of his life Balthasar wrote of the lasting influence on him of the very doctrine of Barth's, that of election, that he had previously criticized: "Barth's doctrine of election, this brilliant overthrow of Calvin, attracted me powerfully and lastingly; it converged with Origen's views and thus also with Adrienne's theology of Holy Saturday."[184] Wainwright describes Balthasar's eschatology as "constantly attracted by the gravitational pull of *apokatastasis,* the possible 'final restoration of all things' — which doctrine is itself inseparable in his case, from his speculations on Christ's 'descent into hell.'" He also notes his longstanding "fascination" with "theologians suspected or accused of universalism: Origen, Gregory of Nyssa, Maximus the Confessor, Karl Barth, on all of whom he wrote significant and path-breaking monographs."[185]

Part of Balthasar's argument, as we have noted, is that if everyone is not saved God will have lost his "gamble." Rejecting the profound reflection found in the tradition on the mystery of human freedom which sees no necessary contradiction between the infinite goodness of God and his infinite justice, between his universal will to salvation and his respect of human freedom, he ends up resolving the tension in such a way that universal salvation becomes all but necessary. As we have seen, he is not just "speculating" but is rather strongly holding for the "infinitely improbable" possibility of anyone ending up in hell. He is thereby neutralizing the Word of God and perhaps unwittingly, encouraging people to continue on the "broad way" that, in his view, almost certainly ends up at the same destination as the "narrow way." This has undoubtedly contributed to the shocking reversal in the contemporary mind of the words of Jesus himself.[186] It appears as if an anthropocentric image of God, shaped by our culture's likes and dislikes, is taking the place of the biblical revelation of who God is.[187] As Cardinal Ratzinger remarked in relationship to a similar tendentious biblical interpretation, "Here, too, Scripture is being read contrary to its own intention."[188]

White thinks that Balthasar's teaching on universalism is "seriously problematic" and singles out what he judges the most serious deficiency in Balthasar.

Most seriously, Balthasar's thought can be seen as clearly intimating that a world in which hell exists is a world in which the love of God has failed.

This touches on the heart of the issue. Who exactly has failed when moral evil occurs, and when the spiritual creature "perseveres" in resistance to the divine good? Is it God or the creature? If, following Damascene and Aquinas, we adopt the distinction between the antecedent and conse-quent will of God, we can say clearly that it is the creature. By refusing the instigations and movements of nature and grace that would rectify his or her use of free will, the human person (or angel) *alone* is to be seen at the *origins* of the mystery of hell. Balthasar seeks at many points to vindicate God against any blame for this condition, yet his theology is fragile at this juncture. He has defended the universal extension of God's goodness as it is revealed in Christ, but does he defend sufficiently his innocence in the wake of the human refusal of love? . . . In refusing to appropriate the above mentioned distinction, he rejects along with it an authentic reception of the Catholic Tradition's teaching on the "resistible" character of saving grace, and the corresponding reality of God's permissive will of evil. Con-sequently, persisting moral evil must necessarily be seen as a reality en-gendered by the *absence of the divine initiative* toward the heart of the creature who "stands under judgment" by an infinite love. We are con-fronted, then, with the possibility of either a restricted election or of a uni-versal restoration. Neither can do justice to the teaching of the Gospel.[189]

Pitstick points out another departure from Scripture and tradition in Balthasar's work. Balthasar claims that even though someone can die in mortal sin, if he did one good act earlier in his life, that may be enough to save him. In this he adopts a radical theory of moral choice that was re-jected by John Paul II in *Veritatis splendor*. As Pitstick points out, the act of charity noted by Balthasar does not even have to be an act of supernatural charity or anything approaching what could count as a "fundamental op-tion" for charity. *Veritatis splendor* rejects the position that without repen-tance an individual "could continue to be morally good, persevere in God's grace and attain salvation, even if certain of his specific kinds of behavior were deliberately and gravely contrary to God's commandments as set forth by the Church."[190]

In point of fact, man does not suffer perdition only by being unfaithful to that fundamental option whereby he has made a "free self-commitment to God" (*Dei Verbum* 5). As the Council of Trent teaches, "the grace of justification once received is lost not only by apostasy, by which faith itself is lost, but also by any other mortal sin" (DS 1544).[191]

The actual text of Trent is worth quoting:

> It must be asserted, against the subtle modes of thinking of certain peo-
> ple, who *by fair and flattering words deceive the hearts of the simple-*
> *minded* (Rom 16:18), that the grace of justification once received is lost
> not only by apostasy, by which faith itself is lost, but also by any other
> mortal sin, though faith is not lost. Thus is defended the teaching of the
> divine law which excludes from God's kingdom not only unbelievers,
> but also the faithful if they are guilty of fornication, adultery, wanton-
> ness, sodomy, theft, avarice, drunkenness, slander, plundering, and all
> others who commit mortal sins from which, with the help of divine
> grace, they can refrain, and because of which they are severed from the
> grace of Christ (1 Cor 6:9-10; 1 Tim 1:9-10).[192]

This section of the Council's teaching on justification ends with the
warning that "unless each one faithfully and firmly accepts it, he cannot
be justified."[193]

Assessing Balthasar's Pastoral Concerns

As we noted at the beginning of this chapter, one of the main sources of
motivation in Balthasar's elaboration of his theory of the possibility of
universal salvation was certain pastoral concerns.[194] Balthasar felt that
these concerns could be met by establishing that we cannot be certain that
anyone is in hell, and that universal salvation remains a real possibility and
therefore an appropriate, indeed necessary, object of hope.

One cluster of his concerns centers on what he considers the inevitable
negative development in those who believe that there are actually some
people in hell, regarding charity toward the other. The fact is that those
who believe, as the entire tradition does, that there are actually people in
hell, do not know from among those who are alive what may be their ultimate destinations; hence unrestricted, universal charity towards all those
currently alive, or who may be alive, is quite possible. In fact, the very
knowledge that it is very likely that there are people in hell serves as an impetus to universal charity for those now living, so that they may avoid such
a tragic end. Where there is life there truly is hope. But the hope that is
born through an acceptance of the certainty (the tradition) or the probability (a possible position) that there are people in hell is directed not only

towards personal meditation on the theoretical possibility of "hell for me" but ushers in intercessory prayer and sacrifice, and most of all, a strong commitment to evangelization personally and as a Church. Where a climate of universalism began to gain sway in the Church after the Vatican II Council, the missionary effort of the Church virtually collapsed. Mission in many places became redefined as primarily directed to improving the structures of life in this world, or even helping people to be better adherents of their own non-Christian religions. The number of missionaries and missionary orders devoted to drawing others to conversion to Christ drastically collapsed.[195]

There is widespread testimony to the collapse of the missionary enterprise in the confusing currents that flowed from certain interpretations of Vatican II.

Already in 1975, ten years after the Council, Paul VI addressed the theological confusion that was already undermining evangelization, in his important Apostolic Exhortation, *Evangelii nuntiandi*.

After noting the interior lack of fervor as a significant obstacle to evangelization, Paul VI identifies the theological confusion that is undermining evangelization.

> The most insidious of these excuses are certainly the ones which people claim to find support for in such and such a teaching of the Council.
>
> Thus one too frequently hears it said, in various terms, that to impose a truth, be it that of the Gospel, or to impose a way, be it that of salvation, cannot but be a violation of religious liberty. Besides, it is added, why proclaim the Gospel when the whole world is saved by uprightness of heart? We know likewise that the world and history are filled with "seeds of the Word"; is it not therefore an illusion to claim to bring the Gospel where it already exists in the seeds that the Lord Himself has sown?
>
> Anyone who takes the trouble to study in the Council's documents the questions upon which these excuses draw too superficially will find quite a different view.[196]

Norman Tanner, in an understatement, notes that *EN* "did not completely solve the crisis of missionary vocations or revive the era of certainty about missionary activity."[197]

Stephen Bevans, the contemporary Catholic missiologist, provides a good overview of the multiple factors that combined to create what he acknowledges was a "crisis" in the "precipitous decline" and missionary collapse that followed Vatican II. He notes that something like a "perfect storm" of circumstances combined to create a "seismic" impact on the Church's understanding of and practice of mission. The age of colonialism was coming to an end, movements of independence were afoot, and a critique of Western imperialism was in the air. Prominent missionaries called for a "moratorium" on missions. Along with calls for "dialogue" with world religions and the revival of some of these previously moribund religions, a state of uncertainty was communicated to Catholic missionaries. Among all these factors, however, Bevans cites the theological confusion as central to the collapse.

> And, perhaps more radically, with Vatican II's acknowledgement of the possibility of salvation outside of explicit faith in Christ and membership in the church [*LG* 16 among other texts are cited here], many Catholics — including missionaries — no longer saw missionary activity as an urgent need. If people could be saved by following their own consciences in the context of their own religions, why try to convert them? How could the traditional understanding of evangelization be harmonized with the new emphasis on invitation and dialogue?[198]

While Bevans does not claim that there has been a resurgence of missionary activity, he thinks that the broader understanding of mission that has emerged by reading together *AG* and *GS*, which includes dimensions of listening, dialogue, inculturation, and working for peace and justice, has now become well established as a new vision of mission. He is clear that mission in the magisterial documents still speaks of proclamation with a view towards conversion as the "permanent priority" and "central" element of mission but acknowledges that there is "much hesitation among missionaries and mission theologians about such a central role, even perhaps a deeply felt aversion." He concludes: "On balance, *Ad Gentes* has been well implemented, although perhaps in ways that might surprise its authors and those who approved it."[199]

In 1990, John Paul II published his encyclical *Redemptoris missio* in order to address this situation and reinvigorate evangelization. He notes that there have been many positive fruits as a result of the Council but that the waning of missionary activity can only be viewed as a negative.

> Nevertheless, in this "new springtime" of Christianity there is an undeniable negative tendency, and the present document is meant to help

overcome it. Missionary activity specifically directed "to the nations" (*ad gentes*) appears to be waning, and this tendency is certainly not in line with the directives of the Council and of subsequent statements of the Magisterium. . . . For in the Church's history, missionary drive has always been a sign of vitality, just as its lessening is a sign of a crisis of faith. . . . We must ask ourselves how it is that in some countries, while monetary contributions are on the increase, missionary vocations, which are the real measure of self-giving to one's brothers and sisters, are in danger of disappearing.[200]

He states that one purpose of the encyclical is "to clear up doubts and ambiguities" regarding preaching the gospel to non-Christians, and goes on to identify what some of these doubts and ambiguities are.

Nowadays the call to conversion which missionaries address to non-Christians is put into question or passed over in silence. It is seen as an act of "proselytizing"; it is claimed that it is enough to help people to become more human or more faithful to their own religion, that it is enough to build communities capable of working for justice, freedom, peace and solidarity.[201]

The truth about heaven and hell determines the shape and content of the hope in question and the response to such hope. When the only destination that is seen as a real possibility for human beings is heaven, it is easy to see that motivation for evangelization would weaken. It is quite possible that in an effort to "improve the concept of God" many have been lulled into a false belief that how they live and how they choose ultimately does not matter. How tragic if the promulgation of a theoretical or practical presumption that almost everyone will be saved actually became the cause of many people being lost.

A major cluster of Balthasar's pastoral concerns revolves around preserving a good image for God. Indeed, many people have very distorted understandings of God, ranging from God as an unpredictable, moralistic, judgmental tyrant, to a permissive, affirming, symbolic image of our own goodness and divinity. The only good image of God is one that is true. The only way of really knowing what God is like is by his own revelation of himself to us. Attempts to correct a particular distorted image of God can, unfortunately, end up by creating a distortion in the opposite direction.

The image of God that emerges from the tradition's reflection on one of the Bible's major themes, the "two ways, two choices, two destinations," is capable of producing a profound, holy, and spiritually and psychologically healthy fear of God, disposing one for the deepest and most intimate gift of loving union. Both fear and love are necessary.

> See, then, the kindness and severity of God: severity toward those who fell, but God's kindness to you, provided you remain in his kindness; otherwise you too will be cut off. (Rom. 11:22)

Balthasar's pastoral concern that people who believe in a populated hell will fail in charity is not well founded; the opposite appears to be the case.[202]

It's time now to draw some conclusions for the pastoral life of the Church.

CHAPTER VII

The Pastoral Strategy of Vatican II: Time for an Adjustment?

This book has been concerned with addressing a certain "atmosphere of universalism" in the Church that undermines motivation for evangelization. It has done so by examining the primary text from Vatican II that is relevant to this issue, *LG* 16. We have considered the history of the development of this text, as well as commentaries on the text, and have offered our own interpretation. In doing so we have examined the important footnote that locates the teaching of *LG* 16 within the doctrinal tradition of the Church, and the important reference to Romans 1, both of which ground the conciliar teaching in Scripture and tradition and are essential to its proper interpretation. We have also analyzed the speculative theology of two very influential theologians, whose teachings on this topic have tended to overshadow the teaching of *LG* 16, and have not taken it sufficiently into account. We would like now, in this concluding chapter, to briefly examine the pastoral strategy of Vatican II and make a suggestion for what we believe to be a necessary and useful adjustment in it, based on the preceding research.

The Pastoral Strategy of Vatican II

There is a general consensus among the commentators on Vatican II that a conscious decision was made, by John XXIII before the Council, affirmed at the Council itself, to change the pastoral strategy of the Catholic Church in an attempt to communicate more effectively with the modern world and make evangelization more successful. That change was spearheaded by Pope John XXIII when he called for the Council to be pastoral and not issue any condemnations. Pope John XXIII and many others sensed that the Church was becoming increasingly alienated from modern culture and locked into a defensive, apologetic stance that was perceived by the world as negative, condemnatory, and unattractive. The Church appeared to many as an archaic institution laden with trappings of an imperial and aristocratic past whose sympathies were with the *ancien régime* of a Church/State symbiosis and far removed from the concerns of "modern man."

Anyone who reads the numerous histories of the Council or theological commentaries on the debates, and then reads the final documents, cannot fail to be impressed by the balance, theological quality, solid scriptural bases, spiritual vitality, and pastoral sensitivity of the final texts. They are, indeed, "compromise" documents, but documents, we believe, that were guided by the Spirit and provide to this day a solid foundation for that true renewal and revitalized evangelization that was the twofold purpose of the Council. The words of Blessed John Paul II remain true:

> What a treasure there is, dear brothers and sisters, in the guidelines offered to us by the Second Vatican Council! . . . With the passing of the years, *the Council documents have lost nothing of their value or brilliance.* They need to be read correctly, to be widely known and taken to heart as important and normative texts of the magisterium within the Church's Tradition . . . the *great grace bestowed on the Church in the twentieth century:* there we find a sure compass by which to take our bearings in the century now beginning.[1]

The Council chose to "accentuate the positive" in its presentation of the gospel, highlighting the great beauty of the Trinity, the Incarnation, the ineffable mercy and goodness of God, and the beauty of the Church as a Sacrament of Christ showing forth his face to the world. It chose to affirm everything it could about the endeavors of the modern world and modern man and not speak much about the consequences of rejecting the good news. As one commentator put it, if this strategy and vision could be successfully presented to the modern world, "men will storm her doors seeking admission."[2]

This pastoral strategy has continued to guide the teaching on evangelization and mission in the postconciliar Church. The reasons given for evangelization in the major postconciliar documents such as *EN* and *RM* are predominantly positive, speaking of how Christianity can enrich or fulfill the human person.

The Pastoral Strategy of Vatican II

Avery Dulles describes this pastoral strategy:

Neither Vatican II nor the present pope [John Paul II] bases the urgency
of missionary proclamation on the peril that the non-evangelized will
incur damnation; rather they stress the self-communicative character of
love for Christ, which gives joy and meaning to human existence (*RM*
10-11; cf. 2 Cor 5:14).[3]

Richard John Neuhaus studied the reasons given for evangelization in
RM and came up with six, none of which speak of the eternal consequences of rejecting the good news, or the fact that those who never hear
the good news are not to be presumed saved. He claims that a study of
Benedict XVI's writings both as Pope and before would be in harmony
with these reasons and this approach as well.[4]

This, of course, is in stark contrast to the traditional focus on the eternal consequences that rest on accepting or rejecting the gospel that motivated almost two thousand years of mission. This emphasis also stands in
stark contrast to the stress placed on the eternal consequences of accepting
or rejecting the gospel, characteristic of the previous modern papal encyclicals devoted to the missionary task of the Church, published prior to 1960.

Pope Benedict XV, on November 30, 1919, promulgated *Maximum
illud* (On the Propagation of the Catholic Faith Throughout the World).
He wrote:

The realization must come as a shock that right now there still remain in
the world immense multitudes of people who dwell in darkness and in
the shadow of death. According to a recent estimate, the number of
non-believers in the world approximates one billion souls. The pitiable
lot of this stupendous number of souls is for Us a source of great sor-
row. . . . You [speaking to missionaries] have been called to carry light to
men who lie in the shadow of death and to open the way to heaven for
souls that are hurtling to destruction. . . . The sacred obligation of assist-
ing in the conversion of the infidels applies also to them [all Catho-
lics]. . . . Now what class of men is more in need of fraternal help than
unbelievers, who live in ignorance of God, and consequently, bound by
the chains of their blind and violent desires, are enslaved in the most
hideous of all the forms of slavery, the service of Satan?[5]

Pope Pius XI, on February 28, 1926, promulgated *Rerum ecclesiae* (On
Catholic Missions). He stated:

We determined to leave nothing undone which might, by means of apostolic preachers, extend farther and farther the light of the Gospel and make easy for heathen nations the way unto salvation. . . . We ask that there should daily arise to heaven the prayer that the Divine Mercy may descend upon so many unhappy beings, inhabitants of the densely populated pagan countries. . . . Pray that the gift of faith be bestowed upon the almost limitless number of pagans.[6]

Pope Pius XII, on June 2, 1951, promulgated *Evangelii praecones* (On Promotion of Catholic Missions). He declared:

The Catholic missionary movement both in Christian and pagan lands has gained such force and momentum and is of such proportions as perhaps was never witnessed before in the annals of Catholic missions. . . . It is a great consolation to Us to know that the number of missionary vocations is happily on the increase. . . . When We consider the countless peoples who are to be called to the one fold and to the one haven of salvation by the preaching of these missionaries . . . we pray: There is no God beside thee, O Lord. . . . The object of missionary activity, as all know, is to bring the light of the Gospel to new races and to form new Christians. . . . Pray earnestly for the salvation of the infidel. . . . You are well aware that almost the whole human race is today allowing itself to be driven into two opposing camps, for Christ or against Christ. The human race is involved today in a supreme crisis, which will issue in its salvation by Christ, or in its dire destruction.[7]

Pius XII's encyclical *Fidei donum* (On the Present Condition of the Catholic Missions, Especially in Africa), promulgated on April 21, 1957, conveys a similar concern for the salvation of the unevangelized, "where some 85,000,000 people still sit in the darkness of idolatry."[8]

Shortly before Vatican II, on November 28, 1959, Pope John XXIII, to commemorate the fortieth anniversary of *Maximum illud*, issued his own encyclical on missions, *Princeps pastorum* (The Prince of Shepherds, On the Missions, Native Clergy, and Lay Participation) in which he states: "We are everywhere confronted by appeals to Us to ensure the eternal salvation of souls in the best way We can, and a cry seems to reach Our ears: 'Help us!' (Acts 16:9)."[9]

Three of these encyclicals *(Maximum illud, Rerum ecclesia, and Fidei donum*) are referenced in a footnote to *LG* 17 that concludes Chapter II of *LG* with a strong call to evangelization.[10]

An Adjustment in Pastoral Strategy Is Needed

While there were many sound reasons to emphasize the positive in the Church's relations with the modern world, it has also become clear that an adjustment in her pastoral strategy is needed. Contemporary culture has not stormed "her doors seeking admission," as one writer we have just cited predicted. Contemporary culture has proven more resistant to the gospel as it has been presented than the Church has been resistant to the secularizing pressures of contemporary culture.

The most important reason, though, for an adjustment in pastoral strategy, is that we have a responsibility to transmit revelation as we have received it, in its integrity, proportion, and balance. Our goal needs to be to transmit in its entirety the whole teaching of Jesus and the Apostles as it comes to us in Scripture, tradition, and the authoritative teaching of the magisterium. Revelation cannot change — although it can be more profoundly understood and expressed — but pastoral strategy can and should change to meet changing circumstances and as the fruits or effectiveness of a particular pastoral strategy can be assessed. Insofar as the Second Vatican Council shaped its message to suit a particular pastoral strategy (radically changing the previous pastoral strategy), it is subject to evaluation and change.

Another important reason to adjust the strategy is that when the eternal consequences that flow from what we choose to believe and how we choose to act are not spoken of for long periods of time, the silence on these dimensions of the gospel is often taken to mean that they are no longer important, true, or relevant.[11]

As one commentator has pointed out, when the eternal consequences of believing and obeying or not believing and obeying are left fuzzy, "the essential faith of Catholics will then amount to no more than a vague theism with little specific moral content; just what it is for a large proportion of Catholics today."[12]

In this connection, Cardinal Ratzinger spoke of the "catastrophic failure of modern catechesis":

The new evangelization we need so urgently today is not to be attained with cleverly thought out ideas, however cunningly these are elaborated:

the catastrophic failure of modern catechesis is all too obvious. It is only the interaction of a truth conclusive in itself with its proof in the life of this truth that can enable that particular evidence of the faith to be illuminated that the human heart awaits: it is only through this door that the Holy Spirit enters the world.[13]

The popularization of theological theories — which are almost always more nuanced in the scholarly works that propound them — that give the impression that almost everybody is saved, and that perhaps only a few especially evil people end up in hell, and that there are many ways to salvation, has done much to contribute to a "culture of universalism" not only in Western society as a whole but within the Church as well.[14]

In addition, when a "practical universalism" holds sway in the minds of people, the zeal for holiness and evangelization will certainly be reduced. Both Paul VI and John Paul II bemoaned this lack of zeal and noted the cause for this lack of zeal as often being rooted in false theological theories. Unfortunately, they both stopped short of the full remedy, a full restatement of the gospel concerning salvation as we find it in Scripture, tradition, and the important sentences of *LG* 16. They, for the most part, remained silent on this aspect of the truth, in all probability, in order to remain within the pastoral strategy of Vatican II.

Paul VI, after exhorting the Church to keep the missionary impulse alive, says: "Let us state this fact [the Church's commitment to keep the missionary spirit alive] with joy at a time when there are not lacking those who think and even say that ardor and the apostolic spirit are exhausted, and that the time of the missions is now past."[15]

As we have previously noted, he clearly identifies the theological currents that are taking away the motivation to evangelize:

Thus one too frequently hears it said, in various terms, that to impose a truth, be it that of the Gospel or to impose a way, be it that of salvation, cannot but be a violation of religious liberty. Besides, it is added, why proclaim the Gospel when the whole world is saved by uprightness of heart? We know likewise that the world and history are filled with "seeds of the Word"; is it not therefore an illusion to claim to bring the Gospel where it already exists in the seeds that the Lord Himself has sown? Anyone who takes the trouble to study in the Council's documents the questions upon which these excuses draw too superficially will find quite a different view.[16]

Paul VI responds to the question of the "imposition of the Gospel" by clarifying that we propose, not impose, disavowing any pressure or coercion, respectful of each person's freedom. His response, though, to the more serious question of "why proclaim the Gospel when the whole world is saved by uprightness of heart" leaves one hanging.

> God can accomplish this salvation in whomsoever He wishes by ways which He alone knows [he cites *AG* 7 here]. And yet, if His Son came, it was precisely in order to reveal to us, by His word and by His life, the ordinary paths of salvation. And He has commanded us to transmit this revelation to others with His own authority. It would be useful if every Christian and every evangelizer were to pray about the following thought: men can gain salvation also in other ways, by God's mercy, even though we do not preach the Gospel to them; but as for us, can we gain salvation if through negligence or fear or shame — what St. Paul called "blushing for the Gospel" (Rom 1:18) — or as a result of false ideas, we fail to preach it?[17]

Paul VI's argument basically comes down to — yes, people can be saved without us evangelizing — but the Lord has asked us to evangelize. There is certainly a force to this argument. But if one simply makes the argument from authority and fails to give the reasons why Christ has asked us to evangelize, then one of the most fundamental reasons of all has not been given, a reason that was the most significant motivation for 2,000 years of heroic evangelization. What motivated the Apostles and the whole history of Christian missions was knowing from divine revelation that the human race is lost, eternally lost, without Christ, and even though it is possible for people to be saved under certain stringent conditions without explicit faith and baptism, "very often" this is not actually the case. Therefore it is urgent that the gospel be preached. Knowing the truth provides the compelling motivation that leads to heroic love in action.

John Paul II also notes the significant negative influence of theological confusion on the will to evangelize. He acknowledges that while the Council intended for there to be a flowering of missionary effort as a fruit of its work, the very opposite has happened, and the Church has seen a waning of missionary fervor since the Council. Despite the many positive fruits of the Council — the Pope explicitly mentions here the emergence of a laity dedicated to evangelization "which is changing ecclesial life" — there is nevertheless a serious impediment to the full realization of a "new spring-time" which the Pope links to a "crisis of faith."

> Nevertheless, in this "new springtime" of Christianity there is an undeniable negative tendency, and the present document is meant to help overcome it. Mission activity specifically directed "to the nations" *(ad gentes)* appears to be waning, and this tendency is certainly not in line with the directives of the Council and of subsequent statements of the Magisterium.[18]

John Paul II indicates that this should be a concern to all since "missionary drive has always been a sign of vitality, just as its lessening is a sign of a crisis of faith."[19] He also hopes by writing this encyclical "to clear up doubts and ambiguities regarding missionary activity *ad gentes*."[20]

Both *EN* and *RM* are truly inspiring documents, and they provide many eloquently stated reasons for continuing the Church's primary service to the human race, namely, evangelization. However, neither one addresses extensively one of the primary underlying reasons for the waning of mission *ad gentes* or the lack of any significant embrace of the call to a "new evangelization" or "re-evangelization" (*RM* 33) of those who perhaps have been baptized but are far from the faith. Neither one elaborates on the Council's main teaching in *LG* 16 on why "very often" the possibility of people being saved without hearing the gospel is not realized.[21]

The Need to Recover the Boldness of Apostolic Preaching

To present adequately the teaching of *LG* 16 would entail an unashamed explication of the teaching of Romans about what the human condition actually is apart from Christ. This would include explaining adequately the horror of sin, immorality, idolatry, and unbelief; the culpable suppression of the truth; the refusal to worship, thank, and submit; the reality of God's wrath properly understood; and our desperate need for Christ in order for us to be reconciled with God, bringing with it an appropriate fear of the Lord.

As Fr. Francis Martin puts it in his study of John's Gospel as it relates to evangelization:

> The essential action of the Paraclete in this passage [John 16:7-11] is to prove that the world is culpably wrong, to establish its culpability as

world. The difficulty arises when we seek to define the recipient of this action. Is it that the world is brought to acknowledge its sin or that the believers are given irrefutable proof that the world is in sin? Basically, it must be the second. If the world were able to acknowledge its sin, it would no longer be the "world," that is, a place which, despite the fact that there is still room for freedom and choice, is nevertheless at its depths a "demonic universe of refusal and rejection. . . ." The root sin of the world is refusal to believe in Jesus and the place he holds next to the Father as the Revelation of the Father, the root sin is to reject the Truth. "Whoever believes in the Son has eternal life, whoever disobeys the Son will not see life, but must endure God's wrath" (Jn 3:36).[22]

Fr. John Michael McDermott has pointed out that John Paul II was not completely silent on these realities — and treated them to some extent in *Dominum et vivificantem* — but seldom related them directly to evangelization. Fr. McDermott summarizes some of this teaching:

Despite this optimism about the salvation of men expressed in other works, Pope John Paul II surely does not overlook the horrors of sin. . . . Naturally the sinner is the least likely to admit his need for conversion. His sin ties him up in knots of self-justification. The word from without, preached in the Spirit's power, must be met with the workings of the Spirit from within sinful men. The horror of sin and the sinner is hidden from man unless the Spirit teaches him. . . . The universality of human sin is presupposed by the universality of salvation effected by Christ. . . . Hence all men have need of salvation. . . . That insight, of course, led St. Paul (Rom 5:12-21) and the Church to affirm the doctrine of original sin, "the sin that according to the revealed Word of God constitutes the principle and root of all the others" (DV, 33). . . . This turning from truth is mirrored in the rejection of the Word made flesh on Calvary.[23]

Cardinal Joseph Ratzinger also expressed concern about the silence about sin that he thinks has been characteristic of the post–Vatican II era. He recounts a recollection of a conversation he had with a fellow bishop about what would be a suitable theme for a future World Synod of Bishops. The words of Mark 1:15 which record the fundamental concern of Jesus' preaching, concerning the need to believe and repent in light of the coming Kingdom, were being considered as a theme.

One of the bishops reflected on these words and said that he had the impression that we had long ago actually halved Jesus' message as it is thus summarized. We speak a great deal — and like to speak — about evangelization and the good news in such a way as to make Christianity attractive to people. But hardly anyone, according to this bishop, dares nowadays to proclaim the prophetic message: Repent! Hardly anyone dares to make to our age this elementary evangelical appeal, with which the Lord wants to induce us to acknowledge our sinfulness, to do penance, and to become other than what we are. Our confrere added that Christian preaching today sounded to him like the recording of a symphony that was missing the initial bars of music, so that the whole symphony was incomplete and its development incomprehensible. With this he touched a weak point of our present-day spiritual situation.

Sin has become almost everywhere today one of those subjects that are not spoken about. Religious education of whatever kind does its best to evade it.[24]

We have devoted a whole chapter to the teaching of Romans as it relates to *LG* 16, but the revelation of the power of sin and the need for repentance is a central theme of the entire Bible. The Bible itself sometimes provides some particularly concise summaries of its own teaching on the truth of the human condition and the need for Christ:

And you he made alive, when you were dead through the trespasses and sins in which you once walked, following the course of this world, following the prince of the power of the air, the spirit that is now at work in the sons of disobedience. Among these we all once lived in the passions of our flesh, following the desires of body and mind, and so we were by nature children of wrath, like the rest of mankind. But God, who is rich in mercy, out of the great love with which he loved us, even when we were dead through our trespasses, made us alive together with Christ (by grace you have been saved), and raised us up with him, and made us sit with him in the heavenly places in Christ Jesus, that in the coming ages he might show the immeasurable riches of his grace in kindness toward us in Christ Jesus. For by grace you have been saved through faith; and this is not your own doing, it is the gift of God — not because of works, lest any man should boast. For we are his workmanship, created in Christ Jesus for good works, which God prepared beforehand, that we should walk in them. (Eph. 2:1-10)

The words of Paul to Titus also provide a concise summary:

For we ourselves were once foolish, disobedient, led astray, slaves to various passions and pleasures, passing our days in malice and envy, hated by men and hating one another; but when the goodness and loving kindness of God our Savior appeared, he saved us, not because of deeds done by us in righteousness, but in virtue of his own mercy, by the washing of regeneration and renewal in the Holy Spirit, which he poured out upon us richly through Jesus Christ our Savior, so that we might be justified by his grace and become heirs in hope of eternal life. The saying is sure. (Titus 3:3-8)

Unless we squarely face the bad news — original sin and personal sin have severe consequences — it is impossible really to appreciate the good news (God is rich in mercy; out of the great love with which he loved us we are saved by grace through faith).[25]

As one commentator puts it:

The trouble with the Council's approach to mission is that although it stresses that Catholics must seek to convert unbelievers, it gives no adequate reason for doing so. It does give Christ's command to evangelize as a reason, but it gives no proper explanation of why that command is given, or of the good that the commandment is supposed to promote. This, of course, means that the command is unlikely to be followed; and it has in fact been largely disregarded since the Council. This lack of an explanation of the reason for evangelization is a departure from Catholic tradition, which has presented evangelization as an activity that should be undertaken in order to save the souls of unbelievers.[26]

An Unwise Silence Should End

Obviously the Council did not intend to depart from the Catholic tradition on this point. The effort to show how the Council is based on Scripture and tradition contained within both the texts and the footnotes of the documents is impressive. Our examination of just one of these texts, *LG* 16, demonstrates this. There was, though, perhaps an unwise silence on important elements of Scripture and tradition — with the best of intentions. It was a matter of a prudential judgment concerning pastoral strategy. In retrospect it might be fair to say that it was an unwise silence, a flawed pastoral strategy, and that we are overdue for a "rebalancing" of our message and strategy.

It was already apparent to some theologians that there were theological theories circulating that went beyond what the Church understood to be the truth about the salvation of unbelievers, and that had the potential to undermine evangelization. As early as 1933 astute observations were being made, and substantial articles being written, pointing out the emergence of new theological theories that assumed the mercy of God would not permit many to be lost. Such theories, these articles suggested, would convert mission to a matter of "a greater fulness of life" and not really a matter of life or death as regards eternal destiny, and would undermine it. As one such article states, written by a French Dominican theologian:

> If missionary preaching is not so much a question of life or death but rather a question of a greater fulness of life; if it is not a question of life or death for a great number of unbelievers, the Church then is no longer the ordinary way of salvation, but only a school of perfection for great souls called to the fulness of Christian life. The most urgent reason for missions disappears; it will not be equivalently replaced by those reasons that people are trying hard to find, which are not without their value, but until now were only secondary reasons for people to carry out mission.[27]

But these prophetic warnings were not heeded and the tendency was to repeat the argument from authority (we are commanded to evangelize) rather than to elaborate the reasons for the true necessity of such evangelization; namely, vast numbers of people within and without the Church do not appear to be seeking God and trying to do his will, following the light of their consciences, but are rather exchanging the truth of God for a lie, suppressing the truth, and living in rebellion and immorality, needing desperately to be invited to faith and repentance in order to be saved.

It is obvious that the Council itself truly hoped for a great flowering of evangelization but also was aware that there were theories circulating that could undermine this hope. Philips, the principal drafter of *LG,* had very strong things to say about the intention of the Council as regards evangelization. While God is at work in the authentic elements of truth to be found in the world's religions and even in atheists, nevertheless, he repeatedly states, we have an obligation to evangelize since we have been commanded by Christ to do so, noting the citation of Mark 16:15 in the actual text. He even says that failure to obey the command to preach the gospel would actually be a form of "blasphemy."[28]

And then, aware of theological undercurrents already undermining evangelization, already discouraging missionaries, Philips emphatically denies that there is any basis in *LG* for this to happen:

> We cannot remain silent on a paradoxical situation, stirred up by a mis-understanding of the doctrine of the Council. Under the influence of an extension of conciliar perspectives, the missionary zeal of some has been weakened. No ecclesial document has ever emphasized with such insistence the universal missionary obligation as *Lumen Gentium* did, not only in this text, but throughout the Constitution, from the first to the last page. True missionary zeal is the fruit of a pure faith and unselfish charity: that is what Vatican II aimed at, not indifference.[29]

Philips, of course, is right, but the section of *LG* 16 (16c) that could have forestalled such theological misadventures, and that grounded the Council's teaching on this point in Scripture and tradition, has been virtually ignored. *LG* 17 forms the conclusion of the related series of sections (13-17) and gives a stirring call to evangelization, obviously based on the truth that despite the "ordering" of the non-Christian religions, and indeed of all humanity towards Christ and the Church, that in itself does not imply salvation.[30] Salvation requires a response to grace, which is most likely to happen in response to the preaching of the gospel. *LG* 16 concluded by citing the "great commission" that Jesus gives his disciples to evangelize in Mark 16:16. *LG* 17 cites the other "great commission" from Matthew 28:18-20.

> The Church has received this solemn command of Christ from the Apostles and she must fulfill it to the very ends of the earth (cf. Acts 1:8). Therefore she makes the words of the apostle her own, "Woe to me if I do not preach the Gospel" (1 Cor. 9:16), and accordingly never ceases to send heralds of the Gospel. . . . By her proclamation of the Gospel, she draws her hearers to receive and profess the faith, she prepares them for baptism, snatches them from the slavery of error, and she incorporates them into Christ so that in love for him they grow to full maturity . . . [to] the confusion of the devil, and the happiness of man. Each disciple of Christ has the obligation of spreading the faith to the best of his ability. (*LG* 17)

Perhaps the reason why these strong calls to evangelization, which do, in a secondary way, mention elements of the "biblical worldview" concerning sin, error, and the work of the devil, were not able to counter successfully the undermining theological currents is that the argument from authority is not a strong enough argument for ordinary human beings. The reasons for the command — namely, that the eternal destinies of human beings are really at stake and for most people the preaching of the gospel can make a life-or-death, heaven-or-hell difference — need to be unashamedly stated. This is certainly why Jesus often spoke of the eternal consequences of not accepting his teaching — being lost forever, hell — and did not just give the command to evangelize. This is why Mark 16:16, which is referenced in *LG* 16 but not directly quoted, makes explicit that what is at stake is being "saved" or "condemned." Jesus makes clear that Christianity is not a game or an optional enrichment opportunity but a precious and urgent opportunity to find salvation and escape damnation. In fidelity to the teaching of Christ this is what motivated two thousand years of heroic missionary work and the heroic witness of countless martyrs.

Fr. Sullivan, in his account of the history of the development of doctrine, draws our attention to the moving prayer of St. Francis Xavier, which he prayed before receiving communion:

> Everlasting God, Creator of all things, remember that you alone have created the souls of infidels, whom you have made to your image and likeness. Behold, O Lord, how hell is being filled with them to your dishonor.[31]

Fr. Sullivan suggests that Xavier prayed this prayer not because they were condemned to hell due to original sin, but because of their personal sins of idolatry and vice.

> The pathos of this prayer can well be explained by the fact that Xavier believed, with St. Paul (cr. Rom 1:18-32), that people would be justly condemned for sins of idolatry and vice. He had seen enough of these in his missionary work to be pessimistic about the chances that many pagans had escaped condemnation to hell. His urgency about preaching the gospel was heightened by his experience that only through the acceptance of Christian faith and the grace of the sacraments were people cured of their tendencies to idolatry and vice.[32]

Ratzinger's analysis of "Schema 13," which became the Pastoral Constitution on the Church in the Modern World, *Gaudium et spes (GS)*, makes some similar points.

> The chief concern of the text was to speak to contemporary man; thus it had tried to express fundamental theological ideas in a modern way, and in doing so got even further away from scriptural language than did its scholastic predecessors. Biblical citations were little more than ornamental. . . . What interest could an outsider find in a theological statement which had largely divorced itself from its own origins?[33]

Norman Tanner provides a good account of the debate on the multiple drafts of "Schema 13" and notes that concerns like Ratzinger's were often raised.

> There was also the question of whether the decree was indulging in superficial humanism and naïve optimism about the human state and being insufficiently attentive to evil and the reality of sin.[34]

Tanner's judgment is that there is sufficient balance in the actual document regarding the reality of sin, but "maybe after the council the pendulum swung to the other extreme."[35]

Tanner also notes that when using certain key concepts such as "signs of the times," and "the world," *GS* was not using them in the way they are used in the Bible, but in a contemporary, secular manner, which inevitably led away from a spiritually discerning, biblically based approach to contemporary culture.[36]

Even Rahner, who participated in drafting *Gaudium et spes*, later had reservations.

> Although I took part in the elaboration of *Gaudium et Spes* at the Council I would not deny that its undertone is too euphoric in its evaluation of humanity and the human condition. What it says may be true, but it produces the overall impression that it is enough to observe its [*GS*'s] norms, and everything will more or less turn out well.[37]

In one of his later interviews, Rahner bluntly admitted the document's weaknesses.

So the Council's decree *Gaudium et Spes* can be blamed, despite all that is right in it, for underestimating sin, the social consequences of human guilt, the horrible possibilities of running into historical dead-ends, and so on.[38]

Ratzinger applauds the document for its effort to move away from what had been the only two kinds of doctrinal pronouncements in the Church's history: "the creed of obligation and the anathema of negation."

Both kinds of pronouncement made sense only within the realm of faith; they were based on faith's claim to authority. Since the beginning of the modern era there had been increasingly smaller circles of people ready to bow to the authority of the teaching Church.

Yet, he wished that the substitutes — authoritative pronouncements now based on natural law as interpreted by the Church and dialogue — had included a clear option for "the proclamation of the Gospel, thus opening up the faith to the nonbeliever and abdicating all claim to authority other than the intrinsic authority of God's truth, manifesting itself to the hearer of the message."[39]

Ratzinger clearly holds that the inspired assertions of the sacred authors of Scripture are indeed God's Word and should be proclaimed with authority and received as authoritative. He draws our attention to the fact that only Jesus sees the Father and the things of the Father, and it is only in our own union with Jesus and our attentive reception of his Word that we, too, can see, by faith and by the Spirit's gifts of wisdom, knowledge, and understanding, what is true.

In its innermost essence, the Christian faith is a participation in this act whereby Jesus *sees*. His act of seeing makes possible his word, which is the authentic expression of what he sees. Accordingly, what Jesus sees is the point of reference for our faith, the specific place where it is anchored.[40]

He also spelled out more explicitly the deficiencies he saw in the document.

Despite all disavowals, [the document exhibits] an almost naïve progressivist optimism which seemed unaware of the ambivalence of all external human progress. . . . Most important, the schema as a whole tended, in its definition of the relationship between the Christian and the technological world, to see the real meaning of the Christological in the sacred aura it confers upon technological achievement. . . . [This is] a horrible perversion of Christianity. . . . The schema speaks of the victories of mankind, and means by this the phases of technological progress. The Scriptures also know the language of victory but what they mean is the victory of faith, of love . . . the great victory of Jesus Christ. . . . The world is not redeemed by machinery but by love.[41]

He applies the biblical worldview that we have examined in Romans to the issues raised by *GS:*

We recognize that the small righteousness we manage to build up in ourselves is nothing but an emergency morality in the midst of our radical unrighteousness. We are directly and forcefully reminded of St. Paul when we find ourselves forced from behind our shell of protective speculation, forced to admit that our righteousness is nothing but a temporary expedient in the midst of unrighteousness. We find ourselves crying for mercy to him who makes just the unjust. . . . The foremost intention of the Council was to reveal this need for Christ in the depth of the human heart so as to make man able to hear Christ's call.[42]

When Ratzinger commented on some of the theories that were undermining evangelization in connection with the document *AG,* he made a significant statement, which we have already had occasion to note in an earlier chapter but deserves further consideration. He comments on theological theories that saw the world religions as salvific.

Here, again, closer reflection will once more demonstrate that not all the ideas characteristic of modern theology are derived from Scripture. This idea is, if anything, alien to the biblical-thought world or even antipathetic to its spirit. The prevailing optimism, which understands the world religions as in some way salvific agencies, is simply irreconcilable with the biblical assessment of these religions.[43]

It is a commonplace to state that Scripture is the soul of theology, but it is easy enough to drift into speculation that eventually departs from both the letter and spirit of Scripture or to adopt a pastoral strategy that does so. Ratzinger's reference to the "biblical-thought world" and its "spirit" is important to note. We have devoted an entire chapter to examining the biblical-thought world that unfolds in such a shocking manner in the early chapters of Romans. We have devoted another chapter to understanding the careful and precise doctrinal reflection that led to the teaching of *LG* 16. We have devoted two chapters to examining some contemporary theological theories as regards their harmony or lack of harmony with Scripture and tradition. We have not seen that "biblical-thought world" or its "spirit" adequately "handed on" in the postconciliar years. This omission needs to be corrected if the urgent call for a new evangelization is to achieve its considerable promise in the traditionally Christian nations that are now in massive apostasy[44] and in the reenergizing of primary evangelization to the unevangelized peoples of the world.

As Cardinal Ratzinger reminds us, the renewal of the Church and the true implementation of Vatican II are not a matter of a "reform of the Church by paper," or a "paper-dominated Christianity," but rather a matter of a deeper "yes" to the call to conversion and holiness and the embodiment in living witnesses of the hope and promise of Christ and the Council.

> Whether or not the Council becomes a positive force in the history of the Church depends only indirectly on texts and organizations; the crucial question is whether there are individuals — saints — who, by their personal willingness, which cannot be forced, are ready to effect something new and living. The ultimate decision about the historical significance of Vatican Council II depends on whether or not there are individuals prepared to experience in themselves the drama of the separation of the wheat from the cockle and thus to give to the whole a singleness of meaning that it cannot gain from words alone.[45]

Lumen gentium *16*

Latin Text

16. Ii tandem qui Evangelium nondum acceperunt, ad Populum Dei diversis rationibus ordinantur.[32] In primis quidem populus ille cui data fuerunt testamenta et promissa et ex quo Christus ortus est secundum carnem (cf. Rom. 9, 4-5), populus secundum electionem carissimus propter patres: sine poenitentia enim sunt dona et vocatio Dei (cf. Rom. 11, 28-29). Sed propositum salutis et eos amplectitur, qui Creatorem agnoscunt, inter quos imprimis Musulmanos, qui fidem Abrahae se tenere profitentes, nobiscum Deum adorant unicum, misericordem, homines die novissimo iudicaturum. Neque ab aliis, qui in umbris et imaginibus Deum ignotum quaerunt, ab huiusmodi Deus ipse longe est, cum det omnibus vitam et inspirationem et omnia (cf. Acts 17, 25-28), et Salvator velit omnes homines salvos fieri (cf. 1 Tim. 2, 4). Qui enim Evangelium Christi Eiusque Ecclesiam sine culpa ignorantes, Deum tamen sincero corde quaerunt, Eiusque voluntatem per conscientiae dictamen agnitam, operibus adimplere, sub gratiae influxu, conantur, aeternam salutem consequi possunt.[33] Nec divina Providentia auxilia ad salutem necessaria denegat his qui sine culpa ad expressam agnitionem Dei nondum pervenerunt et rectam vitam non sine divina gratia assequi nituntur. Quidquid enim boni et veri apud illos invenitur, ab Ecclesia tamquam praeparatio evangelica aestimatur[34] et ab Illo datum qui illuminat omnem hominem, ut tandem vitam habeat. At saepius homines, a Maligno decepti, evanuerunt in cogitationibus suis, et commutaverunt veritatem Dei in mendacium, servientes creaturae magis quam Creatori (cf. Rom. 1, 21 et 25) vel sine Deo

viventes ac morientes in hoc mundo, extremae desperationi exponuntur. Quapropter ad gloriam Dei et salutem istorum omnium promovendam, Ecclesia, memor mandati Domini dicentis: "Praedicate evangelium omni creaturae" (Mc. 16, 15), missiones fovere sedulo curat.

English Text

16. Finally, those who have not yet received the Gospel are related in various ways to the people of God.[18] In the first place we must recall the people to whom the testament and the promises were given and from whom Christ was born according to the flesh. [Cf. Rom. 9:4-5.] On account of their fathers this people remains most dear to God, for God does not repent of the gifts He makes nor of the calls He issues. [Cf. Rom. 11:28-29.] But the plan of salvation also includes those who acknowledge the Creator. In the first place amongst these there are the Mohamedans, who, professing to hold the faith of Abraham, along with us adore the one and merciful God, who on the last day will judge mankind. Nor is God far distant from those who in shadows and images seek the unknown God, for it is He who gives to all men life and breath and all things [cf. Acts 17:25-28], and as the Saviour wills that all men be saved. [Cf. 1 Tim. 2:4.] Those also can attain to salvation who through no fault of their own do not know the Gospel of Christ or His Church, yet sincerely seek God and moved by grace strive by their deeds to do His will as it is known to them through the dictates of conscience.[19] Nor does Divine Providence deny the helps necessary for salvation to those who, without blame on their part, have not yet arrived at an explicit knowledge of God and with His grace strive to live a good life. Whatever good or truth is found amongst them is looked upon by the Church as a preparation for the Gospel.[20] She knows that it is given by Him who enlightens all men so that they may finally have life. But often men, deceived by the Evil One, have become vain in their reasonings and have exchanged the truth of God for a lie, serving the creature rather than the Creator. [Cf. Rom. 1:21, 25.] Or some there are who, living and dying in this world without God, are exposed to final despair. Wherefore to promote the glory of God and procure the salvation of all of these, and mindful of the command of the Lord, "Preach the Gospel to every creature" [cf. Mark 16:16], the Church fosters the missions with care and attention.

Relatio *on* Lumen gentium *16*

ACTA CONC. VATICANI II — PERIODUS III. PARS I
[53] 206-207
Relatio de n. 16, olim n. 10
Congregatio Generalis LXXX

Latin Text

(A) Nonnulli Patres dolent de indole *nimis individualistica* doctrinae propositae. Ita *Animadv.*, p. 59; E/566. Plurimi autem optant ut in numero de non-christianis tractante, diversae categoriae clare distinguantur et ut pressius tactetur: a) *de Iudaeis: Animadv.*, p. 59, E/537; b) de Mahometanis, ut postulant Epp. plures; c) de populis qui revelationem iudaeo-christianam nondum cognoscentes, *Deum* tamen colunt *ut providentem* et retribuentem; d) tandem *de atheis,* vel potius de illis qui profitentur se esse sine ulla religione, sed revera absolutam Iustitiam vel Pacem quaerunt; ita Epp. plures. Quae divisio in textu emendato observata est. Ceterum, ut dicitur in priore textu, ed.1963, nota 36, p. 19, Christus universos homines obiective redemit eosque ad Ecclesiam vocat et dirigit. Omnis autem gratia quondam indolem communitariam induit et ad Ecclesiam respicit.

My thanks to Raymond Kelly III and Dr. Edward Peters for assistance with the English translation of this text.

(B) *De Iudaeis:* existentia alicuius Declarationis, a Secretariatu pro Unione Christianorum propositae, non aestimatur rationem suflicientem praebere, ut schema de Ecclesia omittat loqui de Iudaeis: fundamentum enim theologicum huius quaestionis indicandum est. Curavit Commissio loqui de Iudaeis sub hoc aspectu, non autem modo mere humano aut politico.

(C) Haec phrasis respicit ad *Islamitas.*

(D) Quidam petunt ut de modo quo salvari possunt sicdicti "infideles" nihil decernatur, quia haec quaestio ad theologiam spectat, v. g. E/542. Aliqui volunt ut explicitius dicatur quibusnam rebus careant infideles, nempe viis ordinariis seu normalibus ad sanctificationem. Alii postulant ut differentia conditionis inter christianos et paganos non mere ponatur in faciliori vel meliori conditione, sed ut fortius exprimatur *status abnormalis* paganorum in aera messianic E/535 (152Epp.). Fere in eumdem sensum nonnulli postulant ut penultima phrasis textus prioris, "Quapropter . . . via salutis pro eis latius sternatur" auferatur.

Quibus postulationibus satisfaction praebetur in ultima sententia textus emendati et in paragraph sequente, de missionibus.

(E) Hoc assertum fundatur in Dei voluntate salvifica universali.

(F) Sermonem de *praeparatione evangelica* in culturis non-christianis enixe petierunt i. a. *Animadv.,* pp. 3 et 59; E/566; E/682.

In textu priore, ed. 1963, Cap. I, nota 38 pp. 19-20, exhibetur, secundum antiques Patres, quaenam elementa religiosa Evangelio prae-existere possint et tamquam praeparatio divinitus data considerari. Sunt autem *semina veritatis,* scilicet notiones de Deo et de anima aliaeque "rationes universales" de quibis agunt v. g. S. Iustinus, Tertullianus, Origenes; deinde *affinitas inter Creatorem et creaturam,* quam i. a. explanant Lactantius et S. Augustinus; denique *paedagogia divinia,* quam post S. Iranaeum exprimit v. g. S. Gregorius [54] Nazianzenus. Textus vide. *l. c.* in ed. 1963.

(G) Haec phrasis, cum sequente, introducta est ut habeatur *transitus* ad ideam de missionibus, de quibus agit n. 17.

(H) Textus sub tenore generali finem a missionibus intentum exprimit, nempe gloriam Dei et salute hominum promovendam, non intrando in ulteriores disceptationes. Adducitur etiam textus Evangelii fundamentalis de praecepto praedicandi.

English Text

(53) Report on number 16 (formerly number 10)

(A) Some fathers are distressed about the *excessively individualistic* nature of the proposed doctrine. So in *Notices* (<u>Animadversiones</u>), p. 59; E/566. However, very many wish that in the section dealing with non-christians, various categories be clearly distinguished and be dealt with rather accurately: a) *on the Jews: Notices* (<u>Animadversiones</u>), p. 59; E/537; b) on the Muslims, as many bishops demand; c) on people who do not re-cognise the judaeo-christian revelation but still worship God as providential and rewarding; d) finally *on atheists,* or rather on those who profess that they are without any religion but truly seek absolute Justice or Peace; many bishops (feel) this way. This issue in dispute is seen in the amended text. On the other hand, as was stated in the earlier text of the 1963 edition, note 36, page 19, "Christ actually redeems all human beings and calls and leads them to the Church." Yet every grace carries a certain communitarian aspect and is in reference to the Church.

(B) *On the Jews:* the existence of a certain Declaration proposed by the Secretariat for the Unity of Christians is not considered to provide sufficient reason for the schema on the Church to omit any mention of the Jews: for the theological foundation for the question must be indicated. The Commission has taken care to discuss the Jews from this point of view (and) not just in a purely human or political way.

(C) This phrase is in respect to the *followers of Islam.*

(D) Some seek that there be no decree on the way in which the so-called "non-believers" can be saved, because this question pertains to theology, see as an example E/542. Some want to speak more explicitly about those things that *non-believers* lack, specifically the normal or regular ways to sanctification. Others demand that the difference in nature (or condition) between Christians and pagans not be merely attributed to a better or a more accessible nature (or condition) but that the abnormal status of the pagans in the messianic era should be more strongly expressed E/535 (152 Epp). Almost in the same sense, some demand that the next to the last sentence in the earlier text, "For this reason, the way of salvation should be made more available," be removed. A satisfactory response to such demands is provided in the last sentence of the revised text and in the following paragraph about the missions.

(E) This assertion is based on God's universal, salvific will.

(F) They zealously seek a discussion on <u>evangelical preparation</u> in non-

Christian cultures, among other (citations) *Notices* (<u>Animadversiones</u>), pp. 3 and 59; E/566; E/682.

In the earlier text, the 1963 edition, Chapter 1, note 38, pp. 19-20, it is shown, according to the early Fathers (of the Church), which religious elements in the Gospel could exist earlier (or pre-exist) and be considered handed on like a preparation for divinity. There exist, however, *seeds of the truth*, clearly notions of God and the soul and other "universal concepts" which are handled by, for example, ST. JUSTINUS, TERTULLIAN, ORIGEN; next, an *affinity between the Creator and the creature*, which, among others, LACTANTIUS and ST. AUGUSTINE explain; then the *divine pedagogy* which, after ST. IRENAEUS, is discussed by, for example, ST. GREGORY OF NAZIANZUS. See the text in the cited location in the 1963 edition.

(G) This and the following phrase were introduced in order that there be a *transition* to the idea about the missions, with which Number 17 deals.

(H) The text in its general tenor expresses a conclusion focused on the missions, specifically that the glory of God and the salvation of human beings must be advanced, not by entering into further debates.

Balthasar's Criticism of Rahner

It is interesting to note that Balthasar aggressively attacks Rahner's theory of the anonymous Christian, and his whole theological approach, not in regards to its universalizing tendency, which Balthasar shares, but on the grounds that the particularity of Christ, and specifically his cross, and the Church, their historical reality and significance, are downplayed; the love of God is reduced to love of neighbor, and everything is subsumed into a philosophy marked by the abstractions of German idealism. There are certainly places in Rahner's writings that could give this impression. For example, in "The Church's Commission to Bring Salvation and the Humanization of the World," in *TI*, vol. 14, pp. 309-10, he makes statements that could easily be construed as collapsing Christianity into love of neighbor. Balthasar treats of the limits of philosophy in many places but devotes an entire article to it, "Meeting God in Today's World," in *Fundamental Theology: The Church and the World, Concilium* 6 (New York: Paulist Press, 1965), pp. 23-39. He criticizes Rahner's whole approach in "Current Trends in Catholic Theology and the Responsibility of the Christian," in *Communio* 5, no. 1 (Spring 1978): 78-80. He rather sarcastically dismisses Rahner's theory in "In Retrospect," *Communio* 2, no. 3 (Fall 1975): 200-203. He critiques what he considers to be Rahner's underemphasis on Scripture and on the paschal mystery rather severely in *Theo-Drama: Theological Dramatic Theory*, vol. IV: *The Action* (San Francisco: Ignatius Press, 1994), pp. 273-84. He severely attacks Rahner's theory of the "anonymous Christian" (and his American disciples) in an interview with Angelo Scola: *Test Everything, Hold Fast to What Is Good: An Interview with Hans Urs von Balthasar*, trans. Maria Shrady (San Francisco: Ignatius Press, 1989), pp. 38-40.

Balthasar opposed Rahner's theological methodology throughout their careers, including their time together on the International Theological Commission. Rowan Williams, "Balthasar and Rahner," in *The Analogy of Beauty: The Theology of Hans Urs von Balthasar*, ed. John Riches (Edinburgh: T. & T. Clark, 1986), pp. 11-34, provides a good account of the theological specifics of their career-long tension. Another excellent account is that of Karen Kilby, "Balthasar and Karl Rahner," in *The Cambridge Companion to Hans Urs von Balthasar*, pp. 256-68. Kilby, pp. 260-61, makes the trenchant comment:

> Balthasar can be a subtle and sympathetic reader of the texts of others, but at times . . . he paints with very broad brush strokes, and whatever the benefits of this, fairness to individuals may be one of the costs . . . such criticisms contain elements of misrepresentation and caricature. . . . It is worth noting, as well, that though Balthasar's criticisms on this point [Rahner's theory of the anonymous Christian] are so forceful, it is not in fact easy to work out how his own views differ from Rahner's on questions of non-Christians and their relationship to Christ, grace, and salvation. . . . In fact, he is probably more emphatic than Rahner in maintaining the legitimacy of Christian hope for universal salvation.

It is somewhat startling to find Balthasar accusing Rahner of veering towards *apokatastasis*!

> Like all systems that fail to take the *sacrum commercium* seriously, Rahner's soteriology lacks the decisive dramatic element. Thus God's "wrath" is always, antecedently, overtaken by his will to save men, a will that is always ahead of all human resistance to God in the direction of *apocatastasis*.[1]

Balthasar opposes Rahner most aggressively in his book *The Moment of Christian Witness*. Balthasar, focusing on his own central insight into the significance for salvation of the "descent into hell" and the holiness and "martyrdom" that it calls forth from us as response, attacks Rahner:

> Anyone who says he is pursuing "theology as anthropology" is saying that every statement made about God in this study is also, in the same way, said of man; but he is silently leaving the presupposition of all theology in the shade: namely, that it is the Logos of a God who speaks to

man. . . . Anyone who speaks of "anonymous Christians" cannot avoid (nor doubtless would he want to) the conclusion that there is ultimately no difference between Christians who are such by name and Christians who are not. Hence — despite all subsequent protests — it cannot matter whether one professes the name or not. And anyone who proclaims the identity of the love of God and one's neighbor and presents the love of one's neighbor as the primary meaning of the love of God must not be surprised (and doubtless is not) if it becomes a matter of indifference whether he professes to believe in God or not. . . . A theology that develops from catchword principles is always a theology that levels out, mitigates and cheapens, and finally liquidates and sells out. Whether it wants to or not, it asymptotically approaches atheism.[2]

Balthasar makes clear that he is not disagreeing with the "universalism" of Rahner's theory, but rather its methodology and its alleged implications for undermining a Church of holiness and beauty. "Of course this is not to deny Karl Rahner's legitimate notion that there is a *fides implicita* and a corresponding supernatural love outside the sphere of Christianity (see Lk 21:1-4) and of the Bible (see Mt 15:21-28), as well as those who are theoretically atheists (Rom 2:14-16)."[3]

Rahner never responded in a comprehensive way to Balthasar but did call Balthasar's speculative theology, with its secret knowledge of what happened in the descent based on the mystical revelations of Adrienne von Speyr, "gnostic." "If I wanted to enter into a counter-attack then I would have to say that there is a modern tendency . . . as much with Balthasar as with Adrienne von Speyr . . . which seems to me to be basically gnostic."[4]

In another essay Rahner makes a comment that probably refers to Balthasar. "Every attempt, even an esoteric one, to advance an Origenistic doctrine of an *Apokatastasis* is fundamentally the assuming of a knowledge which is barred to the creature who must work out his salvation in time and not have certain knowledge of it."[5]

Balthasar ignores the numerous statements of Rahner where he calls the Church to a more heroic and holy life. For example, in acknowledging that the Church of the future will be a little flock engulfed by an aggressively secular culture he states: "If martyrdom represents the situation of the most extreme contradiction between faith and the world surrounding the believer, then the situation we are here discussing is the beginning or a type of martyrdom. But it is of martyrdom that Ignatius of Antioch has said (Rom 2:2) that only here does one begin to be in truth a disciple of Christ."[6]

I think that Eamonn Conway and others have adequately refuted Balthasar's extreme judgments about Rahner and shown that he explicitly does not intend in his theology to deny the significance of the historical life, death, and resurrection of Christ for salvation or the necessity of the Church.[7] From another direction Rahner is attacked as being too conservative and triumphalistic in upholding the uniqueness of Christ and the Church as the means of salvation even for those in other religions. Hans Küng and Paul Knitter attack him for not being "pluralist" enough.[8]

Notes

Notes to Chapter I

1. Paul VI, Apostolic Exhortation, *Evangelii nuntiandi* (hereafter *EN*) (On Evangelization in the Modern World), December 8, 1975 (Boston: Pauline Books and Media, 1976), 2. The numbers after references to papal documents and the documents of Vatican II refer to the numbered sections of such documents, not to page numbers.

2. *EN*, 2.

3. John Paul II, Encyclical Letter, *Redemptoris missio* (hereafter *RM*) (Mission of the Redeemer), December 7, 1990 (Boston: Pauline Books and Media, 1991), 2.

4. John Paul II, Apostolic Letter, *Novo millennio ineunte* (hereafter *NMI*) (At the Beginning of a New Millennium), January 6, 2001 (Boston: Pauline Books and Media, 2001), 2.

5. Avery Dulles, "John Paul II and the New Evangelization," in *Church and Society: The Lawrence J. McGinley Lectures, 1988-2007* (New York: Fordham University Press, 2008), pp. 96-100.

6. *RM*, 33. Here John Paul II distinguishes three phases of the Church's mission: the initial and primary preaching of the gospel to those who have never heard it, *ad gentes;* the pastoral care of those already evangelized, catechized, and living the Christian life; and the "new evangelization" or "re-evangelization" needed "where entire groups of the baptized have lost a living sense of the faith, or even no longer consider themselves members of the Church and live a life far removed from Christ and his Gospel."

7. Benedict XVI has referred to this effect of secularism as a "dictatorship of relativism" numerous times, both before and after he was elected Pope. A recent instance is that of the General Audience of December 16, 2009. In a book he wrote shortly before he was elected Pope, *Christianity and the Crisis of Cultures,* trans. Brian McNeil (San Francisco: Ignatius Press, 2006), Joseph Ratzinger provides an analysis of the philosophical and political trends that have led to the current situation.

8. Joseph Ratzinger, *New Outpourings of the Holy Spirit,* trans. Michael J. Miller and Henry Taylor (San Francisco: Ignatius Press, 2007), p. 115.

9. *NMI*, 2.

10. *NMI*, 40.

11. *RM*, 3.

12. *EN*, 22.

13. *EN*, 27.

14. *RM*, 20.

15. *RM*, 46.

16. A recent major study of religious groupings in the United States has shown that the steady or slightly growing Catholic population is masking a steady and significant decline, apart from Hispanic immigration, primarily because so few people are entering the Catholic Church as a result of evangelization. The study shows that there is a lot of flux in all the religious groupings but the Catholic Church stands out from other groups in bringing in so few new members. See John Allen, "America's Religious Marketplace," http://ncronline.org/blogs/all-things-catholic/americas-religious-marketplace-real-catholic-problem-new-sales (accessed February 11, 2011), who in his interview with the directors of the Pew study, summarizes the findings: "For Catholicism, the banner headline was that there are now 22 million ex-Catholics in America, by far the greatest net loss for any religious body. One in three Americans raised Catholic have left the church. Were it not for immigration, Catholicism in America would be contracting dramatically: for every one member the church adds, it loses four." See also Neil J. Ormerod, "'The Times They Are A-Changin'': A Response to O'Malley and Schloesser," in *Vatican II: Did Anything Happen?* ed. David G. Schultenover (New York: Continuum, 2008), p. 175. Ormerod makes the important point that an exclusive emphasis on "communion" and "the reform of the reform" in terms of the liturgy can produce an inward-turning, aesthetically oriented, culturally inflexible model of church that is not effective for evangelization. "I have argued that, at the very least, *communion* ecclesiology requires some balancing by an emphasis on the mission of the Church as defining its identity. . . . I would argue that a proper recovery of the Church's essentially missionary character [*RM* 5] is needed to prevent the Church from slipping back into the classic conservative antitype from which it attempted to escape through Vatican II. It is simply overloading the language of *communio* to expect it to carry forward this missionary aspect." See also Joseph Ratzinger, *Pilgrim Fellowship of Faith: The Church as Communion*, ed. Stephan Otto Horn and Vinzenz Pfnür, trans. Henry Taylor (San Francisco: Ignatius Press, 2005), p. 287, who makes a similar point: "For the Church it is never merely a matter of maintaining her membership or even of increasing or broadening her own membership. The Church is not there for her own sake. She cannot be like an association that in difficult circumstances, is simply trying to keep its head above water. She has a task to perform for the world, for mankind. The only reason she has to survive is because her disappearance would drag humanity into the whirlpool of the eclipse of God and, thus, into the eclipse, indeed the destruction, of all that is human. We are not fighting for our own survival; we know that we have been entrusted with a mission that lays upon us a responsibility for everyone. That is why the Church has to measure herself, and be measured by others, by the extent to which the presence of God, the knowledge of him, and the acceptance of his will are alive within her. A Church that was merely an organization pursuing its own ends would be the caricature of a Church. To the extent to which she is revolving around herself and looks only to the aims necessary for maintaining herself, she is rendering herself redundant and is in decline, even if she disposes of considerable means and skillful management. She can live and be fruitful only if the primacy of God is alive within her."

17. It is beyond the scope of this book to engage in the discussion on the "hermeneutics of continuity" or "discontinuity" in interpreting Vatican II, the literature of which is sizable and growing. The research and argument of this thesis will demonstrate that, at least as regards *LG* 16, we see a great deal of continuity with the tradition, a continuity that is commonly overlooked. We do not intend by this to take a position on the wider issues of interpretation. It does seem clear, though, that there are significant elements of both continuity and discontinuity in the documents of Vatican II. The discontinuity cannot be held to involve discontinuity concerning doctrine, although a discontinuity of methodology, pastoral strategy, attitude, and formulation can certainly be demonstrated. Two recent books that tend to emphasize opposite sides of the "hermeneutical" discussion are John W. O'Malley, *What Happened at Vatican II* (Cambridge, MA: Harvard University Press, 2007), and Matthew Lamb and Matthew Levering, eds., *Vatican II: Renewal Within Tradition* (New York: Oxford University Press, 2008). Taken together, the two books provide a good range of opinions. More recently, Archbishop Agostino Marchetto, *The Second Vatican Ecumenical Council: A Counterpoint for the History of the Council,* trans. Kenneth D. Whitehead (Scranton, PA: University of Scranton Press, 2010), has published a collection of his reviews, articles, and lectures on the literature that has appeared interpreting Vatican II. The book is valuable for its extensive review of the literature that has appeared in European languages, primarily Italian but also some French and German. Marchetto has a strong point of view that is very much opposed to what he considers the dominant interpretations of "discontinuity" influenced by the School of Bologna, typified by Alberigo's five-volume work. He regularly criticizes mentions of Vatican II as an "event" and any opposition of the "spirit" to the letter. We have found useful insights in all of these works. We have also consulted, and found useful, Benedict XVI's major address on the interpretation of the Council, "Address of His Holiness Benedict XVI to the Roman Curia" http://www.vatican.va/holy_father/benedict_xvi/ speeches/2005/december/documents/hf_ben_xvi_spe_20051222_roman-curia_en.html (accessed February 11, 2011), in which he contrasts a "hermeneutics of discontinuity" with a "hermeneutics of reform." Cardinal Ratzinger in his personal writings as theologian offers some profound insights into the interpretation of the Council. While his comments on the danger of discontinuity are well known, less well known, but nevertheless very important, are his insights into the dangers of "integralism" or "traditionalism" in the interpretation of the Council. Ratzinger is clear that there were significant theological shifts in the Council, that something did change, and that a suspicious and sectarian resistance to this change is a significant problem. See particularly *Principles of Catholic Theology: Building Stones for a Fundamental Theology,* trans. Mary Frances McCarthy (San Francisco: Ignatius Press, 1987), pp. 370-78, 389-91. Also useful is Avery Dulles's analysis of the Extraordinary Synod of Bishops held in 1985 to assess the work of Vatican II: "The Reception of Vatican II at the Extraordinary Synod of 1985," in *The Reception of Vatican II,* ed. Giuseppe Alberigo, Jean-Pierre Jossua, and Joseph A. Komonchak, trans. Matthew J. O'Connell (Washington, DC: Catholic University of America Press, 1987), pp. 349-63. We are in agreement with the hermeneutical principles advanced by Ormond Rush, *Still Interpreting Vatican II: Some Hermeneutical Principles* (New York: Paulist Press, 2004), that any sound interpretation of Council documents must take into account: the history of the development of the particular text, the sources used to develop the text, and of course, the final version of the text. The text in question then must be interpreted in light of other relevant texts in other Council documents. Third, attention must be paid to the "reception" of the text in the life of the Church, both in

the subsequent theological literature and in pastoral life. We will employ each of these elements of a sound hermeneutics as they are relevant to our task. See Francis Sullivan, *Creative Fidelity: Weighing and Interpreting Documents of the Magisterium* (Eugene, OR: Wipf & Stock, 2003), pp. 162-74, for a useful chapter on the question of the doctrinal authority of the various documents of Vatican II. See Ladislas Orsy, *Receiving the Council: Theological and Canonical Insights and Debates* (Collegeville, MN: Liturgical Press, 2009) for a canon law perspective. See also John Michael McDermott, "Did That Really Happen at Vatican II? Reflections on John O'Malley's Recent Book," *Nova et Vetera* (English ed.) 8, no. 2 (2010): 425-66, for a lengthy critique of the hermeneutical approach that John O'Malley takes to his interpretation of Vatican II.

18. *RM*, 9.

19. *RM*, 10.

20. Charles Morerod, O.P., "John Paul's Ecclesiology and St. Thomas Aquinas," in *John Paul II and St. Thomas Aquinas*, ed. Michael Dauphinais and Matthew Levering (Naples, FL: Sapientia Press, 2006), p. 63.

21. *NMI*, 40. See also Ralph Martin, "A New Pentecost: Catholic Theology and 'Baptism in the Spirit,'" *Logos: A Journal of Catholic Thought and Culture* 14, no. 3 (Summer 2011): 17-43.

22. Robert Rivers, *From Maintenance to Mission: Evangelization and the Revitalization of the Parish* (New York: Paulist Press, 2005).

Notes to Chapter II

1. The *Catechism of the Catholic Church* (CCC) cites *LG* 16 as the authority for its teaching on the theological points that pertain to the salvation of those who have not heard the gospel. The treatment is straightforward and includes each of the three main units of *LG* 16. Numbers 761, 839, 841-44, 847, 1260, and 1281 of the Catechism all cite *LG* 16. There is, though, one unfortunate mistranslation of a key text that significantly changes the meaning of the original Latin. In #1281 of the 1994 edition of the Catechism, the English translation: "Those who died for the faith, those who are catechumens, and all those who, without knowing of the Church but acting under the inspiration of grace, seek God sincerely and strive to fulfill his will, are saved even if they have not been baptized (cf. *LG* 16)." The official Latin text, though, is this: #1281 *Qui mortem propter fidem patiuntur, catechumeni et omnes homines qui, sub gratiae impulsu, quin Ecclesiam cognoscant, Deum sincere quaerunt et Eius voluntatem implere conantur, salvari possunt, etiamsi Baptismum non receperint.* The key phrase "salvari possunt" should be translated as "may be saved" or "can be saved" not as "are saved." This is how the phrase is translated in the leading English translations of *LG* 16 and also how it is translated in other places where it appears in the Catechism. The jump from possibility to certainty about the salvation of people in this situation, common as it is, is not warranted by the text. This mistake was corrected in the 1997 edition of the Catechism, but as of this writing (April 26, 2011) the mistranslation is still present in the English text published on the official Vatican website. The 1992 French edition also mistranslates the text and has "sont sauvés" rather than "peuvent être sauvés." The French translation on the Vatican website is now correct. According to Norman Tanner, *The Church and the World: Gaudium*

et Spes, Inter Mirifica (New York: Paulist Press, 2005), pp. 64-65, *LG* is the Council document most frequently cited in the CCC.

2. See Gérard Philips, *L'Église et Son Mystère au Deuxième Concile du Vatican: Histoire, texte et commentaire de la Constitution* Lumen Gentium, vol. 1 (Paris: Desclée, 1967), p. 1: "No one would dispute that the Constitution on the Church of Vatican II would be considered the cornerstone of all the published decrees. The other texts . . . depend directly or indirectly on it." (Nul ne contestera que la Constitution de Vatican II 'sur l'Église,' ne soit à considérer comme la pierre d'angle de tous les décrets publiés. Les autres textes . . . appuient directement ou indirectement sur elle.) Also, later on in the text, on page 208, Msgr. Philips notes that, even though some of these issues were elaborated on and taken up in more detail in other decrees and declarations, the treatment in *LG* is the primary doctrinal treatment on which the other texts build and with which they are intended to harmonize. "As to our text, it studies exclusively the dogmatic aspect of these complex problems." (Quant à notre texte, il étudie exclusivement l'aspect dogmatique de ces problèmes complexes.) See also Joseph Ratzinger, "La Mission d'Après les Autres Textes Conciliaires," in *Vatican II: L'Activité Missionnaire de l'Église* (Paris: Cerf, 1967), p. 122, which makes the point that all treatments of mission in the other Council documents depend on sections 13-17 of *LG*. "It's in the Constitution on the Church, numbers 13-17, that one finds the central text of the Council on the nature, task and path for mission. There, as their foundation, are supported all the other texts related to mission, including the Decree on missionary activity." (C'est dans la Constitution sur l'Église, aux numéros 13 à 17, que se trouve le texte central du Concile, sur la nature, la tâche et la voie de la mission. Là, comme sur leur base de départ, s'appuyent tous les autres textes relatives à la mission, y compris le Décret sur l'activité missionnaire.) See also Joseph Ratzinger, "The Ecclesiology of the Constitution *Lumen Gentium,*" in *Pilgrim Fellowship of Faith: The Church as Communion,* ed. Stephan Otto Horn and Vinzenz Pfnür, trans. Henry Taylor (San Francisco: Ignatius Press, 2005), pp. 123-52. Colman O'Neil, "General Introduction," in *Vatican II on the Church,* ed. Austin Flannery (Dublin: Scepter Books, 1966), p. 9, bluntly states: "This constitution is the central pronouncement of the whole council." (All translations from the French and Italian in this book are mine.)

3. Gérard Philips, "History of the Constitution," in *Commentary on the Documents of Vatican II,* vol. 1 of 5, ed. Herbert Vorgrimler, trans. Kevin Smyth (New York: Crossroads, 1967-1969), p. 137.

4. The full Latin text of *LG* 16 with an English translation, from the Vatican website, www.vatican.va, is provided in Appendix I.

5. A recent doctoral dissertation analyzes philosophically the text of *GS* 22, which states: "For, by his incarnation, he, the Son of God, has in a certain way united himself with each man." See Caroline Farey, "A Metaphysical Investigation of the Anthropological Implications of the Phrase: 'Ipse enim, Filius Dei, incarnatione sua cum omni homine quodammodo se univit' (For, by his incarnation, he, the Son of God, has in a certain way united himself with each man — *Gaudium et spes,* 22)" (Ph.D. diss., Pontificia Universitas Lateranensis, 2008), pp. 162-72. Here too it is clear that the nature of the union is not salvific. Her analysis of "in a certain way" shows the multitude of meanings that could be intended, as well as those that clearly are not. While the dissertation is done in the faculty of philosophy, it draws heavily on patristic and scholastic theological sources. Her conclusions mirror Aquinas's understanding of a union that brings with it "potential."

6. The following footnote is inserted here as backing for this text: "See Eusebius of

Caesarea, *Praeparatio Evangelica*, I, 1: PG 21, 28 AB." Joseph Ratzinger, "La Mission d'Après les Autres Textes Conciliaires," in *Vatican II: L'Activité Missionnaire de l'Église* (Paris: Cerf, 1967), p. 129, note 11, indicates that this reference to Eusebius does not really support the point being made, but, of course, the point can be supported in other ways. "The reason for this allusion is not very clear, since in this work Eusebius, in treating of the non-Christian religions, has another emphasis than our text: Eusebius underlines the aberrations of the pagan myths and the insufficiency of Greek philosophy; he shows that Christians are right in neglecting these in order to turn to the sacred writings of the Hebrews which constitute the true 'preparation for the gospel.'" (La raison de cette allusion n'est pas très claire, car dans cet ourvrage l'orientation d'Eusèbe, par rapport aux religions non chrétiennes, est tout autre que dans notre texte: Eusèbe signale les égarements des mythes païens et l'insuffisane de la philosophie grecque; il montre que les chrétiens voint juste en les négligeant pour se tourner vers les livres saints des Hébreux qui constituent las véritable 'préparation évangélique.') The Sources Chrétiennes translation of this text, *La Préparation Évangélique: Livre I*, trans. Jean Sirinelli et Édouard des Places (Paris: Cerf, 1974), pp. 97-105, shows that Eusebius, in the chapter cited, only mentions the non-Christian religions and philosophies as being in dire need of conversion. He speaks of them as representing a piety that is "lying and aberrant" *(mensongère et aberrante)* and cites the Scripture that speaks of "exterminating all the gods of the nations" and making them "prostrate before Him."

7. The Walter Abbott translation that appeared in 1966 translates the Latin phrase as "But rather often." The commonly used Flannery translation of the Council documents translates the Latin *at saepius* as "very often." This is the translation we will be using. (Austin Flannery, ed., *Vatican Council II: The Conciliar and Post Conciliar Documents,* New Revised Edition, vol. 1 [Northport, NY: Costello Publishing, 1996].) Other English translations use "but often," (the translation of the National Catholic Welfare Conference, the precursor of the National Council of Catholic Bishops; contained in *The Sixteen Documents of Vatican II: Introductions by Douglas G. Bushman* (Boston: Pauline Books and Media, 1999). The Vatican website translation which is available in Appendix I also uses "but often." The English translation (by Clarence Gallagher) of *Lumen gentium* in Norman Tanner's two-volume collection of the *Decrees of the Ecumenical Councils* (Washington, DC: Georgetown University Press, 1990) uses "more often, however." The French translation of the text that Congar collaborated on translates *at saepius* as "mais trop souvent." *L'Église de Vatican II,* Tome I, Texte Latin et Traduction, P.-Th. Camelot (Paris: Cerf, 1966). The Vatican website translation uses "bien souvent." The Italian translation on the Vatican website is "ma molto spesso." The Spanish translation on the Vatican website is "pero con mucha frecuencia."

8. Joseph Ratzinger, "Pastoral Constitution on the Church in the Modern World," in *Commentary on the Documents of Vatican II,* ed. Herbert Vorgrimler, trans. W. J. O'Hara, vol. 5 (London: Burns & Oates; New York: Herder & Herder, 1969), pp. 161-63.

9. There are many accounts of the development of *LG* from its initial draft to its final text. One of the best is that of Jorge Medina Estevez, "The Constitution on the Church: Lumen Gentium," in *Vatican II: An Interfaith Appraisal,* ed. John H. Miller (Notre Dame: University of Notre Dame Press, 1966), pp. 101-22. Another comprehensive account of the stages that *LG* went through before its final approval is that of Colman O'Neil, "General Introduction," pp. 10-17. One of the most recent, that of Richard Gaillardetz, *The Church in the Making: Lumen Gentium, Christus Dominus, Orientalium Ecclesiarum* (New York: Paulist Press, 2006), pp. 8-27, 149, in the Paulist Press series commemorating the fortieth anniver-

sary of the Council, also affirms that there was no particular controversy connected with *LG* 16. Now that all the relevant documents have been finally published, Gaillardetz shows once again, in his tracing of the development of the various drafts, forty years after, that the teaching of *LG* 16 was not viewed as controversial. Gaillardetz acknowledges that in this commentary on *LG* he did not communicate its overall missionary context as much as he would have liked.

10. *De Ecclesiae,* chapter 2, #9, "The Members of the Church Militant and Her Necessity for Salvation." I am grateful to Fr. Joseph Komonchak for permitting me to quote his unpublished English translation of *De Ecclesiae.*

11. Karl Rahner, "Observations on the Problem of the 'Anonymous Christian,'" in *Theological Investigations,* vol. 14 (New York: Seabury, 1979), pp. 284, 286.

12. The *relatio* for *LG* 16 in its original Latin along with an English translation is available in Appendix II.

13. *Acta synodalia Sacrosancti Concilii Oecumenici Vaticani II,* Volumen III, Periodus Tertia, Pars I, Sessio Publica IV, Congregationes Generales LXXX-LXXXII, Relatio de n. 15, Olim N. 9, (A) 1, p. 203. The Commission decided that the anxieties of some Council fathers were not well founded.

14. It took 59 lines of text to present the main suggestions and requests for revisions and give the decisions of the Commission for *LG* 13; 69 lines of text for *LG* 14; 92 lines of text for *LG* 15; and 50 lines of text for *LG* 16.

15. Giuseppe Alberigo and Franca Magistretti, *Constitutionis Dogmaticae Lumen Gentium: Synopsis Historica* (Bologna: Istituto per le Scienze Religiose, 1975), provide a well-organized resource for the history of the development of the text, detailing changes that happened over what they determine to have been seven different drafts, including texts that circulated in mimeographed form. Fr. Francis Sullivan, *Salvation Outside the Church?* (Eugene, OR: Wipf & Stock, 1992), pp. 141-61, traces the development of the various texts of what became *LG* through the course of the Council as it pertains to the questions with which we are concerned. He picks out from each of the main drafts the development of teaching that eventually found expression in *LG* 14-16. He provides translations of the Latin texts found in the *Acta* of the Council that pertain to this development: AS I/4, 15, 18; AS II/1, 220-21; AS III/1, 202-3, 206; AS III/2, 335. See also Gaillardetz, *The Church and the World,* pp. 8-27; Ralph M. Wiltgen, *The Rhine Flows into the Tiber: A History of Vatican II* (Rockford, IL: Tan Books and Publishers, 1985), pp. 56-60, 84-109, 153-59, 228-34; Maximilian Heinrich Heim, *Joseph Ratzinger: Life in the Church and Living Theology, Fundamentals of Ecclesiology with Reference to* Lumen Gentium, trans. Michael J. Miller (San Francisco: Ignatius Press, 2007), pp. 29-38. Jerome Theisen, *The Ultimate Church and the Promise of Salvation* (Collegeville, MN: St. John's University Press, 1976), p. 57, also includes a brief discussion on the *relatio* that summarized the input received from Council fathers on the proposed text and the response of the Theological Commission. He notes that some fathers requested that a more communitarian framework be provided (cf. AS III/1, 206), and some fathers requested that the theology behind the teaching here be spelled out more precisely (cf. AS III/1, 206). Others wanted it to be specifically mentioned that unbelievers lacked the ordinary and normal means of salvation, and that since they were living in the times after Christ, their status was abnormal. The response of the Theological Commission was to include a few communitarian comments in their revision of the final text but to decline to provide more theological elaboration. The Commission also said that they thought the strong call to

evangelization in the last sentence of *LG* 16 and the whole of *LG* 17 was adequate to meet other concerns. Theisen concludes: "We need not concern ourselves about this teaching which has been official for more than a century, nor about the theology which the council preferred to presuppose rather than to analyze (against the wishes of some fathers who requested an elaboration of the issue)." He comments that "it is interesting to compare the outlook of the 152 bishops concerning the abnormal state of those living without explicit belief in Christ with the position of some theologians today (and then) who view Christianity as the extraordinary means of salvation and who consider salvational modes outside Christianity as normal and ordinary." He cites a book by H. R. Schlette, *Towards a Theology of Religions* (New York: Herder & Herder, 1966), as an example of this theology.

16. Joseph Ratzinger, *Theological Highlights of Vatican II* (New York: Paulist Press, 1966), pp. 84, 109, 139. The issues that Ratzinger cites that were central to the Council's concerns are as follows: the problems of Divine Worship, centralization in the Church including the major issue of collegiality, relations with non-Catholic Christianity and the ecumenical movement, which in its earlier discussions included texts on relations with the Jews (later to be split off into a separate schema), religious liberty, and the challenge of how to speak to and think about the modern world. As one illustration of this he mentions that in the initial round of voting on *LG* there were only ten ballots taken to decide issues in seven of the eight chapters: 1-2, and 4-8. And yet there were forty-one separate votes taken for chapter 3, which contained the collegiality teaching. In Marchetto's 707-page survey of the interpretive literature on Vatican II (Marchetto, *Vatican Council,* pp. 124, 449-50), there is scarcely a mention of any issue connected with *LG* 16. He notes that the votes on chapters 1 and 2 of *LG* were "easy." And eventually the vote for the entire document, including the controversial chapter 3 on the relationship between Pope and bishops, was "virtually unanimous." He does note that in connection with the consideration of *Ad gentes,* some of the *vota* submitted by the Council fathers raised issues that indicated awareness of theological issues circulating concerning universal salvation, but there was no sustained discussion of this at the Council.

17. Philips, "History of the Constitution," pp. 1, 133, notes that five fathers requested that there be a mention of hell and purgatory in what was to become the chapter on eschatology (chapter 7) of *LG.* See also Xavier Rynne, *Vatican Council II: An Authoritative One-Volume Version of the Four Historic Books* (New York: Farrar, Straus & Giroux, 1968), p. 294. Wiltgen, *The Rhine,* p. 153, cites the intervention of one such Council father, in the discussion of chapter 7 of *LG,* the chapter on eschatology that had been requested by Pope John XXIII: "The Latin-rite Patriarch of Jerusalem, Alberto Gori, objected strongly to the chapter, saying that the text should not be silent 'on the existence of hell, on the eternity of hell,' and on the possibility of 'personal damnation.' These were truths that had been explicitly revealed, he said, and should today be given their proper emphasis. He said that many, in their sermons, seemed to shrink from expressing these doctrines openly and clearly." These suggestions were generally noncontroversial. No one thought the truths were being denied by not being mentioned, but in an effort to keep the orientation "positive" these mentions were kept to a minimum. As John XXIII put it in his opening address to the Council, "Discourse of the Holy Father John XXIII on the Solemn Opening of the Ecumenical Council Vatican II," October 11, 1962: "The salient point of this Council is not, therefore, a discussion of one article or another of the fundamental doctrine of the Church which has repeatedly been taught by the Fathers and by ancient and modern theologians, and which is presumed

to be well known and familiar to all." In other words, in the words of John XXIII, the basic doctrinal tradition is to be presumed, which helps explain why efforts to restate it in Council documents were, on the whole, not thought necessary. When one Council father requested a modification in the text that indicated that some people are actually in hell "lest damnation remain a simple, unrealized possibility" (Modification #40), Bishop Bonaventure Kloppenburg, *The Ecclesiology of Vatican II* (Chicago: Franciscan Herald Press, 1974), p. 331, reports the response of the Theological Commission to this suggestion was to point out that *LG* 48 indeed cites texts "in which the Lord speaks of the damned as of a future fact." In other words, the Commission is assuring the Council fathers that there is no intention to deny that the Lord is not just talking about a future possibility but of a future fact, and that there are indeed those who are or will be, reprobate, damned. See AS III/8, 144-45, for the official text.

18. Related issues surfaced in the debate on *GS* concerning the "overly optimistic" depiction of the world and its progress about which a significant minority of the Council fathers, including some of the most prominent "progressive" theologians, expressed concern. See John O'Malley, *What Happened at Vatican II* (Cambridge, MA: Harvard University Press, 2008), pp. 258-68. Wiltgen, *The Rhine*, pp. 253-54, notes Cardinal Koenig's concerns at the evolution of GS: "Cardinal Koenig called for the inclusion of concepts that had been omitted by those who had prepared the schema, concepts such as 'sin, the truth of the Cross, the need for repentance and the hope of resurrection with Christ.' Only thus could the danger be averted of 'promising a paradise on earth and a solution to all problems, something that cannot be realized save in the world to come.'" Wiltgen also notes that "Cardinal Frings of Cologne called for a substantial reorganization of the entire text because of a dangerous confusion between human progress, resulting from dialogue, and supernatural salvation, wrought by Christ's mission."

19. Philips, "History of the Constitution," p. 112, states that the material on the episcopate was "by far the most hotly debated."

20. O'Malley, *What Happened at Vatican II*, pp. 5-12, 175, points out that the fundamental teaching about the possibility of people being saved without explicit faith in Christ was considered to have already been settled by the summary of doctrinal development on this point that was contained in the *Letter to the Archbishop of Boston* in regard to the Fr. Feeney case, and therefore the teaching of *LG* 16 in this regard was seen as noncontroversial. He points out that all three of the primary drafts of the texts of *De Ecclesia* that became *LG* stated this teaching in basically the same way: "All three versions of the schema indicate in different ways that even the non-baptized who sincerely follow their consciences are somehow joined to the church and saved. The later versions however, make the new and important point that many elements of sanctification are available outside the church, and that the Holy Spirit works for the sanctification of all the baptized. Although this can be interpreted as substantially the same teaching as in the Feeney case, it was expressed less grudgingly and with more explicit theological grounding. It focused on the glass as half full rather than as half empty." O'Malley is here conflating two different issues (that of the nonbaptized being saved, and the way of conceiving non-Catholic Christians' relationship to the Church), and his one-sentence summary concerning the nonbaptized is too incomplete to be an adequate statement of the teaching. Nevertheless, his views on the noncontroversial nature of the teaching of *LG* 16 concur with that of our other commentators. His listing of the most im-

portant and contentious issues also agrees in large part with the other commentators we have cited in this regard.

21. See Robert J. Schreiter, "Changes in Roman Catholic Attitudes toward Proselytism and Mission," in *New Directions in Mission and Evangelization 2: Theological Foundations,* ed. James A. Scherer and Stephen B. Bevans (Maryknoll, NY: Orbis, 1994), pp. 114, 118-19. Schreiter, a well-known Catholic missiologist, describes the crisis that followed Vatican II as it affected the worldwide missionary effort of the Church, attributing it in part to the general questioning of certainties that took place after the Council, and most specifically to "the most profound questioning of the missionary movement, both in its principles and its practice, that the Catholic Church had ever undergone." He cites the shift from a conversion-oriented understanding of mission to an understanding that now included dialogue, inculturation, respect for non-Christian religions, and sensitivity to Western imposition of culture in the name of the gospel as all contributing to the crisis. But he singles out the question about how necessary it is, really, for someone to become a Christian and a member of the Church in order to be saved. "To be sure, the Council documents continue to speak of the necessity of the church and membership in the church as the visible sign of the fullness of salvation to which we might attain here on earth. But in almost the same breath, speaking of the church as pilgrim and provisional necessarily opened up the question of just how necessary the church was — really — to salvation. Might not conversion to a better life along the lines one's life had already taken be a better task for the missionary rather than insisting upon formal membership in the church? And what was to come into greater evidence in the succeeding period was that the boundaries of church itself, once so dear and secure, were now beginning to appear considerably vaguer."

22. Ratzinger, *Theological Highlights,* p. 172.

23. There are many surveys of the tradition on this point. For a thorough but brief survey, see Avery Dulles, "The Population of Hell," *First Things* 133 (May 2003): 36-41. This essay has been reprinted in a collection of Dulles's lectures and articles, in Avery Dulles, *Church and Society: The Lawrence J. McGinley Lectures, 1988-2007* (New York: Fordham University Press, 2008), pp. 387-400. Citations to this article in this book will be based on the article's first publication in *First Things.*

24. Ratzinger, *Theological Highlights,* p. 173. A recent study, *The Catholic Doctrine of Non-Christian Religions: According to the Second Vatican Council* by Mikka Ruokanen (Leiden: E. J. Brill, 1992), pp. 144-45, demonstrates that Vatican II did not teach that non-Christian religions were salvific as religious systems, although individuals within them could of course be in a situation to be saved by meeting the conditions stated in *LG* 16. Ruokanen points out that Paul Knitter, who wishes to claim that these religions are salvific in some ways, agrees with Ruokanen that Vatican II does not teach that non-Christian religions are salvific, although he believes it leaves the door open to such a doctrinal development, a doctrinal development that he thinks should be pursued. Paul VI, *EN* 53, expresses the teaching of Vatican II on this issue in these terms: "In other words, our religion effectively establishes with God an authentic and living relationship which the other religions do not succeed in doing, even though they have, as it were, their arms stretched towards heaven." Congregation for the Doctrine of the Faith, *Dominus Iesus: On the Unicity and Salvific Universality of Jesus Christ and the Church* (hereafter DI), August 6, 2000 (Boston: Pauline Books and Media, 2000) affirms this position: "If it is true that the followers of other religions can receive divine grace, it is also certain that objectively speaking

they are in a gravely deficient situation in comparison with those who, in the Church, have the fullness of the means of salvation" (DI 22). On a secondary matter, but one that is of interest, Ratzinger, *Theological Highlights*, p. 174, expresses an implied concern about a possible overcomplication of the missionary enterprise by paying so much attention to the challenge of cultural adaptation. "A most remarkable feature of our era of history is the fact that another European world religion has succeeded very well in taking root throughout the world. The Marxist idea has conquered the world. It has done this by ignoring all the theories of adaptation and cultural implantation and adjustment which have been so much a part of missionary theology. It has been carried forward on the compelling dynamism of its new promise."

25. Kloppenburg, *The Ecclesiology of Vatican II*, p. 74.

26. Kloppenburg, *The Ecclesiology of Vatican II*, p. 74.

27. Fr. John Michael McDermott, "Lumen Gentium: The Once and Future Constitution," in *After Forty Years: Vatican Council II's Diverse Legacy*, ed. Kenneth D. Whitehead (South Bend, IN: St. Augustine's Press, 2007), pp. 134-64, provides an impressive analysis of *LG* from the point of view of Thomistic metaphysics, but does not explore the point we are mainly interested in. In McDermott, "Did That Really Happen at Vatican II? Reflections on John O'Malley's Recent Book," pp. 425-66, he does make some comments on this issue. Alan Schreck, in *Vatican II: The Crisis and the Promise* (Cincinnati: Servant/St. Anthony, 2005), pp. 226-29, is one of the few commentators who clearly explicate both parts of the *LG* 16 text we are considering, although he does so briefly, in keeping with the plan of his book. One of the principal contributors to *LG*, Philips, in "History of the Constitution," p. 112, does not even mention this section of *LG* 16. He does comment on it in his major work, *L'Église et Son Mystère*, pp. 207-14. Aloys Grillmeier, "The People of God," pp. 182-84, in Vorgrimler, *Commentary*, does not comment on the concluding section of the *LG* 16 text that speaks of the high frequency of the conditions under which the non-evangelized can be saved not being met. Henri de Lubac, "Lumen Gentium and the Fathers," in Miller, *Interfaith*, p. 157, discusses *LG* 16 but does not comment on *LG* 16c either. Theisen, *The Ultimate Church*, p. 54, briefly mentions the last three sentences of *LG* 16 but does not advert to their implications in the rest of his book devoted to the subject of the work of grace outside the Church.

28. Christopher O'Donnell, "The People of God," in *Vatican II on the Church*, ed. Austin Flannery (Dublin: Scepter Books, 1966), pp. 43-44.

29. Francis Cardinal George, "The Decree on the Church's Missionary Activity, Ad Gentes," in *Vatican II: Renewal within Tradition*, ed. Matthew L. Lamb and Matthew Levering (London and New York: Oxford University Press, 2008), p. 297.

30. See Basil Christopher Butler, "Les chrétiens non-catholiques et l'Église," in *L'Église de Vatican II: Études autour de la Constitution conciliaire sur l'Église*, Tome II, ed. Guilherme Baraúna and Y. Congar (Paris: Cerf, 1966), pp. 657, 667-68. In Butler's commentary on this section of *LG* 16 he seems to make such a jump. "The Constitution remains vague in its terms, but suggests probably that a non-negligible number of those (of which the greater part will die without baptism) will be saved and therefore are 'on the way.'" (La Constitution reste vague dans les termes, mais elle suggère probablement qu'un nombre non négligeable de tous ceux-là [dont la plupart mourront sans baptême] seront sauvés et sont donc 'sur la voie.')

31. Kevin McNamara, "The People of God," in *Vatican II: The Constitution on the*

Church: A Theological and Pastoral Commentary, ed. Kevin McNamara (Chicago: Franciscan Herald Press, 1968), p. 158.

32. Gustave Thils, "Ceux qui n'ont pas reçu l'évangile," in *L'Église de Vatican II: Études autour de la Constitution conciliaire sur l'Église*, Tome II, p. 673. (Faut-il ajouter que ces appréciations sont compensées par les jugements défavorables de très nombreux écrivains ecclésiastiques? Et dans la Constitution *Lumen gentium* [II, no. 16], on peut lire que "trop souvent, les hommes trompés par le Malin, ont perdu le sens dans leurs raisonnements, ils ont transformé en mensonge la vérité de Dieu and ont servi la créature plutôt que le Créateur [cf. Rm. 1, 21 et 25]. . . ." Du moins demeure la conclusion qu'une certaine perfection dans le paganisme paraît un idéal réalisable.)

33. Josephine Lombardi, in *The Universal Salvific Will of God in Official Documents of the Roman Catholic Church* (Lewiston, NY: Edwin Mellen Press, 2007), pp. 79-80, the book based on her doctoral dissertation, briefly mentions the full text of *LG* 16 once, but leaves out the critical phrase "very often" and substitutes for it her minimizing paraphrase "some." She refers repeatedly to the teaching of *LG* 16b (more than a dozen times) to reinforce her argument for a development of the Council teaching in the direction that she points out Jacques Dupuis and Paul Knitter have taken, but never adverts to or comments on the significant "third part," the *LG* 16c teaching.

34. Grillmeier, "The People of God," p. 182, in *Commentary*, ed. Vorgrimler.

35. Grillmeier, "The People of God," p. 292. The Cordeiro quote is taken from AS, IV/4, 151.

36. Grillmeier, "The People of God," p. 292. The Suenens quote is from AS, IV/4, 179-80.

37. Philips, "History of the Constitution," p. 128.

38. Philips, *L'Église*, p. 210. (Ils le connaissent à travers la création, écrit saint Paul aux Romains, I, 19-20, et ils accomplissent ce que sa loi a inscrit dans leur coeur [Rom., 2, 14-15]. Le tableau de la perversion païenne, si sombre qu'il soit comme le dépeint saint Paul, ne permet pas d'accuser son auteur de pessimisme. Une exégèse réaliste nous prescrit de tenir compte de l'alternance de lumière et d'ombres dans l'exposé de sa doctrine.)

39. Philips, *L'Église*, pp. 214-15. (Cette soi-disant largeur de vues, si prisée de nos jours, est en réaction contre la prédication antérieure brandissant les foudres à propos de la perversion du monde et prédisant la ruine de l'univers comme si le Sauveur n'était pas venu. D'une position extrême, certains passent à l'autre extrême sans souci de réalisme. L'opposition du Malin contre le Christ et contre ses fidèles n'est pas un mythe moyenâgeux, encore qu'il ne soit pas nécessaire de se présenter le démon avec des cornes et un pied de bouc. Saint Paul n'excuse en aucune manière les adorateurs d'idoles qui dans leurs raisonnements vains et obscurs, ont échangé la vérité pour le mensonge [Rom., I 20 et 25]. Ils ont élevé la créature ou ils se sont élevés eux-mêmes au niveau de Dieu, où ils essayent de supprimer Dieu complètement, si bien qu'il ne leur reste que l'ultime désespoir. L'absurde doit donner la clef du réel. Le temps presse donc de contrer la tentation qui émane des idoles primitives ou de celles de la haute intellectualité.)

40. "(D) Quidam petunt ut de *modo* quo salvari possunt sic dicti 'infideles' nihil dernatur, quia haec quaestio ad theologiam spectat. . . ." See Appendix II.

41. Grillmeier, "The People of God," pp. 183-84.

42. Christopher Butler, *The Theology of Vatican II* (Westminster, MD: Christian Classics, 1981), p. 63.

43. Avery Dulles, "The Church as Locus of Salvation," in *The Thought of John Paul II: A Collection of Essays and Studies,* ed. John M. McDermott (Rome: Editrice Pontificia Università Gregoriana, 1993), pp. 179-80. George Sabra, in *Thomas Aquinas' Vision of the Church* (Mainz: Matthias-Grunewald-Verlag, 1987), pp. 146-82, provides a very thorough survey of all of Thomas's writings on this subject, including a careful analysis of all five instances in which Thomas comments explicitly on EENS.

44. James T. O'Connor, *Land of the Living: A Theology of the Last Things* (New York: Catholic Book Publishing, 1992), p. 73. Candido Pozo, *Theology of the Beyond,* trans. Mark A. Pilon (New York: Alba House, 2009), pp. 419-28, also provides an illuminating discussion of this issue in his lengthy study of eschatology.

45. Catherine of Siena, *The Dialogue,* trans. and intro. Suzanne Noffke (New York: Paulist Press, 1980), #37.

Notes to Chapter III

1. The original text of *De ecclesiae,* which evolved into the text we are now considering, contained very similar teaching. "Although many real relations exist in the juridical and sacramental order, and indeed can exist in the mystical order, by which every baptized person is linked with the Church, still, according to the most ancient tradition, only they are called members of the Church in the true and proper sense in whom the Church, one and indivisible, indefectible and infallible, comes together in unity of faith, sacraments and government. Therefore, they alone are to be said to be truly and properly members of the Church who, washed in the bath of regeneration, professing the true Catholic faith, and acknowledging the authority of the Church, are joined in its visible structure to its Head, Christ, who rules it through his Vicar, and have not been cut off from the structure of the Mystical Body because of very serious offences." *De ecclesiae,* Chapter II, #9. English translation of Fr. Joseph Komonchak used with his kind permission.

2. A footnote in *LG* 14 lists several citations from the works of St. Augustine as support for the phrases quoted here.

3. See Jean-Guy Pagé, *Qui Est L'Église? Le Peuple de Dieu,* vol. 3 of 3 (Montréal: Les Éditions Bellarmin, 1979), p. 52. However, it must be noted that the original text prepared by the curia and presented to the Council Fathers at the beginning of the Council contained very similar teaching. "The Holy Synod teaches, as God's Holy Church has always taught, that the Church is necessary for salvation and that no one can be saved who, knowing that the Catholic Church was founded by God through Jesus Christ, nevertheless refuses to enter her or to persevere in her. Just as no one can be saved except by receiving baptism — by which anyone who does not pose some obstacle to incorporation becomes a member of the Church — or at least by desire for baptism, so also no one can attain salvation unless he is a member of the Church or at least is ordered towards the Church by desire. But for someone to attain to salvation, it is not enough that he be really a member of the Church or be by desire ordered towards it; it is also required that he die in the state of grace, joined to God by faith, hope, and charity." (The *Letter of the Holy Office to the Archbishop of Boston* is cited as support for this point.) *De ecclesiae,* Chapter II, #8. Unpublished English translation used with the kind permission of Fr. Joseph Komonchak.

4. Luke 12:48 is cited as support for this teaching as well as Matthew 5:19-20; 7:21-22;

25:41-46; James 2:14. The wording of *De ecclesiae* is remarkably similar: "Therefore, let all the children of the Church be mindful of their own privileged condition, which they must ascribe not to their own merits but to the special grace of Christ; and, if they do not correspond to this grace in thought, word and deed, not only will they not be saved, they will be the more severely judged." (Matt. 5:19-20; 7:21-22; 25:41-46; James 2:14 are cited in support.) *De ecclesiae*, Chapter II, #10. Unpublished translation of Fr. Joseph Komonchak, used with permission.

5. Yves Congar, *The Wide World My Parish: Salvation and Its Problems* (Baltimore: Helicon Press, 1961), pp. 145-46.

6. *UR*, 1.

7. A two-part article by Alexandra Diriart, "L'Ecclésiologie du Corps du Christ dans Lumen Gentium: Méfiance des Pères conciliaires ou réappropriation? (I)," *Nova et Vetera* 84, no. 4 (October-December 2009): 253-75, and part II, in the same issue, 373-95, explores the meaning of the language used to describe the Church in *LG*, bringing out both its continuity with tradition and yet its newness.

8. Kloppenburg, *The Ecclesiology of Vatican II*, trans. Matthew J. O'Connell (Chicago: Franciscan Herald Press, 1974), p. 66.

9. *UR*, 3.

10. *UR*, 4.

11. *UR*, 3.

12. DS 1351. The Decretal *Firmiter* was the first Conciliar document to bring the Patristic axiom, EENS, into an official magisterial statement, although Pope Innocent III had used similar language a few years earlier in a confession of faith proposed to the Waldensians. DS 792. See George Sabra, *Thomas Aquinas' Vision of the Church* (Mainz: Matthias-Grunewald-Verlag, 1987), pp. 158-59, for a discussion of this.

13. *UR*, 4.

14. For a classic work on the development of doctrine, see John Cardinal Henry Newman, *An Essay on the Development of Christian Doctrine* (Notre Dame: University of Notre Dame Press, 1989). See also the document of the CDF that treats of authentic and inauthentic development of doctrine, making the important distinction between the substance of the faith and its historical expression: *Mysterium Ecclesiae*, AAS 65 (1973). Although we will not consider this question because of our particular focus, legitimate questions have been raised about whether EENS as originally understood, and how it is interpreted today by the magisterium, is not so variant that some further explanation is necessary and that to simply declare it an authentic development stretches the meaning of development. Some ask the question whether what we have here is truly continuity, or actually contradiction. This issue is taken up in a responsible manner by Bernard Sesboué in his book, *Hors de l'Église pas de salut: Histoire d'une formule et problèmes d'interprétation* (Paris: Desclée, 2004). He cites Yves Congar's observations on this question to the effect that we must recognize the historical limitations of the early formulations and also recognize the principle that is contained in these limited formulas that can be carried forward into the future. Sesboué is not satisfied with this approach and raises the question about whether something more forthright is needed to safeguard the honesty of the Church while stopping short of claiming that it at one time formally taught error. Sesboué suggests (p. 363) that an official statement is necessary admitting the gravely inadequate and badly put earlier formulation while not admitting that error was formally taught. "But to acknowledge a limitation

or a seriously badly put formulation is not to admit a formal error." (Mais avouer une limite ou la grave maladresse d'une formulation n'est pas pour autant avouer une erreur formelle.) Jerome P. Theisen, *The Ultimate Church and the Promise of Salvation* (Collegeville, MN: St. John's University Press, 1976), p. 153, recommends "retiring" the axiom since it requires so much explanation and, in his opinion, does not in fact communicate with adequate nuance what has come to be understood as the sensible understanding of the axiom. "It is not only possible for the church but incumbent upon it to relinquish the traditional axiom. It cannot be taken literally; it never could, even in its original formulation. Thus, linguistic honesty requires its abandonment."

15. Avery Dulles, "*Dominus Iesus,* A Catholic Response," *Pro Ecclesia* 10, no. 1 (Winter 2001): 6.

16. Cardinal George, p. 303, believes that *Dominus Iesus* does rule out a future "development of doctrine" that would equate the "belief" of non-Christian religions with the infused supernatural virtue of faith in Christianity. "For this reason, the distinction between theological faith and belief, in the other religions, must be firmly held. If faith is the acceptance in grace of revealed truth, which 'makes it possible to penetrate the mystery in a way that allows us to understand it coherently' (John Paul II, *Fides et Ratio,* 13), then belief, in the other religions is that sum of experience and thought that constitutes the human treasury of wisdom and religious aspiration, which man in his search for truth has conceived and acted upon in his relationship to God and the Absolute (FR, 31-32; DI, 7)."

17. Most commentators on this issue provide an account of the history of the development of this doctrine. The accounts are generally in harmony with one another as they are based on some very objective and well-known "monuments of tradition." I will be drawing on the following sources for the account of this history given in this chapter: Maurice Eminyan, *The Theology of Salvation* (Boston: Daughters of St. Paul, 1960); Francis Sullivan, *Salvation Outside the Church: Tracing the History of the Catholic Response* (Eugene, OR: Wipf & Stock, 2002); Karl Rahner, "Membership of the Church According to the Teaching of Pius XII's Encyclical 'Mystici Corporis Christi,'" in *Theological Investigations,* vol. 2 (Baltimore: Helicon Press, 1963), pp. 1-88; Avery Dulles, "The Church as Locus of Salvation," in *The Theology of John Paul II: A Collection of Essays and Studies,* ed. John M. McDermott (Rome: Editrice Pontificia Università Gregoriana, 1993), pp. 169-87; Jean-Guy Pagé, *Qui Est L'Église?* vol. 3, *L'Église, Peuple de Dieu* (Montréal: Les Éditions Bellarmin, 1979); Gérard Philips, *L'Église et Son Mystère au IIe Concile du Vatican: Histoire, Texte et Commentaire de la Constitution Lumen Gentium,* vol. 1 (Paris: Desclée, 1967); G. Thils, "Ceux qui n'ont pas reçu l'Evangile," in *L'Église de Vatican II,* ed. Guilherme Baraúna (Paris: Cerf, 1966); Kevin McNamara, "The People of God," in *Vatican II: The Constitution on the Church: A Theological and Pastoral Commentary,* ed. Kevin McNamara (Chicago: Franciscan Herald Press, 1968), pp. 142-46; Aloys Grillmeier, "The People of God," trans. Kevin Smyth, in Vorgrimler, *Commentary,* vol. 1, pp. 169-75; Bernard Sesboué, *Hors de l'Église pas de salut: Histoire d'une formule et problèmes d'interprétation* (Paris: Desclée, 2004); and the International Theological Commission's document "Christianity and the World Religions," in *International Theological Commission,* vol. 2, *Texts and Documents 1986-2007,* ed. Michael Sharkey and Thomas Weinandy (San Francisco: Ignatius Press, 2009), pp. 168-70. An excellent doctoral dissertation also exists that very thoroughly explores the history of the development of this doctrine: Richard A. Marzheuser, "The *Votum Ecclesiae* and the Necessity of the Church: An Ex-

amination of *Lumen gentium* of the Second Vatican Council" (S.T.D. dissertation, Catholic University of America, 1988).

18. Francis Sullivan, *Salvation Outside the Church? Tracing the History of the Catholic Response* (Eugene, OR: Wipf & Stock, 2002). The classic texts cited in this area of historical theology are widely known and quoted. Unless otherwise noted and for the sake of consistency, I will use the translations contained in Fr. Francis Sullivan's work (cited simply as Sullivan) and also give the original source. He is using the 34th edition of Denzinger-Schönmetzer published in 1967. He himself acknowledges his debt to the "monumental work" by Louis Capéran, *Le Problème du salut des Infidèles: Essai Historique* (Toulouse, 1934). He cites the lack of an English translation of this book as a reason for writing his book. Fr. Dulles, "The Church as Locus of Salvation," in *The Theology of John Paul II: A Collection of Essays and Studies*, ed. John M. McDermott (Rome: Editrice Pontificia Università Gregoriana, 1993), pp. 169-87, which traces the history of this development, acknowledges the work of Capéran as well.

19. Origen, *Homiliae in Jesu Nave* 3.5; PG 12:841-42. Sullivan, p. 20.

20. The theology of baptism was still developing at this point but a consensus eventually developed, articulated by Augustine, that schism and heresy do not "undo" baptism, and therefore the separation from Christ of heretics and schismatics is not radical. Cyprian, however, believed in rebaptizing the lapsed, which perhaps contributed to his strong interpretation of the status of those separated from the Church.

21. *Epist.* 4.4; CSEL 3, 2:476-77; trans. R. B. Donna, FC 51:13. Sullivan, p. 21.

22. *Epist.* 73.21; CSEL 3, 2:795; FC 51:282. Sullivan, p. 21.

23. *The Unity of the Catholic Church*, p. 14; trans. M. Bévenot, ACW 25:56. Sullivan, p. 21.

24. Bernard Sesboué in his book, previously cited, *Hors de l'Église pas de salut*, pushes the hermeneutical questions even more to the forefront than does Sullivan.

25. Sullivan, p. 23.

26. *In Epist. ad Rom. hom.* 26.3-4; PG 60:641-42. Sullivan, pp. 25-26.

27. Sullivan, p. 27.

28. *Sermo* 341.9,11; PL 76:1154b. Kloppenburg, *The Theology of Vatican II*, p. 27. Jean Daniélou, *Holy Pagans of the Old Testament*, trans. Felix Faber (Baltimore: Helicon Press, 1957), pp. 132-33, has done a remarkable study of some of the "holy pagans" — among them Abel, Enoch, Noah, Job, Melchizedek, Lot, and the Queen of Sheba — all of whom are mentioned in the Bible and most of whom are held up in the New Testament and among the Fathers as heroes of faith and righteousness, but none of whom are Jews or Christians. Daniélou acknowledges, though, that not everyone in this situation responded with faith and righteousness. "Admittedly, as we have said, the revelation [natural] was scarcely ever grasped. The cosmic liturgy was degraded into idolatrous rites, practices of magic and nature myths. Similarly pagan virtue was almost invariably vitiated, as St. Augustine was well aware, by desire for self-glorification, by pressure of public opinion and by self-interest. In any case it must always be inferior to Christian holiness. But none the less the fact remains that holiness of that sort is possible and the Bible gives us examples of it."

29. *Sermo ad Caesariensis ecclesiae plebem* 6; CSEL, 53:174-75. Sullivan, p. 32.

30. Sullivan, p. 35.

31. *Enchiridion ad Laurentium de fide et spe et caritate*, 23.93; CCL 46:99. Sullivan, p. 37.

32. *De correptione et gratia* 7.11-12; PL 44:923. Sullivan, p. 38.

33. *De fide, ad Petrum* 38(79). PL 65:704. Sullivan, p. 43.

34. Sullivan, p. 43.

35. DS 780. Sullivan, p. 46.

36. There has been a contemporary resurgence of debate on the theological issues that led to the postulation of the doctrine of limbo. See the study of the International Theological Commission, "The Hope of Salvation for Infants Who Die Without Being Baptized," January 19, 2007, in *Origins* 36, no. 45 (April 26, 2007): 725-45. And both Avery Cardinal Dulles in "Current Theological Obstacles to Evangelization," in *The New Evangelization: Overcoming the Obstacles,* ed. Steven Boguslawski and Ralph Martin (New York: Paulist Press, 2008), pp. 13-25, and Fr. Basil Cole in "Is Limbo Ready to be Abolished? Limbo Revisited," in *Nova et Vetera,* English Edition, vol. 6, no. 2 (Spring 2008): 403-18, have written important articles on the topic as well. An article by Ralph Martin, "Believing and Praying: The Power of Homilies," *Homiletic & Pastoral Review* 104, no. 3 (December 2003): 64-66, which was cited by Dulles in his above-mentioned article, on the pastoral issues that are connected to the theological questions surrounding limbo, also deals with this question. Another substantial article on the doctrine of limbo was published by Serge-Thomas Bonino, "La Théorie des Limbes et le Mystère du Surnaturel chez Saint Thomas d'Aquin," *Revue Thomiste* 119, no. 1 (January-June 2001): 131-66. There appears to be pressure, even in "high places," to ignore the serious data of revelation concerning original sin which led to the postulation of the hypothesis of limbo in the first place. In most of the contemporary language translations of *Evangelium Vitae* posted on the Vatican website, a battle was going on for a while over how to translate the official Latin text of *EV* 99. The English and other modern-language translations translated it like this for periods of time, with, unfortunately, some of these translations still in print and still being cited: "You will understand that nothing is definitively lost, and you will be able to ask forgiveness from your child, who is now living with the Lord." However, the official Latin text of *EV* 99 reads: *Infantem vestrum potestis Eidem Patri Eiusque misericordiae cum spe committere.* (You can entrust your child to the same Father and His mercy with hope.) The official Latin text reflects the Catechism (CCC 1261). The unofficial translations pushed in a different direction and seriously mistranslated the text. I am grateful to Dr. Robert Fastiggi, a colleague of mine at Sacred Heart Major Seminary, Detroit, for drawing this to my attention and providing the translations. Fr. Francis Sullivan, in "The Development of Doctrine about Infants Who Die Unbaptized," *Theological Studies* 72, no. 1 (March 2011): 3-14, suggests that confessors seeking to console women who had an abortion might consider using the unofficial translation of the above text, before it was corrected in the official Latin edition, a suggestion that I think is unwise and unsound.

37. Thomas O'Meara, "The Presence of Grace Outside Evangelization, Baptism and Church in Thomas Aquinas' Theology," in *That Others May Know and Love: Essays in Honor of Zachary Hayes,* ed. Michael F. Cusato and F. Edward Coughlin (St. Bonaventure, NY: The Franciscan Institute, 1997), p. 10, makes the case that Aquinas's understanding of this theological axiom was in reference to Church members and not to unevangelized peoples. "Aquinas' usage of this ancient formula was intra-ecclesial: it censured church members who had separated or were considering separation from unity. In no citation [O'Meara finds five places in Aquinas's writings where he comments on EENS] is any application made to groups outside Christendom."

38. Of course one of the major themes of the New Testament is the necessity of faith to be saved. See, for example, Romans 1:16-17; 3:21-25; Galatians 2:15-16; John 8:24; 11:25.

39. Philips, *L'Église*, pp. 208-9. (Saint Thomas lui-même enseigne avec insistance: "Quoique les infidèles ne soient pas effectivement [actu] de l'Église, ils en font malgré tout partie en puissance [in potentia]. Cette disposition repose sur deux éléments: premièrement et primordialement sur la force du Christ qui suffit à elle seule pour le salut de tout le genre humain; en second lieu, sur la libre adhésion de l'homme" [*ST* III, q. 8, a. 3, ad 1].) O'Meara, "Grace Outside Evangelization," pp. 113-19, discusses this potentiality as well.

40. Sullivan, p. 51. There are many fine studies that analyze in detail the teaching of St. Thomas on membership in the Church and salvation. The collection of essays edited by Anthony D. Lee, *Vatican II: The Theological Dimension* (Washington, DC: The Thomist Press, 1963), has several chapters devoted to this topic. The essay by Colman O'Neil, "St. Thomas on Membership in the Church," pp. 88-140, is directly on the topic and the articles by Egan and Sauras are also of interest. A more recent treatment of St. Thomas and this issue is that of Charles Morerod, "John Paul II's Ecclesiology and St. Thomas Aquinas," in *John Paul II and St. Thomas Aquinas*, ed. Michael Dauphinais and Matthew Levering (Naples, FL: Sapientia Press, 2006), pp. 45-73.

41. Sullivan, p. 51. O'Meara, "Grace Outside Evangelization," pp. 104-5, 125-31, agrees that Aquinas teaches that after the coming of Christ explicit faith is necessary for salvation. When speaking, though, of the possibility of salvation before the coming of Christ, O'Meara demonstrates that Aquinas saw the possibility of such salvation through an implicit faith and sees this as a principle that can be applied to non-evangelized peoples after the coming of Christ, although he admits that Aquinas himself didn't see this as a possibility. "The perspective here of his theology of exceptions to explicit faith . . . does seem to be that of the past: 'After the time of grace revealed, insightful as well as ordinary people . . . are obligated to have explicit faith in the mysteries of Christ, particularly with regards to those things which are solemnized in the church and publicly proposed' (II-II, 2, 7). . . . Nevertheless, such a theology in its principles calls for a broader application." O'Meara argues explicitly for this application and claims that the basis for this wider application is indeed found in Aquinas. He also notes that fifteen years after Spain's first contact with the Americas, Dominican theologians at Salamanca were already drawing on texts in the *Summa* to argue that "grace can exist outside baptism."

42. *Summa contra gentiles*, 3.159; ed. Parma 5:287. Other texts of Thomas that Sullivan cites that make a similar point are *In III Sent.* D.25, q. 2, a. 1, sol. 1, ad 1; ed. Parma 7:272; *De veritate*, q. 14, a. 11, ad 1; ed. Parma 9:246; *ST* III, q. 67, a. 3. Sullivan, p. 51.

43. Sullivan, p. 52.

44. *De veritate*, q. 14, a. 11, ad 1; ed. Parma 9:246. Sullivan, p. 53.

45. Sullivan, p. 54. Thomas O'Meara, "Grace Outside Evangelization," p. 128, reports Pesch's research on this issue: "Pesch thinks that Aquinas' later views stimulated by the discovery of a wider world beyond lonely forest-folk led to an Augustinian pessimism: many would be lost." (O. Pesch, *Thomas von Aquin* [Mainz, 1988], pp. 56 and 712.) O'Meara, "Grace Outside Evangelization," pp. 91-98, drawing on the research of Capéran and Chenu as well as Pesch, recounts the growing awareness in the mid-thirteenth century of the existence of many unevangelized peoples.

46. *ST* II-II, q. 10, a. 1. Sullivan, p. 57.

47. Sullivan, p. 57.

48. *ST* III, q. 68, a. 2. Sullivan, p. 59.

49. *ST* III, q. 69, a. 4, ad 2. Sullivan, p. 59.

50. Yves Congar, *The Wide World My Parish: Salvation and Its Problems,* trans. Donald Attwater (Baltimore: Helicon Press, 1961), p. 96, tries to explain how despite the patristic and medieval knowledge of unevangelized peoples theological reflection was not stimulated, as it later was to be. "The middle ages *knew* that there were other countries and other peoples beyond the bounds of Christendom, but on the whole they had little curiosity or disquiet about them. They scarcely ever thought of going to have a look at them; unlike us, they did not have an itch to push half-open doors or to go where nobody had been before.... How is this to be explained? No doubt the conspicuousness of the Church and her far-flung triumph were so great in those days that it weakened the vigour of the consciousness one could have of what lay outside Christendom. This consciousness did not, so to say, influence ideas or the theological aspect of questions."

51. DS 875. Sullivan, p. 65.

52. DS 1351. Sullivan, p. 66. The internal quote, marked with an *, is from Fulgentius of Ruspe, who lived about a hundred years after Augustine, and was his theological disciple. Fulgentius of Ruspe, *De Fide,* ad Petrum c. 38-39, nn. 79-80 (PL 65, 704A-B).

53. *De Indis et de Iure Belli Relectiones,* ed. E. Nys, trans. J. P. Bates (Washington, DC: The Classics of International Law, 1917), p. 142. Sullivan, p. 70.

54. Sabra, *Vision of the Church,* p. 166, examines Aquinas's teaching on what would constitute a valid preaching of the gospel so that those who reject it would be culpable. He points out that Aquinas distinguishes between an encounter with the gospel simply as a result of hearing about it *(notitia Christi)* and an encounter that involved an established church *(cum plenu efectu).* Sabra cites *ST,* Ia IIae, q. 106, a. 4. ad 4, as the main text where this distinction is found. Sabra poses the question: "What is of consequence for our purposes here is not so much the applicability of the sin of infidelity to various categories of people, rather the question: does indifference to, or nonacceptance of, the *fama* of the Gospel suffice to condemn someone? Is one's attitude towards the fame of the Gospel decisive for salvation, or is his response to the preaching of the Gospel *cum plenu effectu,* i.e., a confrontation with the church, that is decisive?" As usual with a question that Thomas doesn't exactly pose as contemporary theology would pose it, Thomas's answer to this question is not completely clear. Sabra, pp. 164-68, acknowledges however that certain texts of Thomas, particularly his commentary on Paul's answer to the question of whether the Jews (and then the Gentiles) have effectively heard the gospel, posed in Romans 10:18-19, indicate that Thomas thought both Jews and Gentiles were culpable if they didn't heed the gospel, including a culpability solely based in some cases just on the *fama* of the gospel. There is a third possibility, though, that neither Thomas nor Sabra explores. Besides the simple *fama* of the gospel or the encounter with an established church community there is the encounter with the preaching of the gospel in the power of the Holy Spirit that occurs without the witness of a local church but is considerably more compelling than merely hearing about Christianity. With modern means of communication this encounter with the gospel is increasingly possible. It would seem from various examples in the Acts of the Apostles, Peter's preaching on the day of Pentecost (Acts 2:14-41), his preaching to Cornelius and his household (Acts 10:9-49), Philips's explanation of the Scriptures to the Ethiopian eunuch (Acts 8:26-40), indeed, all the initial missionary work that took place in the spread of Christianity before the establishment of local churches, that such preaching and teaching, apart from a community of faith, can be effective, and therefore incur culpability if rejected.

55. Graphic descriptions of the treachery and cruelty that accompanied the preaching

of the gospel in the New World are recounted by Jared Diamond, *Guns, Germs, and Steel: The Fate of Human Societies* (New York: W. W. Norton, 1999), pp. 70-74. See also Andrew Wilson, "With What Right and with What Justice?" *First Things* 218 (December 2011): 47-52.

56. *De Indis et de Iure Belli Relectiones,* ed. E. Nys, trans. J. P. Bates (Washington, DC: The Classics of International Law, 1917), pp. 142-43. Sullivan, pp. 72-73.

57. Sullivan, p. 73. O'Meara, "Grace Outside Evangelization," pp. 107-8, examines the limited discussion in Augustine, Chrysostom, and Aquinas on what constitutes an adequate preaching of the gospel. He notes that Aquinas made a distinction (*ST* I-II, q. 106, a. 4, ad 4) between the simple promulgation of the idea of Christ and the actual establishment of the Church among each people.

58. Sullivan, p. 76.

59. Sullivan, p. 81.

60. *De virtute fidei divinae,* disp. 20, n. 149, pp. 566-67. Sullivan, p. 80.

61. DS 1524. Sullivan, p. 83. "In these words a description of the justification of a sinner is given as being a translation from that state in which man is born a child of the first Adam to the state of grace and of the 'adoption of the sons' (Rom 8:15) of God through the second Adam, Jesus Christ, our Savior; and this translation after the promulgation of the Gospel cannot be effected except through the laver of regeneration (can. 5 *de bapt.*), or a desire for it, as it is written: 'Unless a man be born again of water and the Holy Spirit, he cannot enter into the Kingdom of God' (John 3:5)." The translation used here is from Denzinger, *The Sources of Catholic Dogma,* trans. Roy J. Deferrari from the 30th edition of Henry Denzinger's *Enchiridion Symbolorum* (St. Louis: Herder, 1957), p. 796. See also, in the same edition, #388, a letter attributed to Innocent II: "We assert without hesitation (on the authority of the holy Fathers Augustine and Ambrose) that the priest whom you indicated had died without the water of baptism, because he persevered in the faith of holy mother the Church and in the confession of the name of Christ, was freed from original sin and attained the joy of the heavenly fatherland. Read in the eighth book of Augustine's 'City of God' where among other things it is written, 'Baptism is ministered invisibly to one whom not contempt of religion but death excludes.' Read again the book also of the blessed Ambrose concerning the death of Valentinian where he says the same thing. Therefore, to questions concerning the dead, you should hold the opinions of the learned Fathers and in your church you should join in prayers and you should have sacrifices offered to God for the priest mentioned." This English translation, made in 1957, was based on the 30th edition. There have since been many more editions. The numbering of the texts in the editions changed in 1963 but most subsequent editions also provide the previous numbering in the margins. The first new English translation since 1957, of the most recent edition of Denzinger, the 41st, is now in preparation and will be forthcoming from Ignatius Press.

62. Robert Bellarmine, *De Ecclesia militante,* cap. 6; ed. Giuliano, vol. 2, p. 76. Sullivan, p. 89.

63. Robert Bellarmine, *De Ecclesia militante,* cap. 6; ed. Giuliano, vol. 2, p. 80. Sullivan, p. 89.

64. Sullivan, pp. 89-90.

65. See Charles Morerod, *The Church and the Human Quest for Truth* (Ave Maria, FL: Sapientia Press, 2008), pp. 93-119, for a fuller description of Bellarmine's ecclesiology and its contrast with that of Aquinas.

66. *De auxiliis gratiae,* lib. 4: *De auxilio sufficient,* n. 17, ed. Vives, vol. 8, p. 318. Sullivan, pp. 93-94.

67. DS 2123. Sullivan, p. 110. The decree was actually issued by the Holy Office with the approval of Innocent XI.

68. Sullivan, p. 95.

69. John F. Perry, "Ripalda and Rahner: 400 Years of Jesuit Reflections on Universal Salvation," *Philosophy and Theology* 13, no. 2 (2001): 344.

70. Sullivan, pp. 103-4. While there were many factors that contributed to the suppression of the Jesuits, it is the case, as argued by Jean Lacouture, *The Jesuits: A Multibiography,* trans. Jeremy Leggatt (Washington, DC: Counterpoint, 1995), pp. 262-63, that the Jesuits were perceived as "liberal" in their understanding of the universal extension of God's grace. One of the most effective attacks on them was written by Blaise Pascal "on behalf of the Jansenists . . . who held that God's grace was limited to a selected few, and for whom the Jesuits' influence as confessors to the kings of France . . . was anathema. . . . For the Jesuits of the Enlightenment were already preaching a message much closer to that of the *philosophes* and the world of learning than their most implacable adversaries, the Jansenists. . . . Most of the French *philosophes* had themselves been trained in Jesuit colleges, where the teachings of Malebranche and of Father Mersenne — who promulgated a 'natural' religion owing little to Revelation — held sway. Indeed the public controversies the Jesuits had been involved in — such as the 'scandal' of the Guarani Republic — had turned them into champions of a universalism in which Montesquieu, Buffon, and even Voltaire saw themselves reflected."

71. *De vera religion,* pars II, prop. XI, n. 284, p. 221. Sullivan, p. 111.

72. Giovanni Perrone, *De vera religione,* pars II, prop. XI, n. 265, in *Praelectiones theologicae,* vol. 1, 34th ed. (Torino: Marietti 1900), p. 214. Sullivan, p. 109.

73. Sullivan, pp. 108-12.

74. *Acta Pii IX,* I/3, 613. Sullivan, p. 114. An English translation of the Encyclical is available in Claudia Carlen, ed., *The Papal Encyclicals: 1740-1878* (Raleigh, NC: McGrath, 1981).

75. *Acta Pii IX,* I/3, 613. Sullivan, p. 114.

76. "Schema of a Dogmatic Constitution on the Church Prepared for the Examination of the Fathers of the Vatican Council," in *The Church: Papal Teachings,* Selected and Arranged by the Benedictine Monks of Solesmes, trans. Mother E. O'Gorman (Boston: St. Paul Editions, 1980), pp. 809, 813-14. O'Donnell, "The People of God," p. 42, puts it like this: "The meaning of the phrase 'outside the church there is no salvation' must thus be understood in positive terms as: if a man is saved, he is saved through the Church."

77. Sullivan, pp. 114-15.

78. The entire text of the letter in its original Latin along with an English translation was first published in *The American Ecclesiastical Review* 127 (October 1952): 307-15. It is also available in Neuner/Dupuis, pp. 854-57, and Denzinger, pp. 3866-72.

79. Pagé, *Qui Est L'Église?* vol. 3, p. 50.

80. Yves Congar, "Principes Doctrinaux," in *L'Activité missionnaire de l'Église* (Paris: Cerf, 1967), p. 214, in speaking about the *Letter* remarks: "The text of the Decree *Ad gentes* makes allusion to this doctrine, which today is common and even official. The text adds, however, that this in no way removes the necessity of missionary activity." (Le texte du Décret *Ad gentes* fait allusion à cette doctrine, aujourd'hui commune et meme officielle. Il ajoute cependant qu'elle n'enlève rien à la nécesssité de l'activité missionnaire.)

81. Fr. Sullivan gives a comprehensive account of this "case" and the documents related

to it in his book on the subject by which we have been guided in this chapter: pp. 3-5, 115-16, 134-40.

82. DS 3869-70. Sullivan, p. 137.

83. DS 3870. Sullivan, p. 137.

84. DS 3871-72. Sullivan, pp. 137-38.

85. Karl Rahner, "Atheism and Implicit Christianity," in *Theological Investigations*, vol. 9, trans. Graham Harrison (New York: Herder & Herder, 1972), p. 151, acknowledges that indeed the Council is teaching that a supernatural faith is necessary for salvation in any and all circumstances. "To a certain degree the Council makes its own case — the possibility of the unbaptized non-Christian's salvation without contact with the Gospel (thus including the atheist) — more difficult to defend by requiring a real supernatural faith even in such a case, i.e., not escaping the issue by saying that such a person attains supernatural salvation at the end of his life on the basis of a mere 'natural' morality." Rahner, "The Christian among Unbelieving Relations," in *TI*, vol. 3, p. 364, also clearly acknowledges that not only is supernatural faith necessary but salvation is impossible apart from grace, which indeed, makes such supernatural faith possible: "There exists in Catholic theology an opinion, up to now uncontested, according to which the faith demanded (as distinct from a merely metaphysical knowledge of God which is insufficient for salvation) [cf. *Denz.* 1173, Innocent XI 1679] is given in a sufficient degree whenever there is given an obedient disposition for faith, an attitude of faith and a readiness for faith, which is possible even where the object of revelation in the strict sense of the specifically evangelical message has not been arrived at. . . . Everyone who is saved is saved only through the grace of Christ."

86. DS 3872. Sullivan, p. 138. See Morerod, *The Church*, pp. 108-9, for a contemporary description of "implicit desire," based on the teaching of Aquinas: "Implicit desire is possible — in the line of St. Thomas — because the articles of faith are included in some most basic truths (God's existence and his providence [*ST* IIa IIae, q. 1, a. 7]), and thus someone may desire implicitly baptism by being firmly attached to the more elementary truths that he already knows [*ST* IIa IIae, q. 2, a. 5]."

87. It must also be noted that even though the overwhelming preponderance of theological opinion interprets this doctrinal development as we do in this thesis (namely that it is possible that saving, supernatural faith and charity may be accessed in an implicit manner that does not involve explicit faith in Christ or the Church), there are serious arguments that are made, such as that of Fr. Brian Harrison in "Can an 'Implicit Faith' in Christ Be Sufficient for Salvation?" Available at: http://www.catholicism.org/downloads/FrHarison_Implicit-Faith.pdf (accessed December 23, 2008), for a more minimalist reading of these texts, which attempts to hold to the Thomistic teaching that requires explicit faith in Christ before death, for salvation to be possible. Fr. Harrison writes within the framework of orthodox Catholicism while pushing the limits on a minimalist interpretation of various magisterial documents. He argues that *Dominus Iesus* when it makes the distinction between supernatural faith and the non-salvific "belief" of the non-Christian religions rules out the possibility of members of such religions having saving faith. It seems, though, that while DI makes this strong distinction about the non-Christian religions as religious systems it by no means intends to rule out that individuals within those religions may respond with supernatural faith to an illumination that God gives them. A professor from the Lefeverite seminary at Econe has written an intelligent but minimalist interpretation of EENS as well: Jean-Marc Rulleau, *Baptism of Desire: A Patristic Commentary* (Kansas City, MO: Angelus

Press, 1999). Charles A. Coulombe, *Desire and Deception* (Arcadia, CA: Tumblar House, 2009), writes from an explicitly Feenyite position questioning the authority of magisterial documents from Pius IX that interpret EENS in what he considers a "novel" way not consonant with the previous tradition. Oftentimes in this literature the point is made that the recent magisterial statements are not infallible and are in fact mistaken. There are many websites that advocate views like this and even more extremely critical views of the recent magisterium and Vatican II as well. One such is that based in Most Holy Family Monastery, in Fillmore, New York, which is dedicated to "Defending the Catholic Faith, exposing the false post–Vatican II Counter Church and more." A "fundamentalist" reading of both Scripture and magisterial documents is characteristic of their attacks on the teaching of Vatican II regarding the salvation of those who die without becoming members of the visible Church. See www.mostholyfamilymonastery.com. Writings like this argue that the earlier magisterial documents have greater weight than the later ones and that the later ones therefore are not binding. Strangely enough, in the name of fidelity to tradition a departure from the Church's role in interpreting its own tradition takes place. A book has appeared recently by Moyra Doorly and Aidan Nichols, *The Council in Question: A Dialogue with Catholic Traditionalism* (Herefordshire, UK: Gracewing, 2011), that, while written on a popular level, nevertheless contains a serious exploration of the traditionalist critique of Vatican II. Moyra Doorly raises the strong objections of the Society of St. Pius X and Fr. Aidan Nichols replies with intelligent and nuanced answers.

88. Sullivan, p. 139.

89. See Stephen Bullivant, "*Sine Culpa?* Vatican II and Inculpable Ignorance," *Theological Studies* 72, no. 1 (March 2011): 70-86, for a recent consideration of how inculpable ignorance may apply to contemporary unbelievers.

90. Karl Rahner, "Forgotten Dogmatic Initiatives of the Second Vatican Council," in *TI*, vol. 22, pp. 9, 99.

91. Pagé, *Qui Est L'Église?* vol. 3, pp. 63-65.

92. Charles Journet, *What Is Dogma?* (New York: Hawthorn, 1964), p. 15.

93. Jacques Maritain, "La Dialectique Immanente du Premier Acte de Liberté," in *Raison et Raisons* (Paris, 1947), pp. 131-56. Also in translation: *The Range of Reason* (New York: Scribner, 1952), pp. 66-85 (cited in Journet, *What Is Dogma?* pp. 130ff.).

94. Thomas O'Meara, in "Grace Outside Evangelization," pp. 119-24, has a useful discussion of this concept in Aquinas. Riccardo Lombardi, in *The Salvation of the Unbeliever* (London: Burns & Oates, 1956), provides a comprehensive study of the question of what constitutes saving faith and how, in various situations, it might be possible for it to come into existence. Lombardi's work particularly focuses on the theological works in Latin and Italian that explored this question before Vatican II.

95. Journet, *What Is Dogma?* p. 35.

96. Étienne Hugueny, "Le scandale édifiant d'une exposition missionnaire," *Revue Thomiste* 76 (1933): 217-42, and 78-79 (1933): 533-67. The citation is on p. 562. (Les bonnes influences du milieu ne suffisent malheureusement pas à empêcher les défaillances et souvent la corruption des volontés en formation; mais très rares sont celles qui résistent aux influences mauvaises du milieu où elles s'épanouissent. C'est donc le plus souvent, que le jeune infidèle, en milieu païen, suivra la pente de sa nature corrompue et les exemples mauvais du milieu où il vit, quand viendra pour lui l'heure de poser la première orientation de sa vie morale. Se dérobant à l'appel de Dieu, il grossira le nombre des infidèles négatifs, qui, par un

premier péché contre le Dieu que leur présentait leur raison, ont mis obstacle à l'illumination intérieure ou à la révélation extérieure qui leur aurait donné le Dieu de la foi, en perfectionnant leur première idée religieuse.)

97. Morerod, *The Church*, p. 138, drawing on the teaching of St. Thomas and Cardinal Journet, points out that genuine supernatural charity actually brings a certain visibility with it, evidencing some of the fruits of life in Christ and the Church, even when these are not explicitly known: "Whoever accepts the divine invitation starts belonging to the Church, and that membership is not totally invisible because the behavior of the person changes: the body of the Church starts being present. This Thomistic ecclesiology makes it possible to understand what is meant by 'No salvation outside the Church': 'to be in the Church' and 'to be saved' mean the same thing, because to be in the Church means to be under the salvific influence of the Head of the Church, that is, Jesus Christ."

98. See Morerod, *The Church*, p. 84: "God's gift can be received only with God's help. It is possible to refuse it, and such a choice is the main point of our present life. Anyone who would refuse to be with God would in fact diminish his own humanity by restricting to finite goods the desire of a heart made for the infinite. If such an attitude is persistent, it can lead to hell."

99. Rahner, "Anonymous Christians," in *TI*, vol. 6, p. 397.

100. Richard McBrien, "The Church *(Lumen Gentium),*" in *Modern Catholicism: Vatican II and After,* ed. Adrian Hastings (New York: Oxford University Press, 1991), p. 90.

101. Sullivan, p. 9; also see pp. 160, 162.

102. Sullivan, pp. 151-61.

103. Sullivan, pp. 141-61.

104. Jacques Dupuis, *Toward a Christian Theology of Religious Pluralism* (Maryknoll, NY: Orbis, 1999); CDF, "Notification, intended to safeguard the doctrine of the Catholic faith from errors, ambiguities or harmful interpretations." February 26, 2001. http://www.vatican.va/roman_curia/congregations/cfaith/documents/rc_con_cfaith_doc_20010124_dupuis_fr.html (accessed February 17, 2011).

105. Francis A. Sullivan, "Ways of Salvation?" *America Magazine* 184, no. 12 (April 9, 2001): 29.

106. Sullivan, p. 202.

Notes to Chapter IV

1. Joseph Ratzinger, *Principles of Catholic Theology: Building Stones for a Fundamental Theology* (San Francisco: Ignatius Press, 1987), p. 53.

2. Gérard Philips, *L'Église et Son Mystère au Deuxième Concile du Vatican: Histoire, texte et commentaire de la Constitution Lumen Gentium,* vol. 1 (Paris: Desclée, 1967), p. 210.

3. C. E. B. Cranfield, *A Critical and Exegetical Commentary on the Epistle to the Romans,* vol. 1, The International Critical Commentary (Edinburgh: T. & T. Clark, 1975), p. 31.

4. We will examine the text a few verses at a time, but the text as a whole is included here:

For the wrath of God is revealed from heaven against all ungodliness and wickedness of men who by their wickedness suppress the truth. For what can be known about God is plain to them, because God has shown it to them. Ever since the creation of the world his invisible nature, namely, his eternal power and deity, has been clearly perceived in the things that have been made. So they are without excuse; for although they knew God they did not honor him as God or give thanks to him, but they became futile in their thinking and their senseless minds were darkened. Claiming to be wise, they became fools, and exchanged the glory of the immortal God for images resembling mortal man or birds or animals or reptiles. Therefore God gave them up in the lusts of their hearts to impurity, to the dishonoring of their bodies among themselves, because they exchanged the truth about God for a lie and worshiped and served the creature rather than the Creator, who is blessed forever! Amen. For this reason God gave them up to dishonorable passions. Their women exchanged natural relations for unnatural, and the men likewise gave up natural relations with women and were consumed with passion for one another, men committing shameless acts with men and receiving in their own persons the due penalty for their error. And since they did not see fit to acknowledge God, God gave them up to a base mind and to improper conduct. They were filled with all manner of wickedness, evil, covetousness, malice. Full of envy, murder, strife, deceit, malignity, they are gossips, slanderers, haters of God, insolent, haughty, boastful, inventors of evil, disobedient to parents, foolish, faithless, heartless, ruthless. Though they know God's decree that those who do such things deserve to die, they not only do them but approve those who practice them. (Rom. 1:14-32)

5. The RSV translation will be utilized for all Scripture passages cited in this book unless otherwise noted.

6. Joseph A. Fitzmyer, *Romans: A New Translation with Introduction and Commentary*, The Anchor Bible (New York: Doubleday, 1992), p. 270.

7. Brendan Byrne, *Romans*, Sacra Pagina Series, vol. 6 (Collegeville, MN: Liturgical Press, 1996), p. 18.

8. Byrne, p. 21. See also p. 85, where Byrne cites the OT and NT references to the day of wrath/judgment.

9. Byrne, pp. 65-66.

10. Robert Jewett, *Romans: A Commentary*, Hermeneia: A Critical and Historical Commentary on the Bible (Minneapolis: Fortress Press, 2007), pp. 149-50.

11. Charles Morerod, *The Church and the Human Quest for Truth* (Ave Maria, FL: Sapientia Press, 2008), pp. 122-24, makes the important point that when it is a question of responding to revelation from God, to accept part but not all of what is being revealed is to engage in a radical form of disobedience and the construction of one's own religion. He cites Aquinas (*ST* IIa IIae, q. 5, a. 3) as foundation for this view and concludes: "Aquinas says that if we refuse one article of faith on the basis of our own judgment, it means that our own judgment and not divine revelation is also the reason why we accept other articles of faith. It is a way of making up our own religion, a religion human and not revealed. Of course Thomas adds that divine revelation is received through the teaching of the Church."

12. Stanislas Lyonnet, *Études sur L'Épître aux Romains* (Rome: Editrice Pontificio Istituto Biblico, 1989), p. 45. (C'est évidemment une métaphore, comme la jalousie, la haine, etc. et elle ne met aucun sentiment changeant en Dieu lui-même, ainsi que S. Thomas le fait souvent remarquer, comme si Dieu s'irritait d'abord, puis s'apaisait; le changement, dit S. Thomas, n'est que dans l'effet, c'est-a-dire l'homme lui-même.)

(En fait, cette métaphore vise à travers l'effet produit dans le pécheur *l'incompatibilité absolue qui existe entre Dieu et le péché,* et par suite entre Dieu et le pécheur, en tant qu'il est séparé de Dieu par son péché.) See also Byrne, *Romans,* p. 66.

13. Cranfield, pp. 109-10; see also pp. 212-17.

14. Fitzmyer, p. 302, emphasizes: "[Paul] confirm[s] the validity of OT teaching about God's eschatological retribution. He does not simply borrow this affirmation in a moment of ardent rhetoric; it is an important part of his teaching." Ernst Käsemann, *Commentary on Romans,* trans. and ed. Geoffrey W. Bromiley (Grand Rapids: Eerdmans, 1980), p. 68, in commenting on Romans 2:16, "on that day when, according to my gospel, God judges the secrets of men by Christ Jesus," states: "what the chapter shows is that, and how far, the proclamation of judgment inseparably belongs to the gospel. This gospel is, of course, constitutive for primitive missionary preaching." See Justyn Terry, *The Justifying Judgement of God: A Reassessment of the Place of Judgement in the Saving Work of Christ* (Bletchley, UK: Paternoster, 2007), for a recent study that argues that the final judgment is the primary optic through which the Scripture presents the saving work of Christ.

15. Joseph Ratzinger, *The Yes of Jesus Christ,* trans. Robert Nowell (New York: Crossroad, 1991), pp. 94-97.

16. Lyonnet, p. 45. Fitzmyer, p. 284.

17. Byrne, p. 66.

18. Francis Martin, "Revelation as Disclosure: Creation," in *Wisdom and Holiness, Science and Scholarship: Essays in Honor of Matthew L. Lamb,* ed. Michael Dauphinais and Matthew Levering (Naples, FL: Sapientia Press, 2007), p. 219.

19. Martin, "Revelation as Disclosure," p. 223.

20. Richard John Neuhaus, on the *First Things* website (www.firstthings.com, *The Coming Kulturkampf,* November 14, 2008), commenting on H. Richard Niebuhr's classic book, *Christ and Culture,* states that we are again entering a time when we need to reassess the relationship between Christ and the Church and culture: "Anytime is the right time for Christians to think anew about the perennial question of Christ and culture. *Christ,* in the phrase *Christ and culture* always means Christ *and* his Church. Christ and the Church constitute a distinct society within the surrounding culture that is Babylon. At least that is the depiction in the New Testament and the Great Tradition of Christian teaching. In this community, the promised *not yet* keeps breaking into the *now.* The surrounding Babylon assumes many different cultural forms that may be viewed as different cultures. To look at the larger picture of the relationship between Christ and culture is, at the beginning of the twenty-first century, a dizzying experience."

21. Lyonnet, p. 48.

22. Ratzinger, *Christianity and the Crisis of Cultures,* pp. 94-95. See also Ratzinger's similar comments on these texts of Romans in *The Yes of Jesus Christ,* pp. 21-27.

23. Cranfield, p. 104.

24. Fitzmyer, p. 270. See also Byrne, p. 72.

25. Lyonnet, p. 179. "It is in this sense that we are able to and must say that the dogma of original sin is the foundation of the entire Christian religion." (C'est en ce sens qu'on peut et doit dire que le dogme du péché original est le fondement de toute la religion chrétienne.) Of course, despite the theological ferment on the question of original sin, it is still a fundamental dogma of the faith, and is taught as such by the Catechism of the Catholic Church.

26. Käsemann, p. 47.

27. Cranfield, p. 111.

28. Jewett, p. 152.

29. Jewett, p. 158.

30. Jewett, p. 152.

31. See Cranfield, pp. 116-17.

32. It is interesting to note that Vatican I cited Romans 1:20 to support the teaching that human beings are able to come to knowledge of God by "natural reason." Lyonnet, pp. 61-70, discusses this issue at length, as does Käsemann, pp. 63-65, and also Byrne, p. 67. Francis Martin, "Revelation as Disclosure," p. 233, makes some perceptive and helpful comments:

> The texts of Vatican II, as well as those of Vatican I, have as their goal to defend the intrinsic ability of the mind to arrive at knowledge of God. Their intent was to deny that the mind was so crippled that it has to rely on faith for certitude in religious and moral matters (fideism) and/or that all knowledge of God derives from a primitive revelation made to humanity and then subsequently obfuscated. As we have seen, this was a *de jure* statement: the mind is capable of knowing God since creation is a revelation of God as the biblical tradition asserts. On the other hand, the *de facto* situation is that human beings need divine help in order to exploit the full potential of their mind.

A recent study on the interplay between reason and revelation by J. Budziszewski, "Natural Law Revealed," appeared in *First Things* 188 (December 2008): 29-33. It is a chapter from a forthcoming book-length study of the question.

Much work has been done in attempting to analyze the supernatural light that may come to those who have not heard the gospel and the type of response that may be salvific, even on a preconceptual level. As we have previously noted, in a well-known essay Jacques Maritain, "La dialectique immanente du premier acte de liberté," *Raison et Raisons* (Paris, 1947), pp. 131-65, comments on the famous texts of St. Thomas on the "first moral decision" (*ST* I-II, q. 89, a. 6). (This essay is also found in English translation as "The Immanent Dialectic of the First Act of Freedom," in *The Range of Reason* [New York: Scribner, 1952], pp. 66-85.) This article of Maritain has been commented on by Jean-Guy Pagé, *Qui Est L'Église? Le Peuple de Dieu*, vol. 3 of 3 (Montréal: Les Éditions Bellarmin, 1979), p. 64, and also by Charles Journet, *What Is Dogma?* (New York: Hawthorn, 1964), pp. 26-37. René Latourelle, *Theology of Revelation* (New York: Alba House, 1966), pp. 332-41, has an insightful discussion on the difference between knowing God by the light of natural reason and by supernatural light, including a discussion of the teaching of Vatican I on this point and also of Romans 1. Latourelle (p. 39) expresses well the difference between the knowledge of God that comes from "natural reason" and the knowledge of God that comes from a supernatural light:

> In contemplating creation, man does not feel that he is addressed; he does not have to answer a call, but to decipher an object placed before him. Creation refers him to God as to its cause. Creation betrays the presence of God, manifests his perfections. It speaks of God, but God Himself does not speak; God does not enter into a dialogue. He is like a person present but silent. And thus the encounter between man and universe does not terminate in the assent of faith, but in an existential attitude: that of homage and adoration. In supernatural revelation, on the other hand, God intervenes, in person, at a given point in time and space; he enters into a *dialogue* of friendship with man, makes known to him the mystery of His inmost life and plan for salvation,

invites him to a personal communion of life. Through faith, man directly called upon thus by God, freely responds to the personal call of God and enters into a covenant with Him. Natural revelation does not have this characteristic of word and testimony.

33. Lyonnet, p. 50 *(par le monde créé et une lumière intérieure)*. See also Fitzmyer, pp. 273-74.

34. Francis Martin, "Revelation as Disclosure: Creation," pp. 225, 227. Pope Pius XII's Encyclical, *Humani generis* (Concerning Some False Opinions Threatening to Undermine the Foundations of Catholic Doctrine), August 12, 1950, #2-4, affirms the teaching of Vatican I (*Dei Filius* [Decree on Divine Revelation]), chapter 2, that in principle God and the moral law can be known through reason, but points out how difficult this is in the actual human condition:

> For though, absolutely speaking, human reason by its own natural force and light can arrive at a true and certain knowledge of the one personal God, Who by His providence watches over and governs the world, and also the natural law, which the Creator has written in our hearts, still there are not a few obstacles to prevent reason from making efficient and fruitful use of its natural ability. The truths that have to do with God and the relations between God and men completely surpass the sensible order and demand self-surrender and self-abnegation in order to be put into practice and to influence practical life. Now the human intellect, in gaining the knowledge of such truths, is hampered both by the activity of the senses and the imagination, and by evil passions arising from original sin. Hence men easily persuade themselves in such matters that what they do not wish to believe is false or at least doubtful.
>
> It is for this reason that divine revelation must be considered morally necessary so that those religious and moral truths which are not of their nature beyond the reach of reason in the present condition of the human race, may be known by all men readily with a firm certainty and with freedom from all error.
>
> Furthermore the human intelligence sometimes experiences difficulties in forming a judgment about the credibility of the Catholic faith, notwithstanding the many wonderful external signs God has given, which are sufficient to prove with certitude by the natural light of reason alone the divine origin of the Christian religion. For man can, whether from prejudice or passion or bad faith, refuse and resist not only the evidence of the external proofs that are available, but also the impulses of actual grace.

35. Byrne, p. 67: "The fleeting recognition given in this Pauline text to a revelation of God in the natural world is theologically significant in its own terms. (The First Vatican Council, opposing fideism in its dogmatic constitution 'On the Catholic Faith,' cited the text in support of its teaching that God can be known by the natural light of human reason apart from positive revelation [DS 3004].) Nevertheless, the judgment to which it leads is inescapably harsh. Modern sensitivity of the very real difficulties attending belief will find it offensive. Paul, however, has no concept of a sincere atheism. He stands within a biblical tradition given classic exposition by the psalmist: 'The fool has said in his heart, "There is no God"' (14:1; 53:2)."

36. Karl Rahner, "Atheism and Implicit Christianity," in *TI*, vol. 9, trans. Graham Harrison (New York: Herder & Herder, 1972), pp. 146-47, recognizes the challenge that Scripture and tradition present to Vatican II's cautious acknowledgments that it may be possible to be a "theoretical atheist" but not to be culpable of a truly "transcendental" rejection of God:

On the one hand one is obliged to appreciate the weight of the official view: in Scripture God's knowability seems so clearly *given* and atheism seems to give evidence so definitely of being man's most terrible aberration, that it was only thought possible to understand it as a *sin* in which a man freely turns away in the *mysterium iniquitatis,* evilly suppressing the truth which everywhere impinges on him (Rom 1:18).

On the other hand it must be said that until now neither text-book theology nor Scripture has been confronted with the experience of a world-wide and militant atheism, confident of its own self-evident nature and because of this it was possible to regard the earlier, ubiquitous, theistic "common opinion" as something necessarily so, as an eternally valid quality of human nature.

37. Fitzmyer, p. 281.

38. Byrne, p. 74. "But in 1 Cor 1:21 (cf. also 1 Thess 4:5; Gal 4:8) the 'knowing' has the fuller Semitic sense that goes beyond intellectual awareness to include the 'glorifying' and 'thanking' which according to Rom 1:21 is the required follow-up to intellectual awareness of God. . . . Paul portrays the 'overflow' of thanksgiving to God on the part of human beings as the goal of the entire Christian mission."

39. Käsemann, p. 51.

40. If I were to attempt to articulate what seems to be the prevailing view of commentators, although not without vigorous dispute, it is that most probably Paul is talking here about Gentile pagans, although with a universal intent in mind, such that the Jews, in their own way, may also be understood to be included. As Käsemann, p. 38, puts it: "To the intensity of the judgment corresponds the totality of the world which stands under it, so that the statement about Gentiles applies to the heathen nature of mankind as such, and hence implies the guilty Jew as well."

41. Jewett, p. 159, claims that the Greek word for "reasonings" is "always taken by the writers of the NT in an unfavorable sense; it denotes the unregulated activity of the *nous,* understanding, in the service of a corrupt heart."

42. Jewett, p. 160.

43. Jewett, p. 160.

44. G. K. Beale, *We Become What We Worship: A Biblical Theology of Idolatry* (Downers Grove, IL: InterVarsity, 2008), pp. 202-16.

45. Byrne, p. 75.

46. Käsemann, p. 38.

47. Jewett, p. 157, citing Epictetus, *Diss.* 1.16.20.

48. There are significant NT passages that underline the importance of giving thanks and glory to God and the gravity of not doing so. Lyonnet, p. 57, points these out: Luke 17:15-18 as a positive example of the grateful healed leper, and Acts 12:21-22 as an example of the judgment of God on Herod who did not glorify God.

49. Jewett, p. 157.

50. Byrne, p. 74.

51. Fitzmyer, p. 283. Emphasis is mine.

52. Käsemann, p. 48.

53. Jewett, p. 158.

54. Jewett, p. 158.

55. Fitzmyer, p. 274, strongly argues against seeing allusions to the Fall of Adam in these texts.

56. Most commentators would agree that there is probably a reference to Psalm 106:20 in verse 23, which refers to Israel's worship of the golden calf, and to Jeremiah 2:11, which speaks of the idolatry of Israel later in her history. See Byrne, p. 68.

57. Philip F. Esler, "The Sodom Tradition in Romans 1:18-32," *Biblical Theology Bulletin* 34 (Spring 2004).

58. Esler, "The Sodom Tradition," pp. 9-10. Esler argues that the Sodom narrative played a larger role in the oral tradition of Israel than strict textual references would indicate.

59. Cranfield, pp. 105-6.

60. Käsemann, pp. 46-47.

61. Käsemann, p. 38: "Paul perceives the assault on divine truth as demonic and he characterizes it with horror as sacrilege."

62. Jewett, p. 170.

63. Käsemann, p. 47.

64. Cranfield, pp. 120-21.

65. Käsemann, p. 37; Jewett, p. 167.

66. Many commentators draw attention to the remarkable parallels between this section of Romans and similar descriptions in Wisdom 13:1-19 and 14:22-31.

67. Fitzmyer, p. 276.

68. Jewett, pp. 172-18, conducts an extensive discussion and review of the literature concerning what exactly Paul is talking about here and what the cultural and religious situation of the time regarding homosexuality contributed to his teaching.

69. Esler, "The Sodom Tradition," p. 13, claims that in the case of male homosexuality the transition from male identity to "shameful effeminacy" constitutes a main part of the punishment. See also Byrne, pp. 69-70.

70. Cranfield, pp. 126-27. Byrne, p. 70, interprets the punishment as "a permanent uncontrollable desire to engage in the activity in question. . . . Idolatry has made human beings exchange the dignity that accompanied being created in the image and likeness of God for a captivity in which they are trapped in a most shameful state."

71. Jewett, p. 165.

72. Jewett, p. 182.

73. Byrne, p. 71.

74. Jewett, p. 182.

75. Jewett, p. 181.

76. Romans 13:13; 1 Corinthians 5:10; 6:9; Galatians 5:19-21; Ephesians 4:31; 5:3-5; Colossians 3:5; 1 Timothy 1:9; 2 Timothy 3:2-5; Titus 3:3; 1 Peter 4:3.

77. Käsemann, pp. 50-51.

78. Jewett, p. 184.

79. The Mosaic law stipulated the death penalty for crimes such as idolatry, murder, and adultery, but also for what it considered the "abomination" of male homosexuality. Leviticus 18:22; 20:13; Deuteronomy 23:17; 1 Kings 14:24; 15:12; 22:46; 2 Kings 23:7. It also stipulated the death penalty for children who were disobedient to their parents (Deut. 21:18-21), but we have no evidence it was enacted.

80. Byrne, p. 72.

81. Käsemann, pp. 51-52.

82. Fitzmyer, pp. 289-90.

83. Cranfield, p. 135.

84. Jewett, p. 191.

85. Byrne, p. 63.

86. Byrne, pp. 64-65, provides a detailed comparison that shows the remarkable similarities between Romans 1:18-32 and Wisdom 11–14. Martin, "Revelation as Disclosure," pp. 213-17, also comments on this at length.

87. Cranfield, pp. 138-39.

88. Cranfield, p. 142. See also Byrne, p. 81.

89. Cranfield, pp. 168-70.

90. Byrne, pp. 81-82.

91. Käsemann, p. 55.

92. Käsemann, p. 56.

93. Catherine of Siena, *The Dialogue*, chapter 41.

94. Bernard of Clairvaux, *On the Song of Songs*, vol. 1, trans. Kilian Walsh, Cistercian Fathers Series, vol. 4 (Kalamazoo, MI: Cistercian Publications, 1971), Sermon 20, no. 1.

95. Cranfield, pp. 139-40, makes the point that while we respect God's faithfulness to the sacraments this does not mean that "he will not judge severely those who have received them, requiring much of all those to whom much has been given (Lk 12:48)." The relevance of what Paul says here about circumcision to Christian baptism has often been noted. Cranfield cites Chrysostom as among these commentators.

96. Lyonnet, p. 72.

97. Thomas Aquinas, *Lectures on the Letter to the Romans*, trans. Fabian Larcher, ed. Jeremy Holmes (soon to be published by Sapientia Press, Ave Maria University), Lecture 3, 216. "But the expression, *by nature*, causes some difficulty. For it seems to favor the Pelagians, who taught that man could observe all the precepts of the Law by his own natural powers. Hence, *by nature*, should mean nature reformed by grace. For he is speaking of gentiles converted to the faith, who began to obey the moral precepts of the Law by the help of Christ's grace." Aquinas, though, seems to acknowledge the possibility of another interpretation as well: "Or *by nature* can mean by the natural law showing them what should be done . . . the light of natural reason, in which is God's image. All this does not rule out the need of grace to move the affections any more than the knowledge of sin through the law (Rom 3:20) exempts from the need of grace to move the affections."

98. Cranfield, pp. 151-52.

99. Lyonnet, pp. 71-88, surveys the range of opinions on this complex question. Fitzmyer, p. 310, argues, against Cranfield, that Paul is talking about Gentiles, and not Gentile Christians, in these verses. Käsemann, p. 54, holds the same interpretation as Fitzmyer.

100. Byrne, p. 90.

101. Byrne, p. 90.

102. Cranfield, pp. 152-53. Jewett, pp. 212-14. Käsemann, pp. 56-59. Note also the comments of Fitzmyer, p. 309: "Paul does not ascribe the Gentile's 'doing of the law' to a human being's unaided effort *(physei)*, because doing the law, even when it is unknown, becomes possible only where 'what can be known about God' (1:19) is the basis of human activity, rather than the rebellion that characterizes humanity as a whole (1:18-23). . . . It is only in the light of divine judgment according to human deeds that the justification of the sinner by

grace through faith is rightly seen. Hence there is no real inconsistency in Paul's teaching about justification by faith and judgment according to deeds" (Fitzmyer, pp. 306-7). Francis Martin also makes this point, "Revelation as Disclosure," p. 19. Fitzmyer points out that the grammar of 2:14 indicates that only "some" of the Gentiles do "some" of the precepts of the law "by nature, instinctively" by the regular, natural order of things, prescinding from any positive revelation.

103. As Fitzmyer, p. 302, puts it: "This is the first Pauline mention of 'eternal life,' an idea derived from his Jewish tradition (Dan 12:2; 2 Macc 15:3) . . . it is life in the *aion*, in the 'age' to come. See further 5:21; 6:22-23; cf. Gal 6:8. So Paul formulates the destiny of Christian existence, which he will further specify in time as a share in the 'glory' of God (3:23; 5:2) and in the life of the risen Christ (6:4), i.e., being 'forever with the Lord' (I Thess 4:17; cf. Rom 5:21; 6:22-23)."

104. Käsemann, p. 59.

105. Ratzinger, *Christianity and the Crisis of Culture*, p. 97.

106. Ratzinger, *The Yes of Jesus Christ*, pp. 24-25.

107. Cranfield, pp. 199-200. See also Cranfield, pp. 212-14.

108. The multiple issues and the innumerable articles, books, and commentaries concerning the endings of Mark's Gospel are not relevant to our purpose here. The Church continues to include the ending that it cites in *LG* 16 in the canonical writings, and for our purposes it is sufficient to utilize it here in such a manner.

109. Fitzmyer, p. 283.

110. Lyonnet, pp. 46-47. "Il n'est donc pas étonnant qu'avant de décrire la révélation de la justice salvifique de Dieu (Rom 3,21 ss.), Paul fasse connaitre une autre révélation, celle de la colère de Dieu.

"Il faut ajouter que dans la dialectique de l'Apôtre la révélation de la colère de Dieu joue un rôle essentiel: pour recevoir la justification comme un *don de Dieu purement gratuit*, il faut que l'homme soit tout à fait conscient de son péché (Rom 3, 19-21)."

111. Matthew 7:13-14 is a very important text for our purposes. The traditional interpretation of this text is that it means what it says; that many are heading to destruction and comparatively fewer are heading to salvation. Some modern commentators, uncomfortable with the traditional interpretation, look for alternate interpretations. The attempts to neutralize the text are well described by B. F. Meyer, "Many (= All) Are Called, but Few (= Not All) Are Chosen," *New Testament Studies* 36, no. 1 (1990): 89-97. Of the various attempts he identifies he thinks only one has any merit, that is, to try to ascertain the underlying Aramaic, which does not have the clarity that the Greek has when referring to the many and the few. But, as the ITC pointed out in its document on eschatology, "Some Current Questions in Eschatology," p. 72, the Greek of the New Testament is no less inspired than the Hebrew of the Old Testament. The Greek words for many and few are not ambiguous in their meaning. Attempts to get behind the Greek to the Aramaic, while of interest, cannot replace our close attention to the inspired Greek text. "Looking at matters from another perspective it cannot be supposed that Hebrew categories alone were the instrument of divine revelation. God has spoken 'in many and varied ways' (Heb 1:1). The books of Sacred Scripture in which inspiration is expressed in Greek words and cultural concepts must be considered as enjoying no less authority than those which were written in Hebrew or Aramaic." John P. Meier, *Matthew: A Biblical-Theological Commentary*, ed. Wilfrid Harrington, Donald Senior, New Testament Message, vol. 3 (Wilmington, DE: Michael Glazier, 1980), pp. 72-75, thinks it is im-

portant to see Matthew 7:13-14 as part of the whole concluding discourse to the Sermon on the Mount with a strong eschatological framework that underlines the seriousness of Jesus' teaching being followed in light of the impending judgment and separation of those who are on very different paths. He sees Matthew as using "antithetical parallelism" contrasting the two gates, the two ways, sheep and wolves, two types of trees, two foundations, as describing two types of disciples who despite external similarities live totally different lives before God. The current mixture in the Church will be revealed and separated at the final judgment. Meier points out that the future tense used in these parables of judgment is important to note. They show that the words of Jesus are not empty threats. The judgment will happen and will happen in accordance with the criteria that Jesus mercifully reveals to us. Daniel J. Harrington, *The Gospel of Matthew*, in Daniel J. Harrington, ed., Sacra Pagina Series, vol. 1 (Collegeville, MN: Liturgical Press, 1991), pp. 108-11, concludes: "The scene is a warning to the audience that to enter the kingdom is hard and only a few do so." He thinks this meaning is confirmed and deepened when we consider the larger section of which Matthew 7:13-14 is a part. Harrington, as do other commentators, points out the very similar message in a second set of Jesus' teachings in Matthew 13:1-52.

112. St. Thomas Aquinas, *ST* III, q. 46, a. 11, comments on the significance of this separation of the human race that was manifested at the crucifixion itself, citing Chrysostom, Jerome, Pope Leo, Augustine, Hilary, and Bede. Thomas's citation of Augustine will give a sense of these patristic commentaries: "The very cross, if thou mark it well, was a judgment-seat: for the judge being set in the midst, the one who believed was delivered, the other who mocked Him was condemned. Already He has signified what He shall do to the quick and the dead, some He will set on His right, others on His left hand (Augustine, Jo. vii. 36)."

Notes to Chapter V

1. See for example the wide-ranging essays in Paul G. Crowley, ed., *Rahner Beyond Rahner* (Lanham, MD: Rowman & Littlefield, 2005), and the very substantial essays in Declan Marmion and Mary E. Hines, eds., *The Cambridge Companion to Karl Rahner* (Cambridge: Cambridge University Press, 2005). Another scholar in a recent book gives an account of Rahner's continuing influence: Thomas F. O'Meara, *God in the World: A Guide to Karl Rahner's Theology* (Collegeville, MN: Liturgical Press, 2007), pp. 1-4, 135-38. See also Conrad T. Gromada, "How Would Karl Rahner Respond to *'Dominus Iesus'*?" *Philosophy and Theology* 13, no. 2 (2001): 425-36, for a commentary on Roger Haight's groundbreaking work as being "clearly in the spirit of Rahner" and Jacques Dupuis's work as being "unabashedly Rahnerian."

2. Eamonn Conway, *The Anonymous Christian: A Relativised Christianity? An Evaluation of Hans Urs von Balthasar's Criticisms of Karl Rahner's Theory of the Anonymous Christian* (Frankfurt am Main: Peter Lang, 1993), p. 10, claims that this is the most important of Rahner's theological concepts. "The supernatural existential, however, is Rahner's most important theological concept, and it provides the basis for, and in Rahner's own opinion, has its most important expression in his theory of the anonymous Christian."

3. Karl Rahner, "Anonymous Christians," in *TI*, vol. 6, p. 393. For a more detailed explanation, see "On the Theology of the Incarnation," in *TI*, vol. 4, pp. 105-20. See also his definition in Karl Rahner and Herbert Vorgrimler, *Theological Dictionary*, ed. Cornelius Ernst,

trans. Richard Strachan (New York: Herder & Herder, 1965), p. 161. See also Karl Rahner et al., *Sacramentum Mundi*, vol. 2 (New York: Herder & Herder, 1969), p. 306.

4. John F. Perry, "Ripalda and Rahner: 400 Years of Jesuit Reflection on Universal Salvation," *Philosophy and Theology* 13, no. 2 (2001): 342-43.

5. Stephen J. Duffy, "Experience of Grace," *The Cambridge Companion to Karl Rahner*, pp. 43-46, provides an account of the Catholic debate on the nature/grace relationship that erupted with the publication of Henri de Lubac's *Surnaturel* in 1946, which helps to contextualize Rahner's attempt to walk a middle path between "extrinsicism" and "intrinsicism."

6. Emerich Coreth, in his interview in Andreas R. Batlogg and Melvin E. Michalski, *Encounters with Karl Rahner: Remembrances of Rahner by Those Who Knew Him*, ed. and trans. Barbara G. Turner (Milwaukee: Marquette University Press, 2009), p. 201, comments on the importance of this for Rahner's work and properly identifies it as an unprovable hypothesis. "Fr. Rahner struggled for years to find an *a priori* for all theology, a starting point, a principle, so to speak, from which you could not unconditionally deduce everything but which would still make everything intelligible. . . . Strictly speaking, a transcendental *a priori* is philosophically unprovable. That is faith. . . . This is the key point for Karl Rahner: all of creation is different, since the Son of God has become human. You can also find this *a priori* difference in Karl Rahner's *theologoumenon* of the anonymous Christian. Somehow, everyone is already in the order of salvation, whether one knows it or not, whether one believes it or not. Fr. Rahner calls this the 'supernatural existential': existential in the strict sense meant by Martin Heidegger. Existential is an ontological determination of existence. Existence is the manner of being of the human person. Heidegger calls a constitutive, ontological determination of human existence an 'existential.' An ontological determination of human existence is simply the act of redemption: life in Christ." See also Harvey Egan, "Theology and Spirituality," *Cambridge Companion to Karl Rahner*, pp. 16-18, for a good summary.

7. Patrick Burke, *Reinterpreting Rahner: A Critical Study of His Major Themes* (New York: Fordham University Press, 2002), p. 61.

8. John M. McDermott, "Karl Rahner in Tradition: The One and the Many," *Fides Quaerens Intellectum* 3, no. 2 (Spring 2007): 23-24, esp. n. 34, notes that there is considerable discussion and disagreement about what kind of entity Rahner actually thought the "supernatural existential" was. "It is not completely clear whether grace provides the supernatural existential or the supernatural existential is the presupposition of grace."

9. Burke, *Reinterpreting Rahner*, p. 69.

10. Rahner has periodically recommended an essay by Klaus Riesenhuber as providing a good summary account of his theology of the anonymous Christian: Klaus Riesenhuber, "The Anonymous Christian According to Karl Rahner," in Anita Röper, *The Anonymous Christian*, trans. Joseph Donceel (New York: Sheed & Ward, 1966), pp. 145-79.

11. Burke, *Reinterpreting Rahner*, p. 62.

12. A number of Rahner's commentators claim that there is no significant variation in his views on this point over the course of his career. See, for example, Norman C. S. Wong, "Karl Rahner's Concept of the 'Anonymous Christian,'" *Church and Society* 4, no. 1 (April 2001): 23-39. O'Meara, *God in the World*, p. 68, detects the first outlines of the theory, although without the terminology, as early as 1947, in Rahner's essay, "Membership of the Church according to Pius XII's Encyclical, '*Mystici Corporis Christi*,'" in *TI*, vol. 2, pp. 1-88. He identifies the first use of the term "anonymous Christian" in the 1962 essay, "Thoughts

on the Possibility of Belief Today," in *TI*, vol. 5, pp. 9-22. Conway, *The Anonymous Christian*, p. 18, finds references to the "anonymous Christian" in sixteen volumes of the *Theological Investigations*. Gavin D'Costa, "Karl Rahner's Anonymous Christian: A Reappraisal," *Modern Theology* 12 (1985): 146, provides a listing of the most important texts in Rahner's *oeuvre* that pertain to the anonymous Christian.

13. Rahner, "Observations on the Problem of the 'Anonymous Christian,'" in *TI*, vol. 14, p. 288.

14. Rahner, "Observations," p. 294.

15. There is an extensive discussion regarding terminology in the scholarly debate concerning "anonymous Christians." The primary criticism is that the term "Christian," by definition, means someone who has explicitly expressed faith in Christ, and therefore it is inappropriate to describe someone who has not done so, as a Christian. Another criticism accepts the phrase "anonymous Christian" but wishes to rule out the phrase "anonymous Christianity" because Christianity is by definition a social, historic, visible entity. Rahner at times defends both terms, at other times, agrees with the criticism regarding "anonymous Christianity," and ultimately suggests that if someone has a better term that is fine with him, since what is important is the reality, not the particular language used to describe it. It is not necessary that we enter into this debate for the purposes of this book. D'Costa, "Rahner's Anonymous Christian," pp. 135-36, among others, provides a good summary of the terminology debate, with references to Rahner's varying opinions on the issue.

16. Rahner, "Christianity and the Non-Christian Religions," in *TI*, vol. 5, p. 125.

17. *ST*, I-II, q. 89, a.6.

18. Rahner, "Anonymous Christians," p. 394.

19. Conway, *The Anonymous Christian*, p. 17.

20. Rahner, "Anonymous Christians," pp. 394-95.

21. The most developed treatment of atheism in the documents of Vatican II is in *Gaudium et spes*, pp. 19-21, in addition to the mention in *LG* 16 on which we have already commented. Concerning the *LG* 16 sentence, Rahner, "Anonymous Christians," p. 397, remarks: "That an inculpable atheism of this kind can last a long time whether individually or collectively is not stated, but not excluded either." See also Walter Kasper, *The God of Jesus Christ*, trans. Matthew J. O'Connell (New York: Crossroad, 1984), p. 53, for a useful summary of the strengths and weaknesses of Rahner's treatment of atheism and the possibility of salvation. He very much values Rahner's efforts to understand and dialogue with atheism, but also thinks it is open to serious ambiguity. "Rahner's theory . . . represents a tremendous advance because it makes it possible for the first time to reflect on the inherent possibilities in the phenomenon of atheism and to do so in theological terms, instead of immediately rejecting it as alien and even absurd. . . . On the other hand, as the entire modern development has made clear, it is highly ambiguous to claim God as the interpretation of human transcendence, for there is the danger either of no longer being able to preserve fully the transcendence of God or — as is rather the danger in Rahner — of turning this transcendence into an ineffable mystery in which man exists but which he must rather be silent about than speak of." See also Walter Kasper, *Jesus the Christ*, trans. V. Green (New York: Paulist Press, 1976), p. 189 for an analysis that expresses similar concerns about Rahner's Christology: "These are all splendid and ingenious projects of a Christocentric total view of reality. Nevertheless, their intrinsic danger must not be overlooked, which consists in transforming the uniqueness of Jesus Christ into something universal and ending with a Christianity which is

found anonymously everywhere in mankind, paying for its universality by the loss of its concreteness and uniqueness of meaning."

22. Karl Rahner, "Forgotten Dogmatic Initiatives of the Second Vatican Council," in *TI*, vol. 22, p. 98. See also Karl Rahner, *Faith in a Wintry Season* (New York: Crossroad, 1990), p. 76.

23. Karl Rahner, "Atheism and Implicit Christianity," in *TI*, vol. 9, p. 150.

24. Marmion and Hines, eds., in their introduction to *The Cambridge Companion to Karl Rahner*, p. 7, acknowledge that Rahner had consciously adopted the theory of "fundamental option" in his theology.

25. Karl Rahner, "Christianity and the Non-Christian Religions," in *TI*, vol. 5, pp. 124-25. Joseph Ratzinger, *Truth and Tolerance: Christian Belief and World Religions* (San Francisco: Ignatius Press, 2004), pp. 21-23.

26. Rahner, "Christianity and the Non-Christian Religions," p. 294.

27. Ratzinger, *Truth and Tolerance*, pp. 21-23.

28. Rahner, "Christianity and the Non-Christian Religions," p. 123.

29. Rahner, "Christianity and the Non-Christian Religions," pp. 123-24.

30. Herbert Vorgrimler, Rahner's pupil and colleague, gives an account of Rahner's life that includes his wartime activities in *Karl Rahner: His Life, Thought and Work*, trans. Edward Quinn (London: Burns & Oates, 1965), pp. 3-32.

31. We will examine this "hope" in the next chapter.

32. Rahner, *Wintry Season*, p. 167.

33. Rahner, *Wintry Season*, p. 168.

34. Karl Rahner, "Reflections on the Unity of the Love of Neighbor and the Love of God," in *TI*, vol. 6 (New York: Seabury, 1974), p. 237.

35. Robert Sears, "Trinitarian Love as Ground of the Church," *Theological Studies* 37, no. 4 (1976): 655. The reference to Freud is Sigmund Freud, "Analysis Terminable and Interminable," *Standard Edition*, ed. James Strachey (London: Hogarth, 1964), 23:252.

36. John C. Bennett, "Two Christianities," *Worldview* (October 1973): 24. Cited by Sears, "Trinitarian Love," p. 656.

37. Sears, "Trinitarian Love," p. 656. The reference to Niebuhr is Reinhold Niebuhr, *Moral Man and Immoral Society* (New York: Scribner's, 1960), p. 272.

38. Sears, "Trinitarian Love," p. 657. The reference to Mahon is found in an unpublished dissertation by Robert J. Delaney, *Pastoral Renewal in a Local Church: Investigation of the Pastoral Principles Involved in the Development of the Local Church in San Miguelito, Panama* (Münster, 1973), esp. pp. 91-92.

39. Richard Schenk, "The Epoché of Factical Damnation," *Logos* 1, no. 3 (1997): 138. See also John Michael McDermott's article, "Metaphysical Conundrums at the Root of Moral Disagreement," *Gregorianum* 71, no. 4 (1990): 713-42, esp. pp. 726-27, which probes the difficulty Rahner has in explaining sin as a factor in his "salvation optimism."

40. See "Anonymous Christianity and the Missionary Task of the Church," in *TI*, vol. 12, pp. 166-67; Rahner, "Observations," pp. 283-84.

41. Rahner, "Missionary Task," p. 167.

42. Rahner, "Anonymous Christians," p. 397. Cardinal Koenig, in Batlogg and Michalski, *Encounters with Karl Rahner*, p. 52, who enlisted Rahner as his *peritus* during the Council, claims that Rahner influenced the section of *LG* 16 that teaches that those who through no fault of their own have not heard the gospel, under certain conditions, may

achieve eternal salvation. Cardinal Karl Lehmann, in Batlogg and Michalski, *Encounters with Karl Rahner,* p. 124, for many years Rahner's assistant, gives an account of Rahner's thoughts on the teaching of *LG* 16. "Rahner occasionally came back to the house and commented that it is astonishing that there are completely new things in the texts that are not taken from the tradition. . . . Rahner was of the opinion that much had changed at the Council and theology had somehow changed as well. It was not just things which Rahner had already formulated, but rather it was ideas that, to a certain extent, were in the air." As this book argues, it is only by ignoring *LG* 16c that one can claim a lack of continuity with the tradition.

43. Rahner, "Anonymous Christians," pp. 397-98.

44. Ratzinger, *Principles of Catholic Theology,* p. 380. John Michael McDermott, "Vatican II and the Theologians on the Church as Sacrament," *Irish Theological Quarterly* 71 (2006): 170, n. 69, notes that Rahner's claim of Conciliar support for his theory is contradicted by Congar's testimony "that at Vatican II in the debate over *Ad Gentes* the Council Fathers were very upset and strongly resisted an attempt to define the missionary's task as a bringing to consciousness of what was already present in non-Christian religions."

45. Rahner, "Anonymous Christians," p. 398.

46. Rahner, "Observations," p. 284.

47. Rahner, "On the Importance of the Non-Christian Religions for Salvation," in *TI,* vol. 18, p. 290.

48. Rahner, "On the Importance of the Non-Christian Religions for Salvation," p. 286.

49. Karl Rahner, "Justification and World Development from a Catholic Viewpoint," in *TI,* vol. 18, p. 261.

50. Conway, *The Anonymous Christian,* pp. 17-18.

51. Conway, *The Anonymous Christian,* pp. 130-31, 134-35, 156.

52. Eamonn Conway, in "So as Not to Despise God's Grace: Re-assessing Rahner's Idea of the 'Anonymous Christian,'" *Louvain Studies* 29 (2004): 111, 126, cites Balthasar, *Dare We Hope,* pp. 225-54, as support for his assertions. *Apokatastasis* is sometimes spelled *apocatastasis* when it is transliterated from the Greek into English. In direct citations from other authors, we will leave the word as the author wrote it.

53. O'Meara in *God in the World,* p. 130, never mentions the qualifications contained in *LG* 16c that forestall a one-sided optimism, or a universalist tilt. For example: "For the Christian, there are not two equal paths leading to two places: heaven and hell. Evil is a dead end, a static perversion. The key issue for the person who has radically chosen evil is change: the absence of any positive change in a life of hatred would hold one in that perverse orientation. Can a negative decision last into the next life? Can an elected orientation take on an eternal duration? God has created us to share his life, he loves us, and Christ died for us — those realities permeate existence. To say 'no' to them — although possible — is much more difficult than to say 'yes' with one's entire being. . . . One might hope that hell is empty." Even the Navarre Bible commentary on the Gospel of Luke, in its comments on Luke 13:22-27, quotes fully in its commentary *LG* 16b, seemingly as a corrective to Jesus' words, while ignoring *LG* 16c, which confirms them.

54. Those who apply Rahner's thought to contemporary expressions of syncretistic religions come to more sweeping positive judgments about their being salvific for their adherents than does Thils in his comments above. There have been some interesting attempts to use Rahner's theories to evaluate what is going on in ambiguous expressions of religion. One such attempt, Claudio M. Burgaleta, "A Rahnerian Reading of *Santeria:* A Proposal for a

Christian Recovery of the Syncretic Elements of Latin American Popular Religiosity Based on Rahner's Concept of 'Anonymous Christianity,'" *Apuntes* 2 (Summer 1993): 147, uses Rahner's thought to evaluate what is going on in *Santeria*, a mixture of Nigerian tribal religion and Christianity commonly found among Hispanics of Caribbean background who are ostensibly "Catholic." Burgaleta's study concludes: "*Santeria* ceases to be merely a syncretistic expression of Christianity which needs to be expunged through renewed evangelization efforts, but rather becomes what Rahner calls a 'lawful religion,' that is, a provisional and partial vehicle by which human beings who have not heard of Jesus Christ at all, or not in a convincing way, can come to salvation."

55. Rahner, "Observations," p. 287.

56. Gerald O'Collins in his book, *Salvation for All: God's Other Peoples* (New York: Oxford University Press, 2008), devotes a great deal of effort assembling and assessing the biblical testimony of God's promise of universal salvation and draws conclusions on the basis of this that seem not well founded since the methodology he adopted was to consider just the "positive" passages and not the "negative." In his introduction, p. v, he states: "But my purpose is not to survey equally and appraise both the 'negative' and the 'positive' witness; to do that would call for a book twice the length of this one." This remarkable "methodology" is similar to what we have seen in people claiming to state the teaching of *LG* 16 while ignoring *LG* 16c.

57. Schenk, "Factical Damnation," p. 139.

58. Jen-Guy Pagé, *Qui Est L'église?: Le Peuple de Dieu*, 3 vols. (Montréal: Les Editions Bellarmin, 1979), vol. 3, p. 53. [Cependant, la Constitution ne verse pas dans un optimisme ridicule qui ne verrait pas les erreurs dont sont menacés ceux qui ne jouissent pas de la pleine révélation évangélique (cf. la fin du paragraphe).]

59. Pagé, *Qui Est L'église?* vol. 3, pp. 82-84.

60. Gérard Philips, *L'Église et Son Mystère au Deuxième Concile du Vatican: Histoire, texte et commentaire de la Constitution* Lumen Gentium, vol. 1 (Paris: Desclée, 1967), p. 211. (Le tableau de la perversion païenne, si sombre qu'il soit comme le dépeint saint Paul, ne permet pas d'accuser son auteur de pessimisme. Une exégèse réaliste nous prescrit de tenir compte de l'alternance de lumière et d'ombres dans l'exposé de sa doctrine.

Il est possible que pour ces hommes honnêtes, Dieu demeure caché sous la forme d'une valeur absolue et impérative, sous le vocable de Justice, de Solidarité, ou d'un autre concept. Que l'on ne s'y méprenne pas cependant. Une fraternité humaine inconditionnée qui ne reconnait aucun fondement divin ne subsistera pas longtemps. Pour être pleinement homme avec les hommes, l'être humain doit se dépasser lui-même.)

61. Karl Rahner, "The Christian among Unbelieving Relations," in *TI*, vol. 3, pp. 355-56.

62. Rahner, "Christianity and the Non-Christian Religions," in *TI*, vol. 5, pp. 116-17.

63. Rahner, "Missionary Task," p. 175.

64. Rahner, "Anonymous Christians," p. 390.

65. Karl Rahner, *The Shape of the Church to Come*, trans. and intro. Edward Quinn (London: SPCK, 1974), pp. 20, 84-89, reveals that in the midst of his "despair" Rahner sometimes catches a glimpse of a more joyful, confident Christianity. When commenting on how priests and others are inclined to ignore the stark reality of death at funerals, he remarks:

> Have you ever once spoken in the joy of the Holy Spirit, in the light of the true, unvarnished situation (I am not saying how I would answer the question myself)? Admit it: are you not happy that for the most part no answer at all is expected of us in the light of

the real situation, that we are allowed to talk again only at the graveside, with due so-lemnity, after the others have overcome their first shock and the scandal of the facts has been suppressed also among the heathens? Have you ever once experienced the terror that makes your heart stop when you hear yourself and when your pious and learned words sound even to yourself like an intolerable blah-blah-blah? Have you ever really come once through this inferno?

Where are the tongues of fire talking of God and his love? Where do men speak of the "commandments" of God, not as a duty to be painfully observed, but as the glori-ous liberation of man from the enslavement of mortal fear and frustrating egoism? Where in the Church do men not only pray but also experience prayer as the pentecos-tal gift of the Spirit, as glorious grace? Where, beyond all rational indoctrination of God's existence is there an initiation into the mystery of that living experience which arises from the centre of our own existence? Where in the priests' seminaries are the ancient classics of the spiritual life read with the conviction that even today they still have something to tell us? . . . We talk too little about God in the Church or we talk about him in a dry, pedantic fashion, without any real vitality. . . . Only when the mes-sage of the living God is preached in the churches with all the power of the Spirit, will the impression disappear that the Church is merely an odd relic from the age of a soci-ety doomed to decline. . . . And in turn the profession of faith in Jesus as Christ and Lord, the decisive and final word of God in history might become more alive, more joyous and spontaneous.

66. Rahner, "Anonymous Christians," p. 396.

67. Joseph Ratzinger, "Salus Extra Ecclesiam Nulla Est," *Documentatie Centrum Concilie*, Series I, no. 88 (Rome, 1963): 2.

68. Ratzinger, "Salus Extra Ecclesiam Nulla Est," pp. 2-3. Ratzinger's solution in this es-say to the question of Christ and the Church's continuing relevance given that explicit ad-herence is no longer seen as necessary for salvation is to see the Church as in some way rep-resentative of all humanity. This solution seems to share in the weaknesses of those theories that ignore *LG* 16c's assertion that even though salvation is possible for people who have not heard the gospel it is not therefore probable and certainly not to be assumed. Ratzinger's own acknowledgment in this essay that even many of the dwindling numbers of sporadi-cally practicing Catholics are not really living according to the gospel would seem to rein-force this point. "Only a small fraction of those who, due to some convention or other, still call themselves Catholics, are in actual fact living according to the Gospel of Jesus Christ."

69. Rahner, "Unbelieving Relations," p. 357.

70. Some interpreters of Rahner state his position in such a way that evangelization seems virtually superfluous. See, for example, Lawrence Kanyike, "The Anonymous Chris-tian and the Mission of the Church" (doctoral dissertation, University of Notre Dame, 1978), p. 92: "In this sense, Rahner, following his system of theologizing by starting from dogmatic formulations, maintains that the dictum, *extra ecclesiam nulla salus* is still valid but under a different interpretation. The 'Church' no longer means as at Florence, 'the holy Roman Church' but properly speaking, rightly understood, fundamentally means all men of good will who all, somehow, belong to the Church and who will be saved through the Church as anonymous members or as anonymous Christians. Hence, the dogma, 'outside the Church no salvation,' is as true as ever because all in fact, are in the Church from the very beginning,

not as formal Christians, but as anonymous Christians." Rahner himself in his early major essay on Pius XII's *Mystici Corporis Christi*, pp. 84-86, after a very careful and detailed account of the traditional interpretation of EENS, in the last part of his essay, proposes that all humanity be considered now as the People of God. He points out the difficulty of reconciling how tied to the visible Church the traditional understanding of EENS is and the modern understanding of the possibility of salvation outside her visible bounds. His solution is to "baptize" humanity, in a certain sense, using language that could easily be understood as almost identifying the Church and the world. "But, according to what has been said, membership of the people of God is one of the determining factors of a concrete human nature, since every human being is necessarily and indissolubly a member of the one human race which really became the people of God by the divine Incarnation." He goes on to say that these members of the "People of God" do need to accept their "concrete human natures" for them to actually become members of the Church. This becomes a "ratification, in an ontologically real sense, of the membership of the people of God." This act of justification, which contains within it a *votum Ecclesiae,* "does not replace real membership of the Church by being 'good will' towards the Church. It replaces it by being the personal acceptance of that membership of the people of God which is already a fact on the historical and visible plane and in which is already given a real reference to membership of the Church as an established society."

71. J. P. Kenny, *Roman Catholicism, Christianity and Anonymous Christianity: The Role of the Christian Today* (Hales Corner, WI: Clergy Book Service, 1973), p. 112.

72. Kenny, *Roman Catholicism, Christianity and Anonymous Christianity,* p. 113.

73. Eugene Hillman, "'Anonymous Christianity' and the Missions," *The Downside Review* 84, no. 277 (1966): 362, 379.

74. Conway, *The Anonymous Christian,* p. 25.

75. D'Costa, in "A Reappraisal," pp. 137-38, discusses several of Rahner's responses to this criticism.

76. Rahner, "Anonymous Christians," p. 395.

77. Rahner, "Unbelieving Relations," p. 363.

78. Rahner, "Christianity and the Non-Christian Religions," p. 132.

79. Rahner, "Missionary Task," p. 171.

80. Rahner, "Observations," pp. 292-93.

81. Rahner, "Unbelieving Relations," p. 371.

82. Rahner, "Missionary Task," p. 177.

83. Rahner, "Unbelieving Relations," p. 370. See also Morerod, *The Church,* p. 115, for a good statement on why, even in the case of those who might be already in a state of justification and "partial" Church membership, despite never having heard the gospel, bringing this implicit faith to explicit consciousness is valuable. "That a partial Church membership can be sufficient for salvation does not mean that Christian 'missions' are not necessary any more, that it is superfluous to preach the Gospel. What has already been received by these 'unconscious' Christians calls for a further development. Initial graces would be better if they would become directly sacramental thanks to a kind of direct 'contact' with the humanity of Christ; the persons who receive them would be more conscious and joyful if what they received were explained to them (what Journet calls 'oriented' graces)." Morerod's reference is to Charles Journet, *The Meaning of Grace* (New York: P. J. Kennedy & Sons, 1960), pp. 118-19.

84. Rahner, "Missionary Task," pp. 176-77.

85. Sears, "Trinitarian Love," pp. 652-79, makes an inspiring case for the quality of life that should characterize the Christian community, as sacrament, and notes the radical conversion that is necessary for the Church as it lives today to manifest Trinitarian love. There is no indication though in the New Testament that the Church has to reach a certain level of perfection in order boldly and continually to preach the gospel. The treasure that is proclaimed will always be contained in an earthen vessel, but the Scripture indicates that there is a power in the proclamation itself that communicates effectively spiritual truth.

86. Joseph Ratzinger, in *Principles of Catholic Theology: Building Stones for a Fundamental Theology*, trans. Mary Frances McCarthy (San Francisco: Ignatius Press, 1987), pp. 44-55, provides a good explication of Vatican II's use of the phrase "Church as Sacrament."

87. Karl Rahner, "The Future of the Church and the Church of the Future," in *TI*, vol. 20, p. 105.

88. Karl Rahner, "The Future of Christian Communities," in *TI*, vol. 22, p. 123.

89. Rahner, "The Future of Christian Communities," pp. 123-24.

90. Karl Rahner, "The Church's Commission to Bring Salvation and the Humanization of the World," in *TI*, vol. 14, p. 305, provides descriptions of what it means to love your neighbor that sometimes seem not so easy to accomplish and not so commonly seen. "In other words: where someone, by recognizing the absolute claims of his conscience in real and selfless love, is able really to rise above himself in reaching out to his neighbour, a movement towards God is already in process and has been accepted in very truth, albeit unconsciously, a movement which is initiated and elevated by grace. And this signifies a salvific event in the strictest sense of the term, and moreover even in those cases in which the man concerned, through no fault of his own, has not yet arrived at any explicit recognition of the first ground and ultimate goal of this movement which proceeds horizontally and vertically *at the same time*. This remains true even if, so far as his conscious awareness is concerned, he still believes that he is an a-theist [*sic*]."

91. Rahner, "The Future of Christian Communities," p. 124.

92. This, of course, is the traditional teaching of the Church, and it is clearly articulated in *LG* 14.

93. Rahner, "The Future of Christian Communities," p. 124.

94. Rahner, "The Future of Christian Communities," p. 125.

95. Avery Dulles, "Who Can Be Saved?" *First Things* 180 (February 2008): 20-21.

96. Peter Phan, *Eternity in Time: A Study of Karl Rahner's Eschatology* (Cranbury, NJ: Associated University Presses, 1988), p. 157.

97. Rahner, "Christianity and the Non-Christian Religions," pp. 123-24.

98. Rahner, "On the Importance of the Non-Christian Religions for Salvation," p. 292.

99. Rahner, "The Abiding Significance of the Second Vatican Council," in *TI*, vol. 20, p. 101.

100. Karl Rahner, "Basic Theological Interpretation of the Second Vatican Council," in *TI*, vol. 20, pp. 88-89. Similarly strong language — "Copernican revolution" — is sometimes used by even recent commentators on the Council. See, for example, Tanner, *The Church and the World*, p. 65: "The development or change — some would call it a Copernican revolution — from a predominantly God-centered religion to one that takes the human condition much more seriously, and as much more the ground of our theology, is undoubtedly

one of the key features of the teaching of Vatican II." Tanner, *The Church and the World: Gaudium et Spes, Inter Mirifica* (New York: Paulist Press, 2005), p. 65.

101. Rahner, "Abiding Significance," p. 97.

102. Rahner, "Abiding Significance," pp. 100-101. Of course the Council did not bury the doctrine of limbo. The recent document of the International Theological Commission, "The Hope of Salvation for Infants Who Die Without Being Baptized," *Origins* 36, no. 45 (April 26, 2007): 41, although it is not a statement of the magisterium but only the considered opinion of respected theologians, acknowledges that this is still one of the legitimate theological hypotheses about the fate of unbaptized babies. See also Rahner's comments on this in *Wintry Season*, p. 77.

Rahner says in *Foundations of Christian Faith: An Introduction to the Idea of Christianity*, trans. William V. Dych (New York: Seabury, 1978), p. 313: "The Council indeed is extraordinarily reserved when it comes to the question of *how* such a salvific faith in a real revelation of God in the strict sense can come about outside the realm of the Old and New Testaments. But this does not forbid the theologian to ask the question how such a universal possibility of faith can come about, nor can it really dispense him from raising the question."

103. Rahner, "Forgotten Dogmatic Initiatives," p. 97. In his approach to what many consider irreformable doctrinal clarifications of the magisterium — such as in the case of artificial contraception or the ordination of women — Rahner, in *The Shape of the Church to Come*, pp. 113-14, states that future development that would move beyond these teachings is indeed possible, and, in his opinion, desirable. See also Karl Rahner, "Perspectives for Pastoral Theology in the Future," in *TI*, vol. 22, pp. 130-31. And also, Rahner, *Wintry Season*, pp. 72, 101, 112-14.

104. Rahner, *The Shape of the Church to Come*, p. 13. He also raises questions, on p. 95, about policies that involve both doctrinal and disciplinary elements pertaining to divorce and remarriage and the Eucharist, open Communion, the possibility of supporting abortion as a state policy, etc.

105. Ratzinger, *Principles of Catholic Theology*, pp. 390-91.

106. Rahner, "Abiding Significance," p. 101.

107. See footnote 111 in Chapter IV for a survey of contemporary Catholic commentary on these two texts.

108. As Newman put it in "Many Called, Few Chosen," *Parochial and Plain Sermons: John Henry Newman* (San Francisco: Ignatius Press, 1987), p. 1118: "Of course we must not press the words of Scripture; we do not know the exact meaning of the word 'chosen'; we do not know what is meant by being saved 'so as by fire'; we do not know what is meant by 'few.' But still the few can never mean the many; and to be called without being chosen cannot but be a misery."

109. This is not to question Rahner's orthodoxy. I would concur with my colleague John M. McDermott, "Karl Rahner in Tradition: The One and the Many," *Fides Quaerens Intellectum* 3, no. 2 (Spring 2007): 57, that despite the serious theological and pastoral problems with Rahner's theory he succeeds in his intention to remain orthodox, even though some of his disciples do not. "Even when the late Rahner yields to Plotinian mystagogy, he never surrenders the need of the visible Church with her creeds and sacraments. Unfortunately, some of his disciples neglect the same balance of polar opposites marking Rahner's dialectical analogy and in their desire to make theological progress draw logical conclusions one-sidedly from partial aspects of Rahner's thought and regress into antiquated heresies."

110. Rahner, "Christian Pessimism," in *TI*, vol. 22, pp. 158, 160.

111. Karl Rahner, "The Experience of a Catholic Theologian," *Communio* 11, no. 4 (1984): 409. See R. Highfield, "The Freedom to Say 'No'? Karl Rahner's Doctrine of Sin," *Theological Studies* 56 (1995): 485-505, and P. C. Phan, "Is Karl Rahner's Doctrine of Sin Orthodox?" *Philosophy & Theology* 9, nos. 1-2 (1995): 223-36.

112. See Appendix III for an account of Balthasar's criticism of Rahner.

Notes to Chapter VI

1. Germain Grisez, *The Way of the Lord Jesus*, vol. 3, *Difficult Moral Questions* (Quincy, IL: Franciscan Press, 1997), pp. 21-22, prefaces his discussion of Balthasar's views on universal salvation by citing the composite example of a CCD teacher who is teaching Balthasar's views to children, an example he constructed to illustrate the pervasive influence on the "grass roots" level of Balthasar's theories.

2. As noted earlier, *apokatastasis* is spelled variably as it is transliterated from the Greek into English. When we use the word we will transliterate it and italicize it as it is at the beginning of this comment. When it is spelled differently in a direct citation from another author we will leave it as the author wrote it.

3. John R. Sachs, "Current Eschatology: Universal Salvation and the Problem of Hell," *Theological Studies* 52 (1991): 252-53. While I am writing this, a well-known theologian, John Fuellenbach, who teaches at a Pontifical University, has taught a group of American priests in Rome for a sabbatical theological updating, very much along the lines of the universalist consensus that Sachs claims. In a book prepared to update wider audiences theologically, Fuellenbach, *Throw Fire* (Manila: Logos Publishing, 1998), p. 191, this same theologian offers this as a discussion question: "How convinced am I that God's saving will is meant for all, and that God will most probably save all human beings effectively?"

4. Richard J. Bauckham, "Universalism: A Historical Survey," *Themelios* 4, no. 2 (January 1979): 48.

5. Bauckham, "Universalism," p. 52.

6. Bauckham, "Universalism," p. 52.

7. Richard Schenk, "The Epoché of Factical Damnation," *Logos* 1, no. 3 (1997): 124-25.

8. *RM*, 46.

9. Jan Ambaum, "An Empty Hell? The Restoration of All Things? Balthasar's Concept of Hope for Salvation," *Communio* 18 (Spring 1991): 42-43, thinks that the renewed interest in universalism "lends itself well to an evolutionary world view because of its dynamic character," and finds the first Catholic traces of it in Teilhard de Chardin. Sachs, "Current Eschatology," p. 227, also emphasizes the consonance of "Christian universalism" to contemporary culture. "My conclusion will stress how a properly understood Christian universalism is not only consonant with several central strands of Christian belief, but is also profoundly relevant to the religious and cultural developments of the present age." Bruce J. Nicholls, "The Exclusiveness and Inclusiveness of the Gospel," *Themelios* 4, no. 2 (January 1979): 64-65, notes a "steady drift towards theological universalism and religious syncretism" that he thinks is particularly prominent in Asia. He points out that in the nineteenth century "it was largely unacceptable, today it is a respectable option." It is worth noting that a common theme of contemporary "new age" spiritualities, rooted in traditional spiritualism, holds for

the eventual union of all with "God." Edgar Cayce's views in *No Soul Left Behind: The Words and Wisdom of Edgar Cayce*, ed. Robert Smith (New York: Kensington Publishing, 2005), pp. 196-97, would be typical: "The soul, then, must return — *will* return — to its Maker. It is a portion of the Creative Forces, which is energized into activity even in materiality, in the flesh. . . . Each soul is destined to become a portion of the First Cause, or back to its Maker."

10. Avery Dulles, "The Population of Hell," *First Things* (May 2003): 41. Since Dulles has expressed these concerns, attempts have been made on both the level of the universal Church and the local Church to eliminate the use of homilies and eulogies to inappropriately declare that the deceased is already in heaven. These efforts have resulted in mixed results.

11. Joseph Ratzinger, *The Yes of Jesus Christ*, trans. Robert Nowell (New York: Crossroad, 1991), pp. 84-87.

12. http://www.dailymail.co.uk/news/article-1255983/How-I-God-peace-atheist-brother -PETER-HITCHENS-traces-journey-Christianity.html#ixzz1BdZBuZIa (accessed January 24, 2011). This is an excerpt from the book by Peter Hitchens, *The Rage against God: How Atheism Led Me to Faith* (Grand Rapids: Zondervan, 2010).

13. Avery Dulles, "Current Trends in Mission Theology," *Theology Digest* 20, no. 1 (Spring 1972): 30.

14. The essays collected by David L. Schindler, ed., *Hans Urs von Balthasar: His Life and Work* (San Francisco: Ignatius Press, 1991), by eminent theologians such as Cardinal de Lubac, and Church leaders such as Marc Ouellet, Christoph Schönborn, Karl Lehmann, and Walter Kasper, all of whom were or became Cardinals and serve in important leadership roles, give evidence of this esteem. Many of the essays can only be described as "effusive" in their praise. Included in the volume is the telegram from John Paul II on the occasion of Balthasar's funeral and the text of the homily given at his funeral by Cardinal Ratzinger. Balthasar died just a few days before the cardinalate could be bestowed on him. As John Paul II put it (p. 289): "All who knew the priest, von Balthasar, are shocked, and grieve over the loss of a great son of the Church, an outstanding man of theology and of the arts, who deserves a special place of honor in contemporary ecclesiastical and cultural life.

"It was my wish to acknowledge and to honor in a solemn fashion the merits he earned through his long and tireless labors as a spiritual teacher and as an esteemed scholar by naming him to the dignity of the cardinalate in the last Consistory. We submit in humility to the judgment of God who now has called this faithful servant of the Church so unexpectedly into eternity." Cardinal Ratzinger in the funeral homily made the strong statement (on p. 295): "But what the Pope intended to express by this mark of distinction, and of honor, remains valid: no longer only private individuals but the Church itself, in its official responsibility, tells us that he is right in what he teaches of the Faith, that he points the way to the sources of living water — a witness to the word which teaches us Christ and which teaches us how to live." None of the essays in Schindler's volume, nor the remarks of John Paul II or Cardinal Ratzinger, directly addresses the theory of Balthasar that we are examining in this chapter.

15. Ambaum, "Hope," pp. 45-46, traces this theme in Balthasar "from 1938 *(Origenes, Geist und Feurer)*, through the Barth study (1951), to 1987 *(Kleiner Diskurs)*. Significant items are found especially in *Theodramatik* IV, 243-73."

16. Hans Urs von Balthasar, *Dare We Hope "That All Men Be Saved"? With a Short Discourse on Hell*, trans. David Kipp and Lothar Krauth (San Francisco: Ignatius Press, 1988).

Henceforth, *Dare We Hope.* (Other authors quoted here use the abbreviation DWH for this text. We will leave each author to his or her own system of abbreviations and will not attempt to standardize.) There are various accounts of the sequence of the publications and their revisions. This chapter will follow the detailed sequence that Kevin Flannery provides in "How to Think about Hell," *New Blackfriars* 72, no. 854 (November 1991): 469-81. Ambaum, "Hope," p. 46, further specifies that it was in connection with Balthasar's reception of the Paul VI award in 1984 "and the publication associated with it of Balthasar's *Kleine Catechese über di Hölle*, in *Oserv. Romano* (German ed.) 14 (1984): 1-2 (previously in *Il Sabato*)" that the controversy intensified. Manfred Hauke, "'Sperare per tutti'? Il ricorso all'esperienza dei santi nell'ultima grande controversia di Hans Urs von Balthasar," *Rivista teologica di Lugano* 6, no. 1 (2001): 196-208, also gives a detailed account of the sequence of the various publications as well as an account of the vigorous theological debate they occasioned in German theological journals.

17. Balthasar, *Dare We Hope*, p. 59, posits that Origen (c. 185–c. 254) "was the first great repudiator of an eternal hell." What exactly Origen taught, and whether he taught it as a hypothesis or as a teaching that he definitively held, is much debated. Balthasar holds that Origen did not certainly teach it but "largely" proposed it as a hypothesis. He acknowledges though that Origen gives the impression that he thought that even the demons would be eventually reconciled and hell would be emptied. However, it appears that Origen's disciples received and promulgated his thinking as a teaching and because of that Origen and his teaching were condemned. Not only is there extensive debate about what exactly Origen taught as opposed to his followers, but there is also extensive debate about the ecclesial status of the condemnations proposed by the Emperor Justinian and accepted by a local synod in Constantinople in 543, which apparently Pope Vigilius signed, and which were later accepted by the bishops gathered for Constantinople II in 553, but before the Council actually convened. An essay by Brian Daley, "Apokatastasis and 'Honorable Silence' in the Eschatology of Maximus the Confessor," in *Maximus Confessor: Actes du Symposium sur Maxime le Confesseur*, ed. Felix Heinzer and Christoph Schönborn (Fribourg, Suisse: Éditions Universitaires Fribourg, 1982), pp. 309-12, details the many conflicting and difficult-to-reconcile statements of Origen on these issues and demonstrates why it is difficult to say what, in the end, Origen actually taught. The fifteen anathemas against the teaching of Origen, along with a discussion of the scholarly debate, can be found in *The Seven Ecumenical Councils of the Undivided Church*, ed. Henry R. Percival, in *A Select Library of Nicene and Post-Nicene Fathers of the Christian Church*, Second Series, vol. 14, ed. Philip Schaff and Henry Wace (Grand Rapids: Eerdmans, 1983), pp. 316-20. Whatever the case, the condemnation of Origen was endorsed by future Councils and was accepted as a clear departure from orthodoxy by the churches of both East and West. James T. O'Connor, *Land of the Living: A Theology of the Last Things* (New York: Catholic Book Publishing, 1992), pp. 76-77, also gives an account of the condemnations of Origen. When the Origenist theories were found in the highly esteemed Gregory of Nyssa, Patriarch Germanos I claimed they were forgeries. See Daley, "Maximus," p. 313. "Gregory's assimilation of the Origenist theory remained a scandal for his Orthodox admirers as late as the eighth century, when Patriarch Germanos I (715-730) composed a treatise, the *Antapodotikos*, to prove that the passages where Gregory seems to teach universal salvation are forgeries." The concern with Origen's orthodoxy included not only his teaching on *apokatastasis* but other views of Origen as well, such as his teaching on the preexistence of souls.

18. It seems that Barth was ambiguous in his work on this point, practically suggesting universalism as a necessary outcome of the sacrifice of Christ, but never so clearly as to be certain. When an interviewer asked him point blank about this he replied, as Justyn Terry reports in *The Justifying Judgment of God* (Eugene, OR: Wipf & Stock, 2007), p. 131: "I do not teach it, but I also do not not teach it." Augustine DiNoia, "Religion and the Religions," in *The Cambridge Companion to Karl Barth*, ed. John Webster (New York: Cambridge University Press, 2000), pp. 243-57, cites a passage from Barth's *Church Dogmatics* that seems to be unambiguously universalist. "Barth affirms, in a strikingly worded passage, that in the end no refusal 'on the part of non-Christians will be strong enough to resist the fulfillment of the promise of the Spirit which is pronounced over them too . . . or to hinder the overthrow of their ignorance of Christ' (CD IV/3, p. 355). K. Barth, *Church Dogmatics*, ed. G. W. Bromiley and T. F. Torrance (Edinburgh: T. & T. Clark, 1956-75), vol. 4, part 3, p. 355." Thomas Joseph White, "Divine Providence: Von Balthasar and Journet on the Universal Possibility of Salvation and the Twofold Will of God," *Nova et Vetera (English ed.)* 4, no. 3 (Summer 2006): 655, cites the correspondence between Maritain and Journet where Journet reports having received a letter from the young Balthasar. "In a letter to Maritain on August 9, 1945, Journet describes a letter he has recently received from the young Jesuit chaplain of Basle in which the latter describes himself as a student of Barth, and claims that he follows the Swiss Protestant thinker in holding to some version of the doctrine of *apokatastasis*, as reinterpreted in light of the mystery of Holy Saturday" (*Journet-Maritain Correspondance*, vol. 3 [Saint-Augustin: St.-Just-Las-Pendue, 1998], pp. 336-37). Balthasar later makes a point (*Dare We Hope*, p. 94) of agreeing that all attempts to deny that Barth taught *apokatastasis* were "rhetorical," or (*Dare We Hope*, p. 197) "come too close to the doctrine of *apokatastasis*. What remains for me an object of hope becomes for him practically a certainty." Also, he explicitly disavows (*Dare We Hope*, pp. 44-45) Barth's teaching that "Jesus, as God's chosen One, is rejected in place of all sinners, 'so that besides him, no one may be lost' [quote from Barth here is from *Church Dogmatics* II/1, p. 551]. This comment is, to be sure, surrounded by others whose tone is less absolute, and the term *apokatastasis*, or 'universal reconciliation,' is carefully avoided, even rejected. Still, one ought to stay well away from so systematic a statement and limit oneself to that Christian hope that does not mask a concealed knowing but rests essentially content with the Church's prayer, as called for in 1 Timothy 2:4, that God wills that all men be saved."

19. Geoffrey Wainwright, "Eschatology," in *The Cambridge Companion to Hans Urs von Balthasar* (New York: Cambridge University Press, 2004), p. 122. James O'Connor, "Von Balthasar and Salvation," *Homiletic and Pastoral Review* 89, no. 10 (July 1989): 16, identifies the 543 gathering as a provincial Synod and explains that "its dogmatic weight is not absolutely clear, although, according to the testimony of Cassiodorus, it was approved by Pope Vigilius during his detention in Constantinople in the years 547-555. Augustine appears to have considered what was taught in this canon to have been, even in his time, a matter of a binding decision of the Church." Tanner in his compilation of the Council's decisions does not include the condemnations of Origen since they were voted on by the bishops assembled before the Council officially convened. It is clear though that subsequent Councils clearly endorsed the condemnation of Origen's teaching. The Second Council of Constantinople's affirmation of Origen's condemnation is typical. "If anyone does not anathematize Arius, Eunomius, Macedonius, Apollinarius, Nestorius, Eutyches and Origen, as well as their heretical books, and also all other heretics, who have already been condemned and anathe-

matized by the holy, catholic and apostolic church and by the four holy synods which have already been mentioned, and also all those who have thought or now think in the same way as the aforesaid heretics and who persist in their error even to death: let him be anathema." Anathema 11. Tanner, p. 553. See also the Third Council of Constantinople (Tanner, p. 125), the Second Council of Nicea (Tanner, p. 135), and the Fourth Council of Constantinople (Tanner, p. 161).

20. In *Dare We Hope*, p. 196, Balthasar writes: "One really has to ask oneself how, given an eternally valid bifurcation of mankind like this, simple human love of one's neighbor, or even love of one's enemy in Christ's sense could still be possible." He also says, on page 166, that if the multiple texts on judgment are more than simply "threats" they would cancel out the positive passages that make hope possible. He quotes, on page 211, another theologian approvingly: "Whoever reckons with the possibility of even only *one* person's being lost besides himself is hardly able to love unreservedly." One hesitates to describe a lack of love to Jesus and the Apostles. And still another, on page 53: "If God is love, as the New Testament teaches us, hell must be impossible. At the least, it represents a supreme anomaly. In no case can being a Christian imply believing more in hell than in Christ. Being a Christian means first of all, believing in Christ and, if the question arises, hoping that it will be impossible that there is a hell for men because the love with which we are loved will ultimately be victorious." Nicholas Healy, "On Hope, Heaven, and Hell," *Logos* 1, no. 3 (1997): 89, in defending Balthasar's position, argues that "if we know with certainty that some men will suffer damnation," it would "attenuate" the force of Vatican II's acknowledgement that people can possibly be saved apart from hearing the gospel, as articulated in *Redemptoris Missio* 9-10. It is unclear why this would be the case.

21. Balthasar, citing words of Blondel, *Dare We Hope*, p. 120.

22. *Dare We Hope*, p. 237.

23. *Dare We Hope*, p. 237.

24. Wainwright, "Eschatology," p. 124, identifies the dilemma in advocating universalism. "The crunch comes with the question of freedom. Balthasar rejects double predestination outright, since he cannot believe that any part of creation was created *in order* to be lost. Has God, then, predestined *all* to beatitude? Such could seem to override the freedom of the creature (at least the human creature). A universalist outlook has to face the problem of a 'forced' salvation in its most extensive and stubborn form." Balthasar, *Explorations in Theology*, vol. IV: *Spirit and Institution*, trans. Edward T. Oakes (San Francisco: Ignatius Press, 1995), pp. 462-63, at times seems to speak about the seriousness of the need to make a choice for or against God in this life, but then often nullifies such statements by speculating on post-death conversion, or God overruling the creature's choice, or somewhat obscure references to what may be the case but we do not realize it, etc. "The decision made in time is and remains the basis of eternity, however much the grace and justice of the eternal judge may transform it and however great the change of condition may be from the Eon of mortality to the Eon of eternal life. No one can exhaust the depths of the temporal situation in which a person makes his decision, but in the resurrection from the dead these depths are now revealed as they already were implicit in the counsels of God." In another section of the same essay, p. 421, he says: "God gives man the capacity to make a (negative) choice against God that seems *for man* to be definitive, but which need not be taken *by God* as definitive." Balthasar, *Explorations IV*, p. 421. Wainwright, "Eschatology," p. 125, concludes: "Balthasar refuses to say whether God can really 'lose the game of creation through the creature's free

choice to be lost' (2 SW, 51)." Wainwright's quote of Balthasar here (2 SW, 51) is from Hans Urs von Balthasar and Joseph Ratzinger, *Two Say Why: "Why I Am Still a Christian," by Hans Urs von Balthasar and "Why I Am Still in the Church," by Joseph Ratzinger,* trans. John Griffiths (Chicago: Franciscan Herald Press, 1973), p. 51. Sachs, "Current Eschatology," pp. 246-54, argues strongly, based on Rahner and Balthasar, that, in fact, human freedom may not be able to persist indefinitely in saying "no" to God, and eventually all will be saved. He speculates that the "process of death" may continue indefinitely until the creature finally says yes to God, thereby avoiding denying the scriptural and magisterial teaching that immediately after death there is the judgment. This speculation seems particularly fanciful, and no reasonable evidence or argumentation is offered in its support.

25. Rahner also acknowledged the strong challenge that Scripture and tradition presented to his position but didn't feel that he needed to address it given what he considered to be the coherency of his theological anthropology and the nature of his work as speculative theology.

26. Book XXI of Augustine's *City of God* remains a fascinating exploration and refutation of all the "moves" that the fallen human mind is tempted to make in denying the reality or eternity of hell. Augustine's thought in Book XXI and elsewhere actually provides underpinning for little-noticed texts of Vatican II, such as *LG* 14, which speaks of even Catholics being lost if they are not living lives of charity, where texts of Augustine are directly cited. The same Book is relevant to the text we are primarily concerned with, *LG* 16. Balthasar, *Dare We Hope,* pp. 65-72, refers to Augustine's work here in a sarcastic, patronizing tone.

27. Dulles, "Hell," p. 39. Later on we will see if Dulles's description of Balthasar's thought as "adventurous" as regards his treatment of Scripture, his relationship to the doctrinal tradition, and his estimation that a "healthy fear of being lost" is preserved really constitutes a suitable word for summing up Balthasar's thought. Dulles does not advert in his article to the fact that Balthasar posits the possibility of other "chances" after death for those who die unrepentant and those condemned to hell (where Christ then "meets them"), and since Dulles is not aware of these texts, or does not advert to them, it is unclear how he would judge the consonance of this opinion with orthodox faith. Flannery, "Hell," p. 476, by contrast, raises the question of orthodoxy more pointedly, if still tentatively: "We cannot accede to Balthasar's way of conceiving the possibility of eternal salvation and remain orthodox." Flannery then considers how the possibility of eternal salvation can be conceived in an orthodox fashion and then, on page 479, concludes his essay: "I do not by any means intend to suggest that Balthasar opposed Church teaching, although the trajectory of his arguments certainly comes into conflict with it."

28. Dulles, "Hell," pp. 37-38.

29. St. Thomas, *ST* I, q.23, a.7, ad 3. "Since their eternal happiness, consisting in the vision of God, exceeds the common state of nature, and especially in so far as this is deprived of grace through the corruption of original sin, those who are saved are in the minority. In this especially, however, appears the mercy of God, that He has chosen some for that salvation, from which very many in accordance with the common course and tendency of nature fall short."

30. Dulles, "Hell," p. 38.

31. Dulles, "Hell," p. 38. See also Candido Pozo, *Theology of the Beyond,* trans. Mark A. Pilon (New York: Alba House, 2009), pp. 376-404, for an account of the development of the doctrine of hell in Scripture, the Fathers, and the subsequent magisterial tradition.

32. Dulles, "Hell," p. 38. This consensus held together longer in the Catholic Church, up until the mid-twentieth century, than it did in the Protestant denominations where it began to break down in the nineteenth century. An examination of the Papal encyclicals published in the twentieth century before Vatican II, which we will review in our concluding chapter, confirms Dulles's point.

33. Dulles, "Hell," p. 38.

34. Dulles, "Hell," p. 37.

35. Balthasar, *Dare We Hope*, pp. 49-50.

36. Balthasar, *Dare We Hope*, p. 64.

37. Edward T. Oakes, *The Pattern of Redemption: The Theology of Hans Urs von Balthasar* (New York: Continuum, 1997), p. 162. See also Pozo's account of the condemnation of Origenism, *Theology of the Beyond*, pp. 386-88.

38. Balthasar, *Dare We Hope*, p. 236.

39. Balthasar, *Dare We Hope*, p. 253.

40. As Grisez, in *The Way*, p. 25, puts it: "Anybody who accepts both sets of passages as God's word must try to synthesize them, and von Balthasar himself tries — precisely in a universalist sense."

41. Balthasar, *Dare We Hope*, p. 218.

42. Edith Stein, *Welt und Person. Beitrag zum christlichen Wahrheitsstreben* [World and person. A contribution to Christian truth seeking], ed. L. Gelber and Romaeus Leuven (Freiburg, 1962), pp. 158ff. Cited by Balthasar, *Dare We Hope*, pp. 219-21.

43. Oakes, *Pattern*, p. 185.

44. See Balthasar, *Theo-Drama: Theological Dramatic Theory*, vol. IV: *The Action* (San Francisco: Ignatius Press, 1994), pp. 273-84.

45. Rahner, "The Hermeneutics of Eschatological Assertions," trans. Kevin Smyth, in *TI*, vol. 4, p. 13 (Baltimore: Helicon Press, 1966), pp. 323-46. Despite the sometimes-bitter disagreement between Rahner and Balthasar on certain issues, Balthasar adopts Rahner's theory that the scriptural texts on final judgment should only be interpreted as warnings, and on this issue at least both end up in remarkably similar places, despite very different methodologies. As Schenk, "Factical Damnation," pp. 130-31, puts it: "Balthasar adopted many of the formulations developed by Rahner in his 1960 essay, 'The Hermeneutics of Eschatological Assertions.'"

46. Rahner, "Hermeneutics," p. 343.

47. Rahner, "Hermeneutics," p. 345.

48. Rahner, "Hermeneutics," p. 340.

49. Rahner, "Hermeneutics," pp. 337-38.

50. Rahner, "Hermeneutics," pp. 339-40.

51. Peter Phan, "Eschatology," in *The Cambridge Companion to Karl Rahner*, ed. Declan Marmion and Mary E. Hines (New York: Cambridge University Press, 2005), pp. 186-87, 189-90. Peter Phan also treats of Rahner's hermeneutics of eschatological assertions in his book, *Eternity in Time* (Cranbury, NJ: Associated University Presses, 1988), pp. 64-76, 205-7.

52. See Balthasar, *Dare We Hope*, p. 177: "Still, in the New Testament there are two series of statements that we cannot bring together into an overall synthesis." Balthasar's approach here, which is fundamental to his argument, is at considerable variance from what he states should be the appropriate approach to Scripture and its interpretation, in, for example, Balthasar, *The Christian State of Life* (San Francisco: Ignatius Press, 2002), p. 16: "We regard

Holy Scripture as an inspired whole — one that is, moreover, [to be] interpreted in the essential tradition and history of the Church."

53. Flannery, "Hell," p. 473.

54. Wainwright, "Eschatology," p. 122.

55. Flannery, "Hell," p. 473.

56. Schenk, "Factical Damnation," pp. 135-36.

57. Rahner also at times indicated a preference for certain parts of Scripture over other parts in what at times seemed also to be an attempt to find the canon within the canon, attempting to get behind the "late" New Testament Christologies to a more primitive understanding of the Christ event. See Eamonn Conway, *The Anonymous Christian — A Relativized Christianity? An Evaluation of Hans Urs von Balthasar's Criticisms of Karl Rahner's Theory of the Anonymous Christian* (Frankfurt: Peter Lang, 1993), p. 90. As Conway puts it (p. 13): "Perhaps both presentations [Balthasar and Rahner] could benefit from closer attention to scriptural exegesis and the proper use of Scripture within dogmatic theology." Conway draws attention to Walter Kasper's insight, *The Methods of Dogmatic Theology* (Shannon: Ecclesia Press, 1969), pp. 27-28, as support for his point: "the initiative and the whole questioning process must start from Scripture; we should not go back to Scripture to find arguments for theses and concepts that have been laid down beforehand. . . . Scripture is not to be utilized within the framework of the Church's teaching; on the contrary, the teaching of the Church must be presented within the framework of Scripture's testimony."

58. Balthasar, *Theo-Drama*, IV:253.

59. Oakes, *Pattern*, pp. 311-12.

60. Balthasar, *Theo-Drama*, IV:253.

61. Oakes, *Pattern*, p. 312.

62. Grisez, *The Way*, pp. 25-26.

63. Oakes, *Pattern*, p. 312.

64. Wainwright, "Eschatology," p. 122.

65. Alyssa Lyra Pitstick, *Light in Darkness: Hans Urs von Balthasar and the Catholic Doctrine of Christ's Descent into Hell* (Grand Rapids: Eerdmans, 2007), p. 318. See also the whole section, pp. 317-22.

66. Pitstick, *Light*, p. 324. Pitstick gives numerous texts of Balthasar where she shows this to be the case.

67. W. T. Dickens, "Balthasar's Biblical Hermeneutics," in *The Cambridge Companion to Hans Urs von Balthasar*, p. 181.

68. O'Connor, "Salvation," pp. 13-14.

69. Schenk, "Factical Damnation," pp. 140-41.

70. Balthasar, *Dare We Hope*, pp. 29, 30, 236.

71. Oakes, *Pattern*, p. 197.

72. Joseph Ratzinger, *Introduction to Christianity*, trans. J. R. Foster (San Francisco: Ignatius Press, 2004), p. 318. "Rudolph Bultmann reckons that the belief in an 'end of the world' signaled by the return of the Lord in judgment is one of those ideas, like the Lord's descent into hell and Ascension into heaven, which for modern man are 'disposed of.'"

73. James T. O'Connor, *The Land of the Living: A Theology of the Last Things* (New York: Catholic Book Publishing, 1992), p. 32. See also pp. 33-37.

74. In 1952 Balthasar published a book, translated into English as *Razing the Bastions* (San Francisco: Ignatius, 1993), which tended to give him, before the Second Vatican Coun-

cil, a "progressive" reputation. In it he pointed out that the razing of certain external bastions — the unity of the Church before the Reformation, of Church and State, of culture and Church — while profound setbacks in certain respects, also provided an opportunity for the razing of internal bastions that kept the Church and individual Christians from proper, active involvement as salt and light in the world. It is clear though, in this book, that Balthasar is not calling for the spurious "revolution" that some interpreters of Vatican II have called for, but a "revolution" that is deeply spiritual and Trinitarian in its foundation.

75. Oakes, *Pattern*, pp. 162-64. See also comments made in Oakes's Introduction on pp. 6-7 that describe Balthasar as both "traditional" and "idiosyncratic." Most of Balthasar's defenders acknowledge that there are "problematic" aspects of Balthasar's eschatology. See, for example, Margaret Turek, "Dare We Hope 'That All Men Be Saved' (1 Tim 2:4)? On von Balthasar's Trinitarian Grounds for Christian Hope," *Logos* 1, no. 3 (1997): 111-13: "Space does not permit us to examine von Balthasar's more problematic proposals concerning the moment of the human being's 'conclusive encounter' with infinite freedom." Turek specifies some of the problematic issues: "Does von Balthasar give an adequate account of why the sinner's opposition to God during his/her lifetime is overcome through this conclusive meeting with the Crucified? Since von Balthasar does not want to allow for a conversion after death, are we to understand the sinner's decisive encounter to occur 'in dying'? . . . As an alternative interpretation does von Balthasar regard the elicited assent to bespeak a retrieval and disclosure 'after death' of a 'yes' already there, albeit hitherto suppressed by the sinner? But then can von Balthasar be accused of trivializing the human being's fundamental decision [*Grundwahl*] as it has been actualized through the choices made in the concrete situations of his/her life? Or are we to understand the 'yes' which is retrieved as the fundamental decision after all? Can this notion be justified? . . . In the end, does this second, alternative interpretation entirely avoid implying a conversion after death?"

76. The Scripture translation used for texts cited in this chapter is that of the NAB.

77. Fr. Christophe Kruijen, who works in the Congregation for the Doctrine of the Faith, completed a doctoral dissertation at the Pontifical University of St. Thomas in Rome that exhaustively analyzes Balthasar's approach to the "two destinations" texts and comes to conclusions similar to my own. My own dissertation on which the current book is based was completed before I had a chance to read Fr. Christophe's dissertation. Christophe J. Kruijen, "Salut universel ou double issue du jugement: Espérer pour tous? Contribution à l'étude critique d'une opinion théologique contemporaine concernant la réalisation de la damnation" (doctoral dissertation, Pontifical University of St. Thomas, Rome, 2008). He has discovered some startling texts where Balthasar acknowledges that his theory of the "descent" is not in accord with the theological tradition and that the Church will not be able to receive it unless he prepares the way carefully. He is consciously aware of the need to "deconstruct" the tradition in order to completely reinterpret it with his own synthesis. The texts are taken from Adrienne von Speyr, *Kreuz und Holle*, vol. II, ed. H. U. von Balthasar (Einsiedeln: Johannes Verlag, 1972), pp. 459-60. They are reproduced in French translation in Kruijen's dissertation on pp. 409-10.

78. Joseph Ratzinger, *Pilgrim Fellowship of Faith: The Church as Communion*, ed. Stephan Otto Horn and Vinzenz Pfnür, trans. Henry Taylor (San Francisco: Ignatius Press, 2005), p. 146.

79. Joseph Ratzinger, *God's Word: Scripture, Tradition, Office*, ed. Peter Hünermann and Thomas Söding, trans. Henry Taylor (San Francisco: Ignatius Press, 2008), pp. 91-126, cites

the principle of the unity of Scripture as central to a truly Catholic approach to the Scriptures. He provides a useful analysis of the main thrust of *Dei verbum* in relationship to the contemporary confusion and conflict in biblical interpretation.

80. Balthasar, *Dare We Hope*, pp. 32-33. Balthasar does not dispute the inspired nature of the text. In any case, there is nothing in the disputed Markan ending that is not contained elsewhere in Scripture.

81. Balthasar, *Dare We Hope*, p. 34.

82. See, for example, Deuteronomy 30:15; Jeremiah 21:8; Proverbs 12:28; Mark 3:29; Matthew 7:13-14; 8:11-12; 11:20-24; 12:32; 13:36-43, 47-50; 24:45-51; Luke 12:8-10; 2 Peter 2:15; 2 Thessalonians 1:6; 1 Corinthians 4:1; Romans 14:10.

83. When the International Theological Commission took up the issue of the normative status of New Testament moral teaching, H. Schürmann, "The Question of the Obligatory Character of the Value Judgments and Moral Directives of the New Testament," in *International Theological Commission*, vol. 1, Texts and Documents, 1969-1985, ed. Michael Sharkey (San Francisco: Ignatius Press, 1989), *ix*, pp. 125-32, it generally agreed that very few of the moral norms of the New Testament (and none that we are citing in this book) were culturally conditioned to such an extent that they should not be regarded as normative today. This document was published by the ITC *in forma generica*, which means that the ITC as a whole "accepts the principal ideas of the text, the rest remains the responsibility of its author."

84. The words of Adrienne von Speyr quoted by Balthasar, *Dare We Hope*, p. 141.

85. Balthasar, *The Theology of Karl Barth: Exposition and Interpretation* (San Francisco: Ignatius Press, 1992), pp. 241-42. Cited in Oakes, *Pattern*, p. 66.

86. Joseph Ratzinger, *Theological Highlights of Vatican II*, trans. Henry Traub, Gerard C. Thormann, and Werner Barzel (New York: Paulist Press, 1966), p. 173.

87. ITC, "Some Current Questions in Eschatology," pp. 79, 84. *LG* 48 is cited as support for the last sentence quoted.

88. Balthasar, *Dare We Hope*, p. 139.

89. 2 Peter 2 lists the content of false teaching that will be severely judged.

90. AS III/8, 144-45. "Unus pater vult aliquam sententiam introduci ex qua appareat *reprobos de facto haberi* (ne damnatio ut mera hypothesis maneat). R. Propositum non quadrat cum hoc contextu. Ceterum in n. 48 Schematis citantur verba evangelica quibus Dominus ipse in forma grammaticaliter futura de reprobis loquitur."

91. O'Connor, "Salvation," pp. 17-18. O'Connor also treats of this issue in his book-length study of eschatology, *Land of the Living*, pp. 78-80. See also Pozo, *Theology of the Beyond*, pp. 394-95, and also Appendix 1, "The Eschatological Doctrine of Vatican II," pp. 477-514, for comments on the debate on *LG* 48 which contain extensive references to the Latin text of the various interventions on the text found in the *Acta* of the Council. See also Grisez, *The Way*, pp. 23-24.

92. O'Connor, "Salvation," p. 18.

93. O'Connor, "Salvation," p. 16, demonstrates this by quoting from the *Creed* of Paul VI (1968) and the CDF *Instruction Concerning Eschatology* (1979): "It is in his treatment of the statements of the *Magisterium* that I find von Balthasar's book most disappointing."

94. "Some Current Questions in Eschatology," in Michael Sharkey and Thomas Weinandy, eds., *International Theological Commission: Texts and Documents 1986-2007*, vol. 2

(San Francisco: Ignatius Press, 2009), p. 66. Pozo, *Theology of the Beyond*, pp. 525-27, provides a commentary on this ITC document in his study of eschatology.

95. ITC, "Eschatology," p. 91.

96. ITC, "Eschatology," pp. 85-91. The widespread belief in "second chances" in the form of various theories of reincarnation caused the ITC to devote substantial attention to this issue in their document on eschatology.

97. ITC, "Eschatology," p. 89.

98. Dulles, "Hell," p. 36.

99. When the ITC, in the document on eschatology, "Some Current Questions in Eschatology," pp. 90-91, attempts to assess the efficacy of the universal offer of salvation, it cautiously says that it has "ample efficacy." It then warns: "But, since hell is a genuine possibility for every person, it is not right — although today this is something which is forgotten in the preaching at exequies — to treat salvation as a kind of quasi-automatic consequence. . . . The Christian ought to be aware of the brevity of life since he knows we have one life only. As we 'all sin . . . in many ways' (Jas 3:2) and since there often was sin in our past lives, we must 'use the present opportunity to the full' (Eph 5:16) and throwing off every encumbrance and the sin that all too readily restricts us, run with resolution the race that lies ahead of us, our eyes fixed on Jesus, the pioneer and perfector of faith' (Heb 12:102). 'We have not here a lasting city, but seek one that is to come' (Heb 13:14). The Christian then as an alien and a pilgrim (cf. 1 Pet 2:11) hurries in holiness of life to his own country (cf. Heb 11:14), where he will be with the Lord (cf. 1 Thes 4:17)."

100. Flannery, "Hell," p. 477.

101. O'Connor, "Salvation," p. 20.

102. Other texts that speak of the universal scope of redemption are John 3:16; 5:24; 6:37-40; 12:32; 17:23; Romans 5:12-21; 11:32; Ephesians 1:10; Colossians 1:20; Titus 2:11.

103. Dulles, "Hell," p. 37.

104. Grisez, *The Way*, p. 25, comments in a similar fashion about Balthasar's interpretation of this text.

105. Balthasar, *The Glory of the Lord: A Theological Aesthetics*, vol. 6 (San Francisco: Ignatius Press, 1991), p. 408, gives an interpretation of this repeated theme from Isaiah that one finds also on the lips of Jesus and throughout the NT that is at variance with prevailing scholarship. "One must bear in mind that the commission to harden hearts which Isaiah and Ezekiel receive is primarily a *missionary* commission from God and thus cannot be anything other than a commission that brings salvation." G. K. Beale, *We Become What We Worship: A Biblical Theology of Idolatry* (Downers Grove, IL: InterVarsity, 2008) provides an extensive summary of the scholarship on this text that is at variance with Balthasar's. In his book Beale thoroughly explores the use of Isaiah 6 in both the Old and New Testaments, showing that it is actually a pronouncement of judgment on those culpably blind and deaf to the Word of God, a culpability which if not repented from will result in their destruction on the day of judgment. The Word spoken is intended to bring salvation but it provokes a crisis, and the rejection of the Word brings with it a deeper blindness and condemnation. See Beale's conclusion, *Idolatry*, p. 38: "Isaiah 6:9-13 [in both the Old and New Testaments] is a pronouncement of judgment on Israel's idolatry."

106. Decrees of the Council of Trent, Session 6, "Decree on Justification," Chapter 2. Tanner, p. 671.

107. Decrees of the Council of Trent, Session 6, "Decree on Justification," Chapter 3. Tanner, p. 672.

108. Decrees of the Council of Trent, Session 6, "Decree on Justification," Chapter 4. Tanner, p. 672.

109. Decrees of the Council of Trent, Session 6, "Decree on Justification," Chapter 1. Tanner, p. 671.

110. See White, "Divine Providence," pp. 643-54, for a discussion of the antecedent/consequent distinction and Balthasar's rejection of it. O'Connor, "Salvation," p. 19, also points out that in order to argue for his thesis Balthasar "must not only ignore the significance of the future mode of speaking in the teaching of Christ and the Church when speaking of humans being damned, he must also (and does) call into question traditional and important theological categories, namely those concerning God's will." This includes the "traditional distinction which says that God's will to save all men is not absolute but conditioned on their free cooperation." O'Connor points out the severe theological problems that denying this distinction occasions regarding questions concerning God's will and sin, human and natural catastrophes, and the like. Schenk, "Factical Damnation," pp. 132-33, also points out that abandoning this distinction has "serious and far-reaching" theological consequences. See Paul K. Jewett, *Election and Predestination* (Grand Rapids: Eerdmans, 1985), p. 97, for a succinct description of the distinction: "God's antecedent will is his general desire that all should be saved. It is the will revealed in the universal promise of salvation contained in the proclamation of the gospel. But this will assumes the readiness of sinners to repent and believe the good news that God in Christ is reconciled to them. What if they do not repent and believe? Then we must say that God does *not* will their salvation. When we so speak, we speak in terms of God's will as consequent — consequent, that is, upon the sinner's response to the gospel. Some of the main texts where St. Thomas makes the distinction are *ST,* Ia, 23, 2-4. Garrigou-Lagrange's *Predestination,* trans. Bede Rose (St. Louis: Herder, 1946) provides an account of the Catholic debate on the issue as it existed in the years before Vatican II.

111. Raymond Brown in his *The Death of the Messiah* (New York: Doubleday, 1994), 2:1286-87, questions the biblical soundness of Balthasar's "descent" speculations. "No theologian has been more interested in the import of what happened on this Holy Saturday than Hans Urs von Balthasar; yet his reflections (guided by the mystical experiences of Adrienne von Speyr) have not been centered on what the canonical evangelists assign to this day." Jean Galot, "Christ's Descent into Hell," *Theology Digest* 13, no. 2 (Summer 1965): 91-92, comments on the interpretation of the descent passage as regards the "preaching" that Christ did (1 Peter 3:19) that was "clearly established" by Gregory the Great: "In the West, Gregory the Great declared that Christ saved only those from prison whom he had saved by his grace during their lives. Man's lot was irrevocably fixed by death, and Christ could save only those who died in grace. . . . From the point of view of what actually happened, Western theology is correct. There was a liberation of the just souls and no possibility of conversion." William Joseph Dalton, *Christ's Proclamation to the Spirits: A Study of 1 Peter 3:18–4:6* (Rome: Pontifical Biblical Institute, 1965), p. 271, provides a detailed account of the history of interpretation, both ancient and contemporary, of the puzzling text of 1 Peter 3:18–4:6 and concludes that the preaching to the dead that is referred to in the text is the preaching to Christians who are now dead but who heard the gospel in their lifetime, which is their salvation, and which will in due time raise them from the dead to eternal life. He interprets Christ's preach-

ing to the "spirits" as announcing to the evil powers that he has defeated them in his Ascension. He does not see a reference to the "Descensus" in this text. In addressing an interpretation attributed to Balthasar, even by his defenders, namely, that of a preaching after death that can lead souls who rejected the gospel in life to have another chance to be converted after death, Dalton firmly concludes: "Again, if the text deals with Christ's preaching to souls, the normal meaning of the term, 'preach the gospel,' would imply the possible conversion of these souls; this is not merely against Christian tradition but against the teaching of the New Testament itself: 'It is appointed for men to die once, and after that comes judgment.'" Dalton cites Hebrews 9:27, and also mentions Matthew 25:31-46 and Romans 2:6 as related texts. N. T. Wright, "Towards a Biblical View of Universalism," *Themelios* 4, no. 2 (January 1979): 55 — citing as an example J. N. D. Kelly, *A Commentary on the Epistles of Peter and Jude* (London: Black's NT Commentaries, 1969), pp. 152-58 — states: "1 Pt 3:18-22 has sometimes been interpreted as offering a 'second chance' to people who do not have faith in this life. But, as has been argued at length by commentators of various outlooks, the writer is most probably referring simply to Christ's proclamation to evil spirits that their power had been broken. In any case, the next chapter (1 Pt 4, especially vv. 17-18) rules out any possibility that 'those who do not obey God's gospel' will be saved. The 'second chance' theory must look outside the Bible for support." See also Daniel Keating, "Christ's Despoiling of Hades: According to Cyril of Alexandria," *St. Vladimir's Theological Quarterly* 55, no. 3 (2011): 253-69.

112. Alyssa Pitstick, *Light*, p. 337, comments on the serious issues being raised: "Balthasar's Christology appears consequently to be a cross between Arianism and monophysitism in that Christ is not perfect God and perfect man, but some third thing. . . . The same failure to maintain the natures' perfections ultimately results in the objective redemption being accomplished through what I have called the 'physical mechanism' of sin-in-itself entering the Trinity through the Son's being 'literally "made sin"'; and in the subjective redemption becoming almost arbitrary in that it is dependent only upon God's choice, and He will not be restricted in His freedom by the negative choice of a creature against Him. In turn, God's absolute freedom coupled with His nature as self-gift (i.e., love) suggests universal salvation is necessary." Pitstick published a summary of her book's main points in the journal *First Things*, accompanied by a response from Oakes, challenging some of her conclusions. Alyssa Lyra Pitstick and Edward T. Oakes, "Balthasar, Hell, and Heresy: An Exchange," *First Things* 168 (December 2006): 25-32. The exchange continued in the next issue, although from Oakes's side there seemed to be more heat than light. Pitstick and Oakes, "More on Balthasar, Hell, and Heresy," *First Things* 169 (January 2007): 16-19. There were some very fine and learned responses to these exchanges, including one by Avery Dulles in "Responses to 'Balthasar, Hell and Heresy,'" *First Things* 171 (March 2007): 5-14.

Rowan Williams, "Balthasar and the Trinity," *The Cambridge Companion to Hans Urs von Balthasar*, p. 50, in a basically sympathetic treatment of Balthasar's Trinitarian theology, nevertheless points out its "idiosyncratic" aspects. "The two most original and significant trinitarian theologians of their age, they [Barth and Balthasar] show how a biblically based theology of the Trinity can veer towards something a bit like Sabellianism (Barth's insistence on 'modes of being' as the proper language for trinitarian distinctiveness) and something a bit like tritheism (the mutual worship of the Persons as Balthasar proposes), and yet be held in a unifying tension by the sheer fact of the narrative of Jesus Christ at the heart of the whole discourse." Jared Wicks, "Christ's Saving Descent to the Dead: Early Witnesses from Ignatius of Antioch to Origen," *Pro Ecclesia* 17, no. 3 (Summer 2008): 308, in response to the debate over Pitstick's work undertook an exhaustive study of ecclesial writers and Fathers from the second century to the year 300, including Irenaeus, Clement of Alexandria, and Origen and concludes: "Regarding the debate over Hans Urs von Balthasar's theology of redemption, these early testimonies give strong support to his critics. They offer no indication at all of the descent being Christ's extreme experience of Godforsakenness in the netherworld. Christ does not go there because of human sin for expiatory suffering in a phase beyond his earthly Passion. He is not passive and suffering in going to the dead, but active soteriologically to bring light, release, and passage to heaven." See also John Yocum, "A Cry of Dereliction? Reconsidering a Recent Theological Commonplace," *International Journal of Systematic Theology* 7, no. 1 (January 2005): 70-78.

113. The central part of this teaching is in *Theodramatics*, vols. 3-5 (San Francisco: Ignatius Press, 1990-1998). Three chapters in Schindler's collection of essays (*Hans Urs von Balthasar: His Life and Work*) provide insight into Balthasar's relationship with Speyr: Peter Henrici, "Hans Urs von Balthasar: A Sketch of His Life," pp. 45-58; Johann Roten, "The Two Halves of the Moon: Marian Anthropological Dimensions in the Common Mission of Adrienne von Speyr and Hans Urs von Balthasar," pp. 65-86; Maximilian Greiner, "The Community of St. John: A Conversation with Cornelia Capol and Martha Gisi," pp. 87-102.

114. Pitstick, *Light*, p. 257.

115. Oakes, *Pattern*, pp. 230-31.

116. Balthasar, *Theo-Logic* II: *Truth of God*, trans. Adrian J. Walker (San Francisco: Ignatius Press, 2004), p. 345, note 75.

117. Balthasar, *Theo-Logic* II, pp. 345-61.

118. Morwenna Ludlow, "Universal Salvation and a Soteriology of Divine Punishment," *Scottish Journal of Theology* 53, no. 4 (2000): 449, points out that "Since most universalists recognize the obvious objection that many (if not most) people appear not to be in a position in this life to be saved, there have been various suggestions as to how salvation can occur after the death of the individual."

119. Oakes, *Pattern*, pp. 241-42.

120. Oakes, *Pattern*, pp. 241-42. John R. Sachs, "Review of *Pattern of Redemption: The Theology of Hans Urs Von Balthasar*," *Theological Studies* 56, no. 4 (December 1995): 788, who is in other respects a strong defender of Balthasar thinks that Oakes is too sympathetic to Balthasar's "rather strong tritheism" and believes that "Balthasar succumbs here to the very sort of vain speculation in theology that he condemns."

121. Oakes, *Pattern*, p. 314. Italics are Oakes's and appear to be Oakes's summary of a key teaching of Balthasar, rather than a direct quotation of him.

122. Oakes, *Pattern*, p. 318, footnote 35.

123. Pitstick, *Light*, p. 53, cites Augustine's conclusion, in considering the various possible interpretations of 1 Peter 3:18–4:6, that if those who die in mortal sin go to hell immediately and their punishment is eternal (DS 857, 1002, 1306; DS 72, 76, 411, 780, 801), to hold that conversion after death is possible is contrary to the faith. "There is no possibility of their conversion after death. Indeed, St. Augustine finds the ideas of conversion after death and the ongoing preaching of the Gospel in hell to be ridiculous, since they militate against the necessity and charity of preaching the Gospel in this earthly life." Pitstick is citing St. Augustine, Ep. 164, contained in *Letters*, vol. 3 (131-64), Writings of St. Augustine 11, The Fathers of the Church 20 (New York: Fathers of the Church, 1953), p. 391. O'Connor, "Salvation," p. 16, does not seem to advert to this aspect of Balthasar's theory when he comments on the

condemnation of the Origenists: "It should be clear that this condemnation is not directly contrary to Fr. von Balthasar's thesis. He does not teach that the damned will be eventually restored. He proposes the hope that no humans are or will be actually damned." It actually seems that Balthasar is suggesting that damned humans may meet Christ in hell and be given another chance. Kereszty, "Response," pp. 231-32, clearly explains the difficulty with positing conversion after death: "According to Scripture and Tradition, our free acceptance and rejection of God's grace takes place here on earth, and conversion in a radical sense after death is impossible. Not even those in purgatory can help their own process of purification; rather they rely on the help of the living. [Kereszty references nn. 26, 506, 2308 in *Christian Faith* in the doctrinal documents of the Catholic Church, ed. J. Neuner and J. Dupuis (Westminster, MD: Christian Classics, 1975).] The explicit magisterial statements reflect a consistent Christian anthropology according to which a human being can act as a human being and thereby decide freely about his destiny only in this life while he is in the body. In contrast, Balthasar seems to say that sheol is contemporaneous to all sinners of all times and their encounter with Christ in sheol decides whether or not sheol becomes for them purgatory or eternal damnation. [Kereszty references *Theologik II*, pp. 314-29.] How he can reconcile his own theory with the Church's teaching remains — to say the least — unclear to me."

124. O'Connor, "Salvation," p. 20.

125. Flannery, "Hell," p. 474.

126. Oakes, *Pattern*, pp. 3-5, 10, 300-305, provides a succinct summary of their relationship and its significance. As Balthasar, "In Retrospect," *Communio* 2, no. 3 (1975): 219, puts it: "It was Adrienne von Speyr who showed the way in which Ignatius is fulfilled by John, and therewith laid the basis for most of what I have published since 1940. Her work and mine are neither psychologically nor philologically to be separated: two halves of a single whole, which has as its center a unique foundation." Jacques Servais, "Per una valutazione dell'influsso di Adrienne von Speyr su Hans Urs von Balthasar," *Rivista Teologico di Lugano* 6, no. 1 (2001): 67-89, has published a detailed account of the growing scholarship on the relationship between Balthasar and von Speyr. He agrees that there is an obvious originality to Balthasar that should not be discounted but also concludes, on page 85, that Speyr's influence on him was decisive *(un influsso decisivo)*.

127. Balthasar, *Dare We Hope*, pp. 237-48.

128. Balthasar, *Dare We Hope*, pp. 245-47.

129. Eberhard Busch, *Karl Barth: His Life from Letters and Autobiographical Texts*, trans. John Bowden (Philadelphia: Fortress Press, 1976), pp. 361-62. Cited in Oakes, *Pattern*, pp. 46, 306.

130. Pitstick, *Light*, p. 338.

131. Daley, "Maximus," p. 318.

132. Brian Daley, *The Hope of the Early Church: A Handbook of Patristic Eschatology* (Peabody, MA: Hendrickson, 2003), p. 202.

133. Balthasar, *Dare We Hope*, pp. 246-47.

134. Hans Urs von Balthasar, *Theo-Drama: Theological Dramatic Theory*, vol. V: *The Last Act*, trans. Graham Harrison (San Francisco: Ignatius Press, 1998), p. 318.

135. White, "Divine Providence," p. 644.

136. Brian E. Daley, "Balthasar's Reading of the Church Fathers," in *Cambridge Companion to Hans Urs von Balthasar*, pp. 202-3.

137. Balthasar, *Dare We Hope*, p. 58.

138. O'Connor, "Salvation," p. 15.

139. *2 Clement* 7:6–8:4. In C. Richardson, *Early Christian Fathers* (New York: Macmillan, 1970), p. 189. Cited by O'Connor, "Salvation," p. 14.

140. Hauke, "Sperare per tutti?" pp. 204-8.

141. O'Connor, "Salvation," p. 12. See also in the same text O'Connor's comments on the *tenor* of Balthasar's work.

142. Kereszty, "Response," pp. 228-30.

143. Flannery, "Hell," pp. 473-74.

144. Balthasar, *Dare We Hope*, pp. 69-70. Jean-Marc Bot, *Osons Reparler de L'Enfer* (Paris: Éditions de L'Emmanuel, 2002), p. 134, appropriately comments: "This refusal of the *principle of non-contradiction* is completely untenable! How can one write such a thing when one is in the school of the one who said: 'Let your yes be yes and your no be no'?" (Ce refus du *principe de non-contradiction* est tout à fait intenable! Comment peut-on écrire ainsi quand on se met à l'école de Celui qui a dit: 'Que votre oui soit oui, que votre non soit non'?)

145. Balthasar, *Dare We Hope*, pp. 215-16. Pitstick, *Light*, p. 345, in summarizing the results of her extensive study of his central teaching concerning the descent into hell, cites these serious methodological flaws in Balthasar's approach: "One notes the exertion necessary for Balthasar to connect his descensus theology even remotely to the larger Catholic theological traditions, including his citation of authors in a mode inconsistent with the context of their thought; his need to redefine terms radically; and his reliance on figures of questionable authority, often precisely with regard to positions of theirs not taken up or even rejected by the received tradition (e.g., Origen and Nicholas of Cusa)." Chapter 10 of Pitstick's work further explores methodological problems in Balthasar. Paul J. Griffiths, "Is There a Doctrine of the Descent into Hell?" *Pro Ecclesia* 17, no. 3 (Summer 2008): 257-68, while admiring the scholarship of Pitstick's work, believes that she overstates the degree of doctrinal authority that the traditional interpretation of the "descent" actually has. White, "Divine Providence," p. 638, questions Balthasar's depiction of Augustine's positions: "It is not the case, however, that Balthasar's historical treatment of St. Augustine is always fair. Many of his theses may be more appropriately attributed to certain disciples of Augustine rather than the Latin doctor himself. Furthermore, Balthasar often affirms or implies that one who believes in selective election must necessarily have an ignoble and even dangerous certitude of his own salvation. (See the censure of Augustine in Balthasar, *Dare We Hope*, p. 191.) This is not true of Augustine's spiritual attitude, historically, nor is it theoretically defensible." In some ways, Balthasar was so struck/fascinated (as was Barth) with his vision of the total magnificence of the paschal mystery in the unusual and unique way in which both he and Speyr understood it, that everything else was made to fit their fundamental "vision." Wainwright, "Eschatology," p. 115, describes it like this: "I shall argue that Balthasar's attraction to a doctrine of *apokatastasis* springs directly from his initial *intuitive and comprehensive* perception of the 'shape' or 'pattern' *(Gestalt)* of the Christian faith. In other words, his first glimpse of the total vision of the Christ event governs his position on individual doctrines, not the reverse." This fascination with the original vision that motivates and inspires Balthasar reminds me of Ignatius's fascination with the visionary, "remarkably beautiful" colored object that he saw, that he at first thought was a consolation from God but later realized was from a different spirit. See St. Ignatius, "The Autobiography," trans. Parmananda R. Divarkar, ed. George E. Ganss, *Ignatius of Loyola: The Spiritual Exercises and Selected Works* (New York: Paulist Press, 1991), pp. 76, 81: "While in this hos-

pice it often happened that in broad daylight he saw something in the air near him. It gave him great consolation because it was very beautiful — remarkably so. . . . He found great pleasure and consolation in seeing this thing and the oftener he saw it the more his consolation grew. When it disappeared, he was displeased." Later on though, at a time of great genuine spiritual consolation and insight he realized that something had insinuated its way into his being that was not from God, although it was mixed in with very great and genuine graces: "There, the vision that had appeared to him many times but which he had never understood, that is, the thing mentioned above which seemed very beautiful to him, with many eyes, now appeared to him. But while before the cross, he saw clearly that the object did not have its usual beautiful color, and he knew very clearly with a strong agreement of his will that it was the devil. Later it would often appear to him for a long time; and by way of contempt he dispelled it with a staff he used to carry in his hand." To the objection that spiritual discernment has no role in scientific theology Balthasar himself would claim that the authentic experience of spiritual reality — that of the saints — needs to have the last word in theology. ("The last word, here as well, will go to the saints" [*Dare We Hope,* p. 169].) Especially when a claim is made that a certain spiritual experience is linked to a theological position — the revelations of Speyr — discernment is not only permissible, but necessary. Recently, the Dominican spiritual theologian Paul Murray, "Aquinas at Prayer: The Interior Life of a 'Mystic on Campus,'" *Logos* 14, no. 1 (Winter 2011): 39, has published an article that discerns that Speyr's vision of St. Thomas at prayer — and her perception of the deficiency of his prayer — is "truly bizarre." I know of no canonized mystic that could be seen as supporting the positions of Speyr/Balthasar. Even a saint and a mystic known for her strong emphasis on mercy, Saint Faustina Kowalska, operates in the traditional framework of biblical revelation. St. Maria Faustina Kowalska's descriptions of hell, *Diary of St. Maria Faustina Kowalska: Divine Mercy in My Soul* (Stockbridge, MA: Marian Press, 2009), #741, which she writes about because commanded by the Father, are remarkably similar to those of Catherine of Siena. "I am writing this at the command of God, so that no soul may find an excuse by saying there is no hell, or that nobody has ever been there, and so no one can say what it is like. . . . I, Sister Faustina, by the order of God, have visited the abysses of hell so that I might tell souls about it and testify to its existence. . . . The devils were full of hatred for me, but they had to obey me at the command of God. What I have written is but a pale shadow of the things I saw. But I noticed one thing: that most of the souls there are those who disbelieved that there is a hell. When I came to, I could hardly recover from the fright. How terribly souls suffer there! Consequently, I pray even more fervently for the conversion of sinners."

146. Balthasar, "Some Points of Eschatology," in *The Word Made Flesh: Explorations in Theology,* vol. 1, trans. A. V. Littledale and Alexander Dru (San Francisco: Ignatius Press, 1989), pp. 268-69. Cited in Pitstick, *Light,* p. 264. Balthasar's claim that Ratzinger is one of his supporters bears some comment. While unquestionably respectful of Balthasar's work on this particular issue, Ratzinger, *Eschatology: Death and Eternal Life,* 2nd ed. (Washington, DC: Catholic University of America Press, 1988), p. 215, had to make clear a particular difference. "No quibbling helps here: the idea of eternal damnation which had taken ever clearer shape in the Judaism of the century or two before Christ, has a firm place in the teaching of Jesus, as well as in the apostolic writings. Dogma takes its stand on solid ground when it speaks of the existence of Hell and of the eternity of its punishments." In the same work, on page 284, footnotes 75-77, Ratzinger details the numerous passages throughout the New Tes-

tament and in the doctrinal statements of the Church that witness to the reality and eternity of hell. Schenk, "Factical Damnation," p. 140, notes that Ratzinger came "at least later, despite continued sympathy for Balthasar's life and work as a whole, to the conviction that such a reduction of one set of texts to a mere, or even an infinitely improbable, possibility runs counter to the texts themselves." Balthasar's defenders cite the fact that John Paul II named him a Cardinal, although he died before receiving the Cardinal's hat, as evidence of the soundness of his theories. Of course, honoring a learned theologian, who has consistently stated that he wants to be faithful to the Church's teaching — although whether he succeeds in this or not is one of the issues we are discussing — does not imply endorsement of all his views. Just as Ratzinger felt the need to recognize the solid foundations of the teaching on hell and its eternity, so did John Paul II. See John Paul II, *Crossing the Threshold of Hope* (New York: Alfred A. Knopf, 1994), pp. 185-86. John Paul II speaks of how the problem of hell has always disturbed great thinkers in the Church and cites Origen and, in our time, Mikhail Bulgakov and Hans Urs von Balthasar. He then points out that the theory of a final *apokatastasis* which holds that every creature would be saved has been rejected by the Church. John Paul II declares that despite our perplexity about how God who is love can permit his creatures to be damned, "the words of Christ are unequivocal." Although we do not know who is in hell, we know that "In Matthew's Gospel He speaks clearly of those who will go to eternal punishment (cf. Mt 25:46)." And the Pope proffers a thought about the necessity of hell. "Is not God who is Love also ultimate Justice? Can He tolerate these terrible crimes, can they go unpunished? Is not final punishment in some way necessary in order to reestablish moral equilibrium in the complex history of humanity? Is not hell in a certain sense the ultimate safeguard of man's moral conscience?"

147. Balthasar, *Dare We Hope*, pp. 216-18.

148. Balthasar, *Dare We Hope*, pp. 168-69.

149. Balthasar, *Dare We Hope*, pp. 168-69.

150. Balthasar, *Dare We Hope*, p. 170.

151. Balthasar, *Dare We Hope*, p. 169.

152. See Ralph Martin, *The Fulfillment of All Desire: A Guidebook for the Journey to God Based on the Wisdom of the Saints* (Steubenville, OH: Emmaus Road Publications, 2006), pp. 47-70. These pages detail the way in which the great mystics carried out their life and writing, with a contemplative understanding of both the final judgment and the final destinations of heaven and hell as actual realities that result in an eternal separation of the redeemed and the damned, and therefore of the urgency of faith and repentance in this life.

153. Larry Chapp, "Revelation," in *Cambridge Companion to Hans Urs von Balthasar*, p. 23.

154. David Moss, "The Saints," in *Cambridge Companion to Hans Urs von Balthasar*, p. 82.

155. Hauke, "Sperare per tutti?" p. 219. (La testimonianza dei santi, però, è decisamente sfavorevole all'opinione che l'inferno potrebbe essere vuoto. Tuttavia, con la sua "tesi più azzardata", provocando il *contradicitur*, il nostro teologo ha messo in rilievo l'importanza della santità per la testimonianza teologica. La proposta balthasariana di mettere in prima fila i santi e la mistica, applicata consequentemente, porta alla falsificazione della speranza nell'apocatastasi e conferma l'esito doppio del giudizio.)

156. O'Meara, "Grace Outside Evangelization," pp. 118-19, discusses Aquinas's explanation of this distinction.

157. Balthasar, *Dare We Hope,* pp. 168, 178, 184-85. So much of this work is filled with *ad hominem* arguments, broad sweeping statements, inflammatory language, mockery, sarcasm, scorn, and emotional reactivity that it is difficult to find a balanced, carefully reasoned exegesis. Those who disagree with his theory are called "infernalists." Those who question the wisdom of Adrienne von Speyr's private mystical revelations being used as a basis for theology are accused of desiring to "burn the witch": "Thus it would be high time to burn the witch before she is beatified." O'Connor, "Salvation," p. 10, notes "the unusual amount of sharp polemic which the author directs against those whose views are at variance with his own, and in the manner which he describes (at times, almost parodies) the convictions opposed to his." Pitstick, *Light,* pp. 434-35, n. 142, notes that O'Connor's article is "accessible" with no loss to its "theological strength" and notes its "clarity and succinctness."

158. In defending himself against the charge that hoping for the salvation of all is in fact an advocacy of universal redemption *(apokatastasis)* Balthasar, *Dare We Hope,* p. 166, points out that since this is condemned by the Church he rejects it. He states that hoping is not knowing and that we "have no right, nor is it possible for us, to peer in advance at the Judge's cards. How can anyone equate hoping with knowing? I hope that my friend will recover from his serious illness — do I therefore know this?" After declaring that it is not possible to peer in advance at the Judge's cards, he then seems to proceed to do so.

159. Pius IX attempted to address the question of the limits of hope by condemning this proposition: "We should at least have good hopes for the eternal salvation of those who are in no way in the true Church of Christ." ND 1013.17; DS 2916.

160. Balthasar, *Dare We Hope,* pp. 76, 178.

161. O'Connor, "Salvation," pp. 11, 20. See also Grisez, *The Way,* p. 26.

162. White, *Divine Providence,* pp. 658-59, 661.

163. Flannery, "Hell," p. 479. The internal quotations of Suarez are taken from F. Suarez, *Opera Omnia,* ed. C. Berton (Paris: L. Vivès, 1856-78), v. 14, 55b.

164. Turek, "Dare We Hope," pp. 101-3.

165. Schenk, "Factical Damnation," p. 152, note 56, makes some important comments regarding the position of the Catechism of the Catholic Church and Balthasar's thesis. Balthasar had claimed support from the regional German Catechism. Schenk comments: "If catechisms despite their inevitable limitations, are to be treated as a theological source, then the formulation of the Roman *Catechism of the Catholic Church,* prepared under the direction of Christoph von Schönborn, who on other issues has been generally sympathetic to Balthasar's theological projects, should be of at least equal interest, where item 1035 reads: 'The teaching of the Church affirms the existence of hell and its eternity.' Item 1038 speaks of the resurrection of the just and the unjust (quoting *Acts* 24:15) and the twofold outcome of the last judgment (referring to *Matt* 25). Items 391 *sqq.* and 414 speak of the personal nature of the fallen angels. Coming after the controversial discussion of Balthasar's theses, the intended differences to theories affirming the sheer but most unlikely possibility of final condemnation of any created persons seems undeniable."

166. Angelo Scola, *Test Everything, Hold Fast to What Is Good: An Interview with Hans Urs von Balthasar,* trans. Maria Shrady (San Francisco: Ignatius Press, 1989), pp. 84-85.

167. Balthasar, *Dare We Hope,* p. 99, makes the claim that even Judas may not be in hell, a claim that seems to be related to Adrienne von Speyr's mystical meditations on Judas. O'Connor, "Salvation," p. 18, discusses why the Church does not see it as her responsibility to do the reverse of canonization, namely, officially declare someone damned.

168. Dulles, "Hell," p. 36. Also, Revelation 20:10 seems to indicate eternal punishment not only for the devil, but also for "the beast and the false prophet."

169. Roch Kereszty, "Response to Professor Scola," *Communio* 18 (Summer 1991): 229.

170. Flannery, "Hell," p. 470.

171. There are multiple anathemas directed to notorious heretics, as well as to those who sin in serious ways, in the canons of the Councils. The Councils, with the approval of the Popes, understood that by the power of the keys they could solemnly excommunicate people and unless there was repentance before they died they were thought to be damned. See, for example, the posthumous anathema directed to John Wycliffe. The Council of Constance, Session 8, May 4, 1415. Tanner, pp. 415-16.

172. Hauke, "Sperare per tutti?" p. 217, also makes this point. In another article, Manfred Hauke, "Shed for Many: An Accurate Rendering of the Pro Multis in the Formula of Consecration," *Antiphon* 14, no. 2 (2010): 173, Hauke comments on the restoration of the biblical phrase *"pro multis"* to the formula of consecration and sees in it a possible theological reserve, in that Christ has died for all, but his sacrifice is not effective for all by virtue of their rejection of it. "The vernacular formula 'for all' is an *interpretation* of the words of consecration, while the words 'for many' correspond to the *biblical text.* Jesus died 'for all' inasmuch as salvation is offered to all men. The actual acceptance of salvation depends, however, on the free will of the recipient, who can also refuse the divine offer. This possibility is left open by the vernacular formula 'for many.'"

173. Balthasar, *Dare We Hope,* pp. 80-81, 85, 211. "From being personally addressed in this way, it follows that I may leave concerns for the salvation of others up to divine mercy and must concentrate on my own situation before God" (p. 87).

174. Balthasar, *Dare We Hope,* pp. 86-87, 251.

175. Edwin A. Blum, "'Shall You Not Surely Die?'" *Themelios* 4, no. 2 (January 1979): 61, points out that the universalist position is characterized by a minimization of the evil of sin. "In universalism sin loses its exceeding sinfulness. Men are so affected by sin that we all trivialize it. Too often sin is seen as ignorance or the result of human finitude. The enormity of sin can only be partially grasped in the light of the colossal Sovereign who framed the universe by His will. Yet in the mystery of iniquity, men and angels have set themselves to do their will and not His. . . . Universalism trivializes sin by effectively denying that sin deserves punishment. If sin deserves infinite punishment, then no sinner has a claim to salvation based on sovereign love. If sin does not deserve infinite punishment, the biblical revelation of the Death of the Son of God is trivialized. What was the necessity of the Cross? Human time and history lose much of their significance in universalism."

176. Oakes, *Pattern,* p. 318, note 35.

177. Ambaum, "Hope for Salvation," p. 51, comments: "It is not easy to bring the hypothesis of Balthasar into agreement with the Constitution *'Benedictus Deus,'* written by Pope Benedict XII in 1336." Ambaum, "Hope for Salvation," p. 51.

178. Session VI, Council of Florence, July 6, 1439. "Definition of the holy ecumenical synod of Florence." Tanner, pp. 527-28.

179. Sacred Congregation for the Doctrine of the Faith, "Letter on Certain Questions Concerning Eschatology," May 17, 1979.

180. Edith Stein, *Welt und Person. Beitrag zum christlichen Wahrheitsstreben* [World and person. A contribution to Christian truth seeking], ed. L. Gelber and Romaeus Leuven

(Freiburg, 1962), pp. 158ff. The quotes from Stein are from the above-mentioned work and are cited by Balthasar, *Dare We Hope*, pp. 218-21.

181. Schenk, "Factical Damnation," p. 150, n. 35, points out that while Balthasar makes this his final position, it was not the final position of Edith Stein herself. Schenk points out that these were passing comments in a work that she herself never published, and that in 1939 in her spiritual testament, she significantly modifies. "The possibility of some final loss appears more real and pressing than one which would seem infinitely improbable." Hauke, "Sperare per tutti?" pp. 207-8, makes the same point as well as the additional point that not everything a saint or Doctor wrote is honored when they are recognized as saints or Doctors.

182. Pitstick, *Light*, p. 270. In a subtly argued section of her work (pp. 263-74) Pitstick discusses the multiple reasons why she thinks universal salvation is necessarily implied, while verbally denied, in Balthasar's writings.

183. Balthasar, *Karl Barth*, p. 186, cited in Oakes, *Pattern*, pp. 247-48.

184. Balthasar, *Unser Auftrag*, p. 85. Trans. and cited in Oakes, *Pattern*, p. 306.

185. Wainwright, "Eschatology," pp. 115, 122.

186. Applying the principles developed by John Henry Newman to discern what is a true development of doctrine and what is a corruption would be a useful exercise in evaluating some of the speculative theology that appears to reverse the clear teaching of Jesus and the Apostles as interpreted by the Church throughout the centuries. It is, however, beyond the scope of this book. The International Theological Commission, "The Interpretation of Dogma," *International Theological Commission: Texts and Documents, 1986-2007*, ed. Michael Sharkey and Thomas Weinandy (San Francisco: Ignatius Press, 2009), p. 52, has distilled seven principles from Newman's work. This study was published *in forma specifica*, which means that not only the principal ideas are accepted but the entire text, including the wording. It indicates a consensus on the present state of the question, not necessarily that all of the approximately thirty members are in exact agreement on the issue.

187. As Blum, " 'Shall You Not Surely Die?' " p. 60, puts it: "The typical universalist definition of God's love is too anthropocentric. It assumes God's love is greater and fuller in the salvation of all men. But the Triune God has within Himself a perfect love which is not added to in the relations He has with His creatures. The argument of the universalist assumes an increase in the perfection of God's love if all mankind is saved. But if God is love, the perfection of His love in universalist thought comes only in creation and redemption. In this way of thought, God's perfection in His being is bound up with His creation and thus His aseity or absolute independence is compromised. This kind of a god bound to his creation can only be a sophisticated idol of the human mind." The contemporary Dominican theologian Gilles Emery, "L'immutabilité du Dieu d'amour et les problèmes du discour sur la 'souffrance de Dieu,' " *Nova et Vetera* (French edition) 74 (1999): 5-37, makes the same point in much greater metaphysical depth in his various books on Trinitarian theology and in particular in this essay. This essay then appeared in English translation as a chapter in a collection of essays: Gilles Emery, "The Immutability of the God of Love and the Problem of Language Concerning the 'Suffering of God,' " in *Divine Impassibility and the Mystery of Human Suffering*, ed. James F. Keating and Thomas Joseph White (Grand Rapids: Eerdmans, 2009), pp. 27-76.

188. Ratzinger, *God's Word: Scripture, Tradition, Office*, p. 96.

189. White, "Divine Providence," p. 665.

190. John Paul II, *VS*, 68.

191. John Paul II, *VS*, 68. See also sections 65-67, 70.

192. Decrees of the Council of Trent, Session 6, "Decree on Justification," chapter 15. Tanner, p. 677.

193. Decrees of the Council of Trent, Session 6, "Decree on Justification," chapter 16. Tanner, p. 678.

194. Another main source of motivation would seem to be the very high regard in which he held the mystical revelations of Adrienne von Speyr, which, because of the uniqueness of her experience and interpretation of Holy Saturday and its centrality in Balthasar's overall theology, inclined towards universal salvation. As Balthasar put it in his interview in Scola, *Test Everything*, p. 89: "I believe the Church will gradually have to adopt substantial parts of her doctrine and, perhaps, wonder why these beautiful and enriching things have not been recognized earlier."

195. Theisen, *The Ultimate Church*, pp. 157-61, speaks of the "crisis" in missions after the Council and describes the various redefinitions of missions that have followed this collapse. See also Ralph Martin, *A Crisis of Truth: The Attack on Faith, Morality, and Mission in the Catholic Church* (Ann Arbor, MI: Servant Books, 1982), pp. 57-113. A recent article chronicles the collapse of missionary work: Jeff Ziegler, "Go and Make Disciples: The Demise of the Missionary Vocation," *Catholic World Report*, July 2011, pp. 17-21.

196. Paul VI, *EN*, 80.

197. Norman Tanner, *The Church and the World: Gaudium et Spes, Inter Mirifica* (New York: Paulist Press, 2005), p. 65.

198. Stephen Bevans and Jeffrey Gros, *Evangelization and Religious Freedom: Ad Gentes, Dignitatis Humanae* (New York: Paulist Press, 2009), pp. 58-59. Bevans on p. 130, note 8, cites Rahner's theory of the "anonymous Christian" as groundbreaking in this regard.

199. Bevans and Gros, *Evangelization and Religious Freedom*, pp. 100, 86.

200. John Paul II, *RM*, 1, 79.

201. John Paul II, *RM*, 46. See also section 4 for another listing of these doubts and ambiguities.

202. Assertions by Balthasar and his defenders that there are no negative consequences to his theory that it is "infinitely improbable" that there is anyone in hell are not plausible. Healy, "On Hope, Heaven, and Hell," p. 90, for example, makes a claim that is representative of Balthasar's defenders: "The hope for the salvation of all as defended by Hans Urs von Balthasar does not entail laxity or presumption in the face of judgment." The lax attitudes towards evangelization and holiness of life that are widespread in the Church today often are based on a presumption that almost everybody will be saved.

Notes to Chapter VII

1. *NMI*, 57.

2. J. P. Kenny, *Roman Catholicism, Christianity and Anonymous Christianity: The Role of the Christian Today* (Hales Corner, WI: Clergy Book Service, 1973), p. 108.

3. Avery Dulles, "The Church as Locus of Salvation," in *The Thought of John Paul II: A Collection of Essays and Studies*, ed. John M. McDermott (Rome: Editrice Pontificia Università Gregoriana, 1993), p. 176.

4. John Richard Neuhaus, "Reviving the Missionary Mandate," in *The New Evangelization: Overcoming the Obstacles*, ed. Steven Boguslawski and Ralph Martin (New York: Paulist Press, 2008), pp. 34-42. The many very fine Pastoral Letters published by a number of American Bishops in recent years on the New Evangelization mostly follow in the same lines, of a positive presentation of life in Christ with virtually no mention of the eternal consequences of rejecting the new life. One such example is the "Pastoral Letter on the New Evangelization," by Archbishop Donald W. Wuerl, *Disciples of the Lord: Sharing the Vision*, published on August 23, 2010, and available on the Archdiocese of Washington, DC, website: www.adw .org (accessed May 2, 2011). Denis Biju-Duval, *Faut-il encore se soucier du salut des âmes? L'urgence de l'évangélisation* (Paris: Éditions de l'Emmanuel, 2012).

5. Pope Benedict XV, encyclical *Maximum illud* (On the Propagation of the Catholic Faith Throughout the World), November 30, 1919; 6, 7, 18, 31.

6. Pope Pius XI, encyclical *Rerum ecclesiae* (On Catholic Missions), February 28, 1926; 3, 8, 12.

7. Pope Pius XII, encyclical *Evangelii praecones* (On Promotion of Catholic Missions), June 2, 1951; 1, 10, 65, 70.

8. Pope Pius XII, encyclical *Fidei donum* (On the Present Condition of the Catholic Missions, Especially in Africa), April 21, 1957; 20.

9. Pope John XXIII, encyclical *Princeps pastorum* (The Prince of Shepherds, On the Missions, Native Clergy, and Lay Participation), November 18, 1959; 6.

10. All five of these pre-1960 mission encyclicals were referenced in the draft of *De ecclesia*, AS III/1, 191-96.

11. Three books that have addressed these issues in greater depth and have provided a measure of statistical and anecdotal backing for these assertions are Ralph Martin, *Unless the Lord Build the House* (Notre Dame: Ave Maria, 1971); Ralph Martin, *A Crisis of Truth: The Undermining of Faith, Morality, and Mission in the Catholic Church* (Ann Arbor: Servant, 1982); Ralph Martin, *The Catholic Church at the End of an Age: What Is the Spirit Saying?* (San Francisco: Ignatius Press, 1994). Avery Dulles, in a foreword to a recent book on evangelization, Timothy E. Byerley, *The Great Commission: Models of Evangelization in American Catholicism* (New York: Paulist Press, 2008), p. ix, cites unsettling statistics, drawn from a book by Nancy T. Ammerman, *Pillars of Faith* (Berkeley: University of California Press, 2005), pp. 117, 134: "Asked whether spreading the faith was a high priority of their parishes, 75 percent of conservative Protestant congregations and 57 percent of African American congregations responded affirmatively, whereas only 6 percent of Catholic parishes did the same. Asked whether they sponsored local evangelistic activities, 39 percent of conservative Protestant congregations and 16 percent of African American congregations responded positively as compared with only 3 percent of Catholic parishes. Converts to Catholicism often report that on their spiritual journey they received little or no encouragement from Catholic clergy whom they consulted. . . . The Council has often been interpreted as if it had discouraged evangelization." The Catherine of Siena Institute in Colorado Springs, Colorado, has interviewed tens of thousands of Catholics and their pastors, and makes the point that even among the minority of Catholics who come to Church somewhat regularly, only about 15 percent could be considered "intentional disciples" who have made Christ the center of their lives (www.siena.org). Cardinal Ratzinger in *The Yes of Jesus Christ*, trans. Robert Nowell (New York: Crossroad, 1991), pp. 39-40, remarked on the strange phenomenon in conjunction with the collapse of the Church in the Netherlands after Vatican II. He pointed out that by every statistical measure the Church in the Neth-

erlands was collapsing and yet, strangely, at the same time an atmosphere of "general optimism" was prevalent that seemed to be blind to the actual situation. "I thought to myself: What would one say of a businessman whose accounts were completely in the red but who, instead of recognizing this evil, finding out its reasons, and courageously taking steps against it, wanted to commend himself to his creditors solely through optimism? What should one's attitude be to an optimism that was quite simply opposed to reality?" In my own country, the United States, the "official optimism" has been quite strong in the midst of radical decline. When the American bishops greeted Pope Benedict XVI on his pastoral visit, they spoke of our "vibrant" Church. The statistics from one large American archdiocese that is quite typical of the Catholic "heartland" of the Middle Atlantic, New England, Midwestern, and Upper Midwestern states are quite sobering. Just in the ten-year period of 2000 to 2010 the following happened: infant baptism declined 42.4 percent; adult baptisms declined 51.2 percent; Catholic marriages declined 45.3 percent; those seeking full communion with the Church declined 43.6 percent; household units that contributed to the annual appeal declined 14.9 percent; and there were 12.8 percent fewer parishes. While there has been growth in the West, Southwest, and South, a growth that is largely due to Hispanic immigration, not growth through evangelization, the statistics about the outflow from the Catholic Church in second- and third-generation Hispanic Catholic immigrants are not encouraging. See Edwin Hernández, with Rebecca Burwell and Jeffrey Smith, "A Study of Hispanic Catholics: Why Are They Leaving the Catholic Church? Implications for the New Evangelization," in *The New Evangelization,* ed. Boguslawski and Martin, pp. 109-41. Shortly before Pope Benedict XVI's visit to the United States, Russell Shaw, a respected author and former spokesman for the American bishops, in "Please Look Behind the Bishops' Potemkin Village," *The Catholic World Report* (February 2008): 19-22, urged the American bishops to stop pretending everything was fine.

12. John Lamont, "What Was Wrong with Vatican II," *New Blackfriars* 99, no. 1013 (January 2007): 92-93. See also John Lamont "Why the Second Vatican Council Was a Good Thing and Is More Important Than Ever," *New Oxford Review* (July/August 2005): 32-36, in which he identifies the positive aspects of Vatican II. For a recent comprehensive study of the religious beliefs of American youth, see Christian Smith with Melinda Lundquist Denton, *Soul Searching: The Religious and Spiritual Lives of American Teenagers* (New York: Oxford University Press, 2005), p. 166, which confirms this judgment and extends it to the parents of such youth. In this study Catholic youth appeared to be in the worst condition of any church group as regards orthodox belief. For example, 57 percent of teenage Catholics stated that they maybe or definitely believed in reincarnation. The authors conclude that even though the "shell" or "form" of traditional religion is there, it has been colonized by an alien spirit which they describe as "Moralistic Therapeutic Deism."

13. Ratzinger, *The Yes of Jesus Christ,* p. 35.

14. Unfortunately some of the remarks of Benedict XVI have furthered this impression, although it appears he may simply be stating theological speculation and not actually teaching in an authoritative way. There are a number of texts that give this impression, but the most prominent appearance of this "supposition" is in the encyclical *Spe salvi*. Sections 45-47 of *Spe salvi* seem to be giving the impression that only a few really evil people are candidates for hell and virtually everybody else will be in purgatory and ultimately heaven. The argument of this book would suggest a need for clarification.

15. *EN,* 53.

16. *EN,* 80.

17. *EN*, 80.

18. *RM*, 2.

19. *RM*, 2.

20. *RM*, 2.

21. Recently, an unpublished text presented by Bishop Thomas Mar Anthonios at a Symposium held at the Pontifical University of Saint Thomas, Rome, March 25, 2011, a document prepared for an upcoming Synod of the Syro-Malankara Church in India, p. 5, cited some of the points we have been making about the need to take into account the complete text of *LG* 16. "*Lumen Gentium* article 16 is often interpreted partially and independently from the rest of the Council teachings on salvation and the 'possibility' of salvation is interpreted to mean probability and presumption giving the impression that salvation can be assumed to 'people who have never heard the Gospel' and the second part 'through no fault of their own' is interpreted lightly and their choice of 'exchanging truth for a lie' is often omitted."

22. Francis Martin, "The Spirit of the Lord Is Upon Me: The Role of the Holy Spirit in the Work of Evangelization," in *The New Evangelization*, ed. Boguslawski and Martin, pp. 72-73. See also pp. 74-76.

23. John M. McDermott, "Reflections on *Dominum et Vivificantem*," in *Pope John Paul II on the Body*, ed. John M. McDermott and John Gavin (Philadelphia: St. Joseph's University Press, 2007), pp. 358-59. See also the whole section on the Holy Spirit and sin, pp. 358-64. Fr. McDermott, "Universal History and the History of Salvation," in *Dictionary of Fundamental Theology*, ed. René Latourelle and Rino Fisichella (New York: Crossroad, 1994), p. 454, draws the connection between original sin and the need for mission: "Knowing how difficult it is to live Christ's sacrificial love even with all the helps of the church, recognizing the power of evil that resulted in the Christ's crucifixion and made clear the absolute need for conversion, and having received Christ's explicit command to make disciples of all nations, believers correctly admit that the gospel's emphasis rests upon the necessity of mission."

24. Joseph Ratzinger, "*In the Beginning* . . .": *A Catholic Understanding of the Story of Creation and the Fall* (Grand Rapids: Eerdmans, 1995), pp. 61-62.

25. As one friend put it: "Before you can preach the Good News, you have to preach the bad news, because if you don't, they'll think that the Good News is not news at all."

26. Lamont, "What Was Wrong with Vatican II," p. 89.

27. Étienne Hugueny, "Le scandale édifiant d'une exposition missionnaire," *Revue Thomiste* 76 (1933): 217-42, and nos. 78-79 (1933): 533-67. The article appeared in two parts and the above citation is from pp. 227-28 of the first part. (Si la prédication missionnaire n'est pas tant une question de vie ou de mort qu'une question de plénitude de vie; si elle n'est pas une question de vie ou de mort pour un grand nombre d'infidèles, l'Église n'est plus la voie normale du salut, mais seulement une école de perfection pour les grandes âmes appelées à la plénitude de la vie chrétienne. La raison la plus urgente des missions disparait; elle ne sera pas équivalemment remplacée par toutes celles qu'on s'efforcera de trouver, qui ne sont pas sans valeur, mais qui jusqu'ici n'étaient que des motifs complémentaires pour tous les missionnaires.)

28. Gérard Philips, *L'Église et Son Mystère au Deuxième Concile du Vatican: Histoire, texte et commentaire de la Constitution Lumen Gentium*, vol. 1 of 2 (Paris: Desclée, 1967), p. 210. "Our free adherence to the will of God imposes on us the duty of preaching the Gospel; the failure to do so makes us culpable of a form of blasphemy." (Notre libre adhésion à la

volonté de Dieu nous impose le devoir de prêcher l'Évangile, faute de quoi nous nous rendons coupables d'une espèce de blasphème.)

29. Philips, *L'Église*, p. 219. (Nous ne pouvons passer sous silence une situation paradoxale, suscitée par une méprise sur la doctrine du Concile. Sous l'influence de l'extension des perspectives conciliaires, il en est chez qui le zèle missionnaire s'est affaibli. Et pourtant jamais document ecclésiastique n'a souligné avec autant d'insistance le devoir missionnaire universel que Lumen Gentium, non seulement à cet endroit mais à travers toute la Constitution, de la première à la dernière page. Le vrai zèle missionnaire est le fruit de la foi pure et de la charité désintéressée: c'est cela que vise Vatican II et non l'indifférence.)

30. Kenny, *Roman Catholicism*, pp. 88-89, provides a very sympathetic account of Rahner's theory of the anonymous Christian, but notes the serious difficulties of a one-sided positive assessment of the non-Christian religions. "History unfolds a long and grim tally of craven fears and terrors, hag-ridden superstitions and inhibitions, taboos, sorcery, human sacrifice and sacred prostitution springing from or cloaked over with the name of religion. . . . Always, even in their most lofty representatives, non-Christian religions are stricken with ambiguity. On the one hand they are embraced, upheld and penetrated by the compassionate love of the unknown Father whom they seek in shadows and images. On the other, they are enmeshed in the web of man's pride and selfishness. Whatever truth they stand for comes from the Spirit of truth, but it needs constantly to be disengaged from false, excessive, depraved accretions. The yearning for God that they voice tends to get stifled or muted by a denial or turning aside from God. Hope impels them to reach out for God's hand, but self-reliance pushes them to have recourse to human devices and techniques of salvation. They want to adore God but not uncommonly they end up by idolatrously manipulating him."

31. Georg Schurhammer, *Francis Xavier, His Life, His Times,* trans. M. Joseph Costelloe, vol. 4 (Rome, 1982), pp. 505-6. Cited by Francis Sullivan, *Salvation Outside the Church: Tracing the History of the Catholic Response* (Eugene, OR: Wipf & Stock, 2002), p. 86.

32. Sullivan, *Salvation Outside the Church*, p. 86.

33. Joseph Ratzinger, *Theological Highlights of Vatican II*, trans. Henry Traub, Gerard C. Thormann, and Werner Barzel (New York: Paulist Press, 1966), p. 153. Avery Dulles, "Pope Benedict XVI: Interpreter of Vatican II," in Dulles, *Church and Society: The Lawrence J. McGinley Lectures*, p. 480, has done a study of the commentary that Ratzinger has done on Vatican II, from the early work right during and after the Council up until that of his papacy. While there have been some shifts in evaluation, Dulles concludes: "Notwithstanding the changes, Benedict XVI has shown a fundamental consistency." Cardinal Ratzinger, *Principles of Catholic Theology: Building Stones for a Fundamental Theology,* trans. Sr. Mary Francis McCarthy (San Francisco: Ignatius Press, 1987), pp. 378-93, also provides a detailed and very helpful evaluation of the final document, and its subsequent reception, in *Principles of Catholic Theology*, pp. 378-93.

34. Norman Tanner, *The Church and the World: Gaudium et Spes, Inter Mirifica* (New York: Paulist Press, 2005), p. 9.

35. Tanner, *The Church and the World*, p. 68.

36. Tanner, *The Church and the World*, pp. 41, 49.

37. Karl Rahner, "Christian Pessimism," in *TI*, vol. 22, pp. 157-58.

38. Karl Rahner, *Faith in a Wintry Season: Conversations and Interviews with Karl*

Rahner in the Last Years of His Life, trans. and ed. Harvey D. Egan (New York: Crossroad, 1990), p. 125.

39. Ratzinger, *Theological Highlights,* pp. 156-57.

40. Joseph Ratzinger, *Christianity and the Crisis of Cultures,* trans. Brian McNeil (San Francisco: Ignatius Press, 2006), pp. 104-5.

41. Ratzinger, *Christianity and the Crisis of Cultures,* pp. 158-59.

42. Ratzinger, *Christianity and the Crisis of Cultures,* p. 171.

43. Ratzinger, *Christianity and the Crisis of Cultures,* p. 173. Thomas O'Meara in "Yves Congar: Theologian of Grace in a Wide World," in *Yves Congar: Theologian of the Church,* ed. Gabriel Flynn (Louvain/Grand Rapids: Peter's Press/Eerdmans, 2005), p. 385, generally sympathizes with Congar's views on the salvation of those who have not heard the gospel, but comments: "In the 1960's, Congar's evaluation of non-Christian or non-Biblical religions followed by billions of the world's inhabitants remains somewhat negative because unfashionably he would not overlook aspects of religions that are destructive, false, or idolatrous." O'Meara is not pleased with Congar's conservatism on this matter: "He sometimes too easily accepts the dichotomy offered by those holding that if you do not have a strong evangelization of an evil world you have no advocacy of the Gospel and no reason for missions." He cites pp. 211-21 of Congar's essay commenting on sections 2 to 9 of *Ad Gentes,* "Principes Doctrinaux," as evidence of Congar's views. Jerome P. Theisen, *The Ultimate Church and the Promise of Salvation* (Collegeville, MN: St. John's University Press, 1976), pp. 65-81, reviews all of Congar's writings that touch on the subject of EENS.

44. As John Paul II stated in *NMI* 40: "Even in countries evangelized many centuries ago, the reality of a 'Christian society' which, amid all the frailties which have always marked human life, measured itself explicitly on Gospel values, is now gone." Tanner, *The Church and the World,* pp. 83-84, 87-89, uncharacteristically speaks rather dramatically of the obvious decline of Christianity in Western Europe and North America since the Council, but cites the theory of the "anonymous Christian" as a reason for consolation. "The wave of immigrants seeking entry into Europe, as well as the marked decline in the birthrate in many parts of this continent, furnish obvious parallels with the decline and fall of the Roman Empire in the fourth and fifth centuries CE. . . . It may well be, indeed, that the Catholic Church in the twenty-first century is heading toward another Babylonian captivity. Diminished and shackled in Europe, its principal home for many centuries, it may live as an exile in much of the rest of the world, harassed and threatened." Tanner thinks that *GS* may in this case help us deal with the diverse, pluralistic situations that we will encounter.

45. Ratzinger, *Principles of Catholic Theology,* pp. 375, 377.

Notes to Appendix I

32. Cf. S. Thomas, Summa Theol. III, q. 8, a. 3, ad 1.

33. Cf. Epist. S. S. C. S. Officii ad Archiep. Boston: DENZ. 3869-72.

34. Cf. Eusebius Caes., Praeparatio Evangelica, 1, I: PG 21, 28AB.

18. Cfr. S. Thomas, Summa Theol. III, q. 8, a. 3, ad 1.

19. Cfr. Epist. S.S.C.S. Officii ad Archiep. Boston: Denz. 3869-72.

20. Cfr. Eusebius Caes., Praeparatio Evangelica, 1, 1: PG 2128 AB.

Notes to Appendix III

1. Hans Urs von Balthasar, *Theo-Drama: Theological Dramatic Theory*, vol. IV: *The Action*, trans. Graham Harrison (San Francisco: Ignatius Press, 1994), pp. 283-84.

2. Hans Urs von Balthasar, *The Moment of Christian Witness*, trans. Richard Beckley (San Francisco: Ignatius Press, 1994), pp. 120-21, p. 113 n. 42.

3. Balthasar, *The Moment of Christian Witness*, p. 113 n. 42. Balthasar also explicitly acknowledges his agreement with Rahner on hope for the salvation of all in *Dare We Hope "That All Men Be Saved"? With a Short Discourse on Hell*, trans. David Kipp and Lothar Krauth (San Francisco: Ignatius Press, 1988), p. 212.

4. Rahner, *Im Gespräch* 1, pp. 245-46, cited in Eamonn Conway, *The Anonymous Christian — A Relativised Christianity? An Evaluation of Hans Urs von Balthasar's Criticisms of Karl Rahner's Theory of the Anonymous Christian* (Frankfurt am Main: Peter Lang, 1993), p. 128.

5. Rahner, "The Christian among Unbelieving Relations," in *Theological Investigations*, vol. 3 of 23, trans. Karl-H. Kruge and Boniface Kruge (Baltimore: Helicon Press, 1967), p. 371.

6. Rahner, "Unbelieving Relations," p. 360.

7. Conway, *The Anonymous Christian*, pp. 107-45.

8. See, for example, Jeannine Hill Fletcher, "Rahner and Religious Diversity," in *The Cambridge Companion to Karl Rahner*, ed. Declan Marmion and Mary E. Hines (New York: Cambridge University Press, 2005), pp. 235-48, esp. 243-44. See also Eamonn Conway's treatment of both Balthasar's and Küng's attack on Rahner in "'So as Not to Despise God's Grace': Re-assessing Rahner's Idea of the 'Anonymous Christian,'" *Louvain Studies* 29 (2004): 107-30.

Select Bibliography

Magisterial Documents

Benedict XV. Encyclical Letter, *Maximum illud* (On the Propagation of the Catholic Faith Throughout the World), November 30, 1919. AAS 11 (1919), 440-55.

Benedict XVI. Encyclical Letter, *Spe salvi* (On Christian Hope), November 30, 2007. Washington DC: USCCB Publishing, 2007. AAS 99 (2007), 985-1027.

————. "Address of His Holiness Benedict XVI to the Roman Curia" December 22, 2005. http://www.vatican.va/holy_father/benedict_xvi/ speeches/2005/december/ documents/hf_ben_xvi_spe_20051222_roman-curia_en.html AAS 98 (2006), 40-53.

Congregation for the Doctrine of the Faith. *Doctrinal Note on Some Aspects of Evangelization*, December 3, 2007.

————. *Dominus Iesus* (On the Unicity and Salvific Universality of Jesus Christ), August 6, 2000. Boston: Pauline Books and Media, 2000. AAS 92 (2000), 742-65.

————. *Instruction on Infant Baptism*. Vatican City, October 20, 1980. AAS 72 (1980), 1137-58.

————. *Letter on Certain Questions Concerning Eschatology*, May 17, 1979. Boston: Daughters of St. Paul, 1979. AAS 71 (1979), 939-43.

————. *Mysterium ecclesiae*. (Declaration in Defense of the Catholic Doctrine on the Church against Certain Errors of the Present Day), June 24, 1973. Washington, DC: United States Catholic Conference, 1973. AAS 65 (1973), 396-408.

Flannery, Austin, ed. *Vatican Council II: The Conciliar and Post Conciliar Documents.* Vol. 1. Northport, NY: Costello Publishing, 1992.

John XXIII. Encyclical Letter, *Princeps pastorum* (On the Missions, Native Clergy, and Lay Participation), November 28, 1959. AAS 51 (1959), 833-64.

————. *Discourse on the Solemn Opening of the Ecumenical Council Vatican II.*

John Paul II. Encyclical Letter, *Redemptoris missio* (Mission of the Redeemer), December 7, 1990. Boston: Pauline Books and Media, 1991. AAS 83 (1991), 249-340.

————. Apostolic Letter, *Novo millennio ineunte* (At the Beginning of a New Millennium), January 6, 2001. Boston: Pauline Books and Media, 2001. AAS 93 (2001), 266-309.

————. Encyclical Letter, *Evangelium vitae* (The Gospel of Life), March 25, 1995. Boston: Pauline Books and Media, 1995. AAS 87 (1995), 401-522.

————. Encyclical Letter, *Fides et ratio* (Faith and Reason), September 14, 1998. Boston: Pauline Books and Media, 1998. AAS 91 (1999), 5-88.

————. Encyclical Letter, *Veritatis Splendor* (Splendor of the Truth), August 6, 1993. Washington DC: United States Catholic Conference, 1993. AAS 85 (1993), 1133-1228.

Paul VI. Apostolic Exhortation, *Evangelii nuntiandi* (On Evangelization in the Modern World), December 8, 1975. Boston: Pauline Books and Media, 1976. AAS 68 (1976), 5-76.

Pius XI. Encyclical Letter, *Rerum ecclesiae* (On Catholic Missions), February 28, 1926. AAS 18 (1926), 64-83.

Pius XII. Encyclical Letter, *Evangelii praecones* (On Promotion of Catholic Missions), June 2, 1951. AAS 43 (1951), 497-528.

————. Encyclical Letter, *Fidei donum* (On the Present Condition of the Catholic Missions, Especially in Africa), April 21, 1957. AAS 49 (1957), 225-48.

————. Encyclical Letter, *Mystici Corporis Christi* (On the Mystical Body of Christ), June 29, 1943. AAS 35 (1943), 193-248.

————. Encyclical Letter, *Humani generis* (Concerning Some False Opinions Threatening to Undermine the Foundations of Catholic Doctrine), August 12, 1950. AAS 42 (1950), 561-78.

The Church: Papal Teachings. Selected and Arranged by the Benedictine Monks of Solesmes, trans. Mother E. O'Gorman. Boston: St. Paul Editions, 1980.

The Papal Encyclicals. Claudia Carlen, ed. 5 vols. Raleigh, NC: McGrath Publishing Co., 1981.

The Seven Ecumenical Councils of the Undivided Church, ed. Henry R. Percival, in *A Select Library of Nicene and Post-Nicene Fathers of the Christian Church, Second Series, vol. 14*, ed. Philip Schaff and Henry Wace (Grand Rapids: Eerdmans, 1983).

Books

Alberigo, Giuseppe, ed. English version edited by Joseph A. Komonchak. *History of Vatican II.* 5 vols. Maryknoll, NY: Orbis, 1995-2003.

Alberigo, Giuseppe, and Franca Magistretti, eds. *Constitutionis Dogmaticae Lumen Gentium: Synopsis Historica.* Bologna: Istituto per le Scienze Religiose, 1975.

Auer, Johann. *The Church: The Universal Sacrament of Salvation.* Translated by Hugh M. Riley and Michael Waldstein. Vol. 8 of 9. Dogmatic Theology. Edited by Johann Auer and Joseph Ratzinger. Washington, DC: Catholic University of America Press, 1993.

Select Bibliography

Balthasar, Hans Urs von. *The Action.* Vol. 4 of 5, *Theo-Drama: Theological Dramatic Theory.* Translated by Graham Harrison. San Francisco: Ignatius Press, 1994.

———. *Credo: Meditations on the Apostles' Creed.* Translated by David Kipp. New York: Crossroad, 1990.

———. *Dare We Hope "That All Men Be Saved"? with "A Short Discourse on Hell."* Translated by Lothar Krauth and David Kipp. San Francisco: Ignatius Press, 1988.

———. *Epilogue.* Translated by Edward T. Oakes. San Francisco: Ignatius Press Press, 2004.

———. *The Glory of the Lord: A Theological Aesthetics.* Vol. 6, *Theology: The Old Covenant.* San Francisco: Ignatius Press, 1991.

———. *The Last Act.* Vol. 5 of 5, *Theo-Drama: Theological Dramatic Theory.* Translated by Graham Harrison. San Francisco: Ignatius Press, 1998.

———. *The Moment of Christian Witness.* Translated by Richard Beckley. San Francisco: Ignatius Press, 1994.

———. *Mysterium Paschale.* Translated by Aidan Nichols. Grand Rapids: Eerdmans, 1993.

———. *Razing the Bastions.* Translated by Brian McNeil. San Francisco: Ignatius, 1993.

———. *The Truth of God.* Vol. 2 of 3, *Theo-Logic: Theological Logical Theory.* Translated by Adrian J. Walker. San Francisco: Ignatius Press, 2004.

Barron, Robert. *The Priority of Christ.* Grand Rapids: Brazos, 2007.

Batlogg, Andreas R., and Melvin E. Michalski, eds. *Encounters with Karl Rahner: Remembrances of Rahner by Those Who Knew Him.* Translated from the German and edited by Barbara G. Turner. Milwaukee: Marquette University Press, 2009.

Beale, G. K. *We Become What We Worship: A Biblical Theology of Idolatry.* Downers Grove, IL: InterVarsity, 2008.

Bevans, Stephen B., and Jeffrey Gros. *Evangelization and Religious Freedom: Ad Gentes, Dignitatis Humanae.* New York: Paulist Press, 2009.

Biju-Duval, Denis. *Faut-il encore se soucier du salut des âmes? L'urgence de l'évangélisation.* Paris: Éditions de l'Emmanuel, 2012.

Boguslawski, Steven, and Ralph Martin, eds. *The New Evangelization: Overcoming the Obstacles.* Mahwah, NJ: Paulist Press, 2008.

Bot, Jean-Marc. *Osons Reparler de L'Enfer.* 21me edition. Paris: Éditions de L'Emmanuel, 2001.

Bray, Gerald. *Romans.* Ancient Christian Commentary on Scripture. Downers Grove, IL: InterVarsity, 1998.

Burke, Patrick. *Reinterpreting Rahner: A Critical Study of His Major Themes.* New York: Fordham University Press, 2002.

Butler, Christopher. *The Theology of Vatican II.* Westminster, MD: Christian Classics, 1981.

Byrne, Brendan. *Romans.* Sacra Pagina Series. Collegeville, MN: Liturgical Press, 1996.

Camelot, P.-Th., ed. and trans. *L'Église de Vatican II,* Tome I, Texte Latin et Traduction. Paris: Cerf, 1966.

Capéran, Louis. *Le Problème du salut des Infidèles: Essai Historique* (Toulouse, 1934).

Catherine of Siena. *The Dialogue*. Translated and introduced by Suzanne Noffke. New York: Paulist Press, 1980.

Congar, Yves, Hans Küng, and Daniel O'Hanlon, eds. *Council Speeches of Vatican II*. New York: Paulist Press, 1964.

Conway, Eamonn. *The Anonymous Christian — A Relativised Christianity? An Evaluation of Hans Urs von Balthasar's Criticisms of Karl Rahner's Theory of the Anonymous Christian*. Frankfurt am Main: Peter Lang, 1993.

Coulombe, Charles A. *Desire and Deception*. Arcadia, CA: Tumblar House, 2009.

Cranfield, C. E. B. *A Critical and Exegetical Commentary on the Epistle to the Romans*. Vol. 1 of 2 vols. The International Critical Commentary. Edinburgh: T. & T. Clark, 1975.

————. *The Gospel According to St. Mark*. Cambridge Greek Testament Commentaries. New York: Cambridge University Press, 1959.

Crowley, Paul G. *Rahner Beyond Rahner*. Lanham, MD: Rowman & Littlefield, 2005.

Daley, Brian E. *The Hope of the Early Church: A Handbook of Patristic Eschatology*. New York: Cambridge University Press, 1991.

Dalton, William Joseph. *Christ's Proclamation to the Spirits: A Study of 1 Peter 3:18–4:6*. Rome: Pontifical Biblical Institute, 1965.

Daniélou, Jean. *Holy Pagans of the Old Testament*. Translated by Felix Faber. Baltimore: Helicon Press, 1957.

Dauphinais, Michael, and Matthew Levering, eds. *John Paul II & St. Thomas Aquinas*. Naples, FL: Sapientia Press, 2006.

Diamond, Jared. *Guns, Germs, and Steel: The Fate of Human Societies*. New York: W. W. Norton, 1999.

DiNoia, J. A. *The Diversity of Religions*. Washington, DC: Catholic University of America Press, 1992.

Doorly, Moyra, and Aidan Nichols. *The Council in Question: A Dialogue with Catholic Traditionalism*. Herefordshire, UK: Gracewing, 2011.

Dulles, Avery. *Church and Society: The Laurence J. McGinley Lectures*. New York: Fordham University Press, 2008.

Eminyan, Maurice. *The Theology of Salvation*. Boston: St. Paul Editions, 1960.

Eusebius. *La Préparation Évangélique: Livre I*. Translated by Jean Sirinelli et Édouard des Places. Paris: Cerf, 1974.

Farey, Caroline. *A Metaphysical Investigation of the Anthropological Implications of the Phrase: "Ipse enim, Filius Dei, incarnatione sua cum omni homine quodammodo se univit" (For, by his incarnation, he, the Son of God has in a certain way united himself with each man — Gaudium et spes, 22)*. Ph.D. diss., Pontificia Universitas Lateranensis, 2008.

Fenton, Joseph Clifford. *The Catholic Church and Salvation: In the Light of Recent Pronouncements by the Holy See*. Round Top, NY: Seminary Press, 2006; original edition 1958.

Fitzmyer, Joseph A. *The Interpretation of Scripture: In Defense of the Historical-Critical Method*. New York: Paulist Press, 2008.

————. *Romans: A New Translation with Introduction and Commentary*. Vol. 33, The

Anchor Bible, edited by David Noel Freedman and William Foxwell Albright. New York: Doubleday, 1993.

Flannery, Austin, ed. *Vatican II on the Church*. Dublin: Scepter Books, 1966.

Fuellenbach, John. *Throw Fire*. Manila: Logos Books, 1998.

Gaillardetz, Richard R. *The Church in the Making: Lumen Gentium, Christus Dominus, Orientalium Ecclesiarum*. New York: Paulist Press, 2006.

Greenman, Timothy, and Jeffrey P. Larsen, eds. *Reading Romans through the Centuries: From the Early Church to Karl Barth*. Grand Rapids: Brazos, 2005.

Grisez, Germain. *The Way of the Lord Jesus: Difficult Moral Questions*. Vol. 3. Quincy, IL: Franciscan Press, 1997.

Harrington, Daniel J. *The Gospel of Matthew*. Sacra Pagina Series. Collegeville, MN: Liturgical Press, 1991.

Heim, Maximilian Heinrich. *Joseph Ratzinger: Life in the Church and Living Theology, Fundamentals of Ecclesiology with Reference to Lumen Gentium*. Translated by Michael J. Miller. San Francisco: Ignatius Press, 2007.

Jewett, Paul K. *Election and Predestination*. Grand Rapids: Eerdmans, 1985.

Jewett, Robert. *Romans: A Commentary*. Hermeneia: A Critical and Historical Commentary on the Bible. Assisted by Roy Kotansky and edited by Elden Jay Epp. Minneapolis: Fortress Press, 2007.

Journet, Charles. *What Is Dogma?* Translated by Mark Pontifex. Vol. 4, Twentieth Century Encyclopedia of Catholicism, edited by Henri Daniel-Rops. New York: Hawthorn, 1964.

Kaiser, Robert. *Inside the Council*. London: Burns & Oates, 1963.

Kanyike, Lawrence. *The Anonymous Christian and the Mission of the Church*. Doctoral dissertation, University of Notre Dame, 1978.

Käsemann, Ernst. *Commentary on Romans*. Translated by Geoffrey W. Bromiley. Grand Rapids: Eerdmans, 1980.

Kasper, Walter. *The God of Jesus Christ*. Translated by Matthew J. O'Connell. New York: Crossroad, 1984.

————. *Jesus the Christ*. Translated by V. Green. New York: Paulist Press, 1976.

————. *The Methods of Dogmatic Theology*. Translated by John Drury. Shannon, Ireland: Ecclesia Press, 1969.

Keating, Daniel, Thomas Weinandy, and John Yocum, eds. *Aquinas on Doctrine: A Critical Introduction*. London and New York: T. & T. Clark, 2004.

Kelly, J. N. D. *Early Christian Doctrines*. New York: Continuum, 1977.

Kenny, J. P. *Roman Catholicism, Christianity and Anonymous Christianity: The Role of the Christian Today*. Hales Corners, WI: Clergy Book Service, 1973.

Kereszty, Roch A. *Jesus Christ: Fundamentals of Christology*. New York: Alba House, 2002.

Kloppenburg, Bonaventure. *The Ecclesiology of Vatican II*. Translated by Matthew J. O'Connell. Chicago: Franciscan Herald Press, 1974.

Knitter, Paul. *No Other Name?* Maryknoll, NY: Orbis, 2003.

Kofsky, Aryeh. *Eusebius of Caesarea Against Paganism*. Leiden: Brill, 2002.

Kruijen, Christophe J. "Salut universel ou double issue du jugement: Espérer pour tous? Contribution à l'étude critique d'une opinion théologique contemporaine concernant la réalisation de la damnation." Doctoral dissertation, Pontifical University of St. Thomas, Rome, Italy, 2008.

Lacouture, Jean. *The Jesuits: A Multibiography.* Translated by Jeremy Leggatt. Washington, DC: Counterpoint, 1995.

Lamb, Matthew L., and Matthew Levering, eds. *Vatican II: Renewal within Tradition.* New York: Oxford University Press, 2008.

Latourelle, René. *Theology of Revelation.* New York: Alba House, 1966.

Lombardi, Josephine. *The Universal Salvific Will of God in Official Documents of the Roman Catholic Church.* Lewiston, NY: Edwin Mellen Press, 2007.

Lombardi, Riccardo. *The Salvation of the Unbeliever.* London: Burns & Oates, 1956.

Lyonnet, Stanislas. *Études sur L'épître aux Romains.* Rome: Editrice Pontificio Istituto Biblico, 1989.

Marchetto, Agostino. *The Second Vatican Ecumenical Council: A Counterpoint for the History of the Council.* Translated by Kenneth D. Whitehead. Scranton, PA: University of Scranton Press, 2010.

Maritain, Jacques. *The Range of Reason.* Translated by Mrs. Pierre Brodin. New York: Scribner's, 1952.

Marmion, Declan, and Mary E. Hines, eds. *The Cambridge Companion to Karl Rahner.* New York: Cambridge University Press, 2005.

Martin, Francis. *Sacred Scripture: The Disclosure of the Word.* Naples, FL: Sapientia Press, 2006.

Martin, Ralph. *The Fulfillment of All Desire: A Guidebook for the Journey to God Based on the Wisdom of the Saints.* Steubenville, OH: Emmaus Road Publications, 2006.

Martin, Ralph, and Peter Williamson, eds. *John Paul II and the New Evangelization.* Cincinnati: Servant/St. Anthony Press, 2006.

Marzheuser, Richard A. "*The Votum Ecclesiae and the Necessity of the Church: An Examination of* Lumen gentium *of the Second Vatican Council.*" STD dissertation, Catholic University of America, 1988.

McDermott, John M., ed. *The Thought of John Paul II: A Collection of Essays and Studies.* Rome: Gregorian University Press, 1983.

Meier, John P. *Matthew: A Biblical-Theological Commentary.* In Wilfrid Harrington and Donald Senior, eds., New Testament Message, vol. 3. Wilmington, DE: Michael Glazier, 1980.

Moens, Jean-Luc, ed. *Si Dieu donne son salut à tout homme pourquoi évangéliser?* Paris: Éditions de L'Emmanuel, 2007.

Morerod, Charles. *The Church and the Human Quest for Truth.* Ave Maria, FL: Sapientia Press, 2008.

Moss, David, and Edward T. Oakes, eds. *The Cambridge Companion to Hans Urs von Balthasar.* New York: Cambridge University Press, 2004.

Murray, John. *The Epistle to the Romans.* Grand Rapids: Eerdmans, 1964.

Newman, John Henry. *An Essay on the Development of Christian Doctrine.* Notre Dame: University of Notre Dame Press, 1989.

Oakes, Edward T. *The Pattern of Redemption: The Theology of Hans Urs von Balthasar.* New York: Continuum, 1997.

O'Collins, Gerald. *Salvation for All.* New York: Oxford University Press, 2008.

O'Connor, James T. *Land of the Living: A Theology of the Last Things.* New York: Catholic Book Publishing, 1992.

O'Malley, John W. *What Happened at Vatican II.* Cambridge, MA: Harvard University Press, 2008.

O'Meara, Thomas K. *God in the World: A Guide to Karl Rahner's Theology.* Collegeville, MN: Liturgical Press, 2007.

Pagé, Jean-Guy. *Qui Est L'église?: Le Peuple de Dieu.* 3 vols. Montréal: Les Éditions Bellarmin, 1979.

Phan, Peter. *Eternity in Time.* Cranbury, NJ: Associated University Presses, 1988.

Philips, Gérard. *L'Église et Son Mystère au Deuxième Concile du Vatican: Histoire, texte et commentaire de la Constitution Lumen Gentium.* Vol. 1 of 2. Paris: Desclée, 1967.

Pitstick, Alyssa Lyra. *Light in Darkness: Hans Urs von Balthasar and the Catholic Doctrine of Christ's Descent into Hell.* Grand Rapids: Eerdmans, 2007.

Pozo, Candido. *Theology of the Beyond.* Translated by Mark A. Pilon. New York: Alba House, 2009.

Rahner, Karl. *Foundations of Christian Faith: An Introduction to the Idea of Christianity.* Translated by William V. Dych. New York: Seabury, 1978.

———. *The Shape of the Church to Come.* Translated by Edward Quinn. London: SPCK, 1974.

Rahner, Karl, et al. *Sacramentum Mundi: An Encyclopedia of Theology.* Vol. 2 of 6. New York: Herder & Herder, 1969.

Rahner, Karl, and Herbert Vorgrimler. *Theological Dictionary.* Edited by Cornelius Ernst, translated by Richard Strachan. New York: Herder & Herder, 1965.

Rahner, Karl, Paul Imhof, and Hubert Biallowons, eds. *Faith in a Wintry Season: Conversations and Interviews with Karl Rahner in the Last Years of His Life.* Translated and edited by Harvey D. Egan. New York: Crossroad, 1990.

Ratzinger, Joseph. *Christianity and the Crisis of Cultures.* Translated by Brian McNeil. San Francisco: Ignatius Press, 2006.

———. *Eschatology: Death and Eternal Life.* Translated by Aidan Nichols and Michael Waldstein. Vol. 9 of 9. Dogmatic Theology. Edited by Joseph Ratzinger and Johann Auer. Washington, DC: Catholic University of America Press, 1988.

———. *God's Word: Scripture, Tradition, Office.* Edited by Peter Hünermann and Thomas Söding, translated by Henry Taylor. San Francisco: Ignatius Press, 2008.

———. *In the Beginning: A Catholic Understanding of Creation and the Fall.* Translated by Boniface Ramsey. Grand Rapids: Eerdmans, 1995.

———. *Introduction to Christianity.* Translated by J. R. Foster. San Francisco: Ignatius Press, 2004.

———. *The Nature and Mission of Theology: Essays to Orient Theology in Today's Debates.* Translated by Adrian Walker. San Francisco: Ignatius Press, 1995.

———. *New Outpourings of the Spirit.* Translated by Michael J. Miller and Henry Taylor. San Francisco: Ignatius Press, 2006.

————. *Principles of Catholic Theology: Building Stones for a Fundamental Theology.* Translated by Sr. Mary Francis McCarthy. San Francisco: Ignatius Press, 1987.

————. *Theological Highlights of Vatican II.* Translated by Henry Traub, Gerard C. Thormann, and Werner Barzel. New York: Paulist Press, 1966.

————. *Truth and Tolerance: Christian Belief and World Religions.* Translated by Henry Taylor. San Francisco: Ignatius Press, 2004.

————. *The Yes of Jesus Christ.* Translated by Robert Nowell. New York: Crossroad, 1991.

Rivers, Robert S. *From Maintenance to Mission.* New York: Paulist Press, 2005.

Roper, Anita. *The Anonymous Christian.* Translated by Joseph Doncell. New York: Sheed & Ward, 1966.

Rousseau, Richard, ed. *Interreligious Dialogue: Facing the Next Frontier.* Scranton, PA: Ridge Row Press, 1981.

Rulleau, Jean-Marc. *Baptism of Desire: A Patristic Commentary.* Kansas City, MO: Angelus Press, 1999.

Ruokanen, Mikka. *The Catholic Doctrine of Non-Christian Religions According to the Second Vatican Council.* Vol. 7. Studies in Christian Mission. Edited by Marc Spindler. Leiden: E. J. Brill, 1992.

Rush, Ormond. *Still Interpreting Vatican II: Some Hermeneutical Principles.* New York: Paulist Press, 2004.

Rynne, Xavier. *Vatican Council II: An Authoritative One-Volume Version of the Four Historic Books.* New York: Farrar, Straus & Giroux, 1968.

Sabra, George. *Thomas Aquinas' Vision of the Church.* Mainz: Matthias-Grunewald-Verlag, 1987.

Schindler, David L., ed. *Hans Urs von Balthasar: His Life and Work.* San Francisco: Ignatius Press, 1991.

Schreck, Alan. *Vatican II: The Crisis and the Promise.* Cincinnati: Servant/St. Anthony, 2005.

Schultenover, David G., ed. *Vatican II: Did Anything Happen?* New York: Continuum, 2008.

Scola, Angelo. *Test Everything, Hold Fast to What Is Good: An Interview with Hans Urs von Balthasar.* Translated by Maria Shrady. San Francisco: Ignatius Press, 1989.

Sesboué, Bernard. *Hors de l'Église pas de salut: Histoire d'une formule et problèmes d'interprétation.* Paris: Desclée de Brouwer, 2004.

Sharkey, Michael, ed. *International Theological Commission: Texts and Documents 1969-1985.* San Francisco: Ignatius Press, 1989.

Sharkey, Michael, and Thomas Weinandy, eds. *International Theological Commission: Texts and Documents 1986-2007.* San Francisco: Ignatius Press, 2009.

Smith, A. Robert, ed. *No Soul Left Behind: The Words and Wisdom of Edgar Cayce.* New York: Kensington Publishing, 2005.

Sullivan, Francis. *Creative Fidelity.* Eugene, OR: Wipf & Stock, 2003.

————. *Magisterium.* Eugene, OR: Wipf & Stock, 1983.

————. *Salvation Outside of the Church? Tracing the History of the Catholic Response.* Eugene, OR: Wipf & Stock, 2002.

Tanner, Norman P. *The Church and the World: Gaudium et Spes, Inter Mirifica.* New York: Paulist Press, 2005.

———. *The Councils of the Church: A Short History.* New York: Crossroad, 2001.

Tanner, Norman P., ed. *Decrees of the Ecumenical Councils: Nicaea I-Lateran V.* Vol. 1 of 2. London/Washington, DC: Sheed & Ward/Georgetown University Press, 1990.

———, ed. *Decrees of the Ecumenical Councils: Trent-Vatican II.* Vol. 2 of 2. London/ Washington, DC: Sheed & Ward/Georgetown University Press, 1990.

Terry, Justyn. *The Justifying Judgement of God: A Reassessment of the Place of Judgement in the Saving Work of Christ.* Bletchley, UK: Paternoster, 2007.

Theisen, Jerome P. *The Ultimate Church and the Promise of Salvation.* Collegeville, MN: St. John's University Press, 1976.

Thomas Aquinas. *The Sermon-Conferences of St. Thomas Aquinas on the Apostles' Creed.* Translated from the Leonine Edition and edited and introduced by Nicholas Ayo. Notre Dame: University of Notre Dame Press, 1988.

———. St. *Summa Theologica.* Translated by Fathers of the English Dominican Province. 5 vols. Allen, TX: Christian Classics, 1948.

Torrell, Jean-Pierre. *Saint Thomas Aquinas: The Person and His Work.* Translated by Robert Royal. Vol. 1 of 2. Washington, DC: Catholic University of America Press, 1996.

———. *Saint Thomas Aquinas: Spiritual Master.* Translated by Robert Royal. Vol. 2 of 2. Washington, DC: Catholic University of America Press, 1996.

Vorgrimler, Herbert. *Karl Rahner: His Life, Thought and Work.* Translated by Edward Quinn. London: Burns & Oates, 1965.

Vorgrimler, Herbert, ed. *Commentary on the Documents of Vatican II.* 6 vols. New York: Herder & Herder, 1967-1969.

Webster, John. *Holiness.* Grand Rapids: Eerdmans, 2003.

Weger, Karl-Heinz. *Karl Rahner: An Introduction to His Theology.* Translated by David Smith. New York: Seabury, 1980.

Whitehead, Kenneth D., ed. *After 40 Years: Vatican Council II's Diverse Legacy.* South Bend, IN: St. Augustine's Press, 2007.

Willimon, William H. *Who Will Be Saved?* Nashville: Abingdon, 2008.

Wiltgen, Ralph M. *The Rhine Flows into the Tiber: A History of Vatican II.* Rockford, IL: Tan Books and Publishers, 1985.

Witherup, Ronald D. *Scripture: Dei Verbum.* New York: Paulist Press, 2006.

Wojtyla, Karol. *Sources of Renewal: The Implementation of the Second Vatican Council.* Translated by P. S. Falla. New York: Harper & Row, 1980.

Articles and Essays in Books

Ambaum, Jan. "An Empty Hell? The Restoration of All Things? Balthasar's Concept of Hope for Salvation," *Communio* 18 (Spring 1991): 35-52.

Balthasar, Hans Urs von. "Current Trends in Catholic Theology and the Responsibility of the Christian," *Communio* 5, no. 1 (Spring 1978): 77-85.

————. "In Retrospect," *Communio* 2, no. 3 (1975): 197-220.

————. "Meeting God in Today's World," *Fundamental Theology: The Church and the World, Concilium* 6 (New York: Paulist Press, 1965): 23-39.

————. "Why I Am Still a Christian," in *Two Say Why*. Translated by John Griffiths. Chicago: Franciscan Herald Press, 1973.

Bauckham, Richard J. "Universalism: A Historical Survey," *Themelios* 4, no. 2 (January 1979): 48-54.

Blum, Edwin A. "'Shall you not surely die?'" *Themelios* 4, no. 2 (January 1979): 58-61.

Budziszewski, J. "Natural Law Revealed," *First Things* 190 (December 2008): 29-33.

Bullivant, Stephen. "*Sine Culpa?* Vatican II and Inculpable Ignorance," *Theological Studies* 72, no. 1 (March 2011): 70-86.

Burgaleta, Claudio M. "A Rahnerian reading of *Santeria:* A proposal for a Christian recovery of the syncretic elements of Latin American popular religiosity based on Rahner's concept of 'anonymous Christianity.'" *Apuntes* 2 (Summer 1993): 139-50.

Butler, Basil Christopher. "Les chrétiens non-catholiques et L'Église." In *L'Église de Vatican II: Études autour de la Constitution conciliaire sur l'Église*, Tome II, edited by Guilherme Baraúna and Yves Congar, pp. 651-68. Paris: Cerf, 1966.

Coffey, David. "The Whole Rahner on the Supernatural Existential," *Theological Studies* 65, no. 1 (March 2004): 95-118.

Congar, Yves. "Principes Doctrinaux." In *L'Activité missionnaire de l'Église*, pp. 185-221. Paris: Cerf, 1967.

Conway, Eamonn. "'So as not to Despise God's Grace': Re-assessing Rahner's Idea of the 'Anonymous Christian.'" *Louvain Studies* 29 (2004): 107-30.

Daley, Brian. "Apokatastasis and 'Honorable Silence' in the Eschatology of Maximus the Confessor." In *Maximus Confessor: Actes du Symposium sur Maxime le Confesseur*, edited by Felix Heinzer and Christoph Schönborn, pp. 309-39. Fribourg, Suisse: Éditions Universitaires Fribourg, 1982.

D'Costa, Gavin. "Karl Rahner's Anonymous Christian: A Reappraisal," *Modern Theology* 12 (1985): 131-48.

DiNoia, J. A. "Religion and the Religions." In *The Cambridge Companion to Karl Barth*, edited by John Webster, pp. 243-57. New York: Cambridge University Press, 2000.

Diriart, Alexandra. "L'ecclésiologie du Corps du Christ dans Lumen Gentium: Méfiance des Pères conciliaires ou réappropriation? (I)," *Nova et Vetera* 84, no. 4 (Octobre-Décembre 2009): 253-75.

————. "L'ecclésiologie du Corps du Christ dans Lumen Gentium: méfiance des Pères conciliares ou réappropriation? (II)," *Nova et Vetera* 84, no. 4 (Octobre-Décembre 2009): 373-95.

Duffy, Stephen J. "Experience of Grace." In *The Cambridge Companion to Karl Rahner*, edited by Declan Marmion and Mary E. Hines, pp. 43-62. New York: Cambridge University Press, 2005.

Dulles, Avery. "The Church as Locus of Salvation." In *The Thought of John Paul II: A Collection of Essays and Studies*, edited by John M. McDermott, pp. 169-96. Rome: Editrice Pontificia Università Gregoriana, 1993.

————. "Current Trends in Mission Theology," *Theology Digest* 20, no. 1 (Spring 1972): 26-34.

————. "*Dominus Iesus*, A Catholic Response," *Pro Ecclesia* 10, no. 1 (Winter 2001): 5-7.

————. "The Population of Hell," *First Things* 133 (May 2003): 36-41.

————. "The Reception of Vatican II at the Extraordinary Synod of 1985." In *The Reception of Vatican II*, edited by Giuseppe Alberigo, Jean-Pierre Jossua, and Joseph A. Komonchak, translated by Matthew J. O'Connell, pp. 349-63. Washington, DC: Catholic University of America Press, 1987.

————. "Vatican II: The Myth and the Reality," *America* 188, no. 6 (February 24, 2003).

————. "Who Can Be Saved?" *First Things* 180 (February 2008): 17-22.

Egan, Harvey D. "Theology and Spirituality." In *The Cambridge Companion to Karl Rahner*, edited by Declan Marmion and Mary E. Hines, pp. 13-28. New York: Cambridge University Press, 2005.

Egan, James M. "The Sin of Schism: A Contribution to the Discussion of Membership in the Church." In *Vatican II: The Theological Dimension*, edited by Anthony D. Lee, pp. 59-77. Washington, DC: Thomist Press, 1963.

Elders, Léon. "Les théories nouvelles de la signification des religions non-chrétiennes," *Nova et Vetera* 23 (Juillet-Sept. 1998): 97-117.

Emery, Gilles. "The Immutability of the God of Love and the Problem of Language Concerning the 'Suffering of God.'" In James F. Keating and Thomas Joseph White, eds., pp. 27-76. *Divine Impassibility and the Mystery of Human Suffering*. Grand Rapids: Eerdmans, 2009.

Esler, P. F. "The Sodom Tradition in Romans 1:18-32," *Biblical Theology Bulletin* 34, no. 1 (2004): 4-16.

Estevez, Jorge Medina. "The Constitution on the Church: Lumen Gentium." In *Vatican II: An Interfaith Appraisal*, edited by John H. Miller, pp. 101-21. Notre Dame: University of Notre Dame Press, 1966.

Flannery, Kevin L. "How to Think about Hell," *New Blackfriars* 72, no. 854 (November 1991): 469-81.

Galot, Jean. "Christ's Descent into Hell," *Theology Digest* 13, no. 2 (Summer 1965): 89-94.

Gaventa, Beverly Roberts. "God Handed Them Over: Reading Romans 1:18-32 Apocalyptically," *Australian Biblical Review* 53 (2005): 42-53.

Griffiths, Paul J. "Is There a Doctrine of the Descent into Hell?" *Pro Ecclesia* 17, no. 3 (Summer 2008): 257-68.

Grillmeier, Aloys. "The People of God." Translated by Kevin Smyth. In *Commentary on the Documents of Vatican II*, vol. 1 of 6, pp. 153-85, edited by Herbert Vorgrimler. New York: Herder & Herder, 1967-1969.

Gromada, Conrad T. "How Would Karl Rahner Respond to '*Dominus Iesus*'?" *Philosophy and Theology* 13, no. 2 (2001): 425-36.

Hauke, Manfred. "Shed for Many: An Accurate Rendering of the *Pro Multis* in the Formula of Consecration," *Antiphon* 14, no. 2 (2010): 169-229.

————. "'Sperare per tutti?' Il ricorso all'esperienza dei santi nell'ultima grande controversia di Hans Urs von Balthasar," *Rivista Teologico di Lugano* 6, no. 1 (2001): 189-214.

Healy, Nicholas J. "On Hope, Heaven, and Hell," *Logos* 1, no. 3 (1997): 80-91.

Highfield, R. "The Freedom to Say 'No'? Karl Rahner's Doctrine of Sin," *Theological Studies* 56 (1995): 485-505.

Hillman, Eugene. "'Anonymous Christianity' and the Missions," *The Downside Review* 84, no. 277 (1966): 361-79.

Hugueny, Étienne. "Le scandale édifiant d'une exposition missionnaire, Part I," *Revue Thomist* 76 (1933): 217-42.

————. "Le scandale édifiant d'une exposition missionnaire, Part II," *Revue Thomist* 78-79 (1933): 533-67.

International Theological Commission. "The Hope of Salvation for Infants Who Die Without Being Baptized," January 19, 2007. *Origins* 36, no. 45 (April 26, 2007): 725-45.

Kereszty, Roch. "Response to Professor Scola," *Communio* 18 (Summer 1991): 227-36.

Lamont, John. "What Was Wrong with Vatican II," *New Blackfriars* 99, no. 1013 (January 2007): 92-93.

————. "Why the Second Vatican Council Was a Good Thing and Is More Important Than Ever," *New Oxford Review* (July/August 2005): 32-36.

Levison, J. R. "Adam and Eve in Romans 1:18-25 and the Greek Life of Adam and Eve," *New Testament Studies* 50, no. 4 (2004): 519-34.

Longacre, Robert E., and Wilber B. Wallis, "Soteriology and Eschatology in Romans," *Journal of the Evangelical Theological Society* 41 (1998): 367-82.

de Lubac, Henri. "Lumen Gentium and the Fathers." In *Vatican II: An Interfaith Appraisal*, edited by John H. Miller, pp. 153-75. Notre Dame: University of Notre Dame Press, 1966.

Ludlow, Morwenna. "Universal Salvation and a Soteriology of Divine Punishment," *Scottish Journal of Theology* 53, no. 4 (2000): 449-71.

Martin, Francis. "Revelation as Disclosure: Creation." In *Wisdom and Holiness, Science and Scholarship: Essays in Honor of Matthew L. Lamb*, edited by Michael Dauphinais and Matthew Levering, pp. 205-47. Naples, FL: Sapientia Press, 2007.

————. "The Spirit of the Lord Is Upon Me: The Role of the Holy Spirit in the Work of Evangelization." In *The New Evangelization: Overcoming the Obstacles*, edited by Steven Boguslawski and Ralph Martin, pp. 59-82. New York: Paulist Press, 2008.

Martin, Ralph. "Believing and Praying: The Power of Homilies," *Homiletic & Pastoral Review* 104, no. 3 (December 2003): 64-66.

Mattox, Mickey L. "Fortuita Misericordia: Martin Luther on the Salvation of Biblical Outsiders," *Pro Ecclesia* 17, no. 4 (Winter 2008): 423-41.

McBrien, Richard P. "The Church *(Lumen Gentium)*." In *Modern Catholicism: Vatican II and After*, edited by Adrian Hastings, pp. 84-95. New York: Oxford University Press, 1991.

McCarthy, Timothy G. "The Church and the Other Religions." In *The Catholic Tradition: The Church in the Twentieth Century*, pp. 139-66. Chicago: Loyola Press, 1998.

McDermott, John M. "II Cor. 3: The Old and New Covenants," *Gregorianum* 86, no. 1 (2006): 25-63.

————. "Did That Really Happen at Vatican II? Reflections on John O'Malley's Recent Book," *Nova et Vetera*, English Edition, 8, no. 2 (2010): 425-66.

———— "Karl Rahner in Tradition: The One and the Many," *Fides Quaerens Intellectum* 3, no. 2 (Spring 2007): 1-60.

————. "Metaphysical Conundrums at the Root of Moral Disagreement," *Gregorianum* 71, no. 4 (1990): 713-42.

————. "Universal History and the History of Salvation." In *Dictionary of Fundamental Theology*, edited by René Latourelle and Rino Fisichella, pp. 446-55. New York: Crossroad, 1994.

————. "Vatican II and the Theologians on the Church as Sacrament," *Irish Theological Quarterly* 71 (2006): 143-78.

McNamara, Kevin. "The People of God." In *Vatican II: The Constitution on the Church: A Theological and Pastoral Commentary*, edited by Kevin McNamara, pp. 106-62. Chicago: Franciscan Herald Press, 1968.

Meyer, B. F. "Many (= All) Are Called, but Few (= Not All) Are Chosen," *New Testament Studies* 36, no. 1 (1990): 89-97.

Moeller, Charles. "History of Lumen Gentium's Structure and Ideas." In *Vatican II: An Interfaith Appraisal*, edited by John H. Miller, pp. 123-52. Notre Dame: University of Notre Dame Press, 1966.

Morerod, Charles. "John Paul II's Ecclesiology and St. Thomas Aquinas." In *John Paul II and St. Thomas Aquinas*, edited by Michael Dauphinais and Matthew Levering, pp. 45-72. Naples, FL: Sapientia Press, 2006.

Murray, Paul. "Aquinas at Prayer: The Interior Life of a 'Mystic on Campus.'" *Logos* 14, no. 1 (Winter 2001): 38-65.

Nicholls, Bruce J. "The Exclusiveness and Inclusiveness of the Gospel," *Themelios* 4, no. 2 (January 1979): 62-68.

Oakes, Edward T., and Alyssa Lyra Pitstick. "Balthasar, Hell, and Heresy: An Exchange," *First Things* 168 (December 2006): 25-32.

————. "More on Balthasar, Hell, and Heresy," *First Things* 169 (January 2007): 16-19.

O'Connor, James T. "Von Balthasar and Salvation," *Homiletic & Pastoral Review* (1989): 10-21. *Land of the Living*

O'Donnell, Christopher. "The People of God." In *Vatican II on the Church*, edited by Austin Flannery, pp. 35-45. Dublin: Scepter Books, 1966.

O'Meara, Thomas. "The Presence of Grace Outside Evangelization, Baptism and Church in Thomas Aquinas' Theology." In *That Others May Know and Love — Essays in Honor of Zachary Hayes OFM*, edited by Michael F. Cusato and F. Edward Coughlin, pp. 91-131. New York: The Franciscan Institute, 1997.

————. "Tarzan, Las Casas and Rahner: Thomas Aquinas' Theology of Wider Grace," *Theology Digest* 45 (1998): 319-28.

————. "Yves Congar: Theologian of Grace in a Vast World." In *Yves Congar: Theologian of the Church*, edited by Gabriel Flynn, pp. 371-99. Grand Rapids: Eerdmans; Leuven: Peter's Press, 2005.

O'Neill, Colman. "General Introduction." In *Vatican II on the Church*, edited by Austin Flannery, pp. 9-17. Dublin: Scepter Books, 1966.

————. "St. Thomas on Membership of the Church." In *Vatican II: The Theological Dimension*, edited by Anthony D. Lee, pp. 88-140. Washington, DC: Thomist Press, 1963.

Ormerod, Neil J. "'The Times They Are a-Changin': A Response to O'Malley and Schloesser." In *Vatican II: Did Anything Happen?* edited by David G. Schultenover, pp. 153-83. New York: Continuum, 2008.

Perry, John F. "Ripalda and Rahner: 400 Years of Jesuit Reflection on Universal Salvation," *Philosophy and Theology* 13, no. 2 (2001): 339-61.

Phan, Peter C. "Eschatology." In *The Cambridge Companion to Karl Rahner*, edited by Declan Marmion and Mary E. Hines, pp. 174-92. New York: Cambridge University Press, 2005.

————. "Is Karl Rahner's Doctrine of Sin Orthodox?" *Philosophy and Theology* 9, nos. 1-2 (1995): 223-36.

Philips, Gérard. "The Church: Mystery and Sacrament." In *Vatican II: An Interfaith Appraisal*, edited by John H. Miller, pp. 187-96. Notre Dame: University of Notre Dame Press, 1966.

————. "Dogmatic Constitution on the Church: History of the Constitution" In *Commentary on the Documents of Vatican II*, edited by Herbert Vorgrimler, vol. 1 of 5, pp. 105-37. New York: Herder & Herder/Palm Publishers, 1967-1969.

Rahner, Karl. "The Abiding Significance of the Second Vatican Council." In *Theological Investigations*, vol. 20 of 23, translated by Edward Quinn, pp. 90-102. New York: Crossroad, 1981.

————. "Anonymous Christians." In *Theological Investigations*, vol. 6 of 23, translated by Karl-H and Boniface Kruger, pp. 390-99. Baltimore: Helicon Press, 1969.

————. "Anonymous Christianity and the Missionary Task of the Church." In *Theological Investigations*, vol. 12 of 23, translated by David Bourke, pp. 161-78. New York: Seabury, 1974.

————. "Atheism and Implicit Christianity." In *Theological Investigations*, vol. 9 of 23, translated by Graham Harrison, pp. 145-64. New York: Herder & Herder, 1972.

————. "Basic Theological Interpretation of the Second Vatican Council." In *Theological Investigations*, vol. 20 of 23, translated by Edward Quinn, pp. 77-89. New York: Crossroad, 1981.

————. "The Christian among Unbelieving Relations." In *Theological Investigations*, vol. 3 of 23, translated by Karl-H. and Boniface Kruge, pp. 355-72. Baltimore: Helicon Press, 1967.

————. "Christianity and the Non-Christian Religions." In *Theological Investigations*, vol. 5 of 23, translated by Karl-H. Kruger, pp. 115-34. Baltimore: Helicon Press, 1966.

————. "Christian Pessimism," In *Theological Investigations*, vol. 22 of 23, translated by Joseph Doncell, pp. 155-62. New York: Crossroad, 1991.

————. "The Church's Commission to Bring Salvation and the Humanization of the

World." In *Theological Investigations,* vol. 14 of 23, translated by David Bourke, pp. 295-313. New York: Seabury, 1976.

————. "The Church of the Future and the Future of the Church." In *Theological Investigations,* vol. 20 of 23, translated by Edward Quinn, pp. 103-14. New York: Crossroad, 1981.

————. "Concerning the Relationship between Nature and Grace." In *Theological Investigations,* vol. 1 of 23, translated by Cornelius Ernst, pp. 297-317. Baltimore: Helicon Press, 1961.

————. "The Experience of a Catholic Theologian," *Communio* 11, no. 4 (1984): 404-14.

————. "Forgotten Dogmatic Initiatives of the Second Vatican Council." In *Theological Investigations,* vol. 22 of 23, translated by Joseph Doncell, pp. 97-105. New York: Crossroad, 1991.

————. "The Future of Christian Communities." In *Theological Investigations,* vol. 22 of 23, translated by Joseph Doncell, pp. 121-33. New York: Crossroad, 1991.

————. "The Hermeneutics of Eschatological Assertions." In *Theological Investigations,* vol. 4 of 23, translated by Kevin Smyth, pp. 323-46. Baltimore: Helicon Press, 1966.

————. "History of the World and Salvation-History." In *Theological Investigations,* vol. 5 of 23, translated by Karl-H. Kruger, pp. 97-114. Baltimore: Helicon Press, 1966.

————. "The Inexhaustible Transcendence of God and Our Concern for the Future." In *Theological Investigations,* vol. 20 of 23, translated by Edward Quinn, pp. 173-85. New York: Crossroad, 1981.

————. "Justification and World Development from a Catholic Viewpoint." In *Theological Investigations,* vol. 18 of 23, translated by Edward Quinn, pp. 259-73. New York: Crossroad, 1983.

————. "Observations on the Problem of the 'Anonymous Christian.'" In *Theological Investigations,* vol. 14 of 23, translated by David Bourke, pp. 280-94. New York: Seabury, 1976.

————. "The One Christ and the Universality of Salvation." In *Theological Investigations,* vol. 16 of 23, translated by David Morland, pp. 199-224. New York: Seabury, 1979.

————. "On the Importance of the Non-Christian Religions for Salvation." In *Theological Investigations,* vol. 18 of 23, translated by Edward Quinn, pp. 288-95. New York: Crossroad, 1983.

————. "Perspectives for Pastoral Theology in the Future." In *Theological Investigations,* vol. 22 of 23, translated by Joseph Doncell, pp. 106-19. New York: Crossroad, 1991.

Ratzinger, Joseph. "Christian Universalism: On Two Collections of Papers by Hans Urs von Balthasar," *Communio* 22 (Fall 1995): 545-57.

————. "The Ecclesiology of the Constitution *Lumen Gentium.*" In *Pilgrim Fellowship of Faith: The Church as Communion,* edited by Stephan Otto Horn and Vinzenz Pfnür, translated by Henry Taylor, pp. 123-52. San Francisco: Ignatius Press, 2005.

———. "La Mission d'après les Autres Textes Conciliaires." In *Vatican II: L'Activité Missionnaire de l'Église*, pp. 121-47. Paris: Cerf, 1967.

———. "Salus Extra Ecclesiam Nulla Est." *Documentatie Centrum Concilie*, Series I, no. 88, Research Papers Published in English in 1963: 1-5.

———. "Why I Am Still in the Church." In *Two Say Why*, translated by John Griffiths. Chicago: Franciscan Herald Press, 1973.

Riesenhuber, Klaus. "'The Anonymous Christian' According to Karl Rahner." In Anita Röper, *The Anonymous Christian*, translated by Joseph Donceel, pp. 145-79. New York: Sheed & Ward, 1966.

Sachs, John R. "Apocatastasis in Patristic Theology," *Theological Studies* 54 (1993): 617-40.

———. "Current Eschatology: Universal Salvation and the Problem of Hell," *Theological Studies* 52 (1991): 227-54.

———. "Pattern of Redemption: The Theology of Hans Urs von Balthasar," *Theological Studies* 56, no. 4 (December 1995): 787-88.

Sau, Norman Wong Cheong. "Karl Rahner's Concept of the 'Anonymous Christian': An Inclusivist View of Religions," *Church & Society* 4, no. 1 (2001): 23-39.

Sauras, Emilio. "The Members of the Church." In *Vatican II: The Theological Dimension*, edited by Anthony D. Lee, pp. 78-87. Washington, DC: Thomist Press, 1963.

Schenk, Richard. "The Epoché of Factical Damnation," *Logos* 1, no. 3 (1997): 122-54.

Schineller, J. Peter. "Christ and Church: A Spectrum of Views," *Theological Studies* 37, no. 4 (1976): 545-66.

Schreiter, Robert J. "The Anonymous Christian and Christology." In *Interreligious Dialogue: Facing the Next Frontier*, edited by Richard W. Rousseau, pp. 175-201. Scranton, PA: Ridge Row Press, 1981.

———. "Changes in Roman Catholic Attitudes toward Proselytism and Mission." In *New Directions in Mission and Evangelization 2: Theological Foundations*, edited by James A. Scherer and Stephen B. Bevans, pp. 113-26. Maryknoll, NY: Orbis, 1994.

Sears, Robert T. "Trinitarian Love as Ground of the Church," *Theological Studies* 37, no. 4 (1976): 652-79.

Servais, Jacques. "Per una valutazione dell'influsso di Adrienne von Speyr su Hans Urs von Balthasar," *Rivista Teologico di Lugano* 6, no. 1 (2001): 67-90.

Sullivan, Francis. "The Development of Doctrine about Infants Who Die Unbaptized," *Theological Studies* 72, no. 1 (March 2011): 3-14.

———. "Ways of Salvation? On the Investigation of Jacques Dupuis," *America* 184, no. 12 (2001): 28-31.

Thils, Gustave. "Ceux qui n'ont pas reçu l'évangile." In *L'Église de Vatican II: Études autour de la Constitution conciliaire sur l'Église*, Tome II, edited by Guilherme Baraúna and Yves Congar, pp. 669-80. Paris: Cerf, 1966.

Tobin, T. H. "Controversy and Continuity in Romans 1:18–3:20," *Catholic Biblical Quarterly* 55, no. 2 (1993): 298-318.

Turek, Margaret M. "Dare We Hope 'That All Men Be Saved' (1 Tim 2:4)? On von Balthasar's Trinitarian Grounds for Christian Hope," *Logos* 1, no. 3 (1997): 92-121.

White, Thomas Joseph. "Divine Providence: Von Balthasar and Journet on the Universal Possibility of Salvation and the Twofold Will of God," *Nova et Vetera,* English Edition 4, no. 3 (Summer 2006): 633-66.

————. "On the Universal Possibility of Salvation," *Pro Ecclesia* 17, no. 3 (Summer 2008): 269-80.

Wicks, Jared. "Christ's Saving Descent to the Dead: Early Witnesses from Ignatius of Antioch to Origen," *Pro Ecclesia* 17, no. 3 (Summer 2008): 281-309.

Williams, Rowan. "Balthasar and Rahner." In *The Analogy of Beauty: The Theology of Hans Urs von Balthasar,* edited by John Riches, pp. 11-34. Edinburgh: T. & T. Clark, 1986.

Wilson, Andrew. "With What Right and with What Justice?" *First Things,* no. 218 (December 2011): 47-52.

Wright, N. T. "Towards a Biblical View of Universalism," *Themelios* 4, no. 2 (January 1979): 54-57.

Index

Index